How We Played Our Pa

on MAY DAY

NEWS FROM THE GROUPS

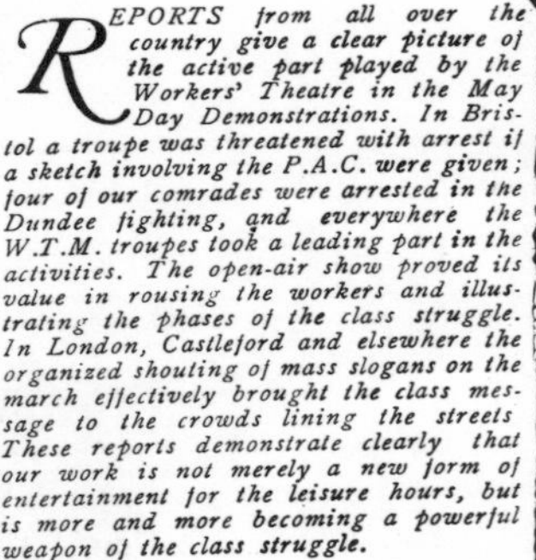

REPORTS from all over the country give a clear picture of the active part played by the Workers' Theatre in the May Day Demonstrations. In Bristol a troupe was threatened with arrest if a sketch involving the P.A.C. were given; four of our comrades were arrested in the Dundee fighting, and everywhere the W.T.M. troupes took a leading part in the activities. The open-air show proved its value in rousing the workers and illustrating the phases of the class struggle. In London, Castleford and elsewhere the organized shouting of mass slogans on the march effectively brought the class message to the crowds lining the streets These reports demonstrate clearly that our work is not merely a new form of entertainment for the leisure hours, but is more and more becoming a powerful weapon of the class struggle.

DUNDEE. There were 21 arrests made in Dundee on May Day. Four of the prisoners were members of the W.T.M.—comrades Helen Whyte, Betty Clark, John Ragan and Frank Clark. As we started singing the " International " the police drew their batons and started smashing at the crowd. The two girl comrades made an attempt to rescue two other comrades; they succeeded in getting one away, then they were arrested. Our comrade carrying the banner was the next one, and was seen lying on the ground. While our four comrades were being marched up the road they started singing the rebel songs together, and that inspired the people. The policeman said to Comrade B. Clark. " Ha ! So you thought you would come out and fight us? " " No," she said, " we came out to fight against the rotten conditions." An inspector told the girls to put on their coats and not to have " any bloody showman tricks here." Owing to the arrests we were unable to put on the sketches because the four comrades had parts in them, but hearty cheers were given for our comrades when the reason was explained.

Above is a photograph of the Manchester Troupe at Preston on May Day. Their show attracted the attention of the local Press, who gave a long editorial account. Comrades are invited to forward photographs of troupes in action and, if possible, the cash for the block. Every group should report regularly to the " New Red Stage."

MANCHESTER. On May Day the troupe went up to Preston and assisted in two open-air demonstrations. The first, which was held in the afternoon, consisted of a march through the town, followed by a meeting in a square. W.T.M. items, notably the P.A.C. sketch and " May Day," were very enthusiastically received.

In the evening a meeting was held in the covered market. An enormous crowd gathered round the lorry, attracted chiefly by the W.T.M., in glaring contrast to a small I.L.P. meeting which was taking place opposite. Our rendering of " Jimmie Maxton and the I.L.P," particularly appropriate, was well applauded. The P.A.C. sketch, the " Timber " sketch, " Meerut," " It's Your Country," and songs made up the rest of our repertoire. Tremendous interest was created, and steps are being taken to set up a troupe in Preston as a result.

We are making arrangements for increasing and consolidating the sales of " Red Stage."

" RED FLAG " TROUPE, ISLINGTON. The Troupe have given two outdoor shows, one at Highbury Corner under its own auspices, at which sales amounted to 4s. 7½d., and the other at Garnault Place, Finsbury, under Y.C.L. auspices. These were our first outdoor shows, and the interest shown has encouraged us to carry on more of this work. There is no need for troupes to wait for bookings. W.T.M. initiative is wanted. This is the way to build " Red Stage " circulation and finance.

THE RED PLAYERS, SOUTH LONDON. On our menc three sketches from a lorry at S Circus, where the contingents attracted a large crowd and thusiasm for the march. We Central London and the We motor-lorry, giving mass slog class war by megaphones en Hyde Park we gave " Mee " 1914 " from No. 1 platform of 3,000. Since May Day we centrated chiefly on open-ai Mitcham, Croydon and Lewis excellent results. We think op is the best way of reaching and while we are still book shows we are giving particula to developing our technique work. We have found it usefu a lorry, which we use for con props. and as a platform. Stage " guarantee fund has m start, and we have sold 18 doz and so far 15 dozen Song-Boo brigades for selling the paper ing on housing estates came surprisingly good results. H to groups whose sales are lagg

" REBEL PLAYERS," LONDON. The we g 1st Hackney B.W.S.F. This wen well, and we were surprised rather critical audience was pl they have booked us up again

We are still doing some c sketches, but are now gettin some new ones—" The Co-op " Nobility of Women," a Cavalry."

We have sold all the Song Bo went really well) and most Stages " for this month.

We do not wear a regular our indoor shows, but now discussed outdoor work—whic to commence in a few weeks sider it necessary to have uniform for all outdoor work.

EMBASSY THEATRE

SWISS COTTAGE, N.W.3
Lessees : Embassy (Swiss Cottage) Ltd.
Buses : 2, 13, 31, 113

Telephone : PRI. 2211
Licensee : ANTHONY HAWTREY
Tube : Bakerloo (Stanmore Line) to Swiss Cottage

Commencing MONDAY, MAY 12th for TWO WEEKS

MICHAEL REDGRAVE

presents

The sensational success of the '51 Edinburgh Festival

THEATRE WORKSHOP

Europe's outstanding group theatre

in

URANIUM 235

A modern morality play for the atomic era

by **EWAN MacCOLL**

Produced by JOAN LITTLEWOOD

"The most exciting theatre group I have ever seen!"

SAM WANAMAKER

OPENING MONDAY, MAY 12th at 7.45
SUBSEQUENT EVENINGS at 7.45 except MONDAYS
Matinee : SATURDAYS at 4.45 — SUNDAYS (Members only) at 7.45
PRICES : Stalls, 10/6, 7/6, 5/3, 3/6, 2/6 Circle, 7/6, 5/3, 3/6

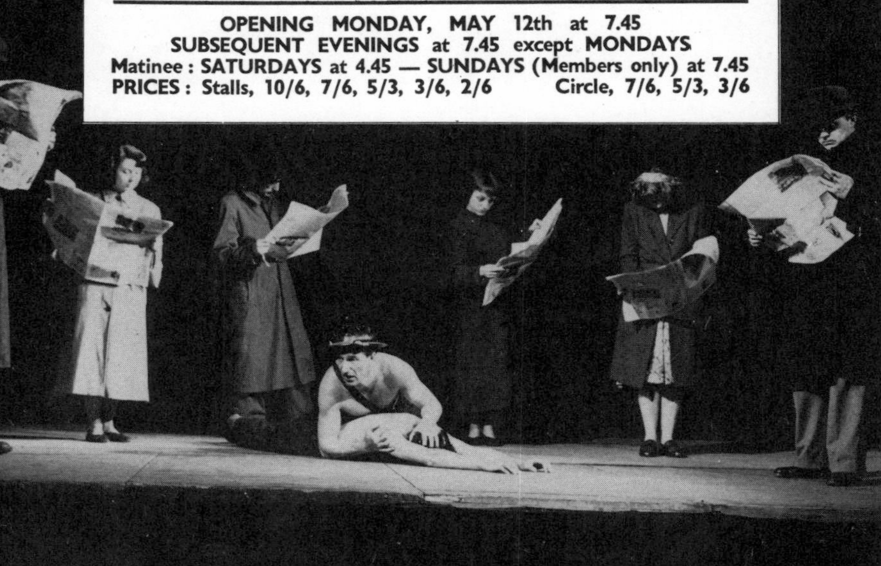

Agit-prop to Theatre Workshop

Theatre
WORKSHOP
Birger Lg
"Uran 235"

Political playscripts 1930–50

Agit-prop *to* Theatre Workshop

edited by **Howard Goorney** *and* **Ewan MacColl**

Published **by Manchester University Press,**
Oxford Road, Manchester, M13 9PL, UK
and
51 Washington Street, Dover, NH 03802, USA

British Library Cataloguing in Publication Data
Agit-prop to Theatre Workshop: political playscripts 1930–50.
1. English drama—20th century
I. Goorney, Howard II. MacColl, Ewan
822′912′08 PR1272

Library of Congress Cataloging in Publication Data
applied for

ISBN 0–7190–1762–9 *hardback*

Photoset in Linotron Plantin with Syntax
by Northern Phototypesetting Co., Bolton

Printed in Great Britain
at the Alden Press, Oxford

Contents

List of illustrations

Preface

Little has been written about the Workers' Theatre Movement of the thirties. My original intention was to help fill the gap by collecting and editing material used by left-wing theatre groups in the Manchester area during that period. I soon discovered that very little had survived the passing of the years. My own involvement from 1938 onwards enabled me to piece together a complete script of *Last Edition* – a living newspaper produced in 1940, and Joan Littlewood was able to come up with her own handwritten script of *John Bullion*. These, plus the American Laboratory Theatre's *Newsboy* and some mass declamations from the late thirties were the only complete scripts available. It was understandable that no written record of the early agit-prop sketches could be traced. They dealt with day-to-day political issues and were by their very nature ephemeral – long-forgotten notes on bits of paper, if written down at all. However, it was disappointing to find that typed scripts from the late thirties had not been kept by those involved, including myself. It became necessary for me to alter my original conception, and I hope I have succeeded in turning my initial disappointment to advantage. Ewan MacColl's early plays written for Theatre Workshop in the 1940's had a direct link in theatrical style with the pre-war agit-prop sketches and living newspapers and he was willing to take on the task of tracing this development. His involvement with the political groups in Manchester and Salford from the late twenties has enabled him to present a personal first-hand account over a much longer period than I would have been able to do.

Lack of space faced us with the choice of including either *Last Edition* or *The Other Animals*. As it happened, Ewan had reservations about the former. Looking at it over forty years on he felt that it contained, as well as much exciting theatre, 'long tedious passages of indigested flab'.

However, it did represent a big step forward from the early agit-prop and it translated into actual production many of the ideas and theatre concepts of the preceding years. It was therefore decided to include extracts from the script.

Last Edition stands as a political statement of its own day, but it is a sad comment on our time that the theme of the three post-war plays – unemployment, the threat of The Bomb, and the use of political torture – are as relevant today as when they were written forty years ago.

Johnny Noble, *Uranium 235*, and *The Other Animals* have an 'epic' quality appropriate to their themes – a form of theatre with great potential which socialist theatre groups in this country have, on the whole, failed to explore. Of course no group in Britain has the resources to emulate the Epic theatre of Piscator in pre-war Germany, with his use of slide projections, moving film, animated cartoons and a double treadmill stage, and this may be not altogether a bad thing. Too much technology can swamp the actor – it can also go wrong, and often did, as Piscator himself admits. However, Theatre Workshop, ploughing a lone furrow and with no subsidy, was able to tour these plays extensively, so their essential requirements in terms of lighting and sound-equipment should be well within the resources of the larger and more established groups. *Johnny Noble* and *Uranium 235* are adaptable to any size of stage area and were played in a great variety of venues, from tiny stages in the Lake District to some of the biggest theatres in Sweden. *The Other Animals*, on the other hand, does require full stage facilities and enough space to accommodate the area of the cage.

But socialist theatre can take many forms. We are beginning to see, as political tensions increase, agit-prop groups again taking to the streets in protest against the injustices in our society and the threat of nuclear holocaust, giving a new meaning to the term 'non-violent direct action'. The Narrator in *Johnny Noble* speaks in the 1940s of '. . . days that linger in the memory like a bad taste in the mouth. Come back with us a dozen years or so. . . . Here is a man of those years, a man without hope, without work, a man burdened with time.'

Only now there is no need to go back. The wheel has come full circle. . . .

Introduction

The evolution of a revolutionary theatre style

manifesto

THE THEATRE must face up to the problems of its time; it cannot ignore the poverty and human suffering which increases every day. It cannot, with sincerity, close its eyes to the disasters of its time. Means Test suicides, wars, fascism and the million sordid accidents reported in the daily press. If the theatre of to-day would reach the heights achieved four thousand years ago in Greece and four hundred years ago in Elizabethan England it must face up to such problems. To those who say that such affairs are not the concern of the theatre or that the theatre should confine itself to treading in the paths of ' beauty ' and ' dignity ', we would say "Read Shakespeare, Marlowe, Webster, Sophocles, Aeschylus, Aristophanes, Calderon, Moliere, Lope-de-Vega, Schiller and the rest." The Theatre Union says that in facing up to the problems of our time and by intensifying our efforts to get at the essence of reality, we are also attempting to solve our own theatrical problems both technical and ideological. By doing this we are ensuring the future of the theatre, a future which will not be born in the genteel atmosphere of retirement and seclusion, but rather in the clash and turmoil of the battles between the oppressors and the oppressed.

theatre union

THE THEATRE OF THE PEOPLE

Each new development in the theatre, however slight that development may be, makes it necessary to evaluate and re-evaluate the immediate past, a process often beset with difficulties. The remote past presents fewer problems since, so to speak, it offers a bird's-eye view of history and allows us to achieve a semblance of objectivity. The point is admirably demonstrated by television where a programme dealing with ancient Egypt or the descent of man presents few pitfalls. When it comes to passing judgement on the ancient world even the most opiniated pundit contrives to appear like Solomon, all cool deliberation and wisdom. With so few facts to deal with, banalities can be made to resonate like eternal truths. The immediate past has to be approached with a good deal more circumspection, for the road which leads to it is cluttered with an embarrassing array of facts, some of which may be mutually exclusive. The problem is to know which to select in order to give a 'balanced report'.

This 'report' does not constitute a history of Theatre Workshop: Howard Goorney's *The Theatre Workshop Story* has already provided us with the main outline of that history. It is an attempt to bring into focus certain of Theatre Workshop's stylistic ideas, to show how they originated and how they influenced the company's development. It is, above all, a personal statement by one who was closely associated with those developments and who was, to some extent, responsible for some of the ideas.

Theatre Workshop was formed in 1945 and, to all intents and purposes, ceased to exist in 1973. In the course of those years it underwent a series of transformations. It would be incorrect to regard its history as a single unbroken line of development or even as a smooth cycle of development and decay. Up until the early fifties, however, Theatre Workshop can be seen to have been fairly consistent in its efforts to create a revolutionary working-class theatre. If that aim was not specifically formulated in the theatre's earliest days, it certainly existed as a less than nebulous idea from the beginning. That beginning is, as far as the editors of this book are concerned, the period which opens the decade of the thirties.

Increasingly, sociologists and historians are preoccupied with the thirties; film-makers and dramatists in search of exotic backgrounds recreate the period in the terms of a *Bonnie and Clyde*, costume departments of television companies ransack their wardrobes for plus-fours and celluloid collars while the cobbled streets of northern mill towns become advertisers' clichés.

It was, in fact, a decade in which enormous changes in the way of living were affecting millions of working people. It was also a period in which many of the ideas and practices of the nineteenth century managed to find a foothold. Indeed the new and the old were to be found existing side by side in comfortable symbiosis. Techniques of mass-production, the conveyor-belt and the assembly-line were being introduced into carefully selected industries but, at the same time, most working-class families took it for granted that at least one son would learn a trade and become a craftsman. Monopoly capitalism had arrived with gigantic enterprises like Imperial Chemical Industries but, if you lived in a city like Manchester, Leeds or Liverpool, the chances were that your milk would be delivered to you by a local farmer or farm-hand riding a horse-drawn float and serving the milk from a churn. Your corner-shop still sold bread which had been baked on the premises and factory-processed cheese was still regarded as an exotic culinary invention.

Children's games and pastimes reflected perfectly the Janus-like visage of the time. They were, on the whole, little changed from the games which had been played down the centuries, though cigarette-cards, those attractive symbols of commercial competition, had been added to the games repertoire and young girls made swings from straw ropes salvaged from orange-boxes and thrown over the arms of lamp-posts, universal symbols of the age of cast iron. These, and the decorating of flagstones with coloured chalks, were innovations effortlessly assimilated into the lives of the post-war generation of children. Perhaps the most significant symbol of the times was the 'steely', the steel ball-bearing which had become an emperor in the game of marbles. For the rest, teenage youths still played chuck-stones on any available piece of waste ground and girls played elaborate ball-bouncing games or, in the days leading up to May the first, would go from house to house carrying a broomstick maypole hung with coloured paper streamers, singing a song in honour of the season. Sometimes on rainy days a group of children would put on a concert in a neighbour's house where, on payment of a piece of broken pottery or a shard of coloured glass, one could hear songs and watch improvised dances and imitations of Charlie Chaplin.

If all this sounds somewhat idyllic then it is time to remind the reader that the past is not unlike one of those king-size sandwiches in which an occasional delicious morsel is concealed in great gobbets of plastic filling. The fact is that the streets through which those little girls carried their broomstick maypoles were mean streets, foul places and whether they were in Manchester, Glasgow, Leeds, Liverpool or Salford no child should have been condemned to grow up in them. Most of them had been built to house the hordes of dispossessed cottagers driven from their homes by successive poor-law acts in the nineteenth century. They were slum-built monuments to the rapacity and inhumanity of those who built them. Those who lived in them had long been familiar with poverty, war, strikes, lockouts, betrayals and defeats. Now they were beginning to experience unemployment on a scale hitherto unknown.

The betrayal and collapse of the general strike in 1926 did incalculable harm to the working-class movement and the demoralization which followed in its wake was still evident at the beginning of the thirties. The Labour Party which still regarded itself as the party of the working class tended to confine its activities to electioneering and skirmishes with the extreme Left. Its lack of a theoretical base had left it unprepared for the savage blows directed against the working class in the course of the deepening economic crisis. The Communist Party, though much more in touch with events, was a very small organisation and was outlawed by both the Labour Party and the T.U.C. The Socialist Party of Great Britain (S.P.G.B.) and the Social Democratic Federation (S.D.F.), each with a handful of members, managed to make themselves heard from time to time as did the Anarchists and Syndicalists, although most of the militant Left tended to regard them as curious survivals from an earlier age. A common meeting ground for members of all the Left organisations as well as for rationalists and freethinkers were the Sunday afternoon debates organised by the Clarion Clubs. These generally took place in a local restaurant and would often attract eighty or a hundred men and a sprinkling of women who would listen and support one or the other of the speakers debating evolutionary theory or Edward Clod's *History of Creation*, or *Colonization and Christianity* or Marx's *Civil War in France*.

And as the seasons came and went, the queues outside the Labour exchanges grew longer and longer, a coalition government was formed, the means test was introduced, the navy mutinied at Invergordon and the hunger-marches began. Those who lived through those years often recall them with a sigh. Ah, the good old days! And yet they didn't exactly offer the average worker a rich full life. For the three million unemployed they were days of despair. For an unemployed youth living in Salford in 1930 the options were, to say the least, limited. Nevertheless the days had to be got through somehow; presupposing that you signed on at the 'broo' at, say, 9 a.m., you still had some fourteen or fifteen hours to dispose of. A number of alternative activities were open to you:

You could call at the library and read the newspapers or you could study there, provided that you knew how to study.

Weather permitting you could go to the public park and lie on the sour grass or sleep on a park-bench. If your friends were unemployed too, then you could do these things together.

From ten o'clock in the morning you could, on payment of a modest threepence, find refuge in the darkness of one of the new super-cinemas.

In the evening, another threepence would get you into 'the Jig', a notorious dance hall situated at the Oldfield Road end of Liverpool Street.

Almost directly opposite there was Hyndman Hall, also known as The Workers' Arts Club. There, threepence would get you a game of billiards or snooker on the solitary table which occupied most of the ground-floor bar-room.

If it was a Saturday or Thursday evening you could spend a 'bob' on a 'hop' (a shilling on a dance) in the first-floor public room or, if it was the second Saturday in the month you could attend a dance-cum-social there.

You could, of course, go up to the top-floor gym where you could stand in as a sparring-partner for some budding fighter without paying anything at all.

If you were totally without money and lacked the inclination to punch and be punched then you could stand at the end of the bar on the ground floor and listen to the pensioned-off warriors arguing the pros and cons of Volney's *Ruins of Empires* or Tom Paine's *Rights of Man*.

These debates were, at times, as entertaining and dramatic as any theatrical presentation. The debaters, rarely numbering more than eight or ten men, would sit in a rough semicircle midway between the billiard-table and the bar. The central figure of the group, the pivot as it were, was Jimmy Tillbrook, a huge mountain of a man who would sit there in his specially built windsor chair like a monarch surrounded by vassal kings. From time to time he would clear his throat and the discussion would cease for a moment so that his heavy breathing and the click of billiard-balls would dominate the silence as he prepared to pass judgement on this or that opinion. He carried a small volume of Proudhon's *Philosopy of Poverty* from which he would, at times, read aloud in a low rumbling voice. From another pocket he would sometimes laboriously extract a slim copy of Kant's *Critique of Pure Reason* which he would hold up in front of his companions while he slowly stared each one of them down. When he felt that they were sufficiently intimidated he would lower his book and, tapping gently upon its cover with a forefinger the size of an overfilled pork sausage, he would make his pronouncement. The smallest of his gestures was loaded with drama, the slow turn of that enormous head with its cascade of chins, the lifting of the hand holding the pint of Tetley's mild-and-bitter, the deliberate exploration of his pockets leading to the majestic flourish of his voluminous silk handkerchief were all actions which gave the impression of having been rehearsed to the point of perfection. I cannot believe that I was the only spectator there who experienced an almost overwhelming compulsion to applaud.

This is not to say that the Workers' Arts Club discussions were one-man performances. They were not. There were other fine performers; Jock Smiley, for example, an unemployed iron-moulder from Falkirk who amused himself and others by baiting Jack Williams, a mercurial Welshman who worked as a maintenance engineer at a local cotton mill and who was given to quoting the *Rubaiyát of Omar Khayyám* and selected passages from Shakespeare's tragedies. Smiley, who had been a youthful disciple of the Scottish Marxist, John MacLean, suspected Williams of holding orthodox Labour Party views. Orthodoxy was, in Smiley's opinion, the worst kind of heresy and he felt obliged to belabour Williams with quotations from Marx and Engels and with some of Burns' satirical poems. In full flight he was a formidable opponent. Though physically small he had an enormous voice and his knowledge of Shakespeare was prodigious. Ridicule was his métier, it became him and he could use it as a rapier or as a bludgeon. There was something horribly fascinating about the way he would use lengthy passages from the bard to reduce Williams before finishing him off with one of the high-kilted pieces from Burns' *Merry Muses*. Jack Williams' face would flame with embarrassment while Smiley's would become chalk white as passion drained the blood from his features. He was dying from tuberculosis and there were times when his fulminations would be interrupted by a fierce bout of coughing. Afterwards he would glare round at the circle defying anyone to comment or show sympathy.

For anyone with a sense of drama these sessions were absolutely invaluable; for a fourteen-year-old hopeful on the threshold of a fifty-year love-affair with the theatre they were unforgettable experiences. Not exactly show business perhaps, but infinitely more important to my education than either of the two examples of legitimate theatre I had seen. The first of these was a production of *Monsieur Beaucaire*, a dreary play by Booth Tarkington and Mrs E. G. Sutherland. I saw it, along with three or four hundred other schoolchildren, when I was eight or nine years of age. I can still remember the tremendous thrill of sitting in that theatre and waiting for the play to begin. I can remember, too, the boredom which enveloped me like a thick, stultifying fog as the play progressed. The antipathy I feel for a great deal of formal theatre was, I think, born at that moment. A few months later I saw my second straight play, a melodrama entitled *The Face at the Window*. The Victoria in Lower Broughton, where it was presented, was a converted cinema which occasionally re-converted and presented short seasons of 'live' theatre. In addition to these two shows I had been taken several times by my parents to the Salford Hippodrome where I had seen some of the most notable comics of the English stage. It was the variety theatre which really made the most profound impression on me; the live music, the wandering limelights, the incredibly beautiful chorus girls, the grotesquely made-up comics and the dashing acrobats – these were indeed the stuff that dreams are made on!

Visits to the theatre, however, were few and far between: they were exceptional experiences. Much more common were the regular performances of street-singers, jugglers, bones-players, fiddlers, trumpeters, step-dancers, escapologists, barrel-organ grinders and Punch-and-Judy men. During the summer months in particular there was a constant procession of these street-entertainers. Their contribution to my theatre background was considerable. Would it be too much to suggest that they formed part of the fabric of working-class culture?

Another vital thread in this fabric were films. This was the era of the growth of Hollywood, the era of the first international stars, the age of the comedians, the celluloid sweethearts and the tough guys. As the lines of unemployed grew longer and longer, so the gigantic baroque palaces of Hollywood's new art form grew more and more sumptuous and the lines of high-kicking chorus girls more and more desirable. The Hollywood film of the late twenties and early thirties was the staple diet of the vast army of unemployed and I would venture to suggest that it provided the main art fare for the entire working class. It was certainly one of the most important artistic influences in my life up until late 1929. In the autumn of that year the Deansgate cinema ran a season of Russian films. This was long before the art-cinema concept first appeared and it must have been a financial flop for I remember going there for several weeks and sitting in splendid isolation as the great epics of Pudovkin, Eisenstein and Dovzhenko unrolled on the screen. It was, I think, Eisenstein's *October* and Pudovkin's *End of St Petersburg* which started me on the road I was to travel for the next twenty years. When, in 1930, the Salford Workers'

Film Society was formed, I was among its foundation members. It was, I believe, on the Labour Party's list of proscribed (communist) organisations and every Sunday morning, in a small flea-pit on Oldfield Road, it presented the cream of the world's best films. There, in the space of the next few months, I saw *Storm over Asia*, *The New Babylon*, Pabst's *Kamaradschaft*, Dziga Vertov's *Man with the Movie Camera*, Aaron Room's *Bed and Sofa* and *The Ghost that Never Returns*, Fritz Lang's *Metropolis* and Dovzhenko's *Earth*. The opportunity of seeing films of such stature compensated for some of the deprivation experienced by an ill-educated adolescent who faced the bleak prospect of trying to earn a living in the arid desert of 1929.

I was fourteen and had left school knowing how to read and write and how to 'do' simple arithmetic. At the same time I was what is called 'well read'. From the time I was eight or nine years old I had been reading the second-hand books which my father bought off the second-hand book-barrows at Pendleton market as he returned from the foundry on a Saturday morning. The books, which never cost more than a couple of coppers, were bought as presents for me and through them I became acquainted with Darwin's *Voyage of the Beagle*, Jack London's *People of the Abyss* and *Martin Eden*, *The Arabian Nights*, *Barnaby Rudge*, *The Golden Ass* of Lucius Apuleius, *Candide* and volume three of Molière's *Collected Plays*. Not typical children's books! But then my father wasn't exactly typical either. He was one of those working-class militants who believed that books were weapons in the armoury of the class-struggle and though he, himself, was not a great reader, he was determined that I should be given the opportunity of becoming one.

Between 1929 and the beginning of 1931 I moved from one dead-end job to another and finally joined the great army of permanently unemployed. It was at this point that my real education began. Three times a week I would stand in the queue outside the Albion Street labour exchange and, after signing-on, beat a path to the local reference library where I was determined to read my way through the stacks. As a plan it left a lot to be desired and I soon abandoned it for the more practical one of using the library for 'serious' reading and borrowing novels and plays to read at home. Shortly after embarking on this project I came across a volume of Gogol's short stories and I remember sitting and weeping at the tale of Akaki Akakyevitch's lost overcoat. That night I took home a copy of *Dead Souls* and in the next few days read everything that Gogol had written. I ready Gorky in the same way, beginning with two short novellas, *The Orloff Couple* and *Malva*. This habit of reading an author's entire output is one which has stayed with me all my life.

My daytime efforts to read Berkeley on *The Principles of Human Knowledge* or Hobbes' *Leviathan* or *The Apologia* of Socrates were not always crowned with success: I fell asleep frequently and would often grow weary of turning the pages of the dictionary as I hunted up the meaning of this or that word. I persevered, however, and occasionally managed to grasp the meaning of some of the ideas hidden in the tortured prose. I was too self-indulgent to be a real scholar and I used to bribe myself with the promise of a half-hour's relaxation with a book of poems as payment for reading another five pages of John Stuart Mill. In this way I became familiar with the works of Chaucer, William Dunbar, D. H. Lawrence, Ezra Pound, Swinburne, Mayakovsky and many others. I owe a lifetime's affection for Alexander Blok's poem *The Twelve* to the tedium generated by Ricardo's *Theory of Rent*.

But how did an unemployed youth with no educational background know which books to choose? Well, it wasn't so difficult. That initial encounter with Gogol had led me to a *History of Russian Literature* and from there I had gone on to read Pushkin, Lermontov, Griboyedov, Chekhov and Gorky. A reference to Balzac in one of Jack London's novels had introduced me to *The Splendours and Miseries of Courtesans* and after that it was inevitable that I should read all fifty-two volumes of *The Human Comedy*. A friend who was working as a rubber-stamp moulder in a small sweat-shop above Manchester's largest second-hand bookseller's began his education by browsing among the stacks of second-hand books during his lunch-hour break. He it was who introduced me to James Joyce, *The Good Soldier Schweik* and to a cheap remaindered copy of *The Satyricon* of Petronius Arbiter. Through him too I discovered Thomas Mann, Sherwood Anderson, Alfred Doblin, Jacob Wasserman, Robert Briffault and Theodore Plivier.

Looking back it seems that I was constantly encountering people whose main aim in life was to encourage me to read. My knowledge of the world's literature was, of course, eclectic and as far as drama was concerned I knew very little outside the works of Pushkin, Griboyedov, Chekhov, Gogol, Aristophanes, Wedekind, Kaiser, Eugene O'Neill and Büchner. A strange assemblage! Of Shakespeare's works I had read only *Macbeth* and *Troilus and Cressida* and Ben Jonson was not even a name to me. I was to reach the age of twenty-four before I was to plunge into the great sea of Elizabethan and Jacobean drama.

I was about fifteen when I joined a socialist drama group called the Clarion Players. My introduction to them was through a young man who lodged with us at the time. He was an unemployed waterproof worker and a member of the tiny communist organisation in our district. I remember him as a man who had learned to live, almost exclusively, on cheese-and-onion sandwiches and whose blue serge suit shone with the lustre of polished pewter. He was a fastidious little man who, six days a week, stood naked in our backyard while he scrubbed himself under a cold hose; on the seventh day he visited the public baths whence he returned boiled scarlet. He owned a hand-cranked portable gramophone – his only luxury – and on this he would play his Parlophone recordings of *I Pagliacci* and selections from Wagner's *Nibelungenlied*. Without much effort I was able to commit both works to memory and amused my friends by singing all the different parts in 'cod' voices. Our lodger must have heard one of these ridiculous renditions for he offered to introduce me to some of his friends, who, he thought, would be able to make use of my talents as a mimic.

His friends were the Clarion Players, all of whom were much older than I was and much better informed about everything except being dirt poor. Not that they were much better off than I was, though most of them had jobs of one kind or another. My first meeting with them left me feeling thoroughly intimidated. The young couple who appeared to be the leading spirits of the group were so self-possessed and so loquacious that I was overwhelmed with a sense of inferiority. Their conversation was larded with the names of writers, most of whom I had never heard of; they tossed them into the conversation with a fine abandon and the more they talked, the more tongue-tied I became. I have a feeling that they were under the impression that I was in some way retarded, not exactly an idiot but not quite all there either. My somewhat grotesque costume may have contributed to their impression; I was wearing a shockingly green sports jacket which had been given to my mother by a lady who employed her as a charwoman. It had been tailored for a giant and enveloped me to mid-calf giving me the appearance of a monstrous aphid. Indeed some time later I wore it for rehearsals of Čapek's *Insect Play*. Everything about that evening conspired against me; even the house in which the meeting took place intimidated me. It seemed enormous. It was, in fact, a house which had seen better days but which had now been absorbed into the surrounding slum. Up until that time I had never been in any dwelling larger than the two-up and two-down in which I lived.

The eight or ten members of the group were engaged in rehearsing *The Ragged-Trousered Philanthropist*. It was all very informal and not, in any way, like the rehearsals I had seen in the films of Hollywood musicals. I was deeply disappointed and regarded the elderly producer with a good deal of disfavour. After what seemed to me to have been a complete shambles the rehearsal ended and coffee was served (the first I had ever tasted!). There followed a discussion in the course of which I heard, for the first time, the names of Ibsen and George Bernard Shaw.

The following week I was given a small part in Upton Sinclair's *Singing Jailbirds*. The rehearsals of this not very good play followed the same pattern as the one I had seen the previous week. I found myself becoming more and more censorious and more impatient. In more prosperous times I might have had the opportunity of being apprenticed to a carpenter or a plasterer or a machine-tool maker but with three million on the dole who could look foward to anything? So perhaps my impatience arose out of the need to master a skill, any kind of skill. Alas! I don't remember a single Clarion Players' rehearsal being anything other than a slovenly performed charade. The fact that I was young and somewhat timorous in the presence of people who knew about Ibsen and Toller and Shaw meant that my criticism never got beyond the grumbling stage. In any case, what did I know about production or running a group?

At some point during my early association with the group we affiliated with the Workers' Theatre Movement and from that time on we ceased to refer to ourselves as the Clarion Players. I cannot remember how long I remained a member of the group, a year perhaps or maybe a little longer. Certainly long enough to take part in a production of *The Ragged-Trousered Philanthropist*. I don't think we ever actually staged the full production though we did present odd scenes from it at dances and socials.

After the *Philanthropist* we began work on Čapek's *Insect Play* but later abandoned it in favour of Toller's *Machine Wreckers*. This too was never actually staged though a Sunday afternoon reading of it was give to a small audience. Toller was the producer's favourite dramatist and it was inevitable that we should rehearse scenes from his most ambitious expressionistic play, *Masses and Man*. For a fifteen-year-old romantic this was very exciting stuff indeed. We never got further than rehearsing two or three of the group choruses but that was enough to convince me of the powerful dramatic effect of mass declamation. Among the other interesting plays read during my stay with the group, I remember Galsworthy's *Strife*, Shaw's *Heartbreak House* and Hauptmann's *The Weavers*. We also staged a political revue written by two members of the group and consisting, for the most part, of Gilbert and Sullivan parodies.

Quite the most interesting and successful show in the group's repertoire was *Still Talking*, a collectively written piece which had been produced prior to my joining the group. All the other items in the group's repertoire were ones which postulated a formal relationship between audience and actors. Even when they were performed in situations where normal theatre facilities were lacking, where there was no special lighting or special décor or costumes, where the players frequently read their lines from a typescript, even then that special theatre relationship was taken for granted. The French window, the Tudor fireplace or the wall lined with simulated books may have been missing but both audience and players recognised that it was meant to be there and, in their imaginations, it still was there. It was there because the author had conceived it as a necessary part of his or her play. *Still Talking*, on the other hand, had been conceived as an open-ended happening at a political meeting. Its presentation required no stage since the entire interior of the hall where it was being performed became a stage. The lack of props, costumes, décor and special lighting effects was not due to a lack of funds or to the inadequacies of the acting area: they were an intrinsic part of the dramatic situation. No signal was given to alert the audience that a play was about to begin. All that happened was that two people, looking like any other two people in the hall, suddenly confronted the audience. One of them called for order and then proceeded to introduce the other as a Labour or Tory politician. The supposed politician then launched into a speech dealing with whatever political or economic issues were most topical. At fixed points in the speech actors planted in the audience would heckle the speaker and then enact small scenes illustrating points raised in the speech. The form was so elastic that almost anything could happen without destroying the structure of the play. It was a fascinating experiment and had we explored it further it might well have led us to discover the road to a truly popular revolutionary theatre form.

Still Talking was only performed on four or five occasions but as far as we were concerned it was a completely successful show. In that success, however, lay the seeds of the Clarion Players' destruction, for the group was now almost evenly divided between those who believed that *Still Talking* was a signpost pointing to the group's future and those who felt that such an approach would result in a theatre where there would be no room for writers other than those who could draft political speeches and pamphlets. The actors would become political orators and all those with a genuine love of theatre would be alienated.

To create such a theatre would, they argued, imply the repudiation of all that had been created in the past by Shakespeare, Ibsen, Shaw and so on. The political faction countered by saying that by pursuing a strong political line, the theatre would be returning to its origins. After all, was not the morality play essentially a political tract?

Exactly, countered the theatre-first faction, a return to feudalism! And so the arguments and counter-arguments thundered over innumerable cups of weak coffee. In the end, the inevitable happened; the theatre-first people abandoned the group leaving the political faction to run things as best they could.

The move to establish a more politically involved theatre wasn't confined to Manchester. In London too there was a healthy Workers' Theatre Movement with several flourishing groups and from them we began to receive a fairly regular supply of sketches written in the agit-prop style. The first of these was a short piece called *R.I.P.* (*Rent, Interest and Profit*), a satirical sketch dealing with the mechanics of capitalist exploitation. It was clever, witty with the kind of political humour that had delighted Elizabethan audiences, the kind of thing, in short, that college-educated comics would be performing on television forty years later. In the space of seven or eight minutes an audience was presented with a schematized picture of a political problem, the specific function of the class forces involved and finally, the solution of the problem. Seven or eight minutes of knockabout comedy, some simplified Marxist analyses, two songs and a mass declamation! Crude? Perhaps, but not without its own rough style. For those of us who had been struggling through the wordy undergrowth of formal drama, these sketches were tremendously exciting.

In October 1931 the first of the mass-unemployed demonstrations which were to sweep the country during the next few months took place in Salford. The following day another enormous demonstration was held on the Liverpool Street gasworks' croft and there, from the back of a horse-drawn coal lorry, three of us enacted a sketch dealing with the means test. It was our first open-air performance and one of our most successful. The occasion was marked with baton-charges by mounted police. I wrote a song about it, a parody of Billy Boy, and it was performed as a duet at a number of unemployed rallies.

As the economic crisis, with its attendant political upheavals, developed and became world-wide we, the radical wing of the group, were possessed by a terrible sense of urgency, a need to create a political theatre which would help to change the world where we found ourselves constantly in danger of drowning. In the months which followed that first open-air performance we took to the streets, or rather to the public parks, city squares and factory gates, performing at anti-war rallies, unemployed demonstrations, political meetings and, occasionally, at the entrance to the Manchester City football ground.

Though our repertoire had changed radically, our approach to rehearsals and production generally was unaltered. The level of presentation was still slapdash; furthermore the slovenliness of production tended to be more obvious in the agit-prop sketches than it had been in the naturalistic plays. Rehearsals were still regarded by some of the older group members as social occasions; the rest of us found the slackness and lack of discipline almost unbearable. Some of the problems undoubtedly arose out of the fact that the group was almost equally divided between younger members who were unemployed and older ones most of whom had jobs. The unemployed had time at their disposal and wanted to make use of it by improving their work on the sketches. The employed, on the other hand, were reluctant to give up any more of their already limited free time. The result was another split; seven unemployed members decided to form an agit-prop group which would concentrate on problems of political immediacy such as unemployment and the gathering storm in the cotton-textile industry. The new group adopted the name Red Megaphones and I, who knew little or nothing about production, became its producer and scriptwriter. The oldest member of the new group was seventeen, the youngest, fifteen. There were four men and three women. Our rehearsal room was a disused cellar in the Salford Workers' Arts Club; it was cold, dark, dirty and it smelled bad. We rehearsed by candlelight.

For our first production we chose a sketch called *Meerut* written by the North-West London Hammer and Sickle Group. It was a simple but extremely effective piece of theatre. Its form was mass declamation, its theme the savage prison sentences given to the leaders of the Indian rail-strike at Meerut. It could be performed by four, five or six actors of either sex. Its 'set' consisted of wooden poles carried by the actors, three of whom would stand with poles held vertically in front of them while the other performers knelt down with their poles held at the horizontal. In this fashion the front of a cage or prison-cell was created. There followed a group declamation lasting five or six minutes at the end of which each of the players would extend a hand through the bars and call for a show of international solidarity with the *Meerut* prisoners. The small cast, the marvellously portable 'set' and the brevity of the sketch made it a perfect item for a street-drama group. At the time, it was quite the most exciting bit of theatre I had ever seen and, looking back over the fifty years that have slipped by since then, I find it still has the power to move and excite me.

From a production point of view *Meerut* presented few problems, even to a beginner such as I was. All that was necessary was to get the cast to speak together like a choir and move together like a platoon of soldiers. So, bawling and shouting like any sergeant-major and generally behaving in a way that no producer should ever behave, I drilled my small cast. It took six sessions of two or three hours each, spread over a fortnight, and then we were ready for the streets.

Our first performance of *Meerut* took place outside the dock gates on Trafford Road, Salford. Our audience numbered about twenty people, six Lascar seamen and the rest dockers. It was time for the morning shift and about half the audience soon left so as to get to the pens where they would stand in the hope of being awarded a day's work. Of those who stayed one or two shouted words of encouragement, one gave a loud raspberry and another dismissed us as 'a bunch of snotty-nosed kids'. One or two applauded at the end of the performance, the others departed without showing either approval or disapproval. Chastened, we moved to the entrance to Howarth's mill and hung around the gates waiting for the lunch-time exodus. Two girls in the group had been weavers and they were recognised by some of their erstwhile mates. As a result, our reception there was an improvement on the docks and we were able to finish our performance before the police arrived. From there we repaired to the corner of Regent Road and Oldfield Road where we were heckled by a postman on a bicycle. We ignored him but he sparked off hecklers in the small crowd and when it looked as if opposing factions were about to start a riot, we left in a hurry.

Looking back, it seems to me that we were, on the whole, received with a distinct lack of enthusiasm by most of the men and women of our own class. Often they would pass us by with heads averted so as not to be involved, occasionally one or two would stop to jeer, others met us with blank apathy and this was harder to take than the abuse. Only a small minority seemed to agree with the things we were saying and with our way of saying them. We consoled ourselves by saying that audiences would improve when we ourselves improved with hard work and rehearsal. We lacked many qualities but humility was not among them. Week-ends were our best times, for then we could be assured of being seen by shoppers in the market-places and week-end bathers at the public baths. The stone steps that were an architectural feature of Manchester and Salford's public baths soon became our favourite venues for performances. For one thing, there were generally queues there on a Saturday morning and, for another, they provided us with a point of vantage where we could be seen and from which we could easily spot 'the law'.

Our most sympathetic audiences were those drawn from the ranks of the unemployed, particularly those organised in the National Unemployed Workers' Movement (N.U.W.M.). From being a small and weak offshoot of the Communist Party, the N.U.W.M. had grown in the space of a few months into an enormous movement numbering tens of thousands. At their meetings, demonstrations and hunger-marches we could always rely on a sympathetic hearing and had it not been for them I doubt whether the Red Megaphones would have surivived. But now a new struggle was developing and the cotton towns round Lancashire and Cheshire began to rumble with talk of strikes and further massive lay-offs.

The cotton industry which had made Lancashire famous was now ailing and the textile barons were withdrawing their capital from towns such as Preston and Burnley and reinvesting it in Tokyo and Hong Kong. Here at home the speed-up and other forms of 'rationalisation' were making the lot of the cotton operatives more and more difficult; their anger and frustration had been building up for years and when the employers announced their intention of introducing the eight-looms system the anger reached boiling-point. The manufacture of cotton textiles was one of our oldest industries and, perhaps because of this, it was difficult to organise its labour force. The main reason for this lay in the fact that from the earliest days unionisation had been on a craft basis. Since there were scores of different processes involved in the manufacture of cotton goods, it followed that there were also scores of different unions. Weavers, ring-spinners, mule-spinners, big piecers, little piecers, back-tenters, combers and others all had their separate organisations. Some of them had tens of thousands of members, some had only a few hundred and one or two counted their membership in tens. The situation was further complicated by the industry having grown up on the basis of regional specialisation. This meant that a town famed for its weaving could have a neighbour six miles to the North of it which specialized in spinning while four miles to the South-East was another town whose workers were mostly employed as finishers. Consequently when it came to adopting industrial action such as a strike, the decision had to be taken by each of the independent unions in turn, which meant virtually by each town and sometimes by each mill.

The two weavers in the Red Megaphones insisted, quite properly, that our duty, as a workers' theatre, was to support the striking cotton workers. Our first attempt at a cotton script was a crude affair even by our standards but we brightened it up by writing new words to a couple of pop tunes and including them. It was mostly mass declamation enlivened by rhythmic movements based on the working actions of a weaver and a mule-spinner. Shortly before the strike some of us had seen a German dance group called, I think, the Bodenweiser. We had watched them, from the 'gods' at the Salford Hippodrome, perform a piece called the Dance of the Machines. It had fascinated us and for quite a long time afterwards its influence could be seen in everything we did. Consequently when we performed our eight-looms sketch outside the Pendleton mill of Elkanah Armitage we were taking our first tentative steps in the field of modern dance.

As the strike gathered momentum we became more and more involved. We were out on the streets almost every night of the week performing, or trying to perform since the police harassed us continuously. Those areas like Earby, Burnley, Nelson and Colne which had been among the first of the towns to come out on strike were soon feeling the pinch, and union funds, which were small, soon gave out. Now was the time for workers throughout Britain to show their solidarity with the strikers. The response to the union's appeal for help was magnificent. Food convoys began to roll in from Glasgow, Tonypandy, Hull, Whitechapel, Newcastle-upon-Tyne, Sunderland and Sheffield. We added the collection of food to our performance routine and after each performance of our eight-looms sketch we went from door to door with an old hand-cart we had acquired and collected food for the strikers. The more active we became the more the police hounded us and scarcely a week went by without one of us being arrested and fined for obstruction, creating a public nuisance or contravening any one of the thousand and one restrictions and by-laws that are there to safeguard the status quo.

The strike dragged on and we found ourselves going further afield at week-ends, to places as far away as Todmorden, Blackburn, Burnley and Great Harwood. More often, however, we would take a threepenny or fourpenny tram or bus ride to a nearby town and play two or three shows there. Where there were three or four towns adjacent to each other we would play all of them in a single afternoon. A typical itinerary would be Ashton-under-Lyne – a show in the market-place and, after a couple of quick appearances in the main shopping area, off to Dukinfield where the pattern would be repeated. If we succeeded in raising a few coppers in the collection we would then take a tram to Hyde where we would repeat the routine again, finishing up in Stockport or Failsworth. The following week we might play Oldham, Rochdale and Bury. During the week we generally confined ourselves to performances in Manchester, Salford and, occasionally, in Eccles, Monton, Pendlebury and Swinton.

At this stage I don't believe that any of us regarded ourselves as artists or, indeed, as being in any way involved with art. We saw ourselves as guerrillas using the theatre as a weapon against the capitalist system. That system had made it perfectly clear that the authorities regarded us as production units which could be used, then thrown away. As far as they were concerned we were zeroes, born to lose. So what the hell had we to do with art, or art with us? On the other hand one needed a skill in order to survive and nobody was going to help you to acquire that skill. You must do it yourself or go under. Now the theatre was the kind of artefact that we could deal with; one could pick up ways of dealing with it just as one could pick up ways of dealing with a lathe or a milling-machine. And that's what we were doing; picking up ways of dealing with a new tool. We knew about tools, about how to fashion them and how to make them work. So we were going to make this new tool work for us. But art . . .!

It was an agit-prop script which contained a passage of writing by Maxim Gorky that first made me aware of the fact that I might be involved in something which could be described as art. The quotation went something like this: 'There is no art in the world today worthy of its name beside the art created by the working-class in the course of its struggle. We are the ones who build this art. By means of it we are working for the great causes of labour, destroying the chains of slavery.' It may strike the reader as incongruous that a small group of unemployed teenagers, wearing bib-and-brace overalls and khaki shirts, should stand on the steps of a decaying bath-house and bawl out such sentiments. And yet there is something quite remarkable too in the fact that these young, under-privileged rejects of a nineteenth-century slum should have been able to preserve such hope, such shining belief, such glorious optimism in a world which offered them nothing but the scrap-heap.

We are, we said, the propertyless theatre of a propertyless class so to hell with art, let's get on with the job, and the immediate job was to collect food, clothing and cash for the besieged strikers. It also meant performing for the strikers themselves and reminding them that they were not alone. It meant, too, explaining the strike to other groups of workers who were not, themselves, directly involved in it. That was the immediate task. The long-term objective was to forge an efficient weapon which could be used to bring about fundamental changes in society. All of us agreed that society needed changing and all of us subscribed to the Marxist theory that such changes could only be brought about by the working class. In the half-century which has passed since that time, nothing has happened to make me alter that point of view.

On the few occasions that I visited the commercial theatre during those years I don't remember seeing anything that wasn't a completely unconvincing sham – badly acted, badly written and badly produced. Obviously one's view of society is determined by one's angle of vision; if one lives under the foot of society one tends to see the entire body as a pair of dwarf-like legs and two enormous, flabby buttocks. I was conscious of all these things but at the same time I remained absolutely convinced that the theatre, in the right hands, could be a symbol of truth, passion and beauty. I am not suggesting that the Red Megaphones were 'the right hands' or that our productions were any more convincing or that they were better written or better acted. In one respect, however, they were infinitely superior: there was no shamming in them, all of us believed passionately in what we were doing and what we were saying and real, unadulterated passion is a rare thing to find, on the stage or anywhere else.

It was this passion which drove us on in the face of constant harassment by police, the jeers and taunts of workers whom we claimed to represent, and the physical attacks by Blackshirts and others. Anyone who believes that street theatre can win an audience more easily than other kinds of theatre has more imagination than experience. Only on rare occasions did we succeed in attracting more than a handful of people to stop whatever they were doing and listen to us. Such rare occasions were unemployed demonstrations or gatherings of strikers. Our most memorable shows were connected with these events. One of them took place in Wigan market-place on the day of the local strike ballot. The entire town was tense with barely concealed excitement and we were met, with a good deal of enthusiasm, by a crowd of three or four hundred women. Small groups of unemployed miners were stationed on the perimeter of the crowd and were there to act as a defence force if necessary. An empty coal-cart had been positioned in the centre of the square and this was to be our platform.

We had scarcely started on our first sketch when we were interrupted by a police sergeant who told us to clear off. Several miners, however, surrounded the platform and, ignoring the policeman, told us to carry on. After a few moments the sergeant went away and returned shortly afterwards with an inspector and several uniformed constables. This time the crowd closed ranks and prevented them from approaching the platform. After a brief argument with a very angry group of women the police withdrew, whereupon a young miner climbed an ornamental lamp-standard and raised our banner on it to the cheers of the crowd. In the course of the next ninety minutes we ran through every item in our repertoire and then, at the insistence of the crowd, repeated it all over again.

Burnley, Lancashire, was the scene of another memorable performance. A very critical point in the eight-looms strike had been reached and, a few days earlier in Earby and Nelson, pitched battles between police and strikers had been fought. On the day of our performance tens of thousands of strikers from the mill towns of Lancashire and Cheshire had poured into Burnley to welcome the food convoys which were due to arrive. We performed our eight-looms sketch from the top of one of these giant pantechnicons, looking out over the sea of faces which filled Burnley's main square and all the roads leading into it. A thrilling experience!

When, eventually, the strikers were defeated we returned to our street-corner performances with occasional shows at anti-war demonstrations or at meetings organised by one or other of the various anti-fascist groups. But times and the political situation were changing rapidly. Unemployment and the demoralising poverty which is part of it were now an established part of our life. The mass demonstrations of hundreds of thousands of unemployed men and women which had highlighted the winter months of 1931–2 had now given way to a different kind of struggle. The emphasis which all through the twenties and the beginning of the thirties had been on economic issues was now shifting to political events, the national and the international were becoming one. Dmitrov, hero of the Reichstag fire trial, speaking at an international anti-fascist congress, gave voice to the hopes and fears of many people when he brought his oration to a close with the words: 'We are entering a period of wars and revolutions.'

In the course of the eight-looms strike the Red Megaphones had been visited by two young German refugees who, until the Nazis came to power, had been actors in a famous German agit-prop group. They were now working as organisers for the International Union of Revolutionary Theatres and were members of a committee which was organising an international Olympiad of Workers' Theatres. Salford was one of the whistle-stops on their international fact-finding tour. They arrived on the week-end of the big meeting and travelled with us to Burnley. They appear to have been impressed by our performance or perhaps they felt that our enthusiasm should be rewarded, for from that time on we were bombarded through the post with scripts and magazines from exiled German theatre groups, from Russia, Czechoslovakia and the United States. One of these scripts, *Wer ist der Dummste*, had been performed by a group led by the distinguished theatre workers Inge and Gustav von Wangenheim. It was an experiment in the kind of theatre that we ourselves had dreamed of creating and were quite incapable of performing. It brought to a head all the discontent with our standards and repertoire which had been building up over several months. Our repertoire now consisted of *Meerut, Rent, Interest and Profit*, *The Spirit of Invergordon*, *Their Theatre and Ours*, *The Fight against the Eight-Looms*, *The Archbishop's Prayer* and *Suppress, Oppress and Depress*. We also had a number of parodies of popular songs and could recite several revolutionary poems.

As a repertoire it left a lot to be desired. The sketches appeared to have been written to a formula which called for loud voices rather than acting ability on the part of the performers. In almost all of them there were some good lines and occasional flashes of real wit. The satire was sometimes crude but it was often very effective indeed though sometimes embedded in stodgy journalese or obscured by horseplay. The message was usually delivered at the top of the human voice in the form of slogans hurled by actors standing head on to the audience. What little movement there was tended to be limited to minor changes in position and absurd capering and this wasn't entirely due to the limited stage area. The fact is we were dealing with literary tracts not very dissimilar in tone and style to those denunciatory broadsides which eighteenth-century pamphleteers were in the habit of hurling at their enemies. The audience was never allowed to forget itself and at the end of each sketch a group of six or more young people would swing towards the onlookers and, with its maximum collective voice, exhort them to do this or do that. We were not asking them, we were commanding them and, not unnaturally, some of them resented us.

Our criticism of our way of working and of our repertoire became increasingly vocal throughout 1933 and when we decided to embark on the production of a piece called *Newsboy* there was a general sigh of relief. This short play had been sent to us by the New York Laboratory Theatre who had taken a poem by V. J. Jerome and made it into a very exciting short drama. It had many features in common with agit-prop theatre and was certainly no less political. But whereas our agit-prop sketches had been largely static, too obviously didactic and over-dependent on caricature, *Newsboy* was full of action and made use of 'real' characters, fairly run-of-the-mill characters but characters none-the-less. The format was simplicity itself: a bare stage lit by a centre-spot in which a newsboy dances and sells newspapers. As he dances he shouts the headlines of the world's news. From time to time he slips out of the light and his place is taken by two, and sometimes three, actors who perform short scenes in which an item of news is 'acted out'. Beyond the rim of the light various representatives of the outside world pass and go about their business. The slogans were still there but they arose naturally out of the play and were not imposed upon it.

The production of *Newsboy* raised problems that we had not had to face before. The central character had to be able to dance! The short scenes demanded actors. It was one thing to learn, parrot-fashion, a mass declamation and one could be drilled into carrying out a series of simple group manoeuvres. But to act! Furthermore, *Newsboy* called for the use of stage lighting, and stage lighting meant an indoor venue. Now we knew nothing about dance, little about acting, less about stage lighting and there was also the matter of length. *Newsboy* was meant to run for fifteen minutes which meant that we needed another seventy-five minutes to make a reasonably full performance. For a group of penniless young people without much knowledge of the theatre, these were enormous problems. The solution of the dance problem came about as the result of a chance meeting. Signing on at the labour exchange I ran into a childhood acquaintance who on leaving school had gone into the building trade and was now a steel-erector. He was one of a large Catholic family, all of whom possessed names which, in our district, were regarded as somewhat high-flown. His parents were actors in a fit-up company and they christened their children with names borrowed from whatever plays they happened to be playing in at the time. My friend's birth had coincided with a tour of *The Fortunes of Gerard*, *Richard the Third* and *Antony and Cleopatra*, hence his name – Gerard Richard Antony Davies. Good names, all of them but not particularly appropriate: they sounded too soft. It wasn't merely that he was a steel-erector, he actually looked as if he had been fashioned in a Bessemer furnace. When I told him about our problems he offered immediately to play the part of the newsboy and he turned out to be a natural-born dancer. His voice too was admirably suited to the part; working outdoors and being forced to make himself heard above the clang of steel girders and the rattle of jack-hammers had given him a voice that could have been heard above a salvo of bombs. He stayed in the group for three or four years, until his job took him to distant parts.

The lighting problems were solved by Alf Armitt, a seventeen-year-old vertical-lathe operator who had once run with the Percy Street mob, one of Salford's most feared juvenile street gangs. He had been a foundation member of the Red Megaphones and was active in the Labour League of Youth. While reading up on lighting in the Manchester Reference Library he came upon a reference to Adolph Appia, the Swiss stage-director and a revolutionary theorist on the nature and function of light in the theatre. Somehow Alf managed to lay his hands on a rough translation of one of Appia's books and from that time on we were all Appia disciples. Alf Armitt's researches didn't only provide us with a theoretical base for what was to be an important element in our work. It also gave us three spotlights which he had made out of ten-pound barrel-type biscuit-tins fitted with 500-watt lamps 'borrowed' from the floodlighting equipment used to illuminate the Salford greyhound-racing track. This was our first foray into the world of theatre lighting: no dimmers, no floods, no switchboard, just three converted biscuit-tins and an off/on wall switch. Later Alf was to demonstrate his ingenuity by building us a switchboard.

The problem of finding enough material to fill an entire evening was solved by making *Newsboy* the centrepiece of a variety show which included a mass declamation calling for the release of Ernst Thaelmann, the German Communist leader who was a prisoner of the Nazis, an agit-prop anti-war sketch, a group of songs of Eisler and Brecht and a surrealistic poem by the American, Funarov. The programme was presented at the Round House, Ancoats, in February or March 1934.

It was during the rehearsals of this show that we were joined by Joan Littlewood. She had come to Manchester to take part in a B.B.C. feature programme and had been taken on by the director of the Rusholme Repertory Theatre to act as A.S.M. and play small roles. Her job occupied most of her evenings but the little free time she managed to get was spent helping us and she was even able to take part in the recitation of the Funarov poem *The Fire Sermon* at the Round House.

In the weeks that followed we took the show to a number of small halls in the Manchester area and added Shelley's *Mask of Anarchy* and Louis Aragon's poem *The Red Front* to the other items.

The comparative success of this first indoor performance and the fact that we no longer were faced with the constant threat of being moved on or arrested produced temporary feelings of euphoria in the group. Shortly before the Round House performance we had reorganised the group and we were now calling ourselves the Theatre of Action, a title which, I believe, we had borrowed from the New York group. Now we were beginning to look around for ideas and models which would help us to arrive at a clearer picture of the kind of theatre we wanted to create. Though we were hostile to the commercial theatre and generally spoke of it with contempt, we really knew very little about it. Most of us had seen three or four plays and a few of us had read quite a lot of plays as well as various critiques and histories of theatre. It was upon these that our opposition was based. We were not, at this stage, opposed to the classical repertoire, the techniques employed or what one might call the machinery of theatre. Our hostility was towards the kind of plays that were being presented in the theatre, towards the kind of people depicted in those plays, to the triviality of the themes and to the kind of audience being catered for. In short our hostility was towards certain products of the theatre and not to the theatre itself. Joan was the only one among us who felt differently about it; four years at R.A.D.A. and the opportunity to see the London theatre at work, followed by her current experience in one of Britain's leading repertory theatres, had convinced her that the theatre was sick in all its parts. It wasn't long before the rest of us were to be converted to Joan's point of view.

Six or seven months after the formation of the Theatre of Action, Ernst Toller, the refugee German dramatist, came to Manchester to supervise a production of his play *Draw the Fires* at the repertory theatre. The play deals with the mutiny of the German fleet in the Kiel canal in 1918. A good deal of its action takes place in the stokehold of the flagship *Von Tirpitz*. Stokers and trimmers, stripped to the waist, shovel coal into the furnaces throughout a complete scene and, indeed, the high point of the drama occurs when the stokers throw down their shovels and refuse to carry on working. The actors, more familiar with a cigarette-case than with shovels, appeared to be incapable of delivering lines and heaving coal at the same time. The disdain with which they regarded these simple tools was scarcely in accord with the surroundings. Actors, at the time, were recruited almost exclusively from the middle classes and they regarded themselves as gentlemen, and it was right and proper that they should have a gentleman's contempt for work and for those who did it. Given a French window or a Tudor fireplace and they would have felt perfectly at home but the stokehold was definitely not their milieu. Toller, alarmed at the prospect of seeing his high drama converted to farce, asked Joan whether there were any actors in the vicinity who didn't appear to be chronic invalids. Joan told him about Theatre of Action and that evening she brought him to our rehearsal. He watched us for ten minutes and then left after telling us to be at the theatre at ten o'clock the following morning.

The awe we felt at being backstage in a 'real' theatre didn't last long. The leading man, an angry boy from one of Britain's lesser public-schools, hated us on sight and most of the company followed his example. It wasn't that they felt, in any way, threatened by us and it wasn't the mild contempt that many professionals feel towards amateurs. They positively hated us and didn't attempt to hide their hatred. Maybe it was because we brought an unwelcome sniff of the real world into their make-believe existence, the world of unemployment, dirt and deprivation. They were contemptuous of the way we spoke and some of them pretended not to understand us when we asked questions. The leading lady held a handkerchief to her nose every time one of us stood near her. For the first hour or two we were suitably humble until we realised just how physically inept they were. We were tempted to show that we too could show a lack of generosity equal to theirs but they looked so weak and ineffectual that we felt sorry for them. One or two of our members felt that we were wasting our time and suggested that we pulled out of the show before we got more involved. The majority, however, voted to stay so as to learn as much as possible about the craft, if not the art, of theatre. During the fortnight's run of the show we were disabused of any illusions we may have had; the general attitude of the rep company to work, the flip dismissal of any serious ideas, the slipshod attitude to rehearsal and the shoddy tricks used as a substitute for acting shocked us profoundly and when we left we had a very clear picture of the kind of theatre we didn't want.

From the beginning Joan's relationship with the repertory company had been an uneasy one and now her employers regarded her as our sponsor; the atmosphere was, to say the least, brittle and it wasn't long before it reached breaking-point. Her resignation was received with relief by the managing committee of the repertory theatre and Joan and I settled down to a period of study and experiment. The bulk of our studying was done at the Manchester Central Reference Library where, for several hours each day, we sat and read everything we could lay our hands on which had any bearing on the theatre: plays, analyses, critical surveys, biographies of dramatists, technical manuals on lighting, lavishly illustrated folios on décor and obsolete essays by forgotten French and German writers.

In the summer of 1934 we attended a Workers' Theatre Movement conference in London where in the course of a speech by a rising West End actor and producer were were advised to abandon the agit-prop technique and 'embrace the techniques of the established theatre'. This advice had already been taken to heart by two of the London groups, and that evening we sat through one of their productions, a mediocre piece called *Hammer*. It was a typical example of the well-made play; typical in the sense that the dialogue was artificial, the plot mechanical and the characters a series of stereotypes. The production was straight, uninspired 'rep' stuff and the acting a typical amateur copy of fashionable west-end posturing. We were appalled and left London raging against the producer and those who had allowed him to 'capture the left theatre'.

Back in Manchester we discussed our experience with the other members of the group who shrugged their shoulders and said: 'What else can you expect from Londoners? No guts! Decadent lot! Not like us Northerners!' And if that suggests that we were typical north-country bigots then it is no less than the truth, for we wrote London off and for the next few years had scarcely any contact with it at all.

We did not, however, feel cut off in any way from the mainstream of socially committed experimental theatre. We were still in touch with groups in the United States and the Soviet Union and with the various groups of exiled German theatre workers. In addition we were avid readers of the theatrical press and magazines like *New Theatre* and *Theatre Arts Monthly* kept us informed about what was happening on the other side of the Atlantic. For European stimulus there was always Leon Moussinac's *New Movement in the Theatre*, a veritable treasure-trove of concepts and ideas. It was through Moussinac's book that we had our first real introduction to Myerhold's theatre and to some extent, at any rate, his ideas were to dominate much of our next production, *John Bullion*. This had started life as *Hammer*, the rather dreary play we had seen in London on the night of the Workers' Theatre Movement conference. The script was quite as bad as the production had been but we were desperately in need of something to produce so we set about adapting it to our needs. For a start, we reduced the number of characters, then cut out all of them and introduced new ones in their place. This necessitated a change of dialogue which, in turn, resulted in several scenes being shortened and then cut out. This called for further changes in the dialogue which, in turn, meant more cuts. We finally cut out all the dialogue and substituted for it catch-phrases spoken by a chorus of typists. The décor, which in the London production had included a naturalistic office with desk, filing-cabinets, chairs, hatstand, doors, windows, etc., now became a bare platform with a raised wooden plane standing along the back wall along which various figures representing the outside world passed. Downstage there were three skeletoid wooden stools, six, seven and eight feet high. Seated on them and attached to them by chains were three young women, clones of the script's original secretary. Their faces and bodies were painted white and they wore black panties and bras. The main character, John Bullion, was made-up to look like a grotesque clown and had a stomach padded to Falstaffian proportions covered by a waistcoat fashioned from a Union Jack. The production was a kind of ménage-à-trois of styles borrowed from agit-prop, constructivism and expressionism. These three elements were to play important roles in many of our productions over the next few years.

Early in 1935 we embarked on a production of *Waiting for Lefty* which had recently opened in New York and was playing there to enthusiastic audiences. Odett's play was an ideal one for us: it was not too long but long enough to fill a substantial part of an evening, it dealt with a significant area of class-struggle and it did so in a way that was direct and uncompromising. Its theme was one which would appeal to almost any working-class audience and its dialogue would be easily comprehended by people whose main theatrical fare was Hollywood films. Like that earlier piece of the Clarion Players, *Still Talking, Waiting for Lefty* contained many agit-prop elements in its make-up. Both plays made use of the public-meeting framework and, consequently, neither needed much in the way of décor and props. Both made use of the auditorium as an acting area and both used the device of the political oration interrupted by short dramatic vignettes. The slogans were still there but they were no longer used as a homiletic epilogue to the main action.

We opened with *Waiting for Lefty* and a supporting programme at the Milton Hall, Deansgate, and, after playing successfully there for three nights, moved to the Houldsworth Hall for a further five nights. Later we presented it at the Hyde Socialist Sunday School and in Haslingden, north-east Lancashire. It was, I believe, in this period that we began to envisage our future ideal theatre as one which toured working-class areas exclusively.

Between the productions of *Newsboy* and *Waiting for Lefty* the group had grown considerably and now numbered some twenty-three members. Furthermore we now had premises, a studio loaned to us by a friendly painter. The organisational structure of the theatre, however, had scarcely changed at all from the days of the Red Megaphones. Rehearsals were called by Joan or me, plays were directed by both of us or by whichever one of us was free at the time. Scripts which arrived through the post were read by us and it was left to us to decide whether they should be produced. There was no secretary, no treasurer (no money either), no technicians, no stage-designer, no wardrobe, no stage-management – just a small collective of would-be political actors. It had worked well enough with a small group of individuals each one of whom related to each other in much the same way that children who are members of the same street gang relate.

But more than working methods had changed. The social composition of the group had changed too and among the new members there were several professional people including two solicitors, a university lecturer and an art-school teacher. Almost all of them were more experienced in the business of running an organisation than were any of the half-dozen adolescents who had graduated through the Red Megaphones. Our way of dealing with our various tasks was very simple: if a job needed doing then whoever was free did it, and that was that! Anarchic? Possibly. Certainly some of our new recruits were shocked to the core by our way of doing things and it wasn't long before we had a management committee and two or three sub-committees. Things progressed smoothly for several weeks after their formation and then the management committee decided that matters concerning production, casting of roles, choice of plays, could no longer be left in the hands of 'a couple of prima donnas'; a production committee was needed. Joan and I treated the suggestion with scorn whereupon an 'extraordinary general meeting' was called in the course of which we were transformed into counter-revolutionaries, Trotskyists, social-fascists, mere formalists and enemies of the working class. It is ironical that those who were most vociferous in their condemnation of us became, in the course of the next decade, pillars of the establishment and solidly reactionary to a man and woman. At the time Joan and I were badly shaken by these events, particularly when, at a pre-arranged point in the meeting, a motion to expel us was proposed and seconded. In the voting which followed, the results were twelve in favour and twelve against. The chairman cast his vote in favour but by now we were sickened by the entire business. We left in disgust.

The attacks on us had left us feeling demoralised and for the next two or three weeks we seriously considered giving up all thought of working in the theatre. Our despair was dissipated by a letter which came from Moscow offering us scholarships to the Academy of Theatre and Cinema. Our spirits soared. Soon we would be studying at first hand the work of Myerhold, Vakhtangov, Stanislavski and Oplopkhov. We would be listening to Pudovkin and Eisenstein lecturing and would be able to watch them at work! Friends who had walked out in protest at the last Theatre of Action meeting, held a farewell party for us and, at a whip-round raised twelve pounds towards our travel expenses.

We arrived in London in November 1935, applied for visas at the Soviet Embassy and settled down to wait. While we were waiting we organised a training class for people who wanted to study our kind of theatre and, on our free nights, gave lectures to anyone who was prepared to listen. I still find myself blushing with embarrassment when I remember the kind of lectures I gave: long, incoherent disquisitions larded with quotations from Aristotle, Diderot, Goethe, Gordon Craig, Richter, Appia and Stanislavski and inapposite references to Moussinac's monumental tome. During one such lecture at the Slade School, I was so overcome with confusion that I couldn't continue. Fortunately Joan was at hand and was able to fill the breach. Her voice could charm birds out of the trees and if her references to Cimabue, Giorgione and Piero della Francesca baffled the listeners, their ears were charmed by her beautiful cadences.

We succeeded in persuading eight or nine trusting souls to become members of our acting school. Two of them were unemployed railway workers from Battersea, one worked as a labourer in the Morgan Crucible works; another, his sister, was a filing-clerk at Nine Elms, one was an art student, one was an unemployed youth from Wandsworth and the names and faces of the rest escape my memory. The instruction consisted mostly of movement classes which were run by Joan who had, at R.A.D.A. taken a movement course which appears to have been based on the Laban method. We also made a few tentative attempts at teaching voice production but abandoned them almost immediately. My teaching role was to lecture on the history of theatre and to conduct classes in Stanislavski's theory of acting. It really was a case of the blind leading the blind.

The fact that we couldn't afford money for premises made life difficult so we decided to live communally and thus solve the problem of living-accommodation and school premises at the same time. So we moved into a rather grand establishment on the west side of Clapham Common. We rattled around in it for a couple of months and then, our meagre travel fund exhausted, found we couldn't pay the rent. Once again our salvation came via the postman. The letter he brought didn't come from Moscow. Our visa application had probably been lost in the frozen waste of the embassy's bureaucracy and we were reconciled to the idea that it might never arrive. Indeed we made a virtue out of necessity and were comforting ourselves by saying that we hadn't really wanted to go to a foreign country to become part of somebody else's theatre. The real need was here in Britain, here where all the conditions existed for the creation of a new theatre, a theatre of the

British working class. So when the Manchester branch of the Peace Pledge Union invited us to produce Hans Schlumberg's *Miracle at Verdun* for them, we were overjoyed. Two days later we were back in Manchester.

The Peace Pledge Union and the Quakers, who were collaborating in this venture, had substantial resources at their disposal, or at least they seemed substantial to us. To begin with, they had an organisation and a secretarial staff who could organise rehearsal schedules, type scripts, deal with correspondents, produce posters and leaflets, arrange newspaper interviews and so on. The Friends' Meeting House, owned by the Quakers, was right in the centre of the city which meant we would have rehearsal premises which would be conveniently situated for just about everybody. This was important for a production which called for a score or more actors. *Miracle at Verdun* hasn't only got an enormous cast but one which includes Africans, French, Germans, Italians, Americans, Russians, Indians, Chinese, Swedes and Turks. Through their membership in the university and technical colleges, the Peace Pledge Union and the Quakers would be able to provide us with students from all the above countries. The big problem was to find a rehearsal room large enough to accommodate so many actors. We solved the problem by rehearsing all the small scenes at the Friends' Meeting House while the mass scenes were reserved for the final week and rehearsed in a large empty warehouse at the corner of Deansgate and Victoria Street.

From the time that Joan had joined the Theatre of Action we had worked together as a production team, often both working on the same unit at the same time. If there were occasional disagreements, they were unimportant. We discussed our ideas so often and at such length that either of us was capable of carrying out the other's wishes. *Miracle at Verdun* called for a different way of working for it had an inordinate number of scenes. So many scenes in fact that we began to doubt whether we had enough time to rehearse them all before the opening date. We solved this problem by sharing out the scenes between us and running simultaneous rehearsals in adjacent rooms. A kind of production-line approach! Not one to be recommended as a general principle though it worked well enough on this particular occasion.

Miracle at Verdun was a rather clumsily constructed play. Its author had not been able to make up his mind about whether he was writing an expressionistic drama or a naturalistic one. He had finally decided to write both and the result, while not entirely satisfactory, had made it a simple matter to divide the play up in the way I have described and when it opened its two-week run at the Lesser Free Trade Hall the critics were enthusiastic. We were less so. We had no reservations about the theme or message of the play but we felt that it was excessively wordy and soft-centred in the main confrontation scene. The fact is that we had a profound distrust of naturalistic theatre and every time we came to grips with it, we failed.

From an organisational point of view *Miracle at Verdun* was a very important stage in the development of our theatre. Not only did it win us a far bigger audience than we'd ever had before but it left us with a skeleton organisation which we could build on. It had, in addition, made it possible for us to reach the student population, it had put us in contact with amateur drama groups throughout the Manchester district and had won us support from a number of painters, sculptors, printers and journalists. A few days after the play's final performance, we called a meeting of all those who had taken part in it and there it was decided to form a new group. The aims of Theatre Union, as this new group was called, are summed up in this manifesto:

> We live in times of great social upheaval; faced with an ever-increasing danger of war and fascism, the democratic people of the world have been forced into action. Their struggle for peace and progress manifests itself in many forms and not the least important of these is the drama.
>
> Theatre Union is Manchester's contribution to the forces of democracy. It has set itself the task of establishing a complete theatre unit consisting of producers, actors, writers, artists and technicians, which will present to the widest possible public, and particularly to that section of the public which has been starved theatrically, plays of social significance. Where the censorship of the period makes it impossible for such productions to be open to the general public they will be given for private audiences of Theatre Union members. All that is most vital in the repertoire of the world's theatre will find expression on the stage of Theatre Union.
>
> It has been said that every society has the theatre it deserves; if that is so, then Manchester, one of the greatest industrial and commercial centres in the world deserves only the best. It is for the people of Manchester to see that Theatre Union's goal is attained. Theatre Union intends that its productions will be made accessible to the broadest possible mass of people in the Manchester district, and consequently it appeals to all Trade Unions and to all parties engaged in the struggle for peace and progress to become affiliated immediately.

This manifesto was still hot from the press when Spain was plunged into civil war. Like many people we were horrified at the turn events were taking and at a meeting of the newly formed Theatre Union, it was decided that we should mount a production which would have the dual function of drawing public attention to the struggle of the

Spanish people against Fascism and raising funds for medical aid. Lope de Vega's *Fuente Ovejuna* (*The Sheep-well*) was the play we chose to produce. It was our first excursion in the field of classical drama, the beginning of a road that was to lead to Marlowe's *Edward the Second*, Marston's *Dutch Courtesan, Arden of Faversham*, *Volpone* and *Macbeth*.

In every respect *Fuente Ovejuna* was the ideal play for the time. Its theme, the revolt of a village community against a ruthless and bloody dictator, was a reflection in microcosm of what was actually taking place in Spain. A colourful play with lots of action and a superb climax, it has a fairly big cast and like *Miracle at Verdun*, there are a number of crowd scenes. But whereas *Miracle* had been a rather static play, relying on a series of tableaus, *Fuente* had a tremendous amount of real action. In *Miracle* most of the roles were lay-figures who delivered speeches; there was no real conversation, instead there was oration. In *Fuente*, on the other hand, the characters were men and women who laughed and wept and cried out in pain and made jokes. Even the crowd was made up of characters who fought and danced and rioted like a crowd of football enthusiasts expressing their devotion to Manchester United. In our agit-prop days we had made great use of songs but had abandoned the practice when we left the streets. In *Fuente* we set Lope's lyrics to the tunes of stirring republican battle songs and used them as a continuous thread throughout the production.

The static nature of *Miracle at Verdun* had called for décor which underlined the play's lack of real physical conflict. The production of *Fuente Ovejuna*, on the other hand, demanded the maximum area of uncluttered stage where the crowds could move and give vent to their violent feelings. The single setting which our newly formed artists' group created for us consisted of a circular drinking-well situated upstage of centre with a large sculpted figure of a rampant sheep towering above it. This and a backcloth of ruffled hessian painted and dyed in autumnal colours of russet, brown and gold provided a wonderfully effective background for Lope's masterpiece.

In addition to extending our stylistic vocabulary, the production of *Fuente Ovejuna* gave us an enormous amount of confidence and won us wider support than we had ever enjoyed before. It occupies a very important place in our calendar of events for not only was it the first time that a play by Spain's most important dramatist had been performed in Britain, it was also the first time that we had dared to step outside the territory of agit-prop-cum-expressionistic theatre.

As the Spanish Civil War dragged on we found ourselves becoming more and more involved with it and soon we were staging pageants and specially written dramatic episodes for public meetings and demonstrations. Indeed, some of the dramatic interludes staged at Medical-Aid for Spain rallies rank among our most successful experiments. In them we carried the agit-prop form to new heights. The group declamations, occasional songs, the tableau-like groupings of the actors had, in our street-theatre days, suffered from sloppy presentation, a lack of nuance; we were either too casual in our approach or too rigidly regimented. We were still dealing with the same basic elements of group declamation, songs and group action but these had become refined, polished and imbued with that special luminescence which a large audience generates. Furthermore we were now using whole batteries of spotlights and they were adding their own kind of excitement. The four or five overworked voices of the Red Megaphones attempting to make themselves heard above traffic and the noise of the streets had now become a choir of fifteen or twenty mixed voices backed by a small band of instrumentalists. The text of the group declamation, which in the past had generally consisted of rather turgid prose, was now the work of Hugh MacDiarmid who could handle words like a Chinese juggler keeping twelve plates in the air with his feet.

There was a new ingredient too, the personal statement or statements made by members of the audience. These were planned and rehearsed interpolations made by two or three individuals seated in different parts of the auditorium and interviewed by us before the actual event. They would be asked several questions about themselves and their answers would then be whittled down to a few short sentences lasting anything from thirty to forty-five seconds. This is the kind of thing:

> My name is Arthur D. I'm a face worker at Agecroft Colliery, Pendleton. I'm on short time, a three-day week. I support the Spanish people's struggle because their fight and my fight is the same.

or:

> My name is Mary Parkinson. I'm thirty-four years old and I'm a back-tenter in Worral's Mill, Salford. I'm married with two children, Norah aged fourteen and Eddie aged twelve. My husband's a brass-moulder but he's out of work. Been idle for two years. I think it's terrible what's happening in Spain, the way our Government's helping the fascists.

At pre-arranged points in the script, these speakers would stand up, spotlights would pick them out and they would say their piece. Their statements would be sandwiched between republican songs sung by the choir or, on some occasions, by Paul Robeson and the whole thing would be given shape by a framework composed of passages from Hugh MacDiarmid's magnificent poem on the Spanish Civil War, *The Flaming Poetaster*. The effect produced by juxtaposing the flat Lancashire accents of housewives and unemployed workers against the soaring voices of the choir, the rich velvety base-baritone of Paul Robeson, or the stinging hail of MacDiarmid's poetry, was riveting. The use of such contrasts was to become an integral feature of many of our productions in the years ahead, particularly in plays like *Johnny Noble* and *Uranium 235*. It was also destined to become a notable feature of the post-war radio-ballads, those B.B.C. documentaries in which the form and spirit of folk-music and recorded actuality strive to become a single entity.

Following the production of *Fuente Ovejuna* we staged, in fairly quick succession, two plays dealing with war and peace, very different from each other in style and content. The first of these was *The Good Soldier Schweik*. Both Joan and I had read Hasek's novel some years before and had fallen in love with it, and when we heard that Piscator had produced a stage version of it in Germany we were determined that we would give it its first British production. We acquired a copy of the script without too much trouble but, unfortunately, it was in German and neither of us could read it. However by using the English translation of the novel and a German dictionary we succeeded in making a reasonable English adaptation.

In his production Piscator had made use of back-projection and life-sized marionettes. We rejected the marionettes but embraced the idea of back-projection with enthusiasm. Our unending discussions and planning for the ultimate theatre had made us receptive to new technical developments and innovations which might lend extra dimensions to the theatre. So we set about investigating the possibility of borrowing or acquiring in some way the special equipment required. The results of our investigations were not encouraging. German refugee actors spoke disparagingly of equipment which kept breaking down and which, when it did work, made so much noise that the actors couldn't be heard. Replies to enquiries were even more discouraging, the cost of hiring was prohibitive – more than we spent on an entire production; furthermore one needed a stage with great depth in order to give the projector an 'adequate throw'. To clinch matters, there was only one such projector in the country and the owners were not prepared to hire it without a team of operating technicians. We decided that we would dispense with back-projection. The following day there appeared in one of the evening papers an item dealing, in some detail, with our unsuccessful quest. That same evening four young men turned up at our rehearsal, engineering research scientists from Metropolitan-Vickers. They wanted details concerning our specific needs. We told them and they went away. Three days before the dress rehearsal they turned up again, this time in a Ford truck with our back-projector which they had built! It worked beautifully, much better than Piscator's, said our German friends.

Schweik fell naturally into our style of production. It contained so many of the basic elements of agit-prop technique. It possessed characters, true! But those characters leaned heavily towards caricature. Its episodic structure was firmly in the agit-prop tradition as was its anabasis. Even the expressionistic side of agit-prop was present, in the form of comic dance-interludes. In the second of our anti-war plays there were few such influences.

I had discovered Aristophanes a few years earlier in a second-hand bookshop in Leeds. It was my first contact with the classical theatre of Greece and what better introduction could there be for an adolescent youth? The pub-crawling episode in *Schweik* had taught us to respect the knockabout-comedy routines of the variety stage; our presentation of the drunken perambulations of Schweik and Woditchka owed a great deal to the various comic turns we had seen at the Salford Hippodrome. Now *Lysistrata's* chorus of old men were being given the same treatment, and it worked splendidly! And wasn't the Magistrate a figure straight out of burlesque? Then there was the singing and dancing which occupied a fair slice of Aristophanes' text: surely that wasn't too far removed from the style of the musicals which were coming out of Hollywood! Unfortunately we lacked the resources which would have allowed us to present *Lysistrata* as a musical. We did the next best thing and produced it as a spirited romp with lots of bawdy jokes and amusing horseplay. It laid the foundations for a more radical reworking of the text in which soldiers' scenes were interpolated between scenes of striking women and where recondite references to obsolete religious practices were cut out in favour of lines and short sequences borrowed from *The Acharnians*, *The Thesmophoriazusae* and *The Peace*.

Lysistrata opened at the Lesser Free Trade Hall at the time Chamberlain and Daladier were preparing to hand Czechoslovakia over to Hitler and the excitement of our play was lost in the rising tide of fear and confusion which accompanied that episode. We were consumed with a terrible sense of urgency and felt we could no longer afford the luxury of producing plays which didn't make an immediate and specific political statement about the danger confronting us all. The oblique parallels of *Schweik* and *Fuente* were all very well but the world was racing headlong towards disaster and we had passed the point where events could be influenced by a reference to the Peloponnesian War or even to that other war which had given birth to Schweik. It's not enough, we said, to have plays which make a generalised exposure of the nature of Capitalism, they must have specific objectives and they must be about events which are taking place now. It wasn't a matter of having less art and more politics but of having more clearly stated politics and more powerful art. The better the politics, we reasoned, the better the art and the nearer we would be to achieving our goal of a truly popular theatre.

Our next pre-war production was to make use of all our newly developed talents. We had often toyed with the idea of producing a living newspaper. The Russians had pioneered the form during the building of the Turksib railway when travelling-theatre groups, faced with audiences of illiterates, had presented shows dealing with the day-to-day politics of the project. The American Federal Theatre had adopted the idea and in 1936 produced *Triple A Ploughed Under* and its most successful living newspaper *One Third of a Nation* had just closed after playing for 237 performances, something of a record for a left theatre at the time. We felt that the time had arrived for us to see what we could do with the form.

The task of collecting newspaper items dealing with the events leading up to the Munich pact and its appalling aftermath was undertaken by the entire company. Everything we had learned about theatre and politics in the years of work was now to be put to use – the mass-declamatory form, the satirical comedy style of agit-prop, the dance-drama of *Newsboy*, the simulated public meetings of *Still Talking* and *Waiting for Lefty*, the constructivism of *John Bullion*, the expressionism of *Miracle at Verdun*, the burlesque comedy of *Lysistrata*, the juxtaposition of song and actuality from the Spanish Civil War pageants and the fast-moving episodic style of *The Good Soldier Schweik*.

From the agit-prop period onwards, we had adopted a somewhat eclectic approach to stage-design. *Newsboy* and the sketches accompanying it had been presented on a bare stage with simple spotlighting marking off the acting areas. *Waiting for Lefty* had also used a bare stage with some action in the auditorium and with two kitchen chairs and a small table for the inset scenes. *Miracle at Verdun* had used a formalised set for the graveyard scenes and some rather nondescript furniture for the League of Nations sequence. *John Bullion* had been unashamedly constructivist. *Fuente Ovejuna* had been architectonic-cum-impressionist and *Schweik* had been played in portable reversible screens. *Last Edition* represented a complete break with formal theatre staging. When it opened at the Lesser Free Trade Hall, it was on a stage which, in addition to the central platform or stage proper, had two further platforms running the full length of each side of the auditorium so that that the audience was enclosed on three sides. There were scenes during which all three stages were in use at the same time; other scenes used only one or two of the stages. Following spots were used for each of the two side-platforms and the overall effect was not unlike a fast-moving variety show, the kind of theatre, that is, with which most of us were familiar. The similarity was reinforced by an added use of song and dance. One or two of the episodes were reworked versions of ideas which had been used in the early days of Theatre of Action when we had neither enough actors nor sufficient resources to carry them out properly. In some instances we combined ideas from *Newsboy* with scenes which had been inspired by early Hollywood musicals like *42nd Street* and *Fox Movietone Follies of 1932*.

The theme of unemployment ran like a thread through *Last Edition*. It was a subject about which we were well informed. Some of us, indeed, were experts on the subject and there was scarcely an actor in the group who hadn't been on the dole at some time or another. For many of us the most potent symbols of the thirties were the unemployed hunger-marches. In the confines of a formal stage structure the presentation of a hunger-march would have involved all kinds of problems; with our three connected stages it became a very simple matter. The hunger-march episodes in *Last Edition* were an amalgam of ideas drawn from agit-prop sketches, *Schweik* and *Waiting for Lefty*.

Among the most effective scenes in the production were those dealing with the Gresford pit disaster. Gresford was one of those mass killings which were a periodic feature of the privately owned coal industry. The annual toll of deaths due to rock-falls, explosions and pneumoconiosis was, apparently, acceptable to the public, provided that only one or two corpses at a time were added to the list. But 265 dead in one fell swoop! Even the Tories couldn't talk that away. We presented the episode in two parts, first as an 'open' scene with simultaneous action on all three stages with writing and acting strongly influenced by the crowd scenes from *Fuente Ovejuna*, and secondly, in marked contrast, as a trial scene with dialogue taken from verbatim accounts which appeared in newspapers at the time of the disaster. The people depicted on the stage are real people.

Specific political events and the individuals associated with them were dealt with in a variety of ways. One of the most interesting was what we called 'acting-out' episodes. These were scenes within scenes in which actors were called upon to step out of a role they were playing in order to assume a completely different role. This parenthetical device had been used frequently in agit-prop sketches such as *Rent, Interest and Profit* and *Their Theatre and Ours* and was used effectively in several Theatre Workshop post-war productions. An example is the 'Politics of Democracy' section printed below.

The staged recitation of poems like *The Fire Sermon*, Shelley's *Mask of Anarchy* and Aragon's *The Red Front* had been a regular feature of the early Theatre of Action shows. In *Aid for Spain* pageants we had made use of MacDiarmid's exhortatory poem on the Spanish Civil War and now we were using it again in *Last Edition* as a link between the several small scenes which made up the civil-war sequence.

The second part of that sequence, the departure of the four International Brigaders, made use of a device which had been a favourite with radio producers ever since Archie Harding had first used it in his brilliant B.B.C. documentary *'Crisis in Spain'*. The device was a simple one: an uncharacterised voice would repeat a phrase at intervals or would read out a list of names or a group of statistics or a catalogue of dates. Inset between the names, or places or dates there would be a naturalistic scene. The juxtaposition of flat statement against dramatic interludes produced a special kind of excitement. It was not unlike the effect of incremental repetition in a traditional ballad. We tended to over-use the device for we were still as poor as church mice and it was a cheap alternative to a change of décor. On the whole it worked well, though there was the odd occasion when it gave the wrong emphasis to a scene by making it unnecessarily portentous.

The Launcelot–Sigismund scene which came prancing at the heels of the Spanish Civil War episode was rooted in the idiom of Christmas pantomime. Indeed, the parodying of popular types of show-biz was an important ingredient of almost all our early shows. The burlesque of the Hollywood gangster film was one we were particularly attached to. It had featured in one of our earliest agit-prop sketches, *Their Theatre and Ours* and we used it in *Last Edition* (as in the Munich Pact episode printed below) and again in *Uranium 235*.

It will be obvious from the above that we tended to use the term 'Living Newspaper' rather loosely. Part documentary and part revue,

Last Edition was, stylistically, an anthology of everything we had ever done in the theatre. While some of it was very exciting, much of it was either ridiculously overwritten or hopelessly pedestrian and tedious. There were episodes when it must have seemed to the audience that the narrator's voice would never stop churning out statistics, items of news and the threadbare clichés which pass for wisdom in the mouths of politicians.

After five performances *Last Edition* was stopped by the police. Joan and I were arrested and fined for behaviour likely to lead to a breach of the peace, and though the company managed to survive for several months longer, the war finally put an end to its activities.

There had never been any doubt in our minds that we would reassemble after the war and continue with our work. When we did so only five of the original Theatre Union company were present. We met in a small rented warehouse near Manchester's Central station and, over a period of several weeks, discussed plans for a new theatre. We were fairly clear in our minds as to the kind of theatre we intended to build; our discussions were mainly about practical issues like finance, finding premises, drawing up training programmes, allocating jobs and responsibilities and deciding on a suitable opening programme. Most of us, I think, still believed that our aims could only be achieved by playing to working-class audiences. All the great theatres of the past, we argued, had been popular theatres and we cited Aeschylus, Sophocles, Aristophanes, Marlowe, Shakespeare, Jonson, Calderón, Lope de Vega, the Commedia dell'arte, Molière, etc. Furthermore, we said, all the great theatres had, in one way or another, been experimental theatres. Think of the way Marlowe's mighty line had streaked across the literary firmament scarcely twenty-five years after the limping cadences of *Gorbuduc* had first sounded in the Inner Temple. And hadn't Shakespeare teased and manipulated the language till it fitted the hands of the age like magic gloves? And how quickly Jonson was off the mark, eager to dissect the new merchant class at the moment of its birth and, in the process, fashioning brilliant new satires out of the old moralities. In Italy the troupes of the Gelosi and I Comici Confidenti had taken the characters from the ancient rituals and had sent them cavorting through sixteenth- and seventeenth-century Europe. Molière had taken those same characters and had worked with them to create a brilliant dramatic literature.

Not that experiment in itself was enough to create popular theatre; nineteenth- and twentieth-century theatrical experiments had proved that. The numerous attempts to change the physical relationship of actors and audience were among the most important of those experiments. The proscenium arch had, in some cases, been banished; apron stages, thrust stages, and central stages had been adopted. Opponents of the illusionist type of theatre had removed everything which might conceal technical aids such as light and sound sources or engineering devices. In some extreme cases actors had been replaced with life-sized puppets and even with cut-out abstract shapes. Less adventurous innovators had settled for a theatre of synthesis where acting, dancing, singing, music, sculpture, painting and architecture would come together in a meaningful fusion.

As far as we were concerned experiment was merely a part of our social and political commitment; it was a tool which would make the theatre more capable of dealing with the reality of the world we were living in. Our emphasis on a working-class audience was part of that reality. We were not concerned with philanthropic gestures or with demonstrating that our hearts were in the right place. We *needed* a working-class audience in order to survive; without it there could be no real development, the theatre could never be anything more than a charming toy. How in the world could one possibly build a great theatre unless one identified with and drew sustenance from the people who, in our society, produce wealth – the working class? Of course, it was also a reality that working people had stayed away from the theatre in large numbers ever since the Elizabethan age or, at least, since Jacobean times. Indeed there were large areas of Britain where no theatre existed at all. Scores of provincial theatres had been converted to cinemas in the years following the First World War and it's doubtful whether more than a handful of folk regretted it. For most working people the basic form of entertainment was the Hollywood film. It might be argued that the films current at the time were in no way superior to the plays produced by provincial theatres. Were they not just as escapist, just as lacking in real ideas as the worst kind of repertory play? The answer must be no. Furthermore, the making of a film demanded a degree of technical expertise which few theatres could match. As an art form film belonged to the age of the internal-combustion engine and the assembly-line, the age of speed and through the use of montages, rapid cross-cutting and speeding up of the projected visual images, it could reflect that speed. It could produce a quick succession of short scenes in a way that was beyond the resources of all but the most splendidly equipped theatres.

More important was the fact that film actors and actresses like James Cagney, Edward G. Robinson, Spencer Tracy, Jean Harlow, Sylvia Sydney were frequently called upon to act working-class roles and could do so convincingly. They were certainly more like the audiences who watched them than were the average hero and heroine of the English stage play of the period or, for that matter, than the top-hatted-and-tailed heroes of many British films. My memory of English films of the early thirties is of endless inane caperings of actors got up to look like butlers disguised as Claude Hulbert or Jack Buchanan and of leading ladies who delivered their lines like well-brought-up children intent on pleasing nanny. Small wonder that we were emotionally prepared for the acculturative invasion of the Hollywood talkie with its tough guys and its wisecracks.

In our theatre, we said, an actor will be able to walk into a steel foundry and pass as a puddler, our actresses will be able to stand at a loom and look like any other Lancashire mill-girl. Perhaps we were a little over-ambitious but the company which we assembled didn't look like a group of actors and they spoke in the accents of Glasgow, Tyneside, Huddersfield, Chichester, Leeds, Salford and South London. This new company we called Theatre Workshop since we intended that it should be both a production unit and a training school where new approaches to acting could be tried out. Our actors would be able to handle their bodies with the same degree of skill and control that was generally regarded as the special domain of ballet-dancers and professional athletes. We were going to find ways of developing our voices so that we could handle the most exacting kind of roles. As for acting proper, we would combine Stanislavski's method of 'living the role' with the improvisational techniques of the Italian Comedy. And for a repertoire – we would create a tailor-made one for ourselves, a repertory consisting of plays which would match at every stage the talents of the company and would extend those talents with each new production. We would, at the same time, carry the lessons learned in *Newsboy*, *Last Edition* and the agit-prop theatre to new heights.

I don't think any of us doubted that we could and would realise our objectives. How else can one explain a dozen young men and women abandoning their various livelihoods in order to become strolling players? We knew, of course, that the work would be hard but we had worked hard in the years before the war and we had done so while doing all kinds of other jobs, jobs which had virtually subsidised our theatre activities. Now we were going to give all our energy and all our attention to building a theatre and, furthermore, we were going to be paid for our work. That, at least, was the theory.

It was taken for granted that Joan would be the producer in the new company and that I should take on the job of Art Director, a title which embraced various functions including being the company dramatist, dramaturg, teacher and songwriter. One of my first tasks was to write material for an opening production. During the period in which the company was being assembled we discussed frequently and at great length the kind of show needed to launch our venture successfully. What was needed was a show in which entertainment and a statement of aims would be combined. It was important to make our political position clear while at the same time underlining our specific theatrical approach. Our introduction to the public should be in a show which, we felt, would lend itself to the kind of production ideas which had made *Last Edition* such an exciting experience. It should also give full scope to our views about the way actors should use their bodies, and make it possible for sound and light to make their full emotional impact. What we really needed was to create a form which was infinitely flexible, which would make it possible for us to move backwards and forwards in time and space as, say, with a film, and which could accommodate improvisations.

I wrote a double bill of two plays, each lasting about an hour. The first of them was an adaptation of Molière's *Flying Doctor*, a very free adaptation owing more to the Marx Brothers and the Commedia dell'arte than to Molière. It also included a scene taken straight from Rabelais's *Gargantua and Pantagruel* ('How a great scholar of England would have argued against Pantagruel and was overcome by Panurge'). In the period between the demise of Theatre Union and the birth of Theatre Workshop, some of us had been studying the history of the Commedia dell'arte and actors like the Andreinis and the Biancholellis had become saints in our calendar. And now we were about to pay homage to them! The other half of the bill was a ballad-opera called *Johnny Noble*.

An offer of premises in Kendal, Westmorland, had been accepted with enthusiasm and we packed and crated our gear ready for the great day when we would be told that our sponsors had completed their arrangements for our reception. The arrangements were never completed, indeed they never got off the ground. In retrospect I doubt whether the sponsorship offer was ever meant seriously. When it finally dawned on us that we had spent several weeks waiting for premises that didn't exist we were in despair. All our plans had been made with Kendal in mind; it had become a kind of Mecca, a promised land where marvellous things could happen. To hell with sponsors, we said, let's go! So early in June 1945 we arrived in Kendal, booked a room in the Conservative Club there and proceeded to rehearse *Johnny Noble* and *The Flying Doctor*.

The launching of these two short plays took place at the Girls' High

School, Kendal, in August 1945. In their different ways they were both typical examples of the early Theatre Workshop style. *The Flying Doctor* was our first attempt at interpreting the ideas of the Commedia dell'arte, or rather what we imagined those ideas to be. The classic roles of Sganarelle, Gorgibus, Doctor Palaprat, Lucille and the rest were played as broad caricatures in the way that we imagined the Gelosi had played Scapino, Dottore, Pantalone and il Inamorata. Movement training which had gone hand-in-hand with rehearsals was now being put to full use, for the production was full of stylised movement, sometimes graceful, sometimes grotesque; indeed the entire production had been as carefully choreographed as any ballet. Costumes for the show owed much of their inspiration and flair to Callot's superb engravings. The set was a small miracle of ingenuity, consisting of a small, manually operated revolving stage. Its surface was made of thin wooden board which made it light enough to be handled with ease. To prevent creaking, the underside was strutted and wired in the manner of an old-fashioned aeroplane wing. The disc was divided into two halves by a cut-out door and window, one side of which represented the street while the other represented a house interior. It was a beautiful set, economic, light and airy; one felt that, at any moment, it might take off and fly.

It would have been difficult to find a more complete contrast than *Johnny Noble*. This hour-long saga of a young, deep-sea fisherman's life in the thirties and forties was played in black drapes without the use of any props or stage furniture. The elaborate use of light and sound provided a setting which was wonderfully versatile; at one moment the stage would represent a working-class street and, a moment later, it would be the deck of a battleship or the execution yard of a Nazi prison. No quick changes of screens or platforms, just an added spot or flood or the sound of a factory siren cross-fading with the cry of gulls. In *The Flying Doctor* the movement style had been consistent throughout; in *Johnny Noble* the actors were called upon to change from modern dance to naturalistic movement and back again without any break in the action of the play. A typical sequence has Johnny, the central character, sitting on a box during a night-watch aboard ship, a short contemplative scene which is shattered by alarum bells signalling the approach of enemy planes. Immediately Johnny becomes a member of the gunnery squad and then, as the bombs begin to crash down, becomes part of the gun's mechanism. A tremendously exciting moment of theatre lasting some three or four minutes, then the stage is a street again with children playing hopscotch, neighbours gossiping and a young woman returning home from work.

In our press handouts we sometimes referred to *Johnny Noble* as 'a simple tale of thwarted love'. Thwarted love was certainly part of the story but the simplicity was achieved by using all our technical resources. New portable switchboards had been built and parallel-beamed lamps specially created so that it could be lit properly. A sound unit consisting of six turntables with speakers and amplifier had been built and there were times when David Scase and his assistant sound-operators were using all six turntables at once. In addition to recorded sounds of factory noises, ships' engines, aeroplanes, artillery and bombs, we also used passages of recorded instrumental music; the contrast between this and the *a capella* singing of the narrators was a sure way of altering the perspective of a scene.

Perhaps our most valuable resource was the fact that we were beginning to function like a real ensemble; the movement training, voice production, acting theory and classes dealing with the history of theatre were combining to weld us into a group with common aims and a common vision of the future. There was also the fact that we were able to draw, to some extent, upon our past work, for *Johnny Noble* was a lineal descendant of *Last Edition* and could trace its ancestry back through *Newsboy* to the Red Megaphones. It wasn't merely a case of having stylistic links with the past, there were actual incidents and scenes in *Johnny Noble* which had first surfaced in *Last Edition*. They had been refined and stripped of all that was superfluous in much the same way that the text of a traditional ballad is stripped down by passing through the mouths of generations of singers. As a production both *Johnny Noble* and *The Flying Doctor* reflected fairly accurately most of our ideas about theatre at that time. After the Kendal opening we toured our double bill through the surrounding district for the next two months. Both productions were kept in the company repertoire for the next five years and played throughout Britain, Norway, Sweden, West Germany and Czechoslovakia.

In the weeks following our first tour we added another short play to our repertoire, Lorca's magnificently erotic *Don Perlimplin's Love for Belisa in her Garden*. We were rehearsing it when the Smythe Report was published. This official account of the events leading up to the creation of the first atom bombs and the destruction of Hiroshima and Nagasaki made horrifying and fascinating reading. Two of the members of the group had been trained as scientists and they were of the opinion that 'The Bomb' was an ideal subject for a play. When I was urged to begin writing it, my immediate reaction was to treat the suggestion as a bad joke. My knowledge of scientific matters was, to say the least, rudimentary; I had once sat in a class with forty other boys and watched a strip of litmus-paper change colour. That was the full extent of my scientific training. It didn't, I felt, equip me to write a play dealing with atomic physics. My two scientist friends, however, were persuasive and they undertook to put me through a crash-course in physics and the history of science. By the time the company was ready to embark on its second tour I had completed the first phase of my scientific education and had begun the actual writing of the script.

I continued to write throughout the tour, mostly in dressing-rooms and rehearsal premises. Occasionally I would have to leave off writing a scene to go on stage and sing the Narrator in *Johnny Noble* or play a zany in *The Flying Doctor*. In December 1945 we were playing at the David Lewis Theatre in Liverpool and it was there that Joan began to rehearse the as yet unfinished *Uranium 235*. We continued to tour through January and early February 1946 and by that time we had reached the point where Joan's production had caught up with me and there was usually someone standing at my elbow waiting to grab the pages from me as soon as they were written.

Uranium 235 was first performed at the Newcastle People's Theatre on 18 February 1946. It ran for just sixty-five minutes and consisted of a short opening sequence similar to the one used later in the two-hour version, and most of the scenes which later formed Part II of the play's final version. Only the gangster-cum-atomic-ballet scene was missing. By our somewhat modest standards it was a great success. As part of a double bill, however, it raised all kinds of problems. Like *Johnny Noble*, *Uranium 235* was played in black drapes but the lighting-rig was different in each show. What suited *Johnny Noble*, *The Flying Doctor* and *Don Perlimplin* didn't suit *Uranium 235* so it was decided that I should extend it to full length so that no changes in the lighting-rig would be necessary once the light settings had been made. Fortunately, by then I had completed my course in the history of science and it was no hardship to sit down and write about Copernicus, Giordano Bruno, Democritus, Mendeleyev and the rest.

The first of the two-hour versions of *Uranium 235* was staged at the Community Theatre, Blackburn, on 22 April 1946. A revised opening and a new ending was written for a production at the Riley Smith Hall, Leeds University, on 23 September and the atomic-ballet sequence was added two or three weeks later.

In Uranium 235 we had again returned to the agit-prop style of theatre and had dug deep into its rich deposits of theatrical ideas. We had, so to speak, struck gold and had come up with sufficient raw material to fashion the kind of play needed to deal with the complex world of politics and atomic physics. *Johnny Noble* had made use of singing, dancing and acting and had succeeded in combining them into a cohesive style; we had, in the words of a newspaper critic, 'evolved a kind of working-class dance drama'. Apart from the final ten minutes of the show when the two roaring boys enter, the style of production had been fairly consistent throughout. In *Uranium 235*, however, a whole variety of styles were used; indeed the clash of different idioms was a vitally important feature of the over-all style.

How does one describe such a piece? An episodic play? A documentary? A historical pageant? A twentieth-century morality play? Almost any of these descriptions would be pertinent, but not completely so. In some ways it resembled the playing of a good jazz ensemble in which, after the theme has been stated, solo instruments take turns in exploring the theme's chordal structure, each one restating the theme in a different way. In *Uranium 235*, however, an actor was expected to be a trombone at one moment and a guitar the next and then to be a trumpet and a piano playing counter-melodies. They were faced with a series of rapidly changing scenes in which they were called upon to dance, sing, act, to speak in unison and to parody themselves doing all these things. A brief breakdown of the play illustrates the extent to which we were indebted to our earlier work in Theatre Union, Theatre of Action and the Red Megaphones.

The play opens with the Firewatcher's monologue, a blank-verse parody of the Watchman's soliloquy in Aeschylus' *Agamemnon*. There follows a short exchange between the Scientist and a 'planted' member of the audience (the Politician and the Heckler from *Still Talking*).

The expressionistic jazz-dance scene which follows is borrowed from the opening scene of *Last Edition* which was based on an idea in *Newsboy*.

There follows a short naturalistic episode in which actors play themselves engaging in an argument with the Scientist. This device for stripping away unnecessary layers of argument was used frequently in agit-prop sketches as was the double acting-out technique of the Greek scene in which parody and burlesque are used to expose false historical romanticism and its nineteenth-century theatrical reflection.

The Microphone Voice reeling off the list of wars and battles fought during the Greek and Roman eras was borrowed from radio-documentary technique and had been used extensively in *Last Edition*.

When the depersonalised Microphone Voice abandons the narration, it is taken up by an actor who talks directly to the audience as he changes his costume. This use of actor-as-narrator was a prominent feature of *Last Edition*.

Abandoning his narrator role, the actor leads us into a scene composed of three vignettes which mirror that early scene in which the Scientist tries to make himself heard above the frenzied chatter of a group of dancers. In the first of these vignettes a spirited fool's jig becomes a lynch-mob and culminates with the burning of a witch. In the second, a group of alchemists performs a slow formalised dance to the chorus of stichomythic gobbledegook, an episode with all the deliberation of a slow-motion film about gymnastics, and contrasting sharply with the scene which preceded it. The last of these historical vignettes has Giordano Bruno and Paracelsus caught up in a band of dancing revellers in which Death sets the pace. Bruno is finally burned at the stake. Elaborate costumes, the clever use of light and shadow and the richly orchestrated music gave these scenes a Goya-like texture and helped to underline the apparent lack of artifice in the actors scene which followed close on their heels.

Once again the passing of historical time was dealt with by actors playing themselves and talking directly to the audience, preparation for the impact of the nineteenth century and John Dalton's atomic theory!

The Dalton scene is played in a style borrowed from *Still Talking* and *Waiting for Lefty*; our audience is transformed into a nineteenth-century audience – members of the Manchester Literary and Philosophical Society. The political orator of *Still Talking* (the corrupt trade-union leader of *Waiting for Lefty*) has become the non-political, uncorrupted John Dalton. He is flanked by two committee members who mime sitting at a non-existent table, an idea borrowed from the Chinese theatre and filtered through Oplopkhov. Only the hecklers of those early productions have remained unchanged.

The final episode of the first part of *Uranium 235* deals with the Royal Society's reception of Mendeleyev's theory of the atomic table. We based it on an idea which had been used in *John Bullion* where the three gibberish-speaking secretaries collapse and melt like wax dummies.

For most of Part II of *Uranium* the stage is dominated by the Puppet Master, his Secretary and his servant Death, three characters whose expressionistic ancestry is obvious. They hold a series of auditions in the course of which we meet some of the leading figures in the history of atomic science.

The first of these auditionees is a duo – Marie and Pierre Curie. They describe their discovery of radium in rhymed verse as they dance a spirited waltz. Finally Pierre is ushered off by Death and Marie is left to complete the account in unrhymed verse to the rhythm of a slow waltz. She too is finally taken off by Death.

There followed a circus-act in which J. J. Thomson, discoverer of the electron, introduces us to his lion-taming act. After him comes Albert Einstein and his two cronies Nils Bohr and Max Planck. They are presented as knockabout comedians who claim to be ballet impresarios who prove their claim by staging their atomic ballet. This simple but effectively choreographed modern dance dealt with the step-by-step discovery of atomic fission. Fission having taken place, the dancers take over the stage and re-enact the fission process in a scene which is a burlesque of the Hollywood gangster movie of the thirties. A somewhat similar type of burlesque has been used in *Last Edition*.

This was the last of the scenes to deal with the purely scientific aspects of nuclear matters. The three short scenes which followed dealt with the social and political background of the events and had their stylistic roots in *Newsboy* and *Last Edition*. The drilling scientists which followed them was pure agit-prop, possibly the most effective example of agit-prop theatre we had ever staged.

The closing scenes of *Uranium 235* deal with the social and political consequences of the discovery of atomic fission. In terms of style they are a kind of simplified diagram of the whole play for they move easily through the expressionism of the modern morality play into the kind of political confrontation which is one of the main features of agit-prop theatre. The scene which actually ended the play was constantly being revised in order to keep pace with the constantly changing political situation.

At some point between Theatre Workshop's first presentation of *Uranium 235* in 1946 and its final performance at the Comedy Theatre in 1952 I wrote *The Other Animals*, a piece in which, for the last time, I attempted to bring together the various disparate elements which had combined to add up to a style.

At first glance it appears to have little in common with *John Bullion*, *Last Edition* or *Uranium 235* and yet, on reflection, one has to acknowledge that there is a family likeness. All of them, for instance, are political and all of them share the same kind of episodic structure, though in *The Other Animals* the episodes do not have the same sharp outline of those in *Last Edition* and *Uranium 235*. Again, all of them require the stage to simultaneously accommodate different times and places without a change of décor. They all call upon their actors to sing and dance as well as act, they all attempt to combine two or more contrasted theatrical idioms and they all incline towards expressionism.

And there the similarity ends. The central theme of *The Other Animals* differs radically from the rest of the plays discussed here. In them specific political events are dealt with and the actions which lead to those events. *The Other Animals*, on the other hand, is not so much concerned with specific political events as with the effects of the impact of political concepts on the inner life of a human being. In terms of real time, the play deals with the last two hours in the life of a condemned political prisoner, Robert Hanau. Prolonged ill-treatment and torture have reduced him to the point where he can no longer distinguish between fantasy and reality; his captors have become less real to him than the phantoms he conjures up in his delirium. The cage he occupies is real enough but no more real than the cage he has erected in his mind, the bars of which are fears, loyalties, beliefs, obligations and the need to maintain an identity. By betraying his comrades he could escape from the cage provided by his enemies; only through self-betrayal could he escape from that other cage.

In each of the plays from *John Bullion* to *Uranium 235* we were concerned to create a series of dramatic metaphors about the political struggles of a society. *The Other Animals* is a single extended metaphor of a man's struggle to create order out of chaos. It was rehearsed in a disused garage on Wilmslow Road, Manchester, and opened at the Library Theatre there on 5 July 1948. It was Theatre Workshop's last serious experiment in the theatre of expressionism.

A ballet with words

John Bullion

by James H. Miller *and* Joan Littlewood

CAST

BIRTHRIGHT, Sir Weldon, an armament's boss
WINMORE, Lord, an aristocratic coupon-clipper
DEAFEN'EM, Mister, a big noise in the Press
FORTUNE, Mister, a large piece of Finance Capital
DANCY PYE, Reverend, a fashionable creeper
BANKS, Miss, a used-up secretary

Four typists, three newsboys, three mannequins, three crippled ex-servicemen, two munition workers, one junior director and one electrician.

A hyper-pathetic voice, an ultra-unpleasant voice, a sanctimonious voice, a BBC announcer's voice and an echo of Pye's voice.

Chorus of children and crowd of workers.

NOTES

The set is constructivist, being designed to facilitate the movement of the actors rather than to represent anything. Curtains are dispensed with and the transitions from one movement to another are achieved by using documented sound sequences. The stage is divided into three levels or planes these being 1. a five-foot level which runs from left to right upstage, which is used for purposes of dramatic generalisation. 2. a level consisting of two sections, the meeting point of the sections being up centre just below the first level; they are placed at an angle of 90 degrees from each other (i.e. each section at an angle of 45 degrees from the first level). The height of the planes at this point is 2 feet. From here they slope down to stage level. These planes are used for stylised dance movements. The ordinary stage level completes the list.

LIGHTING

The lighting should be as rhythmic as possible and must be perfectly timed. The blackouts do not conclude an episode – they are part of the development of the play and therefore need careful rehearsal.

FIRST MOVEMENT. Basic set, no additional furniture.
SECOND MOVEMENT. Basic set plus 2 skeleton desks set down right and down left.
THIRD MOVEMENT. Basic set.
FOURTH MOVEMENT. Basic set plus 3 directors' stools down left and desk down right.
FIFTH MOVEMENT. Same as 4th plus skeleton pulpit set in angle of two sloping planes.
SIXTH MOVEMENT. Basic set plus desk down right.

[THE FIRST MOVEMENT] The auditorium lights are blacked out and the faint reverberation of a native drum is heard accompanied by the low chanting of repetition melody by a chorus. A green spotlight begins to creep over the stage and discovers a native witch-doctor squatting centre stage. He is wearing a black mask painted with white streaks and his body is swaying to the low chanting of the chorus. The rhythm intensifies and the witch-doctor rises to his feet and begins to build up a frenzied war-dance. The tempo and volume increase and, at peak, a second figure enters dressed in evening clothes and tall hat, a huge grotesque caricature of a man. He too wears a mask, the features being the same as the witch-doctor's, the colour, different, being white with black streaks. He dismisses the witch-doctor with a contemptuous hand movement and begins to execute a weird dance symbolising the modern war for profits. At the peak of the dance there is a blackout,

[THE SECOND MOVEMENT] Which lasts for ten seconds. During the blackout two desks are brought on and placed down right and down left. During this movement typing is heard offstage keeping time to the rhythm of the mime. Lights flash up, stylised typist discovered poised in an insouciant attitude on desk down left. 1 – 2 – 3 – Typist takes imaginary powder-puff (1,) flicks it (2,) powders her nose (3). 1 – 2 – Miss Banks enters (1,) takes one step and looks shocked (2,). 3 – 4 – Typist shrugs shoulders (3,) plants hands on hips (4). 1 – 2 – 3 – 4 – Miss Banks takes four determined and offended steps which land her down centre. On (4) she turns and faces the typist grimly.

I / used / to be / his sec - re - tri. /

These words are spoken by a hyper-pathetic voice coming from offstage. Miss Banks makes four movements expressing the sense of the phrase. The voice offstage repeats 'I used to be his secretary' in the same rhythm. This time the typist responds with four movements, then: 1 – 2 – 3 – 4 – Miss Banks moves to desk right, puts down imaginary papers. 1 – 2 – Miss Banks turns (1,) sniffs (2). 3 – 4 – Typist flourishes puff (3,) makes contemptuous hand movement (4).

He'll turn / you over // to the junior / director. /

This is spoken by an ultra-unpleasant voice coming from offstage. Miss Banks acts it in four vicious movements.

He'll turn / you over // to the Junior / Director. /

Repeated by ultra-unpleasant voice on a slightly higher note. Miss Banks and typist freeze. The backplane is faded up to reveal a replica of Birthright (right), and the Junior Director (left). On 'he'll turn / you over' Birthright makes a scornful movement of throwing something over. On 'to the Junior / Director' the Junior Director comes to life: (to the) looks down his nose at Miss Banks, (Junior), cocks his thumb down disparagingly (Director).

He'll turn / you over // to the Junior / Director. /

Good Morning Sir!!!
Good Morning Sir!!

Good Morning Sir!

The lights on the back plane fade down on 'he'll turn you over'. The 'good morning sirs' are spoken, each on a higher note, finishing up simultaneously with 'director'. Miss Banks and the typist react to the 'good morning sirs.'

And so / the day / of toil / begins. /

This is spoken by a sanctimonious voice offstage, cue 'Junior Director'. Simultaneously Birthright enters and makes four lascivious movements towards typist. On 'begins' he embraces her and there is a blackout.

[THE THIRD MOVEMENT] During the blackout the typing from behind the previous movement is carried on. The two desks are cleared and the lights flash up to reveal, in roseate lighting, the four Directors Birthright, Deafen'em, Winmore and Fortune standing on the right sloping plane, Birthright downstage, and the four stylised typists on the left sloping plane. Miss Banks stands centre stage. Prokofiev's 'Chout ballet' commences and the movement begins.

1 – The whole cast stands, fixedly emphasising the various characteristics of the groups.

Miss Banks reacts to all the moves. Birthright remains frozen until 10. The four Directors remain frozen until (6).

2 – The typists poise fingers and point right toes. 3 – The typists place hands on hips. 4 – The typists bend their heads left, sway their hips. 5 – The typists smile coyly, make suggestive flirting movement.

The four typists remain frozen until (10).

6 – Deafen'em, Winmore, Fortune come to life and stare at typists pop-eyed. 7 – Three Directors wink, satisfied, begin to raise their left hands. 8 – Three Directors point their left thumbs at typists, grinning. 9 – Three Directors nudge man on right of them with right elbows. 10 – All four Directors nod heads approvingly, typists exaggerate the invitation of their gestures.

The music breaks into a satirical dance, the Directors and the typists begin to move down the sloping planes and round to meet centre stage. The Directors gambol fatly, throwing their feet up in front of them and behind them. The typists move sexually, first with their hands on their hips then, moving their arms more loosely and expressively. As they meet, centre, they turn and move upstage, still keeping the rhythm of the dance. One after another the typists turn daintily to face the audience. On a rising phrase in the music the typists retreat coyly to the left. The Directors summon them back imperiously, they fly across the stage like butterflies and there is an embrace. Miss Banks has retreated before the dancers and now stands up centre.

A deep motor-horn, sounding once in the rhythm of a telephone bell, is heard above the music. Birthright thrusts his typist away and pirouettes to an imaginary desk down right. The typist falls, like an overturned tailor's dummy on to Miss Banks.

Three other motor-horns, telephone bells are heard one after another and first

Deafen'em, then Winmore, then Fortune pirouette to their imagined stools down left. The typists, thrown aside, have fallen one on top of the other in a flattened diagonal. The music grows louder; to it is added the sound of recurrent motor-horns and sirens and Newsboys' shouts. As the sounds reach peak three newsboys dash across the back plane from right to left shouting topical newspaper slogans (e.g. 'Anglo-German Naval Agreement Reached'). As the newsboys exit, blackout.

[THE FOURTH MOVEMENT] The sounds are sustained during the blackout. Birthright's desk (down right) and the three directors' stools (left centre) are brought on during the blackout. Miss Banks goes off. The lights fade up and the sounds fade down to leave sound of a typewriter which continues behind Fortune's speech. Birthright is seated at his desk, the other three on their stools; as the lights fade up there is the sound of one isolated telephone motor-horn. On this Fortune speaks into an imaginary telephone.

Fortune. Hello Birthright! So Vickers' armament shares are booming, eh? I've just heard from Deafen'em that the price is up to 63. (*Cross-fade typing with sound of machine-gun fire.*) I want another ten thousand if you can get them.

As Fortune begins speaking the four typists slowly come to life and move downstage to their Director. Three of them sit by the stools and mechanically begin typing. Birthright's typist stands by his side and on the cross-fade he gives her a handful of papers, she moves up the right sloping plane; in the rhythm of the machine-gun fire, at the top she chalks ten thousand in huge figures on a blackboard above the upstage plane; she then moves down to stand left of Birthright again.

Winmore. (*Cutting in quickly on Fortune*) Ai say, hello! hello darling boy, is that you? No. Is it *really*? What! Oh yes. Yes quaite! No! Not really! Oh! My dear, it's too utterly incredible. Ai say, old thing (*Cross-fade machine-gun fire with typing.*) Archie's just told me Vickers' are doing frightfully well. No, really! Well, I was just sort of wondering if you could chuck me over a few thousand, say ten thousand. (*Cross-fade typing with machine-gun fire.*) Do sort of try and wangle it for me, darling boy.

Again the typist moves up the plane and down again.

Deafen'em. (*Cutting in quickly on Winmore*) Hallo! Hallo! Welly? Deafen'em of the 'Daily Excess' speaking. Listen! (*Cross-fade machine-gun fire with typing.*) I've got the latest news hot from Geneva; the great International Peace Conference has broken down for the thirteenth and *last* time. What's that? Your representative brought back the news forty-eight hours ago? No. Oh, I get you. So that accounts for the boom in Vickers. (*Cross-fade typing with machine-gun fire.*) Any rise in the prices since this morning? No! Get me ten thousand right away!

Machine-gun fire held behind the following sequence.

Birthright. One thousand, two thousand.

Birthright
Deafen'em. (*Together*) Booming. (*Add sounds of heavy artillery.*)

Deafen'em. Three thousand, four thousand. (*On a higher note*).

Birthright.
Deafen'em.
Winmore. (*Together, loudly*) BOOMING. (*Up heavy artillery.*)

Winmore. Five tharsand, six tharsand. (*Very high note.*)

Birthright.
Deafen'em.
Winmore.
Fortune. (*Together, louder still*) BOOMING (*Hold heavy artillery.*)

Birthright.
Deafen'em. (*Together, very quickly*) Seven thousand, eight thousand.

Winmore.
Fortune. (*Together, very quickly*) Nine thousand, ten thousand.

All. Booming, booming, booming etc. (*Increasing in speed and volume.*)

On 'Eight thousand' the three typists slowly begin to rise to their feet as if impelled. The 'Booming' chorus goes faster and faster and the typists begin to move towards the right in a straight line; they move stiffly, mechanically. To the chorus, sounds of general warfare are added. As the effects reach peak, three mannequins in bathing costumes and hideous gas masks enter right on the upstage plane. The effects drop, 'Booming' is now only hissed, the typists freeze and the sound of children singing

All things bright and beautiful,
All creatures great and small,
All things wise and wonderful,
The Lord God made them all.' –

is heard off stage. As the mannequins exeunt left the sounds of warfare quickly swell up and drown the children's voices. There is a sudden blackout and silence.

[THE FIFTH MOVEMENT] During the silent blackout there is a loud crash and the electrician is heard swearing. He then comes stumbling on to the stage with a torch or flash-lamp. The whole of this speech must be made to sound spontaneous.

Electrician. It's alright everybody, it's alright. Stay there, ______ (*Using the name of the actor who is playing Birthright*). I say, don't move at the back there! We'll be going on in a minute. Excuse me, everybody, but I'm the electrician of this damn show. I've just fallen across a chap, in the wings here! Let me see, what does he call himself? (*Produces a card from his waistcoat pocket.*) The Reverend Dancy Pye; he wants to spout to you about 'Peace'. That alright with you, ______ (*Using the name of the actor who is playing Birthright*)? Right! Ring up the curtain!

The lights flash up. Pye has carried his pulpit on during the blackout and placed it up centre. The Directors have turned their backs on the audience and are seated as if in church. The four typists are kneeling in front of the pulpit. Pye prepares to speak, when the electrician nearly pushes him over by shoving his hand on Pye's shoulder and vaulting on the left sloping plane. (This should momentarily destroy the equilibrium of the set and break down the superficial reality of Pye, turning him into a mere property.) The electrician then chalks a huge cross over the 10,000s on the blackboard; he strolls off along the back plane, whistling, and Pye's second attempt at speech is crushed by a tremendous clatter, as the electrician jumps off the plane into the wings. Again Pye makes elaborate preparations for beginning his sermon but as he opens his mouth sounds of applause and of an orchestra tuning up are heard. He pauses, bows, then as the sounds die away he begins to speak. (The lighting at the beginning of his speech is dim and religious).

Pye. (*In an exaggeratedly sanctimonious voice*) This morning, my dear brethren in Jesus Christ, I am going to address you all on the subject of Peace. Peace the sanctified, Peace the divine.

The parts of Pye's speech set to a narrower measure to the left of the page require an entire change of personality, voice and gesture on the part of the actor. He changes from his heroic, sanctimonious self and twists in servile fashion round the side of the pulpit. The voice which drones on behind his 'business-man' voice, (set to the right) is a caricature of his pulpit manner. It is done by **His Double** *standing behind the back plane (if possible) who should sound almost like a gramophone running down. There should be a change of lighting on the changes of speech, the dim religious lighting for the pulpit speeches and the ordinary stage lighting for the mixed speeches. The typists kneel piously during the sermon parts, but chatter and twist their heads during the business bits.*

What! Birthright, Winmore, Deafen'em, Fortune, you here? Well, well, well!

Birthright opens his mouth and emits a long-drawn-out mocking sound, like the sound of a saxophone.

I – er – trust your armament activities have been successful lately. Ah, but need I ask, need I ask? Your talents as a business man are too well known, my dear Sir Weldon, God be praised that we still have men of such ability to enrich the commerce of our beloved Empire!

His Double. (*See above*)
Peace the sanctified,
Peace the divine.
Peace the sanctified,
Peace the divine . . .
(*Repeat to end of speech.*)

Yea, for the land of our forefathers has always cherished the thought of Peace. It was the first to spread the word of God in those dark deserts of ignorance, where the British flag fluttered triumphant over the benign heads of Christ's missionaries.

Oh, eh, by the way Sir Weldon, I met the – ah – Bishop at Lady Winmore's bridge party last evening. He tells me that Vickers are doing very well indeed. Booming in fact. The Church is in dire need of funds, I am sad to say, and I – er – thought very seriously of investing two thousand pounds of the Church's capital in Vickers. That'll be four hundred shares, yes? Of course this is strictly between . . . ourselves, Sir Weldon. Strictly between ourselves. The fact is . . .

His Double. The flag of our fathers, the flag of Peace. The flag of our fathers, the flag of Peace . . . (*Repeat to end of speech.*)

As Pye's final speech fades down the lighting fades and then grows to a red spotlight. With this comes the voice of:

Radio Announcer. This is the Northern Programme. Here is the first General News Bulletin, copyright reserved. A report from Geneva states that the Peace Conference, for which Sir John Simon left London last night, broke down early today at the first morning's session. It had been decided to postpone the discussion on ______ to a later date. Consequently the first dispute item on the agenda was the discussion on the position between Japan and China. No decision was arrived at and the point was referred back. Princess Marina today opened the extensive new Convalescent Home for Disabled Ex-Servicemen. The Princess was wearing one of the new ostrich-feather muffs. The tension on the Italian–Abyssinian frontier was today heightened by the arrival of one hundred light Italian bombing planes. Market Report: Iron and Steel shares continued to command a big following and in every instance prices soared to still higher levels. Baldwins' rose to 110, Imperial Chemicals hardened at 114. British Oxygens continued to advance as did London Bricks and Tilbury Contracting. Oils were in heavy demand, Anglo-Iranians and Shells being favoured most. Wheat prices were the highest since 1914 and there was frenzied bidding for English Steels and Vickers. The closing prices were: Allied Iron 98, Baldwins 110, massed on . . . Famine sweeps the Balkan states Hitler says German nation will be Vickers 272 avenged France says pact was to be observed only in time of ______ Vickers 298 peace . . . Martial Law declared in Vickers 342 Brest Support your – Vickers by. . . . In time of . . . Vickers 385 . . . strife . . . you owe it to Vickers 395 your Empire Vickers 401–, 409 . . . 412 . . .'

The lights fade up drowning the Mutograph. With the lights 'The Steel Foundry' is faded up again; underneath it can be heard the sound of machine-gun fire. As the effects reach peak there comes a motor-horn telephone bell, then.

Fortune. Hi, Birthright! Vickers have blown up the market. Now we'll see the Germans march on Russia inside a week! Imperial Chemicals are touching 400! Yes sir 400 (*two motor horns on first 400*).

Winmore. (*Cross-fading with Fortune*) I say, Welly dear! I'm too utterly thrilled about your *sweet* company, too thwilled. My dear, how *naice* of them to send the shares up like that, just when I'm so frightfully broke. I say, old boy, do you know Dodie offered to buy my armament holdings at 500? But I'm not selling, old boy, no bally fear. I say, old thing, isn't it awful about those wretched Chinks absolutely impervious to all decent ideas of culture and all that sort of thing? The Pater thinks (*three motor horns*) that the only thing to do is to send half a dozen gunboats down the Kiang and mow the cads down.

Deafen'em. (*Cross-fading with Winmore*) Say, Sir B., yer know that ten thousand of Vickers asked you to get me? Well, can you make it twenty thousand to twenty five thousand? I've just heard that French planes have crossed the German frontier. That should send you up another hundred or so, eh, Birthright? Noni's rather anxious to invest some of the capital she holds, for the War Orphans' Fund. So do you think you could get her some more too?

[THE SIXTH MOVEMENT] As the lights come up on the 'Eh, Birthright' the four typists begin to move, in the rhythm of Mossolov's music. They move in line up the left sloping plane, across and down the right to Birthright's desk. They collect imaginary papers from him which he hands out with robot-like precision. At the beginning of Pye's speech the music fades down and the typists pause and stand, two on either side of Pye's pulpit. The inner two pose in attitudes of Salvation-Army sanctity, the outer two powder their noses. During the whole of Pye's speech the three Directors on the stools keep up a ceaseless and silent activity, miming telephoning, writing cheques etc.

Pye. (*Cross-fading with Deafen'em*) My dearly beloved brethren in Jesus Christ, I exhort you, in this our country's hour of need, to take up the cross of rightenousness and follow our Lord Jesus Christ to the tortured battleground of Golgotha.

Fortune. Hello Birthright! ten thousand more shares you hear? ten thousand more shares. Yes, ten thousand more, ten thousand more, ten thousand more etc. (*Guns on 'Yes, ten thousand more'.*)

Winmore. (*'On first ten thousand more'*) Hello Welly! Do get ten thousand more. What? No ten thousand more, Yes for me and papa what?

Deafen'em. (*On second 'what'*) Yes ten thousand more, ten thousand more etc. (*Increase guns on second 'what'*). Say, Sir B., gimme ten thousand more. Yeah! ten thousand more, ten thousand more etc.

Mossolov is faded up again at the end of Pye's speech. He comes down from his pulpit and embraces two of the typists. One typist sits on Birthright's knees swinging her legs to 'ten thousand more'. The other makes love to Fortune. As Deafen'em speaks, the sound of guns increases; 'ten thousand more' beats on like a hammer. It reaches peak, then drops, as three disabled ex-servicemen enter and cross the back plane from right to left. The 'ten thousand more' is now only hissed, the effects are very faint and the ex-servicemen can be heard whining 'matches, bootlaces, matches'. The lights fade down as they exit, Mossolov is faded up. During the blackout the three stools are taken off. The lights fade up to show two workmen, naked to the waist, throwing imaginary shells from one to the other on the upstage plane. They move to the rhythm of Mossolov and are silhouetted against a red light. Birthright is still seated at his desk down right.

After ten seconds the four typists with Pye behind them enter down right. They droop wearily, with their heads on each other's backs. They drag themselves up the left plane and down the right keeping time to the rhythm of 'the Steel Foundry'. Down left the three Directors enter and follow them. As the line crosses the stage from right to left Birthright rises automatically and leads them. The two workers continue to throw shells. The line drags on until a change of theme in the music, when they become stiff, machine-like automata moving their arms like a piston. At a second change in theme the line breaks up. Their bodies all sway in different directions. They become more and more savage, breaking into a frenzied dance of war like that of the witch-doctor in the first movement. At the height of the dance a savage voice shrieks out 'WAR'. The whole group fling out their hands and cry 'WAR WILL BE DECLARED!' *Mossolov fades out on 'War'. At the end of their shout the group freeze and a Mutograph begins to pass slowly across the back wall.*

Mutograph. French workers demonstrate for peace Martial law declared in Paris Uneasy situation of French Bourse . . . chorus girl says she was . . . British dockers refuse to load munitions . . . asked to dance Slight drop in Vickers . . . without any crisis intensifies Germany paralysed by political mass strikes. Clothes – Sporadic selling of Imperial Chemicals serious ——— . . . Vickers drop to 328.5 Italian strikers occupy munition factories Baldwins offer shares at 176 Baldwin warns the nation – Plan with the Planets Astrologer prophesies Vickers drop to 304 . . . riots . . . in Paris Pitiful case of Woolworth Heiress's Riots in Berlin . . . fifth husband . . . war . . . street chaos frantic . . . . Vickers 272 . . . Japanese soldiers fraternise with Chinese Red soldiers . . . War is the lifeblood of the nation says Mussolini, Italian soldiers say we will not fight Vickers 250 Steady decline in prices . . . Balkan states on verge of Revolution . . . Famous film star divorces Vickers 215 husband because Revolution in Spain . . . he bites his nails . . . British textile workers strike two hundred thousand say we will not work for war Alimony case Vickers 172 . . . . Vickers 164 Anti-war demonstrations and strikes paralyse Britain Riots in Vickers 123 all principal French towns Vickers 101 International anti-war movement's call for action answered by European strikes and demonstrations . . . Vickers 92 Anti-war organisations issue ultimatum Vickers 83 . . . All preparations for war sabotaged Vickers 60 strikes 54 Revolution in 31 30 29 28 the market is declared..................
....
. . . . comrades . . . . the electric newspaper has been taken over by the workers. A manifesto issued by the joint . . .

On the word 'declared' factory sirens are heard offstage. After 'comrades' the 'internationale' is heard faintly. It grows as the lights come up and the sound and light drown the Mutograph. The 'Internationale' flowers into several different languages. Workers march on to the stage from all sides. The two munition workers march forward to join them. The 'Internationale' floods the stage, the typists are lost among the workers. The four Directors and Pye collapse like deflated balloons in a heap down centre. The 'Internationale' reaches peak. The lights fade down to darkness and the voices are heard dying away as if marching on into distance. *[The End]*

Newsboy

Workers' Theatre Movement

Co-ordinated and planned: Workers' Laboratory Theatre, New York, in montage from the poem by V. J. Jerome

English adaptation by G. Bluemenfeld

[SCENE 1] Amber spot thrown on Newsboy. As the play opens the Newsboy, who represents the establishment bourgeois newspapers, stands in the amber spot and shouts in staccato symbolic fashion.

Newsboy. News Chronicle Empire (*repeat*). Plans for royal Jubilee. SIX KINGS AT ROYAL WEDDING. CUP FINAL LATEST.

As he talks the spot grows larger till it covers the entire stage. With the growth of the spot comes the growth of the Newsboy from a symbolic figure of all newsboys to an individual Newsboy, realistically selling his newspapers. This is the transformation to the Second Scene.

[SCENE 2] As the 1st Newsboy shouts his headlines, 2nd Newsboy walks across the stage. They glare at each other for a moment and the 1st Newsboy takes a kick at the 2nd, who runs off the stage.

Enter stage right a pretty girl. At the same time a well-dressed young man, left.

Throughout the entire scene, the Newsboy is shouting his words. The young man bumps into the young lady.

Young Man. (*Lifting his hat*) Awfully sorry. (*Young lady does not reply.*) But I say: I know you. Haven't I met you somewhere before?

Young Lady. No, I haven't been there. (*Sticks her nose in the air. Young man follows patiently behind. Enter blind woman, left.*)

Bl. Woman. (*Nasal whine*) Pity the blind, kind friends. Pity the poor blind. Pity the poor blind.

A charitable fat man comes across the stage from right to the blind woman. He drops a penny in her tin, buys a paper and exit.

[SCENE 3] Ballet scene. As the blind woman comes across the stage and turns to go back, all the figures who have thus far passed in the street scene come on stage and, working on three parallel planes with the same dance movement, go through movements which bring out their individual characteristic movements. All face the audience. They combine voices with characteristic gesture, i.e. the young lady keeps repeating 'Why don't you go away! I'll call a policeman! I'll call a policeman!' *The blind woman repeats her singsong. The 2nd Newsboy shouts* 'News Chronicle Empire. CUP FINAL DRAW. PLANS FOR ROYAL JUBILEE.'

In the meantime, the 1st Newsboy elevates himself above the others, upstairs centre. The characters keep moving back and forth across the stage, intermingling with their own words the words of the Newsboy: 'PLANS FOR ROYAL JUBILEE. SIX KINGS AT ROYAL WEDDING' *etc. until the scene grows, their own words are completely displaced by the words of the Newsboy and all the characters are shouting his slogans. At the height of this chaos, the voices rise to a crescendo, terminating in the words* 'HEY BOY!' *which are the first words of the poem. As they say these words, all the figures veer towards the Newsboy upstage centre.)*

Voice. How long are you going to stand there shouting yer guts out?

All the characters on the stage, still keeping their ballet formation, say the next words with a series of movements which bring out the ideas:

All. BECAUSE SOMEWHERE IN A WEST-END HOTEL A CHORUS GIRL SHOT out the brains of the old rip that kept her.

The figures freeze.

Voice. Don't you get tired, Newsboy, shouting all the time about

Char. Gent. Hold ups

Young Lady. And divorces

All. AND DUCHESSES IN GAMBLING DENS!

All through the play, the characters change from class-conscious workers to symbolic figures of an entirely different nature or realistic characters which vary greatly from scene to scene.

At this point in the play the characters become class workers, representing a picture of the Three Million Unemployed Men and Women. This is done through the characters facing the audience and saying the following words: 'THREE MILLION MEN AND WOMEN' *as in rhythmic tread they form a miserable line outside the labour exchange, constantly repeating in low tones in mass:* 'THREE MILLION MEN AND WOMEN.'

The spotlight changes from amber to green.

1st Voice. Fired from the mills.

2nd Voice. Fired from the docks.

3rd Voice. Fired from the coal mines.

4th Voice. Fired from the shipyards.

All. (*Louder and louder in desperation*) FIRED FIRED FIRED.

Voice (*Offstage*) No jobs today. You've had yer lousy money.

Grumbling rips in voices, then slowly retreating in distance as line breaks up and they all shuffle off the stage, except one.

[SCENE 4] One figure, Unemployed, is left on the stage. Enter well-dressed man.

Unemployed. (*Mumbling*) How about a tanner, Mister, for a bite and bed? I never done this before, Mister, but I gotta eat. Gotta sleep.

Man. Eat! Sleep! Huh!

Exit. A woman hurries by from the other direction, feeling the unemployed man's eyes upon her. Enter charitable gentleman.

Unemployed. (*A little more entreatingly*) How about a tanner, Mister, for a bite and a bed?

Char. Gent. (*Precisely, ethically offended*) I don't believe in it.

Unemployed. (*Not understanding*) What's that, Gov'nor?

Char. Gent. I don't believe in charity.

Unemployed. Oh! (*This strikes him as something new.*)

Char. Gent. (*Sententiously*) Why don't you do something? There must be lots of jobs for big strong fellows like you.

Unemployed. There just ain't, Mister.

Char. Gent. (*Cheerfully patting his shoulder*) Well, don't get downhearted. Keep on pegging away. Something's bound to turn up.

Unemployed. (*Raising his hands, clenching his fists as if he'd like to wring the man's neck*) GOD!

Exit charitable gentleman. Enter 3rd pedestrian.

Unemployed. (*Loud voice, angrily*) Hey, Mister! How about a tanner for a bite and a bed? This ain't charity. I'm hungry.

Pedestrian. Why don't you go to the Workhouse? What about your Parish Relief?

Unemployed (*Harshly*) I told you I ain't looking for Charity.

Pedestrian frightened, searches through his pockets for small change. He finds a sixpence and with hasty fingers offers it to man and starts to back away.

Pedestrian. Here . . . (*The coin drops.*)

Unemployed. (*Furious*) Too good to hand it to me, are yer?

Pedestrian. (*Terrified*) . . . I-It . . . it slipped!

Unemployed. (*Growling*) Get out of my sight.

Pedestrian scampers. Unemployed man looks after him angrily. Enter urchin. Urchin rushes for the money. Unemployed man kicks him away.

Urchin. That's mine. I'm seen it first.

Unemployed. It's mine. THAT'S MY SIXPENCE!

As he stands there, the money in his hand, a sibilant voice right whispers 'THAT'S MY SIXPENCE'. *Following this, voice left ditto. Then voices everywhere. Voices of the three million unemployed. They come on the stage, the same people who were in the labour exchange scene, with their hands stretched out to the unemployed worker, pleading for the sixpence. All the time they keep repeating the phrase* 'THAT'S MY SIXPENCE' *so that it sounds like the murmuring of a hungry mob. Above this noise is heard the following line, repeated at intervals of about 45 seconds;* 'THREE MILLION MEN AND WOMEN'. *As this line is said, the desperation of the mob to get the sixpence rises, and the voices grow with it till by this time they have practically surrounded the unemployed worker.*

Unemployed. (*Raising his fists, crying hysterically*) Tortured in hostels with hymns about Saviours.

All the other figures follow his hands, building a pyramid of grasping hands as they rise to the top. They do so saying the words 'THREE MILLION MEN AND WOMEN'. *Then, deathly silence.*

The silence is broken by the shouts of the Newsboy who is seen above the crowd, in the background, shouting his slogans.

Little by little the group with their hands outstretched draw their hands down and begin to laugh. It begins very quietly – a painful laugh that grows into hysteria as the scene goes on. The following lines are taken by different individuals. The characters again become ordinary workers, people conscious of the roles of the Newsboy.

1st Voice. And he stands up there shouting about Royal Jubilees.

2nd Voice. And Football Cup Draws.

3rd Voice. Six Kings at Royal Wedding.

4th Voice. Another flapper flies to Australia.

Hysterical laughter grows to a high pitch, and is broken by one of the characters who bursts through the mass and comes to the audience with the following lines. The role is still that of a worker who presents these lines with the sense of their class nature.

Worker. In America, 320 men left to burn in a jail so that one won't get away.

Negro Worker. Two hundred white men take a black man for a ride, string him up a tree, and shoot him full of holes because a white woman said he smiled at her.

Indian Worker. In India workers are bludgeoned – thrown in jail for daring to organize unions.

During these lines, those people who are not in the scene which follows move off the stage quietly. Four characters remain on the stage, the Indian worker and three others. The one nearest him grabs him and throws him upstage so that he falls.

[SCENE 5]

Indian Worker. Why are you keeping me here? (*Sitting in chair now.*)

Prosecutor. (*Sits in another chair facing him.*) What's it all about? (*Silence*) I've got some work to do. I've got a job to look after . . . Well, say something, can't you?

Everybody looks at him, except 2nd detective who is cleaning his finger-nails with his keys. After a long pause –

1st Detect. What's your name?

Indian Worker. Ali Singh.

1st Detect. What do you work at?

Indian Worker. On the railway.

1st Detect. You belong to the union? (*No answer*) Come on! Speak up! D'you belong to the union?

Indian Worker. Yes.

2nd Detect. Huh, a Red! I thought so.

Prosecutor. Now tell me, why did you fire those shots?

Indian Worker. Shots?

Prosecutor. Yes. You heard me. You're not deaf?

1st Detect. Come on, Ali Singh, spit it out. We'll see you get off light if you confess.

Prosecutor. Take my advice and don't play innocent. We know you fired those shots at the Governor. Lucky for you he wasn't hurt. So now, speak up. Why did you fire those shots?

Indian Worker. I tell you I don't know anything about any shots.

1st Detect. Where do you live?

Indian Worker. 179 Ragland Street.

1st Detect. Then what were you doing near the racecourse?

Indian Worker. I'm on a job round there, near the station.

2nd Detect. Don't tell lies. You're a Red. You were out to kill the Governor – now tell the truth. You fired those shots!

Indian Worker. No! No!

1st Detect. Then what was this revolver doing in your pocket? (*Taking out revolver.*)

Pause.

Indian Worker (*Jumping up*) That's not mine. I haven't got a revolver. You can't frame me! I was going to my work.

2nd Detect. God-darn you! Shut up. (*Pushes him back in chair.*)

[SCENE 6] *Played in the dark.*

Indian Worker. It's not mine.

Prosecutor. Be sensible, Ali Singh. You know we're going to make you talk.

1st Detect. Do you want us to knock it out of you?

2nd Detect. Come on, own up. Are you looking for a hiding?

Prosecutor. Now be sensible, Ali. Don't waste my time. Say you fired those shots, and get it over.

Indian Worker. No.

1st Detect. You still say this isn't your revolver?

Indian Worker. YES.

2nd Detect. But it was found in your pocket. It must be yours.

Indian Worker. No! I've never seen it before.

2nd Detect. Don't tell bloody lies.

Indian Worker. It's the truth. I swear it isn't mine.

Prosecutor. Then how did it come in your pocket?

Indian Worker. Someone must've put it there.

1st Detect. (*Angrily*) Stop lying. (*Threateningly*) – Now you little brown-skinned bastard, is this your revolver?

Indian Worker. No.

A loud crack. A yelp of pain.

1st Detect. Is it your revolver?

Indian Worker. (*Sullenly*). No.

Another slash. A yelp of pain.

1st Detect. Is it? Refresh your memory.

Indian Worker. No! No!

Two terrified screams, three loud cracks. Worker cries painfully. Silence!

Prosecutor. Now, Ali Singh, perhaps you will tell us. Is this your revolver?

A slight pause.

Indian Worker. (*Almost whispered*) Yes, it's my revolver.

Pause. In the silence, in the darkness, starting very slowly with pauses in between, in a stage whisper, the following lines are heard, each word spoken by a different person: 'Tortured' 'Framed' 'Imprisoned' 'Burned' 'Lynched' 'Murdered'. *These words are repeated three times, growing louder each time until the words are heard:* 'Have you heard of Sacco Vanetti?' *Then the words travel round again until someone takes the line* 'Have you heard of Thomas Mooney?' *Once round again, then* 'Have you heard of tortured Torgler?' *and again* 'Have you heard of Scottsboro? Scottsboro?' *Each time a different voice takes up the line. This continues until the last time round, then the line is* 'Have you heard of Thaelman? Thaelman?' *And then the entire group, in mass* 'HAVE YOU HEARD?' *Lights go up on Scene 7.*

[SCENE 7] As the lights come up on the words 'Have you heard?' all figures are facing the Newsboy, pointing up at him. Their hands slowly go down as Newsboy starts shouting headline: 'PLANS FOR ROYAL JUBILEE'. *He*

comes off chair, still shouting lines, and asks workers to buy papers. As he touches each on the shoulder the worker turns round with the 'Daily Worker' in front, until there is a full line of dailies. Newsboy walks to centre front as voice talks.

Voice. Get yourself a trumpet, sonny, a big red trumpet. Climb to the top of St. Paul's and blare out the news. TIME TO REVOLT! BLACK MEN, WHITE MEN, FIELD MEN, SHOP MEN – TIME TO REVOLT. Get yourself a trumpet, sonny, a big red trumpet and blare out the news –

All. TIME TO REVOLT! TIME TO REVOLT!

Newsboy discards his own placard, takes up trumpet and joins in chorus. Blackout. *[The End]*

Extracts from a Living Newspaper

Last Edition

by Joan Littlewood *and* Ewan MacColl

THEATRE UNION

Presents

LAST EDITION

A LIVING NEWSPAPER

DEALING WITH EVENTS FROM 1934-1940

Edited by Theatre Union

AT THE ROUND HOUSE
EVERY ST., ANCOATS

on MARCH 14th, 15th & 28th, 29th at 7-30 p.m.
MARCH 16th & 30th at 2-30 p.m.

ADMISSION BY MEMBERSHIP CARD ONLY
Collective Membership fee of 2/6 per annum for Trade Union Branches, Co-op. Guilds, Etc.

[THE UNEMPLOYMENT EPISODE]

Narrator. Last week, after vainly searching for work all day, William Castle at his last call, pleaded desperately with tears in his eyes. He was turned away. His wife met him with a brave smile. "Cheer up, Will' she said, "there's a letter for you, perhaps it's a job for the new year." It was an intimation that his employment benefit had ceased. He hid it from his wife, kissed her and left the room. His wife heard a strange noise downstairs. She found him on the floor. He had cut his throat. A verdict of suicide while temporarily insane was recorded.

Music; Vulcan theme

Voice Down with the means test!
Down with the National Starvation Government!

Marchers enter on Platform 'A', singing

Marchers
March, march, men without work,
Scrapped by the cities.
March, march, men of the unemployed committees!

Narrator. Two hundred Scottish hunger-marchers set out from Glasgow.

Voice Men from Govan and Cowcaddens,
Men from the Gorbals and the Broomielaw,
Men from Lanark and Kirkintilloch,
Men from Greenock, Partick and Parkhead.
The Clyde men.

Marchers.
For the right to work!
For the right to live!

Voice. Men from Newcastle, Gateshead, Durham, Morpeth, Willington, Sunderland, Shields; men from the shipyards, idle colliers.

Marchers. We refuse to starve in silence!

Voice: Men from Burnley, Barrow and Whitehaven,
Salford, Oldham, Manchester, Warrington.
Men from the loom and the derelict foundry.
Turners, puddlers, grinders, spinners,
The Northern men!

Marchers.
We've a right to live! We're human beings!
We've a right to work! We're men!

Light on platform 'C'. Hospital accident room. Doctor present. Nurse enters.

Nurse. There's a crowd of injured men outside, Doctor. Hunger-marchers. They've been fighting with the police.

Doctor. Better bring 'em in two at a time.

Exit nurse. She returns with two marchers, both injured.

Hello! You look as if you've been having a spot of bother.

1st Marcher. We've been having a spot of police brutality.

Doctor. That's rather strong, isn't it?

1st Marcher. They were strong men.

Doctor. Well, if you will go about the country disturbing the peace, you can only expect resentment.

2nd Marcher. Which peace? We've not heard about any peace. We only know about war. War with hunger and poverty, a war to keep ourselves and kids alive.

1st Marcher. A war to keep warm in the winter.

Doctor. I appreciate your difficulties, of course. But don't you think your methods of voicing your opinions are rather melodramatic?

2nd Marcher. Not so melodramatic as having your name in the paper with a verdict of 'suicide while of unsound mind' attached to it.

Doctor. That's a nasty blow you've given yourself.

2nd Marcher. I didn't give it myself. A cop gave it me as a sample of his resentment.

Doctor. Y'know, I think you're on the wrong track. These methods may be alright in Russia but the British people will never stand for them.

2nd Marcher. What do you think we are, Fiji Islanders? We *are* the British people; me and my mate here and the others outside.

Doctor. Now look here! You've got to admit that we have the finest democracy in the world here.

The patient slumps in the chair.

He's fainted. Some water nurse!

Nurse brings water.

I'm afraid you'll have to stay here for a few days.

1st Marcher. Don't you think we should leave half a dozen of our lads with him?

Doctor. Whatever for?

1st Marcher. Just in case the police try to get at him again in the interests of democracy.

Blackout.

[THE GRESFORD PIT DISASTER EPISODE] Newsboy dances up platform 'A'.

Newsboy.

All the latest, last edition!
Mr Eden's German mission.
Paris riots, food shops looted,
Van der Lubbe executed.
Loch Ness monster seen again,
Sentence passed on Ludwig Renn.
News a'Chron, Last Edition!
Last edition, Last edition!

A collier enters on platform 'A' carrying a lamp, whistles softly the Vulcan theme. Exit. Another comes and goes. Explosion. Woman runs along platform 'A' to centre stage. Explosion. Blackout.

Voice on Microphone. Hello! Is that the fourteenth district? You've got to get through. There's three hundred men there. Yes, in the Dennis Deep. One of 'em's got to answer. Three hundred men! There's been a second explosion and there's three hundred men there. You've got to get through! You've got to. Three hundred men!

Explosion.

Hello, hello, hello, hello . . . There's been a second explosion in the Dennis Deep. There must be somebody there. There's got to be. There's three hundred men down there. Three hundred men! Hello! Hello! Hello!

Explosion. We hear a woman screaming. Woman runs on platform 'A'. She is in night attire and carries a miner's lamp. Stage lightens to a chill grey. She runs to various parts of platform 'A' knocking on imaginary doors.

1st Woman. The Dennis is on fire! There's fire in the Dennis Deep. The Dennis Deep is on fire! The Dennis Deep is on fire! They're trapped down there! They're trapped!

Women appear at various points along the platform.

Women. Trapped!

1st Woman. It's the pit. Wake up! Wake up! It's the pit!

Women. The pit!

The women slowly, with dance-like movement form a compact group.

1st Woman. The pit's on fire, our men are trapped!

Women. My two sons. My husband and my two sons! All I have in the world!

1st Woman. They're in the Dennis Deep. We've got to get to them . . .

Women. My husband. My sons are down there! Hot as Hellfire! Gas! Falling rock! Burying them! Gassing them! Killing them! We've got to get to them!

As they begin to advance to centre stage there is another explosion and blackout.

Mic. Voice. Hello, hello, hello, answer me. Is that the 14th? Are you in the 14th? No, make for the bottom end, man. Make for the bottom end. Get out by the return airway. Get yourselves out. We'll get through to the Dennis. God help them, there's gas.

Lights up on women standing in two groups as at pit-head.

[THE GRESFORD PIT DISASTER TRIAL SCENE]
Fade up Vulcan theme simultaneously bringing up lights until it is possible to see the shadowy forms of men carrying empty stretchers.

Narrator. The Gresford Disaster. The explosion occurred about 2 a.m. on Saturday, the 22nd of September, 1934, in the Dennis section of the mine. The concussion was felt at the bottom of the pit and in the Slant district. Except for a few persons working near the pit bottom, and one deputy and five men who managed to escape from the 29's district, all the men who were working in the section at the time lost their lives the same day, which brought the total loss of life up to 265.

Towards end of foregoing speech, the light begins to fade again. Blackout. Sustain Vulcan theme then fade slowly behind following speech.

Narrator. The Board of Trade hereby direct that a formal investigation shall be held into the causes and circumstances of the explosion which occurred in the Gresford mine, Denbighshire, on the 22nd of September, 1934, and the board hereby appoint Sir Henry Walker, C.B.E., LL.D., His Majesty's Chief Inspector of Mines, as Commissioner to hold such investigation.

Half-way through foregoing passage lights slowly fade up to reveal group of women on platform 'A'. Group of miners enter downstage right. During the trial scene actors representing company interests use the extreme upstage area while those who appear for the prosecution use the downstage area. Cripps is situated between the two groups.

Cripps. And so, Mr Bonsall, you, the colliery manager at the Gresford pit, admit here that it was due to an oversight that the correct ventilation was not being obtained in this pit.

Bonsall. Yes, I admit it.

Cripps. You, as manager of course, were expected to run the mine as cheaply as possible. Is that so?

Bonsall. Yes, naturally.

Cripps. Mr Bonsall, was it a common practice for men to work overtime on Saturday and Sunday night? Apparently the men were working overtime on the night the explosion occurred, in fact many of them were doubling shifts, were they not? Working two shifts without a break.

Bonsall. They were not exactly doubling.

Cripps. They were working overtime?

Bonsall. Yes.

Cripps. Was it a common practice for the men to work overtime on a Saturday and Sunday night?

Bonsall. Yes, it was common practice.

Cripps. You knew, of course, that a breach of the Act was committed.

Bonsall. Many of them liked it.

Cripps. Did you know that it was a breach of the Act? (*Pause*) Did you know it was a breach of the Act? Did you know it was a breach of the Act?

Light fades. Spotlight on miners' wives who turn and face audience. Up Vulcan theme.

Women. Joseph Andrews, of Wrexham, dead.
Thomas Anders of Wrexham, dead.
George Anderson of Wrexham, dead.
Owen Andrews of Wrexham, dead.

The cause of death in each case was poisoning by carbon-monoxide. They sealed the pit two days after the accident but the force of a new explosion came and threw the seals off again. Sandbags and girders were thrown high in the air. My husband was down that pit.

Vulcan theme out. Women turn and face trial again.

Cripps. Mr Bonsall, there are forty-two days missing of fireman's reports, the forty-two days before the explosion. Those reports are vital to this enquiry. . . . We should like to have them.

Bonsall. They are down the pit.

Cripps. Is that the only excuse you have?

Bonsall. It is not an excuse.

Cripps. Was it not customary to keep those reports at the pithead?

Bonsall. In this case the reports were taken down the pit by a boy and lost in the explosion.

Cripps. Did you allow the pit to be run by boys?

Bonsall. How can I look after every boy?

Cripps. I am not asking you to look after every boy, I am asking you to look after the records.

Bonsall. I haven't the slightest doubt that they have gone down into the bottom.

Cripps. Whose responsibility was this?

Bonsall. The fireman's.

Cripps. I suggest that it was your responsibility. When did you last get the fireman's books to see if your orders were carried out?

Bonsall. I always left that to the clerk.

Cripps. In the same way you left it to the fireman. In the same way you tried to put the responsibility on to the fireman?

Miners' group turn and face audience.

Miners. Joseph Archibald of Wrexham, dead.
Thomas Archibald of Pandy, dead.

They found Thomas Archibald lying close to his tub. Somehow the tub had got turned over. His lamp they found at the face of the drift. All their lamps were at the coal-face. They left them at the coal-face because they were no use to them. Their lamps went out.

Women. They died in the dark.

Blackout.

[THE POLITICS OF DEMOCRACY EPISODE] Newsboy on platform 'B'

Newsboy. Disarmament conference decision! Anglo-German naval agreement reached. Last Edition.

Joe enters from centre stage and approaches Newsboy. Buys paper. Arthur enters from platform 'A'. Buys paper.

Joe. Funny kind of disarmament conference.

Arthur. Bloody funny. Ever since the last war Germany's been asking for equality. While it was a democracy nobody listened but as soon as Hitler comes they get a fleet.

Joe. (*Reading*) Lord Lothian says 'A stable Germany will ensure peace. Hitler has done much to bring order to Germany.'

Arthur. That's another way of saying he smashed the trade unions.

Joe. And now we're going to help him build a new German fleet.

Arthur. Yes, with our money. Listen to this: 'The Bank of England has granted a £750,000 credit to Germany in order to facilitate the mobilisation of German commercial credits.' That money comes from our pockets, every single penny of it.

Joe. They can't squeeze me any more. If there's another rise in the cost of living I'll be paying the boss a wage to let me work for him.

Arthur. They'll squeeze and squeeze until they've milked you dry and then they'll take the skin off your back to make purses with. Hitler's paved the way for this grand ceremony, that's why they're so friendly with him.

Joe. But why call the ceremony disarmament?

Arthur. For the same reason that they call hunger malnutrition or a blackleg a loyal employee. Because they want to give dung a fancy name and make it smell like a wallflower. Have you read what Sir Thomas Inskip said in an article to the press yesterday?

Joe. No.

Arthur. He said: 'In actual fact there is no great difference between the totalitarian and the democratic systems of government.'

Joe. He's talking through his hat.

Arthur. Think so? Listen to this: 'A widespread strike movement has broken out in Trinidad as a result of the rise in the cost of living and the refusal of the companies to increase wages. Serious rioting has occurred and many arrests have been made.' And we're still in the empire, see?

Newsboy. Part of our great democratic system.

Arthur. Right. Only six per cent of the population have a vote so that the only way they have of making themselves heard is to strike. They work in the oilfields. The islands contribute sixty per cent of the entire oil output in the British Empire. The other big industry is sugar. Look at this: 'Rioting still continues in Trinidad and in the police charges which took place last night many natives were killed and wounded.' Now we are going to act Trinidad. You and me will both play company detectives. He will be a Trinidad worker.

Newsboy. Me?

Arthur. Yes.

Newsboy. Can I make my face up?

Arthur. What for? You can be exploited without having a black face, can't you?

Newsboy goes up left. He is in a cul de sac.

We've got you in a side street by a deserted warehouse. There's no one who'll dare to interfere. You are on the strike committee, in touch with the leaders. Somebody's behind the strike, financing it.

Newsboy. That's not true. We made the strike ourselves.

Joe strikes him and he falls to the ground.

Arthur. Who gave the word for the strike? And don't say it was the committee.

Newsboy. We made the strike ourselves.

Joe. You're a liar! (*He hurls him downstage*) I'll make the black bastard talk.

Arthur. Just a minute, the Acting Colonial Secretary wants to talk first.

Spot on platform 'A'.

Act. Col. Secretary. In the past we have tried to ease our consciences with humbug and have had to satisfy Labour with platitudes but I would stress very strongly the view that an industry has no right to pay dividends at all until it pays a fair wage to labour and gives the labourer decent conditions.

Blackout on platform 'A'.

Newsboy. See, even the government is with us.

Joe. (*Kicking him*) Shut up!

Arthur. He's right, y'know. That was Red talk we just heard.

Spot on platform 'A'.

Charlton. I would like to draw the attention of the Secretary of State for the Colonies to the extreme view of the Acting Colonial Secretary for Trinidad.

Blackout on platform 'A'.

Joe. Who was that?

Arthur. It was Mr Alan Charlton, M.P. for Bury, Lancashire, speaking in the House of Commons, London, England.

Joe. How does he come into this?

Arthur. He's the director of the Trinidad Leasehold Limited which owns 85,912 acres of oilfields worth a capital of £1,639,452. His interest in this case is real interest, compound interest. Alright, get to work.

Joe. Who's behind the strike? Who financed it, eh? Who paid for the leaflets? Alright, if you don't want to say. If you want to keep quiet . . . But don't forget we gave you the chance. Don't forget that.

He shoots him. Blackout.

Narrator. Sir Thomas Inskip in a speech at Reading yesterday said that there was no great difference between the totalitarian and the democratic states.

Spot on three men on centre stage, facing audience directly.

Three Men. Which proves that a cabinet minister can sometimes tell the truth.

[THE SPANISH CIVIL WAR EPISODE]

Narrator.

Wonderful days!
So General Mola had to stop the advance on Madrid.
For why? Because he had to wait for his white horse,
So he could ride into Madrid in style.
But while he was waiting, the internationals came in,
And the anarchists from Barcelona,
And the socialists from Asturias,
And the communists from Guaderama,

And Mola's white horse turned out to be
A bloody white elephant.
Have a ride on it Chamberlain!

Spotlights on four men standing on platform 'A'. Each has a rucksack at his feet. They stand without moving.

Mic. Voice. Alec Armstrong of Manchester, building worker, communist. Can you see the people of Spain deserted by the government of your country, left to fight the combined armies of Spanish, Italian and German fascism? (*Pause*) Robert Goodman of Salford, printshop worker, communist. Can you see the women and children of Spain butchered without going to their aid? (*Pause*) George Brown of Manchester, building worker, communist. Can you see the workers of Spain fighting with obsolete weapons against the most modern instruments of war? (*Pause*) Bob Ward of Manchester, building worker, communist. Can you see men of all countries marching to the assistance of Spain and not march with them?

The four men lift up their rucksacks, turn to the audience, raise their hands in farewell.

Four Men. So long.

Slow fade out.

[THE MUNICH PACT EPISODE]

Actor. In accord with our policy of giving you as much variety as possible, what follows is in the style of an American gangster film. Sir Sigismund, or Siggy as he is known to the underworld, is expecting a visit from Sir Launcelot, now known as Lance the Umbrella Man. In the meantime he has summoned to a meeting the Italian killer, Muscle In. This scene is called: Who killed Johnny the Czech?

Central stage. Siggy discovered seated. He is playing patience. Enter Muscle In.

Siggy. Hi, Muscle!

Muscle. Hi, Siggy! I gotta your invitation. Say, what's the idea of all the chairs? A party?

Siggy. Yeah, a party.

Muscle. On my way here I see one of your boys. He says you gotta big job on. Plenty good pickings.

Siggy. Yeah, plenty good. Siddown, Muscle. Thi is the biggest job since we cracked the Spanish bank on 38th street.

Muscle. Yeah?

Siggy. Yeah. I need your help, see.

Muscle. Sure, sure, Boss. A fifty-fifty deal, ugh?

Siggy. What d'ya mean, fifty-fifty? What kinda talk's that? We fixed that you get the pickings from the Spanish job and I take the next. Well, this is it. See?

Muscle. Okay, okay. I get ya boss. I get ya. What's the layout?

Siggy. There's a store at the corner of 18th street and west 39th. It's kept by a guy called Johnny the Czech. You know him?

Muscle. Sure, he's gotta plenty big dough. Not so long ago he live in a cheap tenement joint on 14th street. Now he's on velvet. He gotta plenty cash, plenty boys to take care of him and plenty good business. Sure, sure I know him . . .

Siggy. The guy's poison. He's gotta go.

Muscle. Boss, this guy's plenty tough. Every one of his boys packsa the rod. My boys tell me every joint on his block gotta machine-gun and we wouldn't stand a chance in them streets. Oh no, I think this is not such a good idea. No?

Siggy. Yeah.

Muscle. Listen, Siggy. My boys don'ta feel so good. Look at that Spanish job. I told the boys it was easy but it took them three years, justa the same. Don'ta forget Spanish Joe. He was as full of holes as a sieve before he lay down. I lost plenty of my good boys and plenty cash. Siggy, you know me. Muscle In is your friend but no, I can'ta do this.

Siggy. Ease up, ease up. What do you take me for? A hick from the sticks? (*Pointing to his head*) what do you think this is for, a ball game? Now look. (*He arranges bottles and glasses on table*.)

This is Johnny the Czech's joint. And this is a speakeasy I control – the Viennese Cafe. This is the territory of Lance the Umbrella Man and just across the street is Eddy, his echo. Now Johnny the Czech thinks these two guys are his buddies. See? Well, are they?

Muscle. Boss, those-a guys is nobody's buddies.

Siggy. That's just what I think. Now listen. Who is it that nobody loves?

Muscle. I don'ta think that nobody loves me, Boss.

Siggy. Don't be so dumb. The guy nobody loves is Joe the Red. See?

Muscle. Oh, sure. That guy gives me a pain.

Siggy. He gives Lance and Eddy a worse pain. Them two guys is scared stiff of him. They'll play ball with any guy who's willing to take a poke at him.

Muscle. I geta you, boss. I geta you. You means that you're the guy.

Siggy. I mean I want them guys to think I'm going to take a poke at him . . . And in exchange, they double-cross Johnny the Czech. And then . . . well, I double cross them. A double double-cross.

Muscle. Gee, Siggy, that'sa beautiful. You tell 'em you fighta Joe the Red if they take a run-out powder on Johnny the Czech and thena you take a powder on them. You know what I think? I thinka that'sa beautiful. Boss, you're a genius.

Siggy. Sure, we got the Indian sign on 'em.

There's a knock on the door. They dive for their guns.

Siggy. Come in.

Enter Lance and Eddy.

Well, boys, you know what my terms are. Johnny the Czech's joint in return for a battle with Joe the Red. O.K.?

Lance. Well, we don't know. Eddy here aint so sure. I aint so sure we can trust you, Sig.

Siggy. I'm trusting you, aint I?

Lance. What d'ya mean?

Siggy. Siddown, punk! Right now my boys are breaking in on Johnny's territory. All you gotta do is send some of your boys over and tell Johnny to quit or else. Tell him you say so.

Eddy. I think Monsieur Siggy does not realise that this job is so difficult. Do not forget Johnny the Czech is under the impression that I am his friend. The double-cross is not so good for one's reputation.

Siggy. Aw, can the bull. Stop talking like a sky pilot. Let's have the answer, yes or no . . .

Eddy. Monsieur, you forget Joe the Red. He also is Johnny's friend.

Siggy. That's where you come in. You gotta make Johnny break with the Red.

Eddy. But how?

Siggy. You know how. Just give him some of that highfalutin talk. Put it over big. Tell him Joe's bad for his health. And if that don't work, threaten him. Tell him he'll be taken for a ride.

Lance. What about Joe? When do we start operations on him?

Siggy. As soon as I've cleaned out Johnny.

Lance. Can we count on that?

Siggy. Yes, I give you my word.

Muscle. Sure and I givea my word too. My boy's shirts may be blacka but they sure do hate that Red nogood.

Siggy. Is it a deal then?

Lance.
Eddy. (*together*) It's a deal.

Eddy. And now that's settled I think we'd better be getting back.

Siggy. Just a minute, the job aint finished yet. I gotta make sure you guys don't double-cross me and I gotta way of making sure . . . (*He shouts into the wings*). Okay, bring him in, boys.

Two henchmen drag in Johnny the Czech.

Lance.
Eddy. (*together*) Johnny the Czech!

Siggy. Yeah, Johnny the Czech. We're gonna bump him off, the four of us.

Johnny. Listen Eddy, you too Lance. You're my buddies. This guy's nuts. You can't let him croak me just like that.

Lance. No? You were tied up with Joe the Red, weren't you?

Johnny. Sure. But I was tied up with you too. Look I ain't done a thing. I kept out of your territory, didn't I? I kept to myself. All I did was run my own joint and try to keep the peace with you boys.

Siggy. Aw, can the sob stuff. You gotta go, Johnny.

Lance. Sure and after you, Joe the Red.

Eddy. I'm afraid so, Johnny, It is destiny.

Muscle. That's very good worda.

Johnny. Okay, okay. But don't forget, you birds, that Siggy'll double-cross you. He'll two-time ya. Then you'll be on the spot.

Siggy. Shut up! Okay, boys. Give him the works.

All four draw their pistols.

Lance. Hold on a minute.

He opens his umbrella and covers the four guns. They fire. Johnny falls, Lance takes a rubber ball out of his pocket.

He's all washed up. Okay, let's play ball.

He throws the ball to Eddy who throws it to Muscle. He is about the throw it to Siggy who turns his back on him.

Siggy. What's the prize?

Lance. Joe the Red's territory.

Siggy. No. I don't play.

Lance. Did you hear what I did? He won't play ball. You dirty little double-crossing rat! What about you, Muscle?

Muscle. If he don'ta play, I don'ta play.

Lance. Okay. This is war, war to the knife! This is war! *[The End]*

An episodic play with singing

Johnny Noble

by Ewan MacColl

The curtain opens on a completely dark stage draped in black curtains. On either side of the stage stand two Narrators, a man and a woman dressed in black oilskins. They are pin-pointed by two spotlights. Very simply the man begins to sing.

[MUSIC CUE 1]

1st Narrator. (*Singing*)
Here is a stage –

2nd Narrator. (*Speaking*) A platform twenty-five feet by fifteen.

1st Narrator. (*Singing*)
A microcosm of the world.

2nd Narrator. (*Speaking*) Here the sun is an amber flood and the moon a thousand-watt spot.

1st Narrator. (*Singing*)
Here shall be space,
Here we shall act time.

2nd Narrator. (*Speaking*) From nothing everything will come.

1st Narrator. (*Singing*)
On this dead stage we'll make society appear.

An acting-area flood fades up, discovering three youths playing pitch-and-toss upstage centre.

The world is here –

2nd Narrator. (*Speaking*) Our world.

Up boogie-woogie music. A woman enters, dances across the stage and off. Fade out music.

1st Narrator. (*Singing*)
A little gesture from an actor's hand creates a rolling landscape:
(*Speaking*) or a desert.

2nd Narrator. (*Singing*)
A word from us and cities will arise;
The night be broken by screaming factories.

Up burst of machinery. A red spot is faded up discovering a half-naked figure of a man. He mimes raking out a furnace in time to machinery. The light and machine-noise fade out together. The man goes off.

1st Narrator. (*Speaking*) Yes, we speak of days that linger in the memory like a bad taste in the mouth. Come back with us a dozen years or so, back to the early thirties, to the derelict towns and the idle hands, the rusting lathes and the silent turbines.

An unemployed man enters, stands left centre, yawning.

Unemp. Man. Time to sign on. (*He exits*)

A child enters, a small lonely figure in a pool of white light. She begins a queer abstracted hopping dance.

2nd Narrator. (*Speaking*) Here a child grows up in a desolate land.

1st Narrator. (*Singing*)
Here is a street
In any seaport town.

Two distant blasts of a ship's siren.

It could be anywhere
Where a man's work is the sea.

The pitch-and-toss players begin to intone their calls.

1st youth. Heads.

2nd youth. Tails.

1st youth. It's mine.

2nd youth. What is it?

1st youth. Heads.

2nd youth. Tails it is.

1st youth. My shout.

2nd youth. Shout!

1st youth. Tails.

2nd youth. It's mine.

Fade and hold behind following sequence. Two small girls enter and are joined by the first little girl in a singing game.

[MUSIC CUE 2]

Three girls. (*Singing*)
Have you seen owt o' my bonnie lad,
And are you sure that he's weel, O?
He's gone ower land wiv his stick in his hand,
He's gone to moor the keel, O.

One girl. (*Singing*)
Yes, I've seen your bonny lad,
Upon the sea I spied him,
His grave is green but not wiv grass
And thou'll never lie beside him.

The song fades but is held faintly behind following sequence. The unemployed man enters, takes a newspaper out of his pocket and begins to read it. Johnny Noble enters and starts to watch the gambling game.

Unemp. man. Hello, Johnny.

Johnny. Hullo.

[MUSIC CUE 3]

1st Narrator. (*Singing*)

Now come all you good people and listen to my song,
It's of young Johnny Noble and I won't detain you long,
Young Johnny lived on the north-east coast where trawler men are made,
And he was quite determined for to follow the sailor's trade.

Unemp. man. Courting again, Johnny?

Johnny. You can call it that.

Unemp. man. If you ask me, it's a mug's game.

Johnny. Nobody asked you.

2nd youth. It's still a mug's game.

Mary enters. The youths whistle appreciatively.

Johnny. Hullo, Mary.

Mary and Johnny dance. The gamblers play. The unemployed man reads his newspaper. The children play.

[MUSIC CUE 4]

2nd Narrator. (*Singing*).

Now Johnny loved a neighbour's lass, young Mary was her name.
His love was deep and tender and burned him like a flame
And Mary had loved her Johnny since she was but a lass,
But you shall soon know their tale of woe and all that came to pass.

2nd youth. You're a liar! It was tails.

1st youth. I tell you it was heads.

2nd youth. Don't try and fool me. I saw you turn it over!

1st youth. Are you calling me a cheat?

2nd youth. Yes, and a dirty rotten one at that!

The 1st youth strikes the 2nd.

2nd youth. You pig!

1st youth. Take your coat off and I'll show you!

They prepare to fight.

Little girls. A fight! A fight!

Mary. O stop them, Johnny!

1st youth. Him and who else?

The other characters form a ring round the fighters.

Unemp. man. Now take it easy. Do it proper. Make it a fair fight.

2nd youth. I'll kill him!

They dance a fight. A fisherman enters, watches the fight for a moment and is then noticed by Johnny.

Johnny. Whitey!

Seaman. Hi, Johnny!

The others crowd around the newcomer, the fight forgotten.

1st youth. I'll settle with you later.

2nd youth. Any time you like.

Johnny. When did you get in?

Seaman. About an hour ago. We've been lying off the point since early this morning.

Unemp. man. What kind of a catch did you have?

Seaman. More than four hundred cran.

2nd youth. Then there'll be work at the fish dock! Come on, let's go.

Seaman. You won't be needed.

2nd youth. Not with a load like that?

Seaman. They're back in the sea.

Johnny. You mean you dumped the whole catch?

Seaman. The whole catch. Five shiploads of dead herring caught off the Faroes.

Mary. But why?

Seaman. Owner's orders.

Enter Mary's mother.

Mother. Ted White! I didn't know you were back. Where's Dan?

Seaman. He's not with us.

Mother. Didn't he come back with you?

Seaman. No.

Mother. Well, where is he?

Seaman. Big John was to break the news. He'll be waiting back at your house now.

Mother. Ted, what is it? He's not . . .

Seaman. Tuesday night it was. The wind came up as we were drawing our nets just north of the Skerries. One minute it was dead quiet with nothing but the slip-slap of the water against the ship and the next it was all wind and thick sky bruised and angry. I never saw the sea in such a rage. It looked as if we'd have to cut the nets, but Dan was for facing it out. We worked there till the wind howled and the sky was in ribbons. By the time we got the nets aboard the sea was in the sky and roaring like a beast and then there came a great black blast and the sea gathered into one big fist of wave. It caught young Syms, the deckie, and crushed him against the cabin. He went limp and spun round like a stick in a cross-current. I saw Dan leap at the wave as a swimmer with a knife might leap to gut a barracuda. I tried to shout a warning but there was no room in the world for any voice but the sea's. The wave took them both.

While he has been speaking, the general lighting has faded leaving only Whitey and the mother spotlit. The other characters have retreated and formed a large semicircle half-hidden in shadow.

Mother. Dead!

Chorus. (*whispering*). Dead! Dead!

Mother. First my son and then his father. Lost, both of them lost, for a handful of fishes. For twenty years I have lived with a fear of this night and cursed the cunning of it. I've prayed that the sea would be swallowed up and silenced forever. Curse on the sea that a man should be less to it than a fish.

Mary. O, Mother!

Johnny. Mary . . .

Mother. Stay away from her! The sea's taken all it's going to take of my life. Stay away from her. No child of mine is ever going to suffer what I've suffered. I'll wash clothes, I'll scrub floors, I'll beg in the street, but no child of mine will ever give her life to the sea or to anything or anyone that belongs to the sea.

During the foregoing passage the lights have faded, leaving only mother and Mary and Johnny surrounded by shadows. Mother and Mary go off. Johnny stands centre stage. He looks round in perplexity. In the distance a barrel-organ plays. The stage becomes dark.

[MUSIC CUE 5]

2nd Narrator. (*Singing*)

Now two years pass and Johnny Noble's
Parted from his dearie;
And still she yearns for his return
And her heart is sad and weary.

The lads all throng at Mary's side
For she has grown full bonny,
But the fairest flower amang them a'
Is the sailor lad called Johnny.

Distant blast of ships' sirens. Enter Mary and Eddie, laughing.

Mary. I live just near here.

Eddie. That's a pity.

Mary. Why?

Eddie. Do you have to ask?

Mary. Well . . . goodnight.

Eddie. Don't go. It's early yet.

Mary. Do you call this early?

Eddie. Look, when am I going to see you again?

Mary. Oh, some time.

Eddie. How about tomorrow night?

Mary. No, I can't, I . . .

Eddie. Thursday, then. Listen, I'll tell you what. Let's have tea in town and then go on to the Plaza. They've got a marvellous band there; not like that bunch of amateurs at The Jig. Well, what do you say?

Mary. I'm sorry, but I can't.

Eddie. Why not? You like dancing, don't you?

Mary. I love it.

Eddie. Well, say you'll come. I'll see that you have a good time. Look Mary, I want to get to know you better.

Mary. You'd better ask someone else.

Eddie. I don't want anybody else, that's why I'm asking you. You know, you're too good to waste your time dancing with a bunch of louts at social club hops. I knew that the first time I saw you. You've got style and when you and me dance together I feel like we've been practising all our lives just for that one dance. You see, dancing with you isn't just routine, it's . . . O, I can't explain it but when I get that beat . . . one . . . two . . . da di di, da di . . .

Faint dance music.

. . . and feel you in my arms. (*He takes her in his arms.*) Well, it's more than just dancing.

The music grows louder. They dance. Johnny advances out of the shadows.

Johnny. Mary!

The music stops. The dancers fall apart.

Eddie. What's the idea?

Johnny. Mary, I've got to talk with you.

Eddie. Now look here, whatever your name is . . .

Mary. Alright, Johnny . . .

Eddie. I seem to be in the way. If you'd told me about him in the first place I wouldn't have bothered.

Johnny. Beat it!

Eddie. I seem to be losing my grip. (*He goes.*)

Mary. Well?

Johnny. Mary, I had to see you.

Mary. Did you have to spy on me?

Johnny. I wasn't spying. I've been waiting here for hours in the hope that I might see you.

Mary. You're shivering. You'll catch cold.

Johnny. I'm on fire Mary, I can't go on like this.

Mary. But what can I do? I told you everything was finished between us.

Johnny. I don't believe it. If you said it a thousand times I still wouldn't believe it. You and me couldn't live in the same world and not be close to each other. If you and me were finished then the sun would hide its face and the sea stop rolling, the wind would never blow again and every man and woman in this town would talk in whispers. Listen, you can hear the town breathing in its sleep. Do you think it would be so quiet if we were really through?

Mary. Is this what you wanted to say?

Johnny. I'm trying to wake you up out of this bad dream.

Mary. I'm sorry.

Johnny. Don't talk as if I am trying to sell you something. You remember me? I'm Johnny, the bloke who loves you. Remember?

Mary. I don't want to remember anything.

Johnny. Why not?

Mary. Because remembering hurts and I'm tired . . .

Johnny. Not too tired to dance.

Mary. Is this all you've got to say?

Johnny. I once knew a girl who looked just like you. Her hair was softer than a summer's night and her eyes were as deep as the ocean. Even to look at her made me feel good.

Mary. Don't, Johnny!

Johnny. Her voice was like yours too, only warmer.

Mary. Oh, why don't you let me forget?

Johnny. I keep remembering the things she used to say, the memory of her words won't let me sleep.

Mary. Forget her, Johnny, forget her.

Johnny. Sometimes we would walk together along the old moorland road and the feel of her arm in mine made the stars nearer and the sky wider. Everything was different when I was with her. This place wasn't half so dark nor the streets nearly so deserted . . .

Mary. Please, Johnny, please don't go on.

Johnny. Have you forgotten, Mary?

Mary. How could I forget?

Johnny. I love you, Mary.

Mary. No, don't say it . . . it's no good . . .

Johnny. I love you like the earth loves the sun, or the sea the sky, and what's more, you love me, don't you?

Mary. Yes, yes, but what's the good? Oh, Johnny, I'm so miserable I wish I could die. I'm tired of all the pain and hurt that's in loving. Do you think I don't feel all the things that you feel? I think of you all the time. Sleeping and waking, you are part of me, a part that never lets me rest.

Johnny. Then why do we act like strangers to each other?

Mary. Because it's the only way for us.

Johnny. Mary, you can't let your mother come between us like this. It's our lives . . . Oh, I know how she feels about the sea, but . . .

Mary. It's not how she feels. It's the way *I* feel. I hate the sea, too. Not just because it took my father but because of you. When I was little I used to lie awake at night and listen to my mother in the next room, lying awake and waiting. Sometimes I'd hear her moaning in her sleep and . . . Oh, don't you see I couldn't live like that? I couldn't. I love you too much.

Johnny. Alright, you won't have to.

Mary. What do you mean?

Johnny. Mary, if I could get a regular job, a land job, do you think you and me could get together again?

Mary. Do you mean it?

Johnny. Of course I mean it. Trawling's finished. They tied up another five boats last month, that means the end of the fleet. I've worked fifteen days in the last four months and three of those were a dead loss. I can't sit around waiting forever, and in any case if I have to choose between you and the sea . . . I don't care if I never see the sea again.

Mary. But where will you find work?

Johnny. There must be one job somewhere that I can do. Anyway, if there is, I'll find it.

Mary. You mean you're going away?

Johnny. Yes, Mary, I'm going to fish for work the way we fish for herring. I'll drag a net over the whole country if I have to, and one of these days I'll be writing to you and asking you to come to me. Will you?

Mary. To the end of the earth.

Johnny. And you'll wait?

Mary. Till the seas run dry.

They dance to the following song.

[MUSIC CUE 6]
1st Narrator. (*Singing*)
Fare you well, my dear, I must be gone,
And leave you for a while.
If I roam away I will come back again
Though I roam a thousand miles, my dear,
Though I roam a thousand miles.

2nd Narrator. (*Singing*)
The salt sea will run dry, my dear,
And the rocks melt in the sun;
But I never will prove false to the lad I love
Till all these things be done, my dear,
Till all these things be done.

The lights fade. Up music behind the following. The lights fade up and a chorus of unemployed men enter dancing.

Microphone voice. Crew of the Trawler 'Mary Ellis': Paid off!

Chorus. No change! No work!

Mic. voice. Trawler 'Sun-bird', in dry dock, all repairs at a standstill.

Chorus. No change! No work!

Mic. voice. Crew of the trawler *Merrily*: paid off!

Chorus. No change! No work!

Mic. voice. In future, trawlermen will apply for work at their labour exchange. Ships' husbandmen will no longer book their crews at this dock.

Chorus. No change! No work!

Johnny. What's wrong with the world? What's wrong with me? Don't people need clothes and shoes and houses any more? Don't they need fish out of the sea and coal out of the earth?

Mic. voice. The unemployment figures can now be said to be stabilised at two and a half million. No immediate deterioration is expected.

Roll of drums. The chorus fall into line.

Mic. voice. Two hundred Scottish hunger-marchers set out from Glasgow.

The chorus begin to march, marking time.

Mic. voice. November 1931. The unemployed of the north-east coast are marching.

1st man. Men from Newcastle!

2nd man. Gateshead!

3rd man. Durham!

4th man. Jarrow!

5th man. Morpeth!

6th man. Sunderland!

All chorus. Shields!

Mary. (*Offstage*) Wait, Johnny! Wait!

A newsboy carrying papers and a poster dances on.

Newsboy.

All the latest! Last Edition!
Mr Eden's German Mission.
Paris riots, foodshops looted,
Van de Lubbe executed.
Loch Ness Monster seen again.
Sentence passed on Ludwig Renn.
All the latest!
All the latest!
All the latest!

He goes off. The chorus read their newspapers.

1st man. Plenty of words!

2nd man. Plenty of promises!

3rd man. Plenty of circuses!

All chorus. But no bread!

Mary. (*Offstage*) Wait, Johnny! Wait!

Johnny. Not me, I'm not waiting. I'm going out to find what's wrong with the world. And if there's a job anywhere, I'll find it!

Chorus retreat, waving slowly as light fades.

Chorus. So long, Johnny! So long, Johnny!
So long!

Chorus goes off.

[MUSIC CUE 7]

1st Narrator. (*Singing*)
Johnny Noble has left his home,
He has walked over moss and moor;
And he has gone to the banks of Clyde,
To try his luck in the shipyards there.

Johnny dances across to the Narrator who suddenly takes the character of an unemployed man.

Johnny. How's things around here, Mac?

Clydesider. Deadly.

Johnny. Anything doing in the yards?

Clydesider. No, we've been idle for the last six years. Where are you from?

Johnny. Hull way.

Clydesider. Engineer?

Johnny. Fisherman.

Clydesider. No work?

Johnny. That's right. I thought I'd try the shipbuilding game.

Clydesider. It's a lost trade, chum.

Johnny. Are there no jobs at all?

Clydesider. None at all.

Johnny. They sound busy enough in there.

Clydesider. That's the wrecking gang. They're breaking up the equipment. Better go south. I'd be there myself if it wasnae for the wife.

The light and the Narrator fade. Johnny dances.

[MUSIC CUE 8]

2nd Narrator (*Singing*)
In Durham County it is the same,
The pithead gear is standing still,
And men are filled with a sense of shame
For idle hands and wasted skill.

A miner enters and stands in a pool of light, centre stage.

Durham miner. Why, but you've come to the wrong place, mon. There's no work here. Number Three was working until a year ago but that's finished now. The Ballarat seam's flooded out. They'll never get it working again. Why, there's not enough work to keep three men and a boy busy.

Johnny. How do you manage to keep going?

Durham Miner. Well, we've got our bit of dole and we scratch for coal on the screens to keep a bit fire in the house. Why . . . aye, but it's bad . . . it is that . . . bad all over, though they say things are better in the south . . .

Music. Man goes off. Unemployed men enter, dancing.

Johnny. Which is the road to Darlington, mate?

1st man. Follow the road . . . straight on.

Dance.

Johnny. Which is the road to Leeds, mate?

2nd man. Follow the road . . . straight on.

Dance.

Johnny. How do I get to Manchester?

3rd man. Follow the road.

All. Follow the road, chum. Follow the road. Follow the road, straight on.

Johnny. Where are YOU going?

All. We don't know, chum. We don't know. We just keep going.

Johnny. Well, good luck!

All. Good luck, chum!

Slow blackout.

[MUSIC CUE 9]

2nd Narrator. (*Singing*)

Winter is past and the leaves are green,
The time is past that we have seen.
But still I hope the time will come,
When you and I shall be as one.

The light fades up to half, showing a group of men sitting and lying on the stage.

Narrator. Men on the roads, men on the streets. The traversing of the endless circle. Hey, you there!

Chorus. Yes?

Narrator. What are you waiting for?

Chorus. For time to pass.

Narrator. Who are you?

Chorus. We are the disinherited.

Narrator. Where are you from?

Chorus. From everywhere.

Narrator. Where are you bound for?

Chorus. Anywhere. We walk between one meal and the next.

Narrator. And this is your life?

Chorus. We sign away our lives . . . every morning.

They lie down and sleep.

[MUSIC CUE 10]

2nd Narrator. (*Singing*)
My Johnny's gone, I mourn and weep,
But satisfied I ne'er can sleep.
I'll write to you in a few short lines,
I suffer death ten thousand times.

One of the men sits up and begins filling his pipe.

Johnny. My, but I could do with a breath of air.

Taffy. Well, there's no shortage of that outside, and no charge either.

Johnny. I like my air to be well seasoned.

Taffy. What do you mean by that?

Johnny. My lungs are in need of salt . . . Oh, for some sea air!

Taffy. Are you a matlo then?

Johnny. Fisherman.

Taffy. You are a long way from home, bach, there are no fish here.

Johnny. No . . .

Taffy. You are looking for work.

Johnny. Work? What's that?

Taffy. Yes, things are bad. Tell me, have you ever heard of Potato Jones?

Johnny. Potato Jones? Isn't he the skipper of the 'Seven Seas Spray'?

Taffy. The very man. Captain Jones, the blockade runner. I am sailing with him next trip.

Johnny. Oh, you're a seaman.

Taffy. Ship's cook for thirty-seven years. A galley-slave, my boy.

Johnny. Where are you bound for?

Taffy. Barcelona. We're carrying a cargo of canned milk.

Johnny. Dangerous work, isn't it?

Taffy. Well, I've known safer trips. Master Franco doesn't like people who feed children. Captain Jones makes him very angry.

Johnny. It's good work.

Taffy. You know, I think the captain is short of a deckhand. (*Pause*). I thought you might be interested. (*Pause*). Perhaps I shouldn't have mentioned it. Just forget everything I told you.

Johnny. Where are you sailing from?

Taffy. Liverpool.

Johnny. When?

Taffy. Thursday night.

Johnny. We'll have to be on the road early, then.

Taffy. I thought you were the right sort.

Johnny. Good night, Taffy.

Taffy. Good night, bach.

The light fades.

[MUSIC CUE 11]

1st Narrator. (*Singing*)

So Johnny shipped aboard a craft well known in the coasting trade,
She sailed for Barcelona through the fascist sea blockade.
They beat the German submarines, and floating mines as well,
And then they lay in the sheltered bay, a-heaving on the swell.

[MUSIC CUE 12]

2nd Narrator. (*Singing*)

But back in the home town,
Where time passes slow,
There Mary sits waiting
For Johnny, her jo.

Her trust has not faded
Though they are apart
And the love has not withered
That grows in her heart.

The stage is flooded with light. Two youths stand upstage right, arguing. Mary sits downstage left. Her mother sits nearby gossiping with a neighbour. The unemployed man stands upstage reading a newspaper.

1st youth. It was in the fourth round.

2nd youth. No, you're wrong –

1st youth. But I tell you, I saw the film four times!

2nd youth. I don't care if you saw it twenty times, it was at the beginning of the fifth round, a technical knockout.

1st youth. That wasn't the Baer fight – it was the Mexican champion.

2nd youth. It was the Baer-Louis fight!

1st youth. Now look, in the third round, Joe Louis began to work on Baer, didn't he? He got Baer into a corner, see, and began by giving him a few short jabs to the side, I tell you. I can remember every single punch in that fight. He stands there like this, see, crowding Baer . . .

2nd youth. So?

1st youth. So Maxie's getting tanned good and proper, so he tries to slip by on the ropes. Well, Louis waits till he's off-balance, see, and then he wades in with a smashing left drive. Maxie tries to side-step it, but Joe follows through with his right and closes Maxie's left eye for him.

2nd youth. Well, who's arguing about that?

1st youth. You are. Anyway, Maxie's minus a lamp now, see, and this time he doesn't know what day it is. He's been punched around so much. Well, the bell goes for the fourth round. 'Seconds out of the ring! Time!' Clang! Louis crossing the ring looking determined, like, but not tough. He looks like what he's going to do is for Maxie's own good. Now Maxie comes in sparring, but Joe won't play. He leads with his left to Maxie's side. Bang! Bang! Then with his right he breaks Maxie's guard. Bang! Wallop! And then that terrific left swing comes from nowhere and Maxie's out for good. One-two-three-four. . . I tell you, the referee could have counted up to a thousand. The fourth round it was, and still three-quarters of a minute to go.

2nd youth. It was the fifth round.

1st youth. You're punch-drunk.

The 1st youth takes a newspaper from his pocket and begins to study it. The 2nd smokes a cigarette.

Mother. My, but it's close, isn't it?

Neighbour. Terrible. It's just like an oven in the house.

Mother. Mary, why don't you go for a walk in the park?

Mary. I'm alright.

Mother. It would do you more good than sitting around here brooding.

A man enters reading a newspaper.

1st youth. What won the 3.30, Larry?

Man. Castle in Spain at 8–1.

1st youth. I had a bob on Blue Silk!

Man. Didn't stand a chance. Came in sixth.

Enter Eddie.

Eddie. Hello, Mary. Going to the dance?

Mary. No, I don't think I'll bother.

Eddie. Still waiting for Johnny?

Mary. What if I am?

Eddie. I think you're crazy. I bet you've almost forgotten how to dance.

Mary. I'm not complaining.

Eddie. Mary, how would you like to take a run into the country this weekend?

Mary. No, Eddie, I've told you, I . . .

Eddie. Alright, alright! I know the answer. It's a pity though, I've just bought a car.

Mary. A car? Well!

Eddie. Yes, I've been doing alright.

Mary. You certainly have.

Eddie. Seriously, though, Mary – you look as if you need some air.

Mary. Well, some other time.

Eddie. Some other time! I seem to have heard that before. How's Johnny going on? Got a job yet?

Mary. Not yet.

Eddie. What a mug you are. Hullo girls? Looking for me?

Enter two girls.

1st girl. Hullo, Eddie.

2nd girl. Coming to the dance, Mary?

Eddie. No, she's got a date with a ghost.

1st girl. How's Johnny?

Mary. He's alright, thanks.

Mother. Why don't you tell them he never writes?

Mary. Why should he? He said he wouldn't write till he found something.

2nd girl. I'd want a better excuse than that.

A youth enters playing a mouth organ. The two girls dance.

1st youth. Break it up, the experts are here.

They partner the girls.

Eddie. Come on, Mary, you're safe enough here.

They dance. Enter 1st Narrator with a letter.

[MUSIC CUE 13]

1st Narrator. (*Singing*)
Which of you is Mary Marsden?
I've a letter for you.

Girls. (*Singing*)
Mary, hear what he is saying:
Here's a letter for you.

1st Narrator. (*Singing*)
The lad that gave it to me said
His name was Johnny Noble.

Girls (*Singing*)
Well she knew her love was true,
Her handsome Johnny Noble.
Oh, oh, oh, oh, Seaman Johnny Noble.

Mary. Oh, let me see it quickly!

She opens the letter.

Girls. Oh, read it quickly, Mary, do
And tell us what Johnny says to you.

Man. Is his search for work now done?

Girls. And does he write for you to come?

All. Oh, read it quickly, Mary.

Girls. Oh tell us, Mary, do!

[MUSIC CUE 14]

1st Narrator.
Why do you grow so pale?
What is so alarming?

1st girl. (*Singing*)
Is it then bad news
Makes you weep and mourn?

2nd girl. (*Singing*)
Here begins the grief,
Pain without relief –
Has he then forsaken his love?

Girls. (*Singing*)
She is left forsaken,
Another she is taken,
Johnny, Oh why do you so?

Mary. This letter – it's from Spain.

1st Narrator. Well?

Mary. He promised me that he was finished with the sea.

Men. (*Singing*)
Oh, oh, oh, oh, faithless Johnny Noble.

[END OF SONG SEQUENCE]

Mother. I warned you, you should have left him when I told you.

1st Narrator. But why? What's he done except try and keep famine from the door of a brave people?

Mother. That's not his business.

1st Narrator. If a man in Spain dies because he opens his mouth to speak his mind, that's everybody's business.

Eddie. We've enough trouble of our own without going out to look for more.

1st Narrator. You don't have to go out to look for it. It's staring you in the face every time you open a newspaper. Look!

He takes a newspaper out of his pocket.

'Men and women are dying in China.'

A girl. That's a long way from here.

1st Narrator. They are dying in Spain and that's not so far away. Aye, and Germany and Austria aren't far away. Look at these four lines in a newspaper: 'It is reported from Hamburg that Rudolph Schwartz was executed this morning for attempting to organise a trade union.' Instead of Rudolph Schwartz it could be you – or Johnny. And we would be his executioners.

1st youth. Who, me?

1st Narrator. Yes, you. Look, we'll act it.

1st youth. But don't I need a black shirt?

1st Narrator. Don't worry – Fascism doesn't always wear a black shirt.

Mic. voice. It is early morning. The city is still asleep. You have lain awake all night waiting for this moment, the moment when time stops. This is the last time you will ever know the cold air of morning or the streets in the moment between sleeping and waking. This is your last walk.

During the foregoing passage, the lights fade until only the condemned man and the guards are clearly visible – the chorus stands on the periphery of the light. A man advances from the body of the chorus and begins to sing. The rest of the scene is danced.

[MUSIC CUE 15]

Singer. In the yard of a prison
That at last they might shoot him.
He stood, back to a wall,
Built by men such as he was.

Guard. Eins! Zwei! Drei!

Chorus. We mixed the lime and carried the hod
We laid the bricks for seventeen pfennig a day.

Singer. Even the rifles that were levelled against his breast
And the bullets had been made by men like himself –

Guard. Vier! Funf! Sechs!

Chorus. We watched the lathe and turned the steel
For twenty-two pfennig a day.

Singer. They were by this time long departed or were scattered,
Yet for him they lingered,
Still present in the work of their hands . . .

Guard. Achtung!

Singer. Even the men who would shoot him
They were not other than he
Nor forever cut off in their blindness.

Chorus. Kill him! Kill him! Kill him! Kill him!

A woman leaves the chorus and advances downstage.

Woman. Now memory comes, sharp and poignant
Filling his eyes with tears,
Trembling with distant music.
The suns of past summers
Stir in the blood
And the little roots of remembered springs tear at the soul.

Chorus. (*Gives a long shuddering sigh.*)

Woman. Oh, let there be night without stars
Body without movement,
Mind without thought.
Let me die unseen in the night
Feeling nothing but the body's anguish
Under the teeth of the wolves of darkness.

Chorus. (*Moans*).

[MUSIC CUE 16]

Bravely he walked still encumbered with fetters,
With fetters forged by his comrades,
And hung on him by his comrades,
And though it was morning then
For at daybreak they marshalled them out,
The buildings were empty and still.

Guard. Links! Recht! Links! Recht! Links! Recht!

Woman. Remember the days of hope,
When the night had ears to hear the words
That leap from house to house
In little blades of fire,
And men had the keen, sharp sight of birds
To recognise the first, trembling spasm of revolt.
Remember the song that thrilled the heart
And made the air itself respond
With brittle murmurings of dreams.

Remember the shared desires and the shared hunger,
The shared belief that all men are brothers,

Remember the sudden crack of voice
That made the streets rise up
And bar the way to soldiers.
These same streets, these same houses.

Guard. Links! Recht! Links! Recht! Halt!

[MUSIC CUE 17]

Singer. But to his eyes they sheltered now
A numberless host of workers,
whose strivings and aims are his own –
Now they led him forth against the wall,
And all this he perceived,
Yet understood it not.

The guard dances the shooting of the prisoner. The prisoner falls. Blackout. Up music and hold until the lights go up again. All the persons on the stage are discovered in their original positions, asleep.

Singer. You see?

Mary. They're asleep.

[MUSIC CUE 18]

1st Narrator. (*Singing*)
Wake you up! Wake you up!
You seven sleepers!
And do take a warning from me,

Be prepared to defend
Your freedom to the end,
Make a stand now for your liberty.

Sound of aeroplane.

2nd Narrator. (*Singing*)
The night is disturbed,
The calmness is broken,
And death overshadows the world,
You can hear the beat
Of an army's marching feet
And the war flags are being unfurled.

Sound of distant bombing.

Mary. What was that?

Unemployed man. It sounded like thunder.

Eddie. We could do with a storm. My, but it's close.

Mother. This kind of weather always puts me on edge. I think I'll go in.

She goes in.

1st youth. It's a good night for a swim. What do you say?

2nd youth. O.K.

They go.

Eddie. Sure you won't change your mind about the dance, Mary?

Mary. Not tonight.

Eddie. (*To first girl*) Come on, kid. You and me's going places. So long, Mary!

They go.

Mary. (*Reading Johnny's letter*) O, Johnny, I wish you were here.

Johnny has entered silently.

Johnny. Do you?

Mary. Johnny! (*They embrace.*) I can't believe you're here!

Johnny. Oh, I'm here, alright. (*He kisses her.*) Does that convince you?

Mary. Oh, Johnny, I've missed you so much. Don't ever go away again, will you?

Johnny. I had to go, Mary. I had to find out. You know, Mary, I used to feel lost, as if there was no place in the world for me. There seemed to be no sense in being born. But I've learned something. There's a lot of people like me in the world. We're everywhere, and we're important. Yes, we are, Mary! Oh, I know they let us starve and they don't care what happens to us, but when there's big trouble anywhere we are the ones they call upon for help. You know what, Mary? I've discovered that everything that's worth looking at in all the towns and cities of the world was built by people like us. I don't feel lonely any more because I know there's a man in Madrid just like me and at this moment he's fighting a German tank with a bottle of petrol. There's a million like me in China picking off stray Japs with obsolete rifles. I used to walk around like a mongrel dog begging for a bone but that's all over. I know who I am now, and I know why I'm here. I don't know why I'm saying all this to you, but . . .

Mary. I want to hear it.

Johnny. It's funny, but it's not what I intended to say.

Mary. No?

Johnny. No – I was going to ask you to marry me.

Mary. What, now?

Johnny. Well, not tonight, say in a week's time.

Mary. Ah . . . (*She weeps.*)

Johnny. What's wrong? Did I say something?

Mary. Oh, I'm so happy.

Johnny. Then you will?

Mary. Of course.

Johnny. I've done it! I've done it! I've done it!

First youth enters.

Johnny. Hey, cocky! I'm going to be married!

He whirls the youth in a dance.

1st youth. Hey, Johnny's gone crazy.

Enter 2nd youth.

2nd youth. What's wrong?

1st youth. He's getting married.

2nd youth. Larry, they've fixed up. They're getting hitched.

Unemployed man enters.

Man. Congratulations, Mary – and you too, Johnny.

Both. Thanks, Larry.

Enter Mary's mother.

Mother. What's happening?

Mary. Johnny's asked me to marry him.

Mother. Ah, well, I knew it would come to it some day.

Mother kisses Johnny. The others enter.

1st girl. Is it true, Mary?

Mary. Aye, it's true.

Johnny. And the whole street's invited to the wedding.

1st youth. Will there be a dance?

Johnny. Aye, you can dance yourself down to the knees.

He plays a jig on a mouth organ. The others dance until suddenly the jig is drowned out in a great sustained phrase of music. Slow fade-out.

Mic. voice. I am speaking to you from the Cabinet Room of Number 10 Downing Street. This morning the British Ambassador in Berlin handed to the German Government a final note stating that unless their troops were withdrawn from Poland by eleven o'clock this morning a state of war would exist between us. I have to tell you now that no such undertaking has been received and that, consequently, this country is at war with Germany.

Up level drone of planes behind the foregoing sequence. Cut in on last word with music, hold at peak and cross-fade with heavy ticking of clock. Hold behind the following.

Mic. voice. Passengers for Preston, Lancaster, Carlisle and Glasgow will leave on number 3 platform at 5.43. The train for Preston, Lancaster, Carlisle and Glasgow will leave number 3 platform at 5.43.

Another voice. Not much time left.

Two groups of figures, each composed of a man and a woman, are discovered embracing in two yellow pools of light.

1st woman. Don't forget your sandwiches, Jim. I've put them at the top of your case. And let me know your address as soon as you get there. I'll send you a parcel. Must keep talking, Jim, we must keep talking. It's queer, the minutes are bleeding away and all I can talk about are the things furthest from my mind. Do look after yourself, Jim, and don't forget to send anything you want washed. Four more minutes and it'll be the end. Oh, God!

Towards conclusion of foregoing fade up clock backed by voice.

Voice. (*Whispering*) Hurry, etc.

Mic. voice. The train for Crewe, Hereford, Birmingham, Pontypool and Bristol, will leave number 11 platform at 5.58.

Mary. Go on talking, Johnny, please go on talking. If we stop talking we'll start thinking. Take care of yourself, Johnny. And please write as often as you can. Oh, so much to be said and no words to say with. If you need anything just write and I'll send it to you. Only a few minutes left and then

. . . Perhaps it won't be for long. I'll be waiting for you. Oh, if only the clocks would stop forever!

Ticking of clock at peak. Sudden high-pitched blast of train whistle.

Mic. voice. Johnny Noble, able seaman!

Johnny looks round.

Johnny. It's time, Mary.

Mic. Voice. James Munroe, bricklayer!

1st man. It's time, lass.

Mic. voice. Young men, it's time to say goodbye.

The couples embrace. The men go off. The two women, lonely figures in the pools of yellow light, stand without moving. There is a sudden, loud, blast of escaping steam and the women begin waving handkerchiefs. The train gets under way and as the light fades there are two, short, melancholy blasts of the engine's whistle as it passes into a long tunnel.

Mic. voice. If only one could choose one's moments of eternity – but inexorable time divides and sub-divides and sub-divides again until nothing is left of a moment but an insubstantial memory.

Complete blackout.

Mic. voice. And everything is left unsaid except – Goodbye.

[MUSIC CUE 19]

2nd Narrator. (*Singing*)
Westryn wind, when wilt thou blow?
The small rain down doth rain,
Oh, that my love were in my arms,
And I in my bed again.

Deep and wide the river runs
That steals my lad away,
And I must bide it here alone
And cannot bid him stay.

[MUSIC CUE 20]

1st Narrator. (*Singing*)
In nineteen hundred and forty two,
In November, the thirteenth day;
The 'Liberty Star' her anchor weighed
And for Murmansk bore away, brave boys,
And for Murmansk bore away.

Our course was set for nor'-nor' east,
Through the raging arctic sea, brave boys,
Through the raging arctic sea.

Fade up throb of ship's engines. Light fades up discovering Johnny seated on a box playing 'On top of Old Smokey' on a mouth organ. A stoker enters. Johnny stops playing.

Stoker. Go on playing, Johnny. I just came up for a breather.

Johnny. My hands are too cold.

Stoker. What's her name, Johnny?

Johnny. Mary.

Stoker. The wife?

Johnny. Not yet.

Short blast of ship's siren.

Stoker. That'll be the 'Sverdrup'. She should be astern of us.

Two short blasts of ship's siren.

Johnny. My, but it's cold!

Stoker. Is this your first trip up here?

Johnny. Well, I was up as far as Iceland once.

Stoker. Iceland! That's the tropics. Wait till we reach the Behring Sea, then you'll know what cold is.

Johnny. How long have you been at this job, Frank?

Stoker. Thirty-seven years.

Johnny. That's a long time.

Three short blasts of ship's siren.

Stoker. Yes, I know these waters better than I know the back streets of Salford. I remember sailing up into the Kara Sea when the insurance risk was only three shillings to the ton. That's going back a bit. And I'd been up to the Chukotsk Sea twice by the time I was twenty. The first skipper I ever sailed with was one of the old timers of the Hull whaling fleet, never felt happy unless he was freezing off the coast of Greenland. A fine man. I was off Bear Island with the trawlers when this lot started. We were lucky to get home. I'll bet the halibut wondered what was happening.

The repeated alarm signal of a destroyer is heard. The clanging of bells. Red and green warning-lights flash.

Stoker. Back again!

Johnny. Well, come on then.

They race off. Blackout. Fade in droning of plane. Build to peak and hold with backing of music.

Voice. (*Above music*) Enemy, Green Nine-O!

Siren. Music out.

Voice. Action station!

Fade up lights. Gun crew discovered stage centre. In the following scene they dance a gun crew in action. Up sound of circling plane.

1st Seaman. What is it? Dornier 109?

Gunner. Well, it's not a seagull.

Voice. Bearing Green Nine-O!

Gunner. Bearing Green Nine-O!

1st loader. Bearing Green Nine-O!

Music. In dance mime the crew load and fire the gun.

1st loader. Load!

2nd loader. Load!

1st loader. On!

2nd loader. On!

Gunner. Fire!

Music.

1st loader. Load!

2nd loader. Load!

1st loader. On!

2nd loader. On!

Gunner. Fire!

Bomb explosion.

Voice. Bearing Red Five-O!

Loaders. Bearing Red Five-O!

Gunner. Red Five-O!

1st loader. Load!

2nd loader. Load!

1st loader. On!

2nd loader. On!

Gunner. Fire!

1st loader. Load!

2nd loader. Load!

1st loader. On!

2nd loader. On!

Gunner. Fire!

Sound of dive-bombing and machine-gun fire. Crew drops to ground. One loader is killed.

[MUSIC CUE 21]

Narrator. (*Singing*)
The Nazi planes from Christiansund
Above our ships did fly,
But our ack-ack guns got the measure of the Huns,
And we blew them from the sky, brave boys
And we blew them from the sky.

The members of the gun-crew re-form and resume the dance.

1st loader. Load!

2nd loader. Load!

1st loader. On!

2nd loader. On!

Gunner. Fire!

Seaman. He's falling! Look! Look!

2nd Seaman. There he goes!

Drone of plane falling followed by explosion. The crew cheer and the lights fade out.

[MUSIC CUE 22]

2nd Narrator. (*Singing*)
And back in the homeland,
Where time passes slow,
There Mary sits waiting
For Johnny, her jo.

Her trust has not faded,
Though they are apart,
And the love has not withered
That grows in her heart.

Full lighting. Johnny and a woman neighbour enter from opposite directions, dancing.

[MUSIC CUE 23]

Neighbour. (*Singing*)
O Johnny, O Johnny, O Johnny,
And is it yourself that I see?
I thought you were on the Atlantic.

Johnny (*Singing*)
I've been up through the cold northern sea.

Two girls enter, dancing.

Two girls. (*Singing*)
It's Johnny, it's Johnny, Johnny Noble's come home,
He left his love, Mary, the wide world to roam;
But now he's come back from the ocean.
You're a welcome sight, Johnny, to me.

Two youths enter, dancing.

1st youth. (*Singing*)
Tonight let's all go out upon a binder.

Two girls. (*Singing*)
There's a girl who's waiting patiently
To hear that you are safe.

All. (*Singing*)
Hurry up, man, hurry up, man,
And find her.

Mary enters, dancing. She dances with Johnny.

[MUSIC CUE 24]

Two girls. (*Singing*)
Winter is past and the leaves are green,
The worst is past that we have seen;
And now at last the time has come
When these two hearts shall be as one.

Unemployed man. (*Singing*)
O Johnny lad, and are you glad
To be with us back home?

Johnny. (*Singing*)
Why aye, but man, of course I am,
No more I wish to roam.
I've done my share of freezing
As you may understand,
And I've known some cold Nor'westers
On the banks of Newfoundland.

All. (*Singing*)
He's done his share of freezing
As you may understand,
And he's known some cold Nor'westers
On the banks of Newfoundland.

Youth. (*Speaking*). Never mind, Johnny, that's all over and done with. You're back home and that's all that matters.

The roaring boys, two grotesque figures wearing black tights and bowler hats, leap on to the stage.

Roaring boys. Yes, it's over and done with.

All. The war is over now.

1st R. boy. No more government attacks.

2nd R. boy. No more excess profits tax.

1st R. boy. No more joint production groups.

2nd R. boy. No more nonsense from the troops.

All. No?

R. boys. No!

1st R. boy. Time we got back to normal. Can't go on being a hero forever, Johnny. The heroes have had their day. Now it's our turn. Business as usual, that's our slogan.

All. Which business?

R. boys. Money business.

1st R. boy. Time we got back to normal.

2nd R. boy.

Time we got back to the good old days,
The happy-go-lucky production ways.

1st R. boy.

Back to the dignified position
Of unrestricted competition.

2nd R. boy.

Back to surplus and higher rent,
And a profit of eighty-four per cent.
Back to normal.

1st R. boy. Back to normal.

Both R. boys. Back!

The chorus have retreated in the face of their dance. Now, the 1st Roaring boy produces a whistle and blows a sharp blast on it. The chorus turn stiffly and go through the motions of clocking-in. Each time one moves a bell rings. When they have all clocked in he blows another blast on the whistle. The chorus dance a machine which the two Roaring boys accompany with the rhythmic reiterations of:

R. boys. Time! Time! Time! Time!

The machine speeds up. At peak, Johnny interrupts.

Johnny. Stop!

The members of the chorus straighten up like men coming out of a dream.

Johnny. The war wasn't fought for this. They said it would be different. They said . . .

1st R. boy. Time to forget. Time to get back to the good old days. The days of plenty.

Johnny. Plenty of what?

Chorus. Hungry bellies and long queues,
Plenty of time and nothing to do with it.

1st R. boy. That's life, Johnny. Survival of the fittest.

Johnny. We fought for something better.

Chorus. Yes!

2nd R. boy. Time you forgot the fighting, Johnny. You can't fight tradition. You can't fight history.

Johnny. But they said . . .

Bell clangs.

1st R. boy. Time to forget! Seconds out of the ring! Time! On my right, ladies and gentlemen, standing in the shadows of protective might is Battling Johnny Privilege the heavyweight champion of the world. On my left, the challenger Johnny Noble, representing the pipe-dreamers. The prize is the Universe. Seconds out! Time!

A bell clangs. Johnny comes out fighting and then drops his guard and looks round in daze.

Johnny. I can't see him.

1st R. boy. Never mind, kid. Forget it. We've got a boom on our hands. A trade boom. Now you go home and leave everything to me. I'll fix things so that you don't have to think about anything.

He begins to shepherd Johnny off the stage.

Man. (*In audience*) Hey Johnny!

Johnny. Who was that?

Man. It's me, Johnny.

Johnny. I seem to recognise the voice.

Man. Do you remember a trimmer called Johnson who was drowned in the Barents Sea. That was me, Johnny. I was a little-piecer from Bolton called Arkroyd. I died screaming in the Burmese jungle. There was a bricklayer called Brown with a wife and three kids in Birmingham. The Germans burned him with a flame-thrower. That was me, Johnny.

1st R. boy. It's time we forgot about the war.

Man. It's time you remembered why the war was fought. There's a job to be done, Johnny.

Johnny. But what can I do?

Man. You've two hands and a brain and there's plenty of you. Take the world in your hands. Johnny, and wipe it clean. It's up to you, Johnny.

Johnny. Do you hear that? It's our world. It's up to us. We can do it, can't we?

Chorus. Yes!

Johnny. Thanks, pal, for reminding me.

Man. That's all right.

Man turns and walks slowly up the centre aisle. Turning, he addresses the stage.

Man. So long, Johnny. Good luck!

Johnny. So long, pal.

Chorus. So long.

[MUSIC CUE 25]

Man. (*Singing*) This is the end.

2nd Narrator. (*Singing*) The end of the story of Mary Marsdon and Johnny Noble.

[The End]

MUSIC CUE 1

MUSIC CUE 2

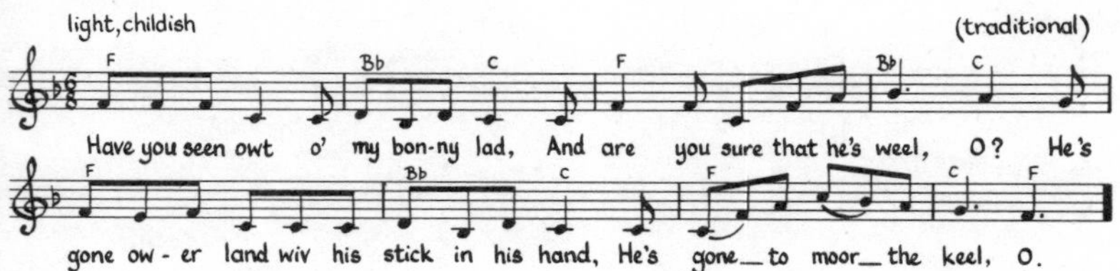
light, childish
(traditional)
F Bb C F Bb C
Have you seen owt o' my bon-ny lad, And are you sure that he's weel, O? He's
F Bb C F C F
gone ow - er land wiv his stick in his hand, He's gone_ to moor_ the keel, O.

MUSIC CUES 3, 4, 11

steadily
(traditional)
C G C
Now, come all_ you good peo-ple and lis-ten to my song, It's of young Johnny
Bb F G C
No-ble and I won't de-tain_you long, Young John-ny lived in the North East coast where
Bb F G C F G C
traw-ler men_are made, And he was quite de-ter-mined for to fol-low the sail-or's trade.

MUSIC CUE 5

somewhat freely
(traditional)
Now, two years pass and John-ny No-ble's Part-ed from_his dear - ie;
And still she yearns for his_ re - turn And her heart is_ sad and_weary.

MUSIC CUE 6

(freely)
(traditional)
Fare you well, my dear, I must be_gone And_leave you_for a - while. If I
roam a - way I will come back a-gain, Though I roam a thousand miles, my dear, Tho' I roam a thou-sand_
miles.
second verse
(etc., as first verse)

MUSIC CUES 7, 8
freely
(traditional)
John-ny No-ble has left his home, He has walked_ov-er moss and moor; And
he has gone to the banks of Clyde, To try his luck in the ship - yards there.
MUSIC CUE 9
freely
(traditional)
Win - ter is past and the leaves are green, The time___ is past that we have seen. But
still I___ hope the__ time__ will__ come, when you____ and I shall be as one.
MUSIC CUE 10
same as cue 9, with alternative ending from *
...I suf-fer death ten thousand times.
MUSIC CUES 12, 22
smoothly
(traditional)
C7
F
C
G7
But back in the home town, Where time pass-es slow, There Ma-ry sits
wait - ing For John-ny, her jo.
MUSIC CUE 13
gaily
(traditional)
Which of you is Ma - ry Mars-don? I've a let-ter for you. Ma - ry, hear what
he is say-ing: Here's a let - ter for you. The lad that gave it to me said His
name was John-ny No - ble. Well she knew her love was true, Her hand-some John-ny
No - ble. Oh, oh, oh, oh, Sea -man John - ny No - ble.

MUSIC CUE 14

MUSIC CUE 15

MUSIC CUE 16

MUSIC CUE 17

MUSIC CUE 18

MUSIC CUE 19

MUSIC CUES 20, 21

with determination
(traditional)
In nine - teen hun - dred and for - ty two, In No - vem - ber the thir - teenth day; The
'Li - ber - ty Star' her an - chor weighed And for Murmansk bore a - way, brave boys, And for
Mur - mansk bore _ a - way. Our course was set _ for _ Nor' Nor' East, Through the
rag - ing Arc - tic _ Sea, brave boys, Through the rag - ing Arc - tic Sea.

MUSIC CUE 23

cheerily
(by Ewan MacColl)
O, John - ny, O John - ny, O John - ny And is it your - self that I see? I
thought you were on the At - lan - tic. I've been up through the cold nor - thern sea. It's
John - ny, it's Johnny, Johnny No - ble's come home, He left his love, Ma - ry, the wide world to roam; But
now he's come back from the o - cean. You're a wel - come sight, Johnny, to me. To -
SPEED UP
- night let's all go out up - on a bin - der. There's a girl who's waiting pa — tient - ly To
hear that you are safe, Hur - ry up, man, hur - ry up, man And find her.

MUSIC CUE 24

moderate
(traditional)
Win - ter is past and the leaves are green, The worst is past that we have seen; And
now at last the time has come When these two hearts shall be as one.
O John-ny lad, and are you glad To be with us back home? Why
aye, but man, of course I am, No more I wish to roam. I've
done my share of freez-ing As you may un - der - stand, And I've
known some cold Nor' wes - ters On the banks of New- found-land. He's
done his share of freez-ing As you may un - der - stand, And he's
known some cold Nor' wes - ters On the banks of New - found - land.

MUSIC CUE 25

heroically
(by Ewan MacColl)
This is the end. The
end of the sto-ry of Ma-ry Marsdon and John-ny No - - - - ble.

An episodic play in two parts

Uranium 235

by Ewan MacColl

NOTE ON CASTING

A company of twelve actors, seven men and five women, made up the original cast of the Theatre Workshop production. Occasionally, this number would be enlarged by the addition of one or two more actors. On other occasions, the cast was reduced to ten.

AUTHOR'S NOTE

Uranium 235 was written for Theatre Workshop and produced by Joan Littlewood in 1946. During the four years it was in the company's repertoire, it underwent constant revision. The present script is the result of yet another revision, the most extensive to date.

[**PART ONE**] *The stage is dark. Spot comes up on the Firewatcher and then, on another level, Scientist is seen at a bench covered with apparatus. Air-raid sirens are heard. A girl hurries past.*

Firewatcher. Good night.

Exit girl.

God, what an empty wilderness is time.
A universe of endless desolation
In which the hours are weary refugees
Bent in a hopeless search for lost relations.
Six till six my shift and three hours gone.
This is no occupation for a man,
This senseless peering into night
As still and imperturbable as death itself.

A plane is heard.

This is the hour
When death is rationed out,
When iron eggs, fruit of some monstrous coupling in Hell
Are hatched in blood.
This is the hour when cities rise up
Shrieking in the night
And lamentations sound from iron throats,
This is destruction's hour.
Oh God, protect this night
From evil birds of prey,
If not for man's sake
Then for the sake of heaven's dignity.
Dignity. What word is that?
A hollow echo, a forgotten dream.
A horse has dignity, a tree, a rock,
An ant, a fly, a dog, a metal bar,
Even a codfish, bleeding at the gills,
Just gutted, outdoes man in dignity.
Tonight they'll come again
Chanting their bloody serenade
And all the stars and wheeling suns of space
Will vanish from men's minds
As night stares down at us with bloodshot eyes.
No more.
This night will pass and so will other nights,
Just as this war will pass.
Men have survived catastrophes before
And those who crouched despairing in a pit
Have often lived to tell their friends of it.

Crash of bombs. Blackout on Firewatcher.

Man in Audience. Hey, there! You in the white coat! Is it always to be like this? Nothing but death and destruction?

Scientist. It depends.

Man in Audience. On what?

Scientist. On you.

Man in Audience. Us? Come off it! You're the ones who're supposed to know all the answers.

Scientist. Not *all* the answers but some of them . . . yes. We have, if I may say so, in the course of the last few years brought about considerable changes in what might be called the map of human knowledge. We have conquered power and explored the innermost secrets of the origin of matter. There are no closed doors to us now. We can choose our own road and send fate scurrying before us like an idiot beggar. We have opened a door on the future and on that door is written Uranium 235.

Blast of jazz music. Enter a couple jitterbugging. Music stops. They embrace. The scene should be played with frantic excitement.

Frank. Jessie, I love you. Honest to God, I love you. Gimme a kiss, Jessie. Do you love me, Jessie?

Jessie. Of course I do. I love you, Frank.

Frank. Do you, Jessie?

Jessie. You know I do, Frank.

Frank. Gimme a kiss, Jessie.

Jessie. I love you, Frank.

Frank. I love you, Jessie.

Scientist. Excuse me, but . . .

Frank. Look at the moon, Jessie.

Jessie. The moon in June . . .

Frank. And time to spoon,
My heart goes boom,
Honest it does, Jessie!
Boom diddy boom
Diddy diddy diddy boom,
Boom, boom, boom!

Music blares up. They execute hysterical dance.

Scientist. I wonder if you could spare a minute . . .

Frank. Are you an eyeful tonight! Honest, Jessie, you knocked 'em cold back there.

Jessie. Did I Frank?

Frank. Honest you did, Jessie, and you're my girl.

Jessie. Your girl . . .

Frank. With your teeth like pearls
My heart's in a whirl . . .

Scientist. I hate disturbing you, but . . .

Jessie. Gimme a kiss. (*They kiss.*)
You awaken such bliss.

Frank. On a night like this.
Just wait till the war's over, Jessie,
And the lights go on again
All over the world.
I love you, Jessie,
I love your eyes
Blue as summer skies.
And the touch of your hand
Makes me understand
And your bonnet of blue
Reminds me of you . . .

Scientist.
Now look here . . .

Frank. I like your little turned-up nose
Your little these and those,
I like your lips, I like your hips,
I like your feet, I think they're sweet,
I like the way you take a chance,
I like the smashing way you dance,
I like your boundless energy.

Scientist.
It's about energy I wanted to talk . . . (*Music and dance drown him. He continues to talk unheard.*) We can change the face of the earth in two generations.

Man in Audience. Speak up!

Scientist. (*Shouting*) I wanted to tell you that . . .

Two girls enter. They dance like sleepwalkers.

1st Girl. Tyrone Power's nice.

2nd Girl. Errol Flynn's nicer.

1st Girl. He's rough.

2nd Girl. He makes me feel all funny inside.

1st Girl. I dream of Tyrone Power.

Scientist. Now about power – I've discovered something very interesting . . .

1st Girl. He's got lovely eyes.

2nd Girl. Van Johnson's nice.

1st Girl. In his last film, Tyrone Power got killed in the last scene. I cried all night.

2nd Girl. Errol Flynn's nice.

1st Girl. I like Laurence Olivier – he's so handsome.

2nd Girl. I like Clark Gable – he's so strong.

1st Girl. James Mason's nice.

2nd Girl. Franchot Tone's nice.

1st Girl. Frank Sinatra's nice.

2nd Girl. Ray Milland's nice.

Both Girls. Nice. Nice. Nice. Nice . . .

Enter Every Girl's Uncle/Aunt reading newspaper. He walks around reading while crooner sings.

Crooner. (*Singing*)

Love, love alone,
Causes me to weep and moan.
Love, love alone,
Causes me to weep and moan.
You can have my brain,
You can have my bone,
But leave me and my sweetie alone,
Love, love alone,
Causes me to weep and moan.

Every Girl's Uncle. The defendants first became intimate in the autumn of 1939 when they met at a reception given by Herr von Ribbentrop at the German Embassy. The plaintiff states that he visited the Conservatory between the soup and the fish at dinner and discovered his wife lying in a bed of arum maculatum. He attempted to remonstrate with her, but . . .

He turns a page.

Scientist.

I should hate to be thought importunate . .

Every Girl's Uncle. Chats with the stars. Lovely ladies learn basic English. Film fans fan flames for Flynn. Knock his eye out with a teenage bra . . . let Priscilla take care of your pimples . . . let me take two stone off your middle . . . let me add six inches to your bust . . . Advice to the lovelorn.

Don't worry, little miss Eighteen, the one man is more important than half-a-dozen others . . . Do you envy her streamlined figure? The new Orion belt will take ten years off your stomach.

Scientist. Now for the last time . . .

Every Girl's Uncle.

Tales of vice,
Tales of spice,
Juicy details, very nice.
Facts about an opium den,
Special remedy for men.
All the latest rapes and killings.
Seaman said: 'The girl was willing.'
Strip-tease dancer's bravery.
Exposure of white-slavery.
Girl says she acted under dope.
Higher birth-rate Britain's hope.
Cottage slayer gets the rope.
Murder weapon found in soap.

Enter sportsman.

Scientist. Is no one interested in what goes on in the world? I tell you, the entire race is in danger!

Sportsman. What race?

Scientist. The human race.

Sportsman. God! For a moment I thought you meant the two-thirty. Got five bob on Whirlwind. Dead cert, eight to one. Inside information, but don't let it get round or the price'll drop.

Scientist. I too have inside information.

Sportsman. Reliable source?

Scientist. Very! Direct from the solar system.

Sportsman. Don't talk to me about systems. I've tried 'em all. It's just a matter of luck. If it's your turn, yet get it. If it isn't, you've had it. Take the Pools – who wins the big money? The experts? Not on your life! It's the mugs who've never even seen a game of football. Last week an old biddy in Liverpool won ninety thousand quid! Think of it!

Scientist. It's not important.

Sportsman. Not important? Listen to him! Ninety thousand quid not important!

Scientist. Listen . . .

Sportsman. Take me, now – been studying form for years and what have I won? Not a bloody sausage! Last week I should have won a packet by all the rules. I'd got Arsenal to win. Dead cert! Five minutes to go and the score even. Matthews gives Stevenson the ball and he's got a clear field. Thompson tries to intercept him – not a chance! Stevie has him cork-legged. Right down the field he goes with the ball at his feet. The crowd's going crazy.

All. Come on, Stevie! Come on!

Sportsman. Parker's coming up behind him like a bleedin' tank. Stevie makes like he's going to shoot. Parker swerves and Stevie gives the ball to the Bomber. He gives it back to Stevie. There's nobody between him and the goal.

All. Shoot! Shoot!

Sportsman. Terrific kick! The ball goes sailing through the air, straight as a bloody arrow to the top left-hand corner of the net. Impossible to miss! Beautiful goal!

All. Goal! Goal!

Sportsman. No . . . no! Just at the last minute there's a sudden gust of wind and the ball curves and misses the net.

Groans from everybody.

Luck! Just luck. That goal would have won me a fortune. Could happen to anybody.

Scientist. Listen, everybody. What happens during the next few months depends upon your decision. There is very little time left.

Crooner enters with microphone on a long lead. He dances as he sings.

Crooner. (*Singing*)

Enjoy yourself, it's later than you think,
Enjoy yourself, while you're still in the pink.

The people on stage reassume their mantles of frantic gaiety, reciting their characteristic lines at greater and greater speed. Build up to a peak. Explosion and simultaneous blackout. After a short pause, a spotlight beam begins to wander aimlessly across the stage area. It finally comes to rest on a female, headless lay-figure. The head, wearing a blond wig, lies at the mannikin's feet. Close by is an old-fashioned portable gramophone on which turns a cracked record so all that we hear is the repeated phrase, 'Enjoy yourself, it's later than you think.' It finally runs out of power. During the narration which follows, members of the cast drift on to the stage.

Microphone Voice. 1945–Atomic bombs on Hiroshima and Nagasaki. 1946–the Cold War begins. 1947–Chiang Kai Shek launches full-scale offensive against the reds. War in Burma. 1948–Extension of the Cold War. British troops fighting in Malaya. France defends Indo-China . . . from the Indo-Chinese. Dutch troops defend Indonesia against the

Indonesians. 1949–Britain saves Greece . . . from the Greeks. 1950–War in Korea. 1951 . . . 52 . . . 53?

1st Actress. Must it happen?

2nd Actress. I can't bear to think of it.

1st Actor. You have to think of it or you won't have anything to think with. That's the way it's always been. People couldn't bear to think about it. So they turned their faces away and refused to see what lay under their noses. It was none of their business, they said, and by the time events had proved them wrong, it was too late. They were either dead or dying, killing or being killed. Their homes were rubble and their towns were graveyards. Men, women and children dying in countless millions because we couldn't be bothered to think.

2nd Actress. And now there's fission.

Mic. Voice. Calculations for the case of masses properly located at the initial instant indicate that between one and five per cent of the fission energy of the Uranium should be released at a fission explosion. This means from two to ten times 108 kilo calories per kilogram of Uranium 235. The available explosive energy per kilogram of Uranium is thus equivalent to about two thousand tons of T.N.T.

1st Actor. That's Greek to me.

Scientist. Actors, of course, are not meant to be physicists.

3rd Actress. They're not supposed to be anything but actors, but it isn't enough.

2nd Actress. It should be.

1st Actor. I don't agree.

3rd Actress. We are part of society whether we like it or not. If we don't eat we go hungry, and according to you (*indicating the Scientist*), if we don't think, we die.

2nd Actor. And now there's fission.

2nd Actress. Yes, and who gave us that great gift?

Scientist. Atomic fission doesn't necessarily mean atomic bombs.

1st Actress. What else does it mean?

Scientist. Why are you so aggressive?

1st Actor. Maybe she's prejudiced against people who make things that kill other people, if you see what I mean.

Scientist. But you can't just shift the responsibility for progress and . . .

3rd Actress. Progress! Is that what you call it?

Scientist. There are problems, I grant you that, but . . .

2nd Actor. Perhaps we ought to examine those problems in our own way.

2nd Actress. Which way's that?

2nd Actor. As actors.

1st Actress. Where do we begin?

2nd Actor. At the beginning, where else?

1st Actor. That's about three thousand years ago, isn't it?

Scientist. It begins with Democritus of Abdera. (*He is handed a chiton by one of the actors. He puts it on.*) In the course of putting on this chiton I have ceased to be a twentieth-century physicist, gone through a transition phase of being myself playing an actor, and finally taken on the external habiliments of an old Greek gentleman.

2nd Actor. Athens, 470 BC., a city built on a rock. Houses of white stone, stucco and marble, occasionally alabaster. Wide streets flanked with statues. The pillar of the ancient world.

A pillar which has been lying on its side upstage centre is raised upright by two actors. On a raised platform which runs against the back wall of the stage a priest enters, followed by a group of worshippers. They sing and dance across the stage.

Priest. City of wise Athene.

Chorus. Io, Io, Io, Io.

Priest. Child of Zeus and Ceres,

Chorus. Io, Io, Io, Io.

Priest. Mother of birds and the wise owl,

Chorus. Io, Io,

Priest. Master of the golden ocean,

Chorus. Io, Io.

Priest. Out of the void and the chaos of nothing,

Chorus. Io, Io, Io, ayee.

Priest. Out of the darkness and the night,

Chorus. Io, Io, Io, ho.

Priest. Zeus, the father and begetter of Gods,

Chorus. Io, ayee, ayee,

Priest. Fashioned the earth from a pebble of clay.

Chorus. Ayee, ayee,

Priest. Fashioned the earth with the sun to warm it;

Chorus. Ayee, ayee,

Priest. Fashioned the moon as a lamp of night.

Chorus. Io, Io, Io, ayee.

They kneel.

Democritus.
All this is false.

Priest. Who speaks against the Gods?

Democritus.
I, Democritus of Abdera.

Priest. Who is greater than Zeus?

1st Chorister.
Did man fashion the earth out of nothing?

Democritus.
Nothing can come from nothing.
Nothing can be reduced to nothing.
The universe does not change.

Throughout that period of time long past elements have existed out of which our world of things is composed and remade. These atoms are endowed with an immortal nature, none of them can turn to nothing.

An eternal substance holds them fast,
A substance interwoven part with part
by bonds more or less close;
But since the mutual fastenings of the atoms are dissimilar,
and their substance is everlasting,
things endure with bodies uninjured
till some force arrives which proves
strong enough to dissolve the texture of each.
Therefore no single thing ever returns to nothing
but at their disruption, all pass back
into the particles of matter.
None of these things that seem to perish
utterly perishes, since nature forms
one thing to another and permits nothing to be forgotten
unless first she has been recruited by another's death.

The 1st actor suddenly steps out of his role and interrupts the proceedings.

1st Actor. God! What a load of codswallop!

1st Actress. Why? What's wrong?

1st Actor. The whole bloody scene's wrong.

3rd Actress. I thought it was quite effective.

1st Actor. Oh, come on! It's an absolute travesty of the truth. What are we trying to show?

2nd Actor. We're helping to perpetuate a myth.

1st Actor. That isn't our job. Can you imagine the rulers of the ancient world wafting around like a bunch of flat-footed Isadoras, spouting bad poetry?

2nd Actress. You got a better idea?

1st Actor. We could try using some common sense. Athens wasn't the paradise the Victorians cracked it up to be. It was a powerful military state founded on slave labour.

The 2nd actor assumes the gestures and vocal delivery of a market-spieler. He grabs hold of the arm of the 3rd actress.

2nd Actor. Ladies and gentlemen, what am I offered for this choice piece of merchandise? This is no sullen captive from the stews of Syracuse but a willing servant, the result of scientific breeding on our state farm at Pylos. As you know, ladies and gentlemen, we deal only in pedigree stock. Strength plus comeliness, that is what we offer you. Look at her, friends – not a blemish anywhere. Feel that firm flesh. Prime condition! Look at the hair; see how it glows. And the teeth! Look at the teeth! There's thirty years' hard work in her, maybe more. And she's fully trained. Guaranteed to give satisfaction both in the kitchen and the bed. She can cook, carry, wash, launder, is proficient at needlework and is an excellent proposition for breeding purposes. Now, what am I offered?

During the foregoing passage, the rest of the company have entered into the spirit of the scene and created the atmosphere of a busy and colourful market. A woman calls her wares: 'Ripe melons, whole or by the piece!' Another carries a basket and advertises ripe figs.

Silk Merchant. Genuine Persian silk! The last piece! You'll never see workmanship like this again. They've stopped producing it. Twenty drachma! That's all I'm asking for, twenty drachma! A bargain at double the price!

Woman. I'll give you ten.

Silk Merchant. Ah, a lady who's fond of a joke, eh? Well, I like a joke myself, but we live in a hard world, lady. Ten drachma wouldn't pay the tax. I'm giving it away at twenty!

Woman. I'll give you ten.

Silk Merchant. I'll tell you what I'll do . . .

They move upstage, still bargaining. Two businessmen stroll downstage, deep in conversation.

1st Businessman. I think it would be a mistake to sell now.

2nd Businessman. The market's good!

1st Businessman. It'll be better still if you wait.

2nd Businessman. You're really banking on the rumours of war, aren't you?

1st Businessman. War is necessary to the economy, it's inevitable.

2nd Businessman. But the cost!

1st Businessman. The cost will be shared by a great number of citizens; the profits, on the other hand, will belong to a small group of far-seeing investors like ourselves.

They move off upstage, talking. Democritus and a youth walk downstage, talking.

Youth. And these atoms – what exactly are they?

Democritus. They are the elements out of which everything is made.

Youth. Everything?

Democritus. Everything. The soil and the seed in it. The sun which warms it and the rain which moistens it. The rocks and mountains, the seas, the birds in the air and the blind worm. All are made of the same elements.

Youth. And man?

Democritus. Yes, man too. All men, the senator, the merchant, the soldier, the slave.

1st Businessman. What's that you say?

Democritus. We were discussing philosophy.

1st Businessman. Philosophy? It sounded like treason.

Silk Merchant. Did somebody say 'treason'?

Democritus. I assure you, sir, you are mistaken. I am Democritus, a philosopher and no politician.

1st Businessman. I distinctly heard him say that the slave is equal to the senator.

Democritus. I merely said that, in my opinion, all men – indeed all things – shared a common origin.

Woman. Does that include women?

Democritus. Everything that is.

2nd Businessman. Is this slave my equal then?

Democritus. In the eyes of nature, yes.

Silk Merchant. Treason!

1st Businessman. And more than treason, for what this man says strikes at the very heart of religion, our social order, our thinking, our way of life. For if everything that is has a common origin then there is no difference between Gods and men, between men and women, between rulers and ruled, between master and slave. Can you imagine what will happen if such ideas are allowed to pass unchallenged? Every slave in Athens would soon be asserting his right to equality; women would question their husbands' authority; the poor would demand a seat in the Senate and the soldier would challenge the general's right to give orders!

All. Treason! To the Senate with him! Stone him!

Democritus. My friends . . .

Silk Merchant. No slave-lover calls me a friend!

Democritus. If you choose to interpret an abstract philosophical idea in social terms, then the fault is not mine. I am not responsible for the way nature organises her resources and neither threats nor arguments can alter the fact that life is constituted in a particular way. I am an old man and I have pondered deeply on these matters and my observations . . .

Priest. Why do you listen to this old fool! Will you match your strength against the high ones on Olympus? Athens asks more of her sons than idle speculations on things that are not. Let us have men like the heroes of antiquity, men like those who fought at Troy awhile back. Not broken seers but warriors like Achilles and he that darkened the Cyclops' eye and trampled the great oceans under his feet. Give us men of the sharp sword and the swift galley . . . men who tame rivers and the high mountains. Would you be great? Would you be noble and remembered in the songs of the bards? Then rise up against the barbarians of Lacedaemon, strike down all the false traitors throughout the Peloponnese. Listen to the drums and the sound of many feet. That is the Thebans on the march. The men of Chios and Lesbos are ready. The Acharnians are waiting for the word. Ionia and Thracia wait only for the men of Athens to begin the war that will carry our power to the uttermost ends of the earth!

Towards the end of the above speech, the crowd encircle Democritus and the murmurs of approval of the priest's remarks turn into shouts of anger directed at the philosopher. They finally close in on him and trample him underfoot as the light fades.

After a moment of complete darkness, the roving spotlight fades up and its beam wanders about the stage, finally revealing a skeleton holding a tattered flag and occupying the place on which the priest stood to deliver his tirade. Blackout.

Mic. Voice. War! Athens against Sparta. Broken Thebans dying of cold on the tracks of mountains. Corcyrian sailors – food for fishes at Syracuse. Siege, hunger, plague! Athenian bodies rotting on the roads of Sparta. Ionian dead feeding the Cretan vines. War and more war! Rome against Greece, against Gaul, against the Iberian peninsula, against the Scythians. Rome against the world. And everywhere the sword triumphant, everywhere the tramp of legions, from the equatorial forests to the congealed sea of Thule. War everywhere! The last flicker of learning and then . . . darkness.

Halfway through the speech the light has faded up again and the Singer has entered half-dressed in mediaeval costume. He carries a doublet over his arm.

Singer. I must apologise for not being properly dressed, but who would have thought the glory that was Greece would have passed by so quickly. But that is the way things happen – events won't wait for the last button to be buttoned and momentous happenings often catch one with an unzipped fly. Hence the ruins of empires. The next scene should, by rights, deal with the Romans, you know the kind of thing, the legions on the march.

(*Singing*)

Twenty leagues a day, that's the Roman way,
Our swords are sharp, our enemies are weak,
Make the vanquished pay, that's the Roman way,
The world is there to win and travel's cheap.

But you probably know all about Rome and the Romans, how they brought civilisation to the inferior peoples of Europe and Africa. I would guess you've all read about the wonderful roads they built and how their barracks were bigger and better than anybody else's and how their plumbing was the wonder of the age. Therefore we'll pass on without comment. In any case we couldn't afford to put Roman soldiers on the stage. For that kind of thing you need subsidies, which we don't have. We're not a rich company, at least not rich enough to be able to afford armour and weapons. And so we pass the Roman era and feel our way through the darkness of seven hundred years, years which passed like a bad dream. And now that I'm suitably dressed, the play can continue. The time is . . . let's say 1300 A.D. The place? Anywhere in Europe. The characters . . .

(*Singing*)

The people whose names are not remembered,
Names that don't get in the history books;
The smith whose shoulder bears the baron's brand,
The serf who nourishes his master's land,
Villeins, sundry servants, greasy cooks.
The woman bending double in the field,
The handless beggar tapping with his hooks,
The legless soldier limping on the road,
The porter dragging at his load,
The brutal, toiling, uncomplaining band
Who, by and large . . .

(*Speaking*) . . . make up the population of this land.

During the above, various characters enter and move about the stage.

Singer. (*Singing*)
The cripple crawls upon his knees.

Cripple. Alms! Alms!

Singer. (*Singing*)
The leper parades his foul disease.

Leper. Unclean! Unclean!

Singer. (*Singing*)
The spotted plague walks through the land,
And hunger's rife on every hand.

Blind Man.
A crust, for the love of Christ!

Singer. (*Singing*)
Death is each man's neighbour,
Death it is who plays the pipe
And beats the tabor.

Music: The Fool's Jig. Ragged figure enters playing pipe and tabor followed by beggars, serfs, etc., dancing. All except the Singer join in.

Blind Man. For the love of Christ!

Mad woman enters carrying bundle as though it were a child.

Mad Woman. Sweet Jesus, restore my babe!

The music fades out but all continue to dance to the slower rhythm of the Singer's tune.

Singer. (*Singing*)
New-risen from the rags she calls a bed
The babe she bore and bears is newly dead.

Mad Woman. No! No! No! No!

Singer. (*Singing*)
And now she needs a scapegoat for her blame,
Someone to bear the burden of her pain.

An old woman enters.

Old Woman. Tibby! Tibby! Come on, Tibby!

Singer. (*Speaking*) Most convenient.

(*Singing*)
And now this feeble-minded, poor old bitch
Must stand accused and die,

(*Speaking*) for she's both old and helpless – must be a witch.

Mad Woman. (*Pointing at the old woman*) Witch!

All. Witch!

The old woman laughs, bewildered.

Man. In the book it says: 'Thou shalt not suffer a witch to live.'

Old Woman. Tibby! Tibby!

Woman. Her familiar – she calls on her familiar.

Mad Woman. Murderer!

Man. Let her burn!

Ali. To the fire!

They drag the old woman off. The light dims until only the Singer can be seen.

Singer. (*Abandoning his role*) What we might call 'The Years of Darkness'. A convenient label though a less than accurate one since the years in question are illuminated by the ruddy glare of fires used to burn old ladies, heretics, scholars, philosophers, towns, villages, cities, libraries – and eccentrics who refused to believe the world was a flat platter on the sideboard of the Lord. As for science, it was taking some odd turns, though things began to improve by 1450 when the first translations of the Arabic manuscripts began to appear in Europe and the art of Alchemy was reborn.

The lights go up and discover Bernard Trevisan who stands upstage centre and forms the pivot of a group of six alchemists who throughout the scene which follows perform a slow, ritual dance, the movements of which are largely made up of cabbalistic signs.

Alchemists. Who art thou?

Trevisan. Bernard Trevisan.

Alchemists. From whence art thou come?

Trevisan. From the city of Padua.

Alchemists. For what art thou searching?

Trevisan. For the philosopher's stone. For the father of rocks and the mother of metals in the same organism.

Trevisan attempts to dance but his way is constantly blocked by the cloaked alchemists.

I shall find the seed which will grow into great harvests of gold. For doth not a metal grow like a plant? Lead would be gold if it had time to grow. For it is absurd to think that nature in the earth bred gold perfect in the instant. Something went before. There must be matter more remote. Nature doth first beget the imperfect then proceeds she to the perfect. Hast thou the secret of the stone?

1st Alchemist. Hast thou rectified spirits of wine?

Trevisan. Thrice ten times till I could not find glasses strong enough to hold it.

2nd Alchemist. Then thou should search at Avignon in the books of Pope John the Twelfth.

Tevisan. Hast thou the secret of the stone?

3rd Alchemist. Go thou to the shores of the Baltic Sea. Take thou the salt of the sea, rectify it day and night until it is as clear as crystal. That is the dark secret of the stone.

Trevisan. I seek the philosopher's stone. Hast thou the secret of the nature of it?

4th Alchemist. Dissolve silver and mercury in aqua fortis. Concentrate the solution over hot ashes and reduce them to half. Pour the mixture into a clay crucible and leave in the sun's rays. For gold is merely the rays of the sun condensed to a yellow solid.

Trevisan. Hast thou the secret of the stone?

5th Alchemist. Whatever is below is like that which is above. And that which is above is like that which is below, to accomplish the miracle of one thing.

Trevisan. The stone . . . the philosopher's stone . . . I must find the secret.

6th Alchemist. The father thereof is the sun and the mother thereof is the moon. The wind carries in it his belly and the nurse thereof is the earth. This thing has more fortitude than fortitude itself for it will overcome every subtle thing and penetrate every solid thing. By it this world was formed.

Trevisan. The stone . . . the stone . . . what is the secret?

The alchemists make cabbalistic signs.

Alchemists. God made one and ten, one hundred and one thousand and then multiplied the whole by ten.

Trevisan. But I do not understand this mummery.

Alchemists. We can tell you no more.

They exit. Trevisan sinks to the ground.

Trevisan. I have burned out my life at a laboratory furnace and I still have not the secret, but a time will come when nature will unloose the bonds of things and man will stand triumphant on the peak of a great mountain.

Snatch of a Gregorian chant. The lights fade.

Bruno. Oh, black wall of ignorance, night of fear! Who will tear the shroud off the world?

Lights go up and discover Giordano Bruno standing centre in a monk's habit. Near him lies a figure half-emerged from a tomb. Death holds him in an embrace.

Is there in all Christendom a place where man can speak his mind? Is there a village anywhere where ignorance does not parade the streets in silks and golden mantle of authority? Is there? In the places of learning I have spoken and my voice was lost in a wilderness of skulls. The universities of

Paris, Prague and Pisa have become night stools where darkness can relieve himself. Truth is banished to the stews where apes can use her for their pleasure and reason is scourged through the streets in a fool's cap.

Recumbent figure moves and then laughs.

Why do you laugh?

Paracelsus. I see myself in you.

Bruno. A sponge made like a man. Another drunken fool whose breath poisons wisdom.

Paracelsus. I am drunk with dust and worms have made me wise.

Bruno. What do they call thee, wineskin?

Paracelsus. Paracelsus, a dust mote caught in the sun's web, a voice riding the wind.

Bruno. Paracelsus – he that is called the sword of reason, the Luther of Chemistry?

Paracelsus. The same.

Bruno. Thou hast been dead a hundred years

Paraclesus. I speak across a grave with a voice full of earth and stars.

Bruno. From what deep hell hast thou returned?.

Paracelsus. I have lain in a worm's belly with the dreamers of dreams, with Copernicus who rode a galactic ride and bloodied the sun's flanks with jewelled spurs, with da Vinci whose brain was a crystal span across the universe.

Bruno laughs.

Why do you laugh?

Bruno. I speak of the seed of life and my only audience is a dead man.

Paracelsus. Thy voice is still unblunted and can cut holes in the night.

Bruno. But the living?

Paracelsus. Fools for the most part, pathetic fools who walk a road of terror between one breath and the next.

Bruno. Is there no hope then?

Paracelsus. There are always some who listen, whose eyes can penetrate the shades. You know that, Bruno.

Bruno. I am a hunted man, an exile. I walk the road by night to avoid the church's spies. I speak to men in Genoa, Florence, Milan, but wherever I go the Inquisition's ears are cocked wide to snare my words. I, who love men, am ringed about with loneliness. Those whom I would teach look at me with fear.

Paracelsus. What would you teach them?

Bruno. A single truth so that all truth should prosper. I would teach them the law of Copernicus which says that the sun is immovable in the centre of the universe and the earth has a diurnal movement of rotation.

Paracelsus. And it is for this . . . truth you would sacrifice your liberty?

Bruno. There can be no liberty without knowledge. Only by understanding the world can we learn to understand ourselves.

Towards the end of this speech, a hooded figure, an officer of the Inquisition, is revealed.

Inquisitor. The truth you teach is heresy! It is an evil lie!

Bruno. The violation of reason is the real heresy and what you call evil is the degradation of man. By denying men the truth, you make them vulnerable.

Inquisitor. It is not the church which seeks to dethrone man as the image of God. It is not the church that would banish the earth to a lower place in the universe and make the sun the centre of the world.

Bruno. It is the church which burdens the mind of man with chains.

Inquisitor. Silence, heretic!

Bruno. I will not be silenced!

Inquisitor. Perhaps when you feel the fire . . .

Bruno. You cannot burn the truth. Rome has excommunicated me, Geneva has stoned me – but while I have breath in my body I will speak the truth for men to hear. I will sing a song of truth as will charm the shackles off their leaden souls.

Inquisitor. You poor, stupid fool! They will not listen.

Bruno. I will make them listen!

Music: The Fool's Jig played on pipe and tabor. Fool enters dancing, leading a procession of dancing men and women. Bringing up the rear is the figure of Death.

Listen, and I'll slake your thirst with wisdom's vintage. I'll spin you an endless universe – on the loom Copernicus built.

Paracelsus. Dance, my pert flesher! Jig it, my she-cadaver! Give us the dunghill galliard!

Bruno. Good people, I have a wondrous tale of sun and stars that will amaze you.

Paracelsus. In upon them, Bruno! Breach the walls of their stupidity with the culverins of reason!

Bruno. Here is a charge of cavalry to put ignorance to flight: the sun is immovable in the centre of the universe and the earth has a diurnal movement of rotation.

The Inquisitor throws off his cloak and reveals himself dressed in the military costume of the period.

Inquisitor. Here is a fine jigging madcap folic for a man of mettle. Here is a lusty hot-breathed gallop for a spirited wench. Come, you lusty boys! Come, you dams of future Alexanders and lend your hearts for drums. Would you be kings and emperors? There are kingdoms waiting for each of you in the Americas. Will you be noble and great and have your name the title of a ballad? Let him that will win renown and a king's booty follow me! I have wars for you in France, in Spain, in the Low Countries, on the seas and oceans of the world.

During this speech a drum has begun to beat. It gets louder and louder. The dancers, led by Death, go off.

Bruno. Fools! How they love the darkness and hold in contempt all that is not contemptible. But it is inconceivable that . . . they will not dance forever. A time will come!

Paracelsus. You will have to die for them first, Bruno. They understand no language but the language of violence.

Fade to darkness.

Mic. Voice. 1550 – War!

Music.

England against France. Poland against Hungary. 1560 – War! Spain against Tripoli. The first religious war in France. 1570 – War! Spain against Turkey. England against Scotland. Venice against the Porte. 1580 – War! Spain against Portugal. Poland against Russia. The seventh religious war in France. 1590 – War! Turkey against Persia. Spain against Aragon. Italy against Provence. 1600 – War! France against Savoy. Spain against Africa. Sweden against Poland. 1600 – Giordano Bruno burnt at the stake.

The recorded voice of Paracelsus is heard whispering.

Paracelsus' Voice. You will have to die for them first, Bruno.

Lights fade up. The actor who plays the Scientist strolls on stage with the 3rd actress. An actor enters from the opposite side of the stage, only half-dressed.

3rd Actress. We seem to have mislaid the atom and . . . what was it you called it . . . fission.

Scientist. Ah yes, the atom. To see the next stage of the development of atomic theory, we have to go forward in time about 250 years.

1st Businessman. November 16th, 1807, to be precise. Where the hell's George? (*Calling into the wings*) George!

2nd Businessman. (*Offstage*) Won't be a minute.

1st Businessman. Hurry up!

2nd Businessman. I'm being as quick as I can.

Scientist. He'll have to move a lot quicker if he's going to keep up with the times. The Industrial Revolution's getting into its stride. Hargreaves' spinning jenny is forty years old and James Watt's steam engine is busy transforming the face of Britain. So unless George really gets moving . . . well, he's going to miss making a fortune.

The 2nd businessman enters.

2nd Businessman. Give me a hand with this cravat, will you.

1st Businessman. Relax, relax.

Scientist. We'll leave them to it.

All leave except the two businessmen.

2nd Businessman. Damn! Look at my hands. They're filthy!

1st Businessman. Well, I don't suppose many early nineteenth-century factory owners had clean hands. Where there's muck, lad, there's brass. And it's brass that counts.

2nd Businessman. How do I look?

1st Businessman. You'll pass. Where's Dalton?

2nd Businessman. He's got a difficult costume change. This jumping about from one character to another is bloody confusing. One of these performances I'm going to come on in the Greek scene dressed as a Manchester businessman. That'd shake 'em! A quick-change artist, that's me.

1st Businessman. Right, cut the chat and let's get the scene moving.

2nd Businessman. Right. November, 1807. Manchester, a meeting of the Literary and Philosophical Society at 35 George Street.

1st Businessman. That's here.

2nd Businessman. Right.

1st Businessman. We're waiting for tonight's lecturer to arrive.

2nd Businessman. Mr John Dalton, schoolmaster.

1st Businessman. We'd better get the table.

They go to the edge of the stage and mime picking up and carrying a table.

1st Businessman. You're not trying! This is a heavy table, solid mahogany. Everything connected with the Literary and Philosophical Society is solid, including the members: self-made, solid as the Stock Exchange, honest-to-God businessmen. Let's try again.

They repeat the mime.

2nd Businessman. Sceneshifters!

1st Businessman. The shifting Manchester scene.

He produces a square of velvet from his pocket and it becomes their table. They mime sitting at it. From now on, they speak in Lancashire dialect.

Both Businessman. Manchester, city of cotton.

Voice. (*Offstage*) City of Peterloo, city of poverty, four-fifths of the population living in cellars!

1st Businessman. Better close the window. We don't want any interruptions.

He rises, mimes closing window and returns to his seat.

Must try and preserve the right atmosphere for scientific speculation.

2nd Businessman. Aye.

1st Businessman. Pays to keep an eye on scientific progress.

2nd Businessman. Aye.

1st Businessman. What Manchester thinks today!

2nd Businessman. Aye. Anything in this Dalton chap's ideas?

1st Businessman. 'Appen there is.

2nd Businessman. Chemist, did you say?

1st Businessman. Schoolteacher.

2nd Businessman. Not too pedantic, I hope. I like a speaker who can make you sit up. No frills or fancies, mind.

1st Businessman. Might be summat in his atomic theory.

2nd Businessman. Where's Dicky Howarth? Ain't he coming?

1st Businessman. Havin' troubles with his weavers. Tried to burn down his mill on Tuesday.

2nd Businessman. Aye, I heard summat about it.

1st Businessman. Five arrested.

2nd Businessman. Well, they'll have plenty of time to repent. Dicky's their magistrate, i'n't he?

1st Businessman. Likely.

Dalton enters.

Ah, here's Dalton now! Good evening, Mr Dalton.

Dalton. Good evening.

1st Businessman. I don't think you've met Mr Butterworth, our membership secretary.

2nd Businessman. How d'ye do. I'm looking forward to hearing all about your . . . what d'ye call 'em?

1st Businessman. Atoms.

2nd Businessman. Atoms, of course! Stupid of me. I've a dreadful memory.

1st Businessman. If you're ready, Mr Dalton . . .?

Dalton. Yes. Perfectly ready.

1st Businessman. Fellow members, ladies and gentlemen. It gives me great pleasure to introduce tonight's speaker, Mr John Dalton, who will speak on 'The Atomic Theory of Matter'. Mr Dalton.

Dalton. Friends, I am a poor lecturer and not very gifted with amusing anecdotes – consequently, I must approach my subject in the only way I know how, that is, directly and without circumlocution. For more years than I care to remember I have been a keen student and observer of the atmosphere, and this has led me to speculate on a problem which no one has yet made clear. We all know that the atmosphere is composed of four gases – oxygen, nitrogen, carbon dioxide and water vapour. Priestley, Cavendish and Lavoisier have proved that point. But how are these gases held together? Are they chemically united or are they just mixed together as one mixes sand and clay? My own observations had led me to believe that air was a mechanical mixture of gases . . . and yet the chemical composition of the atmosphere is constant. My records prove that without question. I have analysed the atmosphere taken from hundreds of different places in England, over mountains, lakes, in valleys, in sparsely settled regions and in crowded towns and always the composition has been the same. Now why does not the heavier carbon dioxide sink to the bottom of the sea of air to be covered in turn by the lighter oxygen, nitrogen and water vapour? You must all have observed how oil floats on the surface of a heavier liquid such as water . . . and yet this does not happen with the gases which compose the air. Why?

Interrupter. (*From the audience*) Because of atoms?

Dalton. Exactly! Because of atoms! Everything in nature is composed of minute particles called atoms and the atoms of the different gases diffuse through each other and thoroughly mix, thus keeping the composition of the atmosphere uniform.

Interrupter. Show us these atoms.

Dalton. That is impossible, my dear sir. Even the most delicate instrument cannot render them visible to the naked eye.

Interrupter. And yet you would have us believe in these intangible toys.

Dalton. They are far from intangible. These atoms are indivisible – even in the most violent chemical change the atoms remain intact. Furthermore, the atoms of the same element are all alike, but the atoms of different elements differ in both size and shape.

Interrupter. How do you deduce that? By their smell?

Dalton. No, by their weight. I have drawn up a table of the atomic weights of the elements – that is their relative weights.

Interrupter. This is absurd: Mr Dalton admits that his atoms are smaller than anything ever seen even under the most delicate microscope, and yet suggests that he can weigh them. Mr Dalton, I'm afraid, is suffering from hallucinations, or something worse. What is Mr Dalton's theory but ridiculous pictorial juggling? Can any serious-minded chemist accept such a theory, which is, in fact, as baseless as the four elements of Aristotle? I am astonished that any man of science can be taken up with such a tissue of absurdities.

1st Businessman. I think the last speaker is being somewhat harsh in his criticism of our guest. At the same time, Mr Dalton, I feel there's summat in what he says. Don't misunderstand me, Mr Dalton, we're all interested in progress. Indeed, I would go so far as to say that without chaps like us there wouldn't be any progress.

2nd Businessman. Hear, hear.

1st Businessman. For while it's true that you are the chaps who do the dreaming, we are the ones who do the doing.

Interrupter. Hear, hear!

Woman in Audience. Don't take any notice of them, Dalton! You were right. Time has proved you right.

The Scientist enters. The two businessmen exeunt.

They were the ones who dealt in absurdities.

Scientist. Please, please, I'm afraid you're interrupting our play. In any case they can't hear you. Oh, the actors can but Dalton and the others . . . as far as they're concerned you don't exist except as a kind of generalised possibility.

Dissatisfied Playgoer. Get on with the play!

Scientist. We're trying to do just that.

Diss. Playgoer. All this awful speechifying! If I wanted to listen to that kind of thing I would go to the appropriate place for it, a lecture hall. The theatre is hardly the place for it.

Scientist. Ah, you wish to be entertained!

Diss. Playgoer. Isn't that what one normally goes to the theatre for?

Scientist. Have patience. We have a love story for you, the love of the proton for the neutron. The most enduring love story in history. And, if you like a good murder, we'll show you the greatest killing the world has ever seen, with the most efficient murder weapon. Just bear with us a little longer. Now, where were we?

Woman in Audience. Dalton and his atomic theory.

Scientist. Ah, yes. Were you able to follow him?

Woman in Audience. Yes, I think so. But where do we go from here?

Enter five scientists, wearing white coats and grotesque masks. They walk deep in thought and move like jerky puppets.

1st Scientist. Well?

Group of Scientists (Chorus). Exactly. Where do we go from here?

Enter Mendeleyev.

Mendeleyev. To the ends of the earth. Search in the bowels of the earth, in the dust of factories, in the waters of the oceans, search.

Chorus. For what?

Mendeleyev. There is an element as yet undiscovered. I have named it eka-aluminium. It will be easily fusible, it will form alums and its chloride will be volatile.

Derisive laughter from chorus.

1st Scientist. The age of miracles. Science has acquired a prophet, gentlemen; he can foretell the properties of elements even before they are discovered.

Chorus. That is ridiculous . . . that is absurd!

Mendeleyev. Seek it, I say, and it will be found.

2nd Scientist. Who is he?

3rd Scientist. Dmitri Ivanovich Mendeleyev. He's a Kalmuk or one of those outlandish creatures.

Mic. Voice. 1875 – Professor Duboisbaudron discovers the eka-aluminium in a zinc ore found in the Pyrenees. He has called the new element gallium.

Chorus dances, expressing consternation.

1st Scientist. Coincidence . . . mere coincidence! One of those lucky guesses which prove the law of averages.

Mendeleyev. There is another undiscovered element which I have called eka-silicon. It is dirty grey in colour with an atomic weight of 72, a density of 5.5 and is slightly acted upon by acids.

Chorus laughs derisively.

1st Scientist. Moses speaks from the laboratory. He gives us the tables of the law before the law is written. He brings metaphysics to bear on the science of chemistry.

Chorus. That is ridiculous . . . that is absurd!

Mic. Voice. 1876 – Winkler has isolated a new element from the silver ore, argyrodite. It has an atomic weight of 72.3 and a density of 5.5. Winkler has called the new element germanium.

1st Scientist. A lucky guess.

Chorus dances and exhibits first signs of panic.

Mendeleyev. The third undiscovered element I have called eka-boron. Its atomic weight is 45, its valency 3.

Chorus laughs weakly.

1st Scientist. I am afraid that our colleague Professor Mendeleyev has allowed himself to become intoxicated by the success of his first two guesses. He would reduce chemistry to the level of the crystal-gazer's art.

Chorus. That is ridiculous . . . that is absurd!

They slowly collapse like wax figures during the following speech.

Mic. Voice. 1878 – Professor Nilsen has isolated a new element from the ore euxanite. It has an atomic weight of 45.1 and a valency of 3. Nilsen has called it scandium.

Mendeleyev. Gentlemen.

Chorus begin to come to life again.

There is no secret, gentlemen. I have discovered that the properties of the elements are a periodic function of their atomic weights; that is, the properties repeat themselves periodically after every seventh element.

Chorus. This is amazing!

2nd Scientist. So beautifully simple!

Chorus. So obvious! This is our goal . . . the end of our search!

Mendeleyev. It is only a stage on the journey, a resting place while material is gathered for the next advance.

Lights fade. Music.

Mic. Voice. A stage in the journey.

Actor. (*Taking off mask and addressing the audience*) At this stage, we could, on this stage, show you the many detailed stages through which the science of physics passed before it reached the present interesting stage. But time and space, or to be more precise, space time, does not permit. And so we follow your example, take the events of the next few years for granted and draw a curtain over half a century. The curtain will be closed for ten minutes during which the lights in the auditorium will go up so that you may move about and restore your circulation. For the mind is always more receptive to ideas when the blood circulates freely. And although ten minutes is not long, it gives an audience time to pick the author's bones quite clean . . . don't you agree? In ten minutes then, we meet again at history's crossroads where we shall endeavour to show you the point at which dreams and reality meet. Blackout please.

Lights fade. *[End of Part One]*

[PART TWO] *The Puppet Master, his Secretary and Death are discovered.*

Puppet Master. This looks like the place . . . what time is it?

Secretary. 1901, sir.

Puppet Master. Then there is no time to be lost . . . the show must open in 1914 . . . that's the deadline.

Scientist enters.

Secretary. Have you an appointment?

Scientist. Appointment? Isn't there some mistake?

Secretary. Everyone has to have an appointment.

Scientist. But look here, this is our stage, we're doing a show . . . you can't just come in here and commandeer the stage . . . the audience is waiting . . . they've paid to be entertained.

Puppet Master. Don't worry about the audience . . . I'm planning a big show for them.

Scientist. What kind of show?

Puppet Master. A tragi-comedy with massed bands and fireworks. A passion play of steel in which the audience are actors and the actors are children lost in a wilderness of fire and screams. My play will draw your heart out of your body and turn your eyes to scalding pools of salt. I'll touch your mind with horror so that every tortured second will extend into eternity. Oh, and there will be laughter too, shrill as a gull's cry; laughter that will cut like a scythe and beat like a hammer against the roof of despair. Dancing I'll show you, such as you've never seen! Jigs of legless men and eightsome reels performed by faceless ghosts and over open graves of broken earth one-armed heroes will tread in slow pavanes to the stinking songs of last year's flowers.

Scientist. But this is our stage.

Puppet Master. Come sir, all the world's a stage.

Scientist. Yes, but we haven't booked the world for our production.

Puppet Master. No, but I have. (*He laughs.*)

Scientist. Who are you?

Puppet Master. My name is Legion. I am sometimes known as James Pierrepoint Rockerfeller Thyssen Zaharoff Vanderbilt Power. My friends call me Order, my enemies, Chaos. I'm the managing director of the biggest show on earth, I.P.I.

Scientist. I.P.I.?

Puppet Master. International Puppets Incorporated.

Scientist. (*Pointing to Death*) And who is that?

Puppet Master. He is the leading man in my next production.

Scientist. Why is his faced masked?

Puppet Master. He lives in the shadows. His skin dislikes the light. And now, if you are satisfied with our credentials, we'll proceed with our auditions.

Scientist. But what about *our* show?

Puppet Master. I'm sorry.

Scientist. Can't your auditions wait?

Puppet Master. Time will not wait . . . these auditions were fixed a hundred years ago.

Scientist. But look here, we have certain rights . . .!

Puppet Master. You have no rights.

Scientist. We have a contract with the management.

Puppet Master. I am the management.

Scientist. Suppose I refuse to leave?

Puppet Master. I think my secretary will convince you that that would be unwise.

Scientist. Are you threatening me?

Puppet Master. That won't be necessary.

Secretary interposes herself between the two men and produces a cigarette case.

Secretary. Cigarette?

Scientist. I don't smoke. Look here, this is a preposterous situation.

Secretary. Do you have a light?

The Puppet Master produces a lighter and thumbs a flame. He then withdraws to the shadows upstage. The Secretary blows smoke in the Scientist's face.

Secretary. Please don't be angry. There's nothing to be angry about.

Scientist. Nothing to . . . do you consider it normal behaviour to . . .

Secretary. Please! We want to help you.

Scientist. Help me? What do you mean?

Secretary. Just think of all the help you've given to others!

Scientist. I don't know what you're talking about!

Secretary. You work miracles with your science. The small flame that lit my cigarette, the lift which carries me to my apartment, the shaded light which stands beside my bed, the music carried on the air.

Music.

Scientist. You're confusing technology with science.

She begins to drift around in a kind of half-dance.

Secretary. How pleasant it is to let one's body be carried along on the music, to move silently hearing only the whisper of the blood.

Scientist. What are you trying to do?

Secretary. I am trying to make you forget the discomfort of knowing. I would like to stroke your mind with dreams.

Scientist. I have my own dreams, thank you!

Secretary. Why are you afraid?

Scientist. You're being ridiculous!

Secretary. Do your dreams frighten you?

Scientist. Not in the least. In any case, my dreams are my own. They are the logical outcome of my work.

Secretary. There are other things. Turn away from the things that disturb you. Is it for you to die of other men's complaints, to weep knives of tears and slow your blood with ice? Somewhere for you is a turquoise sky where the sun sings with the lark's voice. There are rivers and jewelled streams where the slender reeds whisper secrets. Nights when the moon caresses the thighs of hills with silver hands.

In the course of speaking the above lines she has moved close to the Scientist. Now they are both dancing together.

We dance well together.

Scientist. I feel rather hazy about . . . about . . .

Secretary. Don't worry about anything. I'll take care of you.

She dances off with him and after a moment returns alone.

Puppet Master. Well, is he quiet?

Secretary. Sleeping like a child.

Puppet Master. Good. We can begin the auditions. If the talent's good the show'll be good and if the show's good the money'll be good. Did you notify the applicants?

Secretary. Yes, sir.

Puppet Master. Are there many of them?

Secretary. The entire population of Europe.

We'll need more for the second act but that can wait. Let's have the double-act first. What do they call themselves?

Secretary. The Curies. Marie Curie of Warsaw and Pierre Curie of Paris.

Waltz music. Pierre and Marie Curie enter. They wear formal ballroom costume of the period and speak their lines as they dance.

Pierre. To serve humanity, that is the aim.

Marie. We speak in civilisation's name.

Pierre. A secret lies in uranium ore.

Marie. A secret imprisoned within the core

Pierre. Holding the secret of matter in store.

Marie. Together we'll find it!

Pierre. Pitchblende brought to the cleansing flame,

Marie. Dissolved in acids, boiled again.

Pierre. Banish impurities, crystallise,

Marie. Dissolved again, the crystal dies.

Pierre. Crystallise with barium salts,

Marie. Dissolve and remove the impure faults.

Pierre. At this first stage
The pitchblende takes
The form
Of crystalline concentrates.

Marie. Day after day
Week after week
We repeat the process,
We who seek:

Pierre. The shed is red with the furnace glow

Marie. But the seed in the crucible starts to grow.

Pierre. In return for the sweat and toil we've spent
A newly discovered element –

Marie. I will name it after my native land – Poland.

Pierre. But the restless, unfettered mind pursues
Still more reactive residues.

Marie. Seeking for matters' final grain
Repeating the process again and again.

Pierre. Purify further, no cessation.

Marie. Concentrate through crystallisation,

Pierre. Solution,

Marie. Fractional separation.

Pierre. Reduce still further, refine, distil,

Marie. Repeat the process again until

Pierre. There in the heart of the crucible
A steady phosphorescent gleam

Marie. The track where minuscular comets stream –

Pierre. Here is reward,

Marie. The final sum
Of all our labours,
Radium.

Puppet Master. Take the man away, he's spoiling the act.

Death dances off with Pierre, to the waltz tune.

Marie. Pierre, Pierre, where are you? Come back into the light, Pierre . . . oh, my love.

Puppet Master. Carry on, miss. Time's precious.

Marie. But my Pierre?

Puppet Master. Sorry, but the show must go on.

Mic. Voice. To serve humanity, that is the aim.

Marie (*Dancing*)
The long road is my road.
Mine the long journey.
Through the spinning void
I walk,
Through the great silences
Of matter's universe.
Behind are the low lands
The known lands of measured days
And landscapes of nights
Without feature.
Here there is no teacher
Lending experience,
No constant compass,
No dexterous hand
Sharing the net's drag.
Mine is the unshared dream,
And dreams are made of formulae
And hollow glass
Where little suns and blazing stars
Revolve and scatter
Microscopic nebulae.
Oh, there is music in my ears
And brittle songs of dying particles.
Hear how a metal sings
Under the acid's kiss,
Hear how the elements
Repeat their whispered
Scales of secrets.
Now through a darkness of numbers
I walk

Where X is the moon which harries the clouds
With planet packs.
Oh, scythe of wind,
Keen blade of wind,
Reason of wind,
You stir the leaves
With radioactive ecstasy.
And the mind leaps
With the speed of light,
And overtakes
The dream,
And the night
Recedes before
The impact of new suns,
And the mountains
Are broken
By the roads.

Shall I follow the sodium trail or the trail of mercury! Which is my road? How shall I go?

Puppet Master. That's enough, miss, we're short of time. Your act, I'm afraid, lacks popular appeal. Needs a little comic relief . . . and yet . . . and yet . . . we might build you up in a few years' time as a gallant little lady, a silver-haired old lady, the world's sweetheart. I'll think about it. Goodnight . . . the gentleman will show you out.

Death waltzes out with Marie.

Who's next?

Secretary. Joseph John Thomson of Manchester.

Enter Thomson, as ring-master. Circus music.

Puppet Master. Thomson?

Thomson. That is my name.

Puppet Master. What do you do?

Thomson. I am a small-game hunter in the borderlands where force and matter meet. I am an atom tamer.

Trumpets sound.

Puppet Master. What experience?

Thomson. The experience of Faraday in electrolysis. The experience of Helmholtz of Potsdam. Also many years as ring-master in the Cavendish Laboratory.

Puppet Master. I don't think we can use a circus act.

Thomson. My circus is in a cathode tube.

Puppet Master. Circuses are out of date. Horses have no sex appeal and clowns are corny.

Thomson. Sir, you are referring to my public.

Puppet Master. Why do you wear a bandage over your eyes?

Thomson. I move in an unseen world where only the mind's eye sees.

Puppet Master. All right. Let's have your act.

Fanfare. Thomson goes into his 'act', making like a circus-spieler.

Thomson. Ladies and gentlemen, walk up, walk up! See the greatest show on earth. For the first time in any public place of entertainment we present the smallest, fastest, most amazing particle the world has ever not seen. It's terrific, it's gigantic, it's infinitesimal! Ladies and gentlemen . . . the Electron!

Tremendous fanfare. Thomson ushers in the invisible Electron. He bows and kisses her hand and applauds. . . . Puppet Master begins to protest.

Ah, and you are wondering where I found her! Years ago, when I was prospecting in the heart of Darkest Electricity I discovered that an electrical charge possesses inertia, the distinguishing characteristic of all matter. Ever since that day I have hunted in the deserts of space, in the jungles of calculation, in the wastes of gases for this ever-elusive Electron and now, at the cost of great personal danger and sacrifice, I have torn such a corpuscle from the heart of that great continent, the Atom. Look, my friends, look and marvel! See how effortlessly she will speed round the ring at a breathtaking speed of 160,000 miles a second. Ladies and gentlemen, may I present the only Electron in captivity, about to perform in John Thomson's Cathode Circus!

Long roll of drums. Thomson rotates on his heels, apparently following the progress of the Electron. Finally he bows.

Puppet Master. Just a moment, my friend, I didn't see your Electron.

Thomson. Why do you wear a bandage over your mind's eye?

Puppet Master. Not what I would call amusing.

Thomson. I didn't claim that it was amusing, merely miraculous.

Puppet Master. A miracle without crowd-appeal is unacceptable.

Thomson. Peasant!

Secretary. I'm afraid your time is up, sir.

Puppet Master. (*To Death*) Show him out.

Thomson. I can find my own way.

Puppet Master. My friend will help you. Like you, he has solved many problems in his time.

Death dances off with Thomson.

Circus acts! Electron tamers! Are there no tightrope-walkers on the list?

Secretary. None tonight, sir. There'll be plenty next week when we hold the political auditions.

Puppet Master. Pity they're so second rate. Still, what would a circus be without clowns? I'm going out for some refreshment. Carry on with the auditions. You know what I'm looking for.

Death makes to follow him.

No, you stay here. I'm arranging a big banquet for you and I wouldn't want to spoil your appetite.

He goes off. The following scene should be played as knockabout comedy. Enter Einstein.

Einstein. Ah, guten abend, fraulein. Wo is der Herr Direktor?

Secretary. I beg your pardon?

Einstein. The Direktor, he is here, yes?

Secretary. No, he's engaged at the moment. I am his assistant. Who are you?

Einstein. Ich bin Einstein. Albert Einstein.

Secretary. You are a comedian?

Einstein. Bitte, was ist ein comedian?

Secretary. You are a funny man?

Einstein. Oh ja, please, sehr lustige man. Morgan früh hab' ich eine kleine joke gemacht. You like jokes?

Secretary. If they're funny.

Einstein. So. Hier ist eine kleine dichte, a poem I have made . . . listen:

Der was ein young fraulein called Bright
Who could travel much faster than light,
She started one day
In a relative way
Und came back ze previous night.

(*He laughs*) Es is gut, no?

Secretary. It doesn't make sense.

Einstein. More than sense it makes. It makes scientific history. For you I will prove it mit die mathematik. There is a curvature in space . . .

Secretary. We have very little time . . .

Einstein. Please, there is no such thing as your 'time' – everything is a point-event in a space-time continuum.

Secretary. Is that supposed to be funny?

Einstein. The truth is never funny.

Enter the Puppet Master.

Puppet Master. On the contrary, the truth is always funny.

Secretary. This is Mr Einstein, sir. He is a comedian.

Einstein. But please, it is a mistake you make. Only in my spare time am I funny.

Puppet Master. Oh, an amateur.

Einstein. By profession I am an impresario for ze ballet. For you the greatest ballet of the age we have gebracht.

Enter Max Planck and Nils Bohr, arguing.

Planck. Nils, you are mein guter Freund; for you ze greatest admiration I have, but in this thing I must insist . . . ze electrons pirouette.

Bohr. For seventy times have I told you that this is not pirouette, but gargouillade, the spin around the fixed orbit.

Planck. Spin, pirouette, gargouillade, what you like call it, but the sequence follows so . . . first the spin, then the grand jetée en l'air tournant . . . then the spin again in the new orbit. Agreed, ja?

Einstein. Herr Direktor, meet my colleagues: Professor Max Planck and Nils Bohr, choreographers-in-chief of the great atomic ballet.

Puppet Master. How do you do?

Planck. How do we do what?

Einstein. This 'how do you do', it is idiomatic, no?

Puppet Master. Yes. Do you think you could explain to your friends that I am a very busy man?

Einstein. But of course. Der Herr Direktor sagt dass er sehr beschäftig ist und Mann muss zur Sache kommen – der Dummkopf! Aber, naturlich mussen wir die Ungestaltung der Masse in Energie-abgabe verstandlich machen, in Ubereinstimmung meiner Energie-gielchung . . .

Planck. But of course, we are all busy men.

Puppet Master. Well, go ahead then, show us your act.

Planck. Ein moment. First we must explain ze Quantum Theory.

Puppet Master. Is that necessary?

Einstein. It is very important.

Planck. (*With demoniacal intensity*) You think that energy can be divided up indefinitely, do you not? But you are wrong . . . this energy, it is discontinuous. It is atomic in structure.

Puppet Master. Really?

Planck. Ja wohl. It is emitted not in a continuous wave, but only in small, finite units which I have called quanta. So the amount of energy in a system is the number of quanta in it.

Bohr. Stop! Maxie, my friend, for me everything is clear. Your Quantum Theory explains why the electrons give off light and heat. It is so – the electron revolves in an elliptical orbit around the nucleus – yes?

Planck.
Einstein. (*together*) Ja wohl.

Bohr. Until it is disturbed by some outside force like the cathode rays or even heat. Und when it is disturbed so, the electron leaps from one orbit to another orbit farther from the nucleus.

Planck. So.

Bohr. So it is this leaping of the electrons to new orbits which causes the emission of light and heat. Es ist gut, nicht wahr?

Planck.
Einstein. (*together with enormous enthusiasm*) Wunderbar!

Puppet Master. Gentlemen, if you really have a ballet, I should like to see it.

Planck. But of course.

Bohr. Come, together we will go and prepare them for the audition.

They exit.

Puppet Master. What's the theme of your ballet?

Einstein. MC squared equals E.

Puppet Master. What?

Einstein. Here is the story. Attend! I will elaborate.

He calls to offstage.

Anastasia!

A pretty girl wearing a spangled leotard enters.

This is my assistant, Fraulein Mass. Now, together we will prove that a very small mass is equivalent to a great amount of energy, no? Now, please, very carefully you will attend!

He makes passes with his hands like a magician.

MC squared equals E!

A gong is struck and the light is blacked out. When, after a moment, it goes on again, Miss Mass has disappeared and in her place stands Energy, a muscular male figure.

You see! It is sehr simple, no? Und now the corps de ballet I will call. Ah, already they are here. So much activity, yes?

The corps de ballet have entered while he has been speaking. They immediately begin to limber up.

Puppet Master. Ballet, I'm afraid, is a little too precious for what we're looking for. Ours is a mass audience. And for that, a certain robustness is called for.

1st Neutron. But you haven't even seen us. How can you possibly judge us without seeing what we can do?

Puppet Master. And who might you be?

1st Neutron. Well, I might be Eleonora Duse or Catherine the Great, but I'm not. I am a neutron, one of Professor Chadwick's discoveries. I'm the neutral counterpart of the positive proton.

1st Proton. That's me, positively.

Alpha Particle. The pushy type.

Energy. Now you two, don't start again!

Puppet Master. And what do you do?

Energy. I'm Energy. I keep this lot under control.

Puppet Master. And the electron, where is he?

2nd Proton. Oh, you can't see him. He's whizzing round outside in a ten-mile radius.

2nd Neutron. If you're wondering who I am, I'm the extra neutron. I get shot into the heart of the nucleus.

Puppet Master. And I take it that all of you form an atom of uranium.

3rd Proton. Not really. A uranium atom has ninety-two protons and a hundred and forty-three neutrons. Who could afford a cast of that size?

1st Neutron. So you'll have to use your imagination.

Energy. O.K. Let's get on with it. (*Calling*) Music!

Music. Two neutrons, dressed in white, and two protons, dressed in red, whirl round the stage and finally form a compact group. They are joined by other protons and neutrons. An alpha particle attempts to penetrate the group but is deflected by an invisible force. Finally, Chadwick's neutron dances into the centre of the group and all leap away from her and land on their knees. End of music.

Puppet Master. Is that it?

Energy. What more do you want, the end of the world?

Puppet Master. Too abstract, too . . . it lacks . . . zing!

The rest of the scene is played like a 'thirties gangster film.

Energy. Quit shootin' off your mouth. Stick around, bub, and we'll go through the whole routine in another way. O.K., kids, let's show this mug what happens.

2nd Proton. Sure, we'll run a floorshow and mebbe get to Hollywood.

3rd Neutron. You don't object to a little naturalism with just a soupçon of symbolism . . .

Energy. Button up, Gabby, I do the talking in this outfit.

1st Proton. O.K., boss, O.K.

Energy. Get some furniture for this dump.

Protons go off and return with a table. Neutrons bring in chairs. Energy draws a semicircle in white chalk. Protons are now wearing gangster hats and the neutrons very modish headgear.

Now, if any of you mugs cross that line, I'll bust you wide open . . . see?

2nd Proton. Gee, boss, I'm getting tired of sitting around here doing nothing . . . I wanna go out and see the world.

Energy. Yeah? Now listen, sucker, I'm giving the orders around here, see? And nobody complains. There's plenty of guys would give their right arm to be in this outfit . . . how would you like to be a hydrogen proton and live in solitary confinement, eh?

2nd Proton. I wouldn't like that, boss.

Energy. Well, quit bellyaching.

He begins to play patience.

1st Neutron. It ain't so bad, honey . . . you still got me.

2nd Proton. Oh, sure, sure . . . still a change of scenery wouldn't do no harm.

1st Neutron. I think you're tired of me. (*She weeps.*)

2nd Proton. Aw, quit bawling!

1st Neutron weeps all the more.

1st Proton. That ain't the way a gentleman talks to a lady!

2nd Proton. No? D'ye wanna make something of it?

1st Proton. Sure I do.

2nd Proton. Why, you dumb flat-top . . .

Energy. Take it easy, take it easy, or I'll croak the both of you.

The two Protons retire.

2nd Proton. Gee, babe, I ain't tired of you. Honest, kid, I love you, don't I? Do you remember the promise I made when we first teamed up? Wherever you go, I go, and wherever I go, you go. Well, that's still O.K. by me.

1st Neutron. Oh, honey . . .

They embrace.

Mic. Voice. Calling Energy 235! This is the electron guard calling Energy. Reporting unsuccessful attempt by rival electrons to crash the outer ring. Signing off! Signing off!

Energy. Gate-crashers, eh? That's that guy Thomson again . . . imagine it! Trying to send a couple of dumb electrons into my territory . . . some people have no respect for private property.

Pause.

2nd Neutron. Do you know what day it is, sugar?

1st Proton. Sure, it's Thursday.

2nd Neutron. Yeah, but it's kind of special . . .

1st Proton. How come?

2nd Neutron. It's our anniversary.

1st Proton. Yeah? Imagine that.

2nd Neutron. You don't sound very interested.

1st Proton. Oh, sure, sure.

2nd Neutron. I bought a new hat . . . do you like it?

1st Proton. It stinks.

2nd Neutron. Why, you dumb cluck . . .

Energy. Pipe down!

2nd Neutron. But the dirty . . .

1st Proton. You heard: pipe down!

Enter Alfie Particle.

2nd Neutron. (*Flashing the old 'come hither' look*) Well, if it ain't Alfie Particle!

Alfie. Hiya, babe! You still stringing along with that heel?

2nd Neutron. He don't bother me.

Alfie. Why don't you give him the air, kid? I could show you the big time.

2nd Neutron. Mebbe.

Alfie. Aw, come on, babe, I got big ideas . . . this guy's just a stick-in-the-mud.

Energy. Beat it, punk!

1st Proton. Yeah, beat it!

Alfie. Why, I've a good mind to come in there and . . .

First Proton. Listen, needlenose, this is a high-class outfit and we don't take bums, so beat it before things get tough.

Alfie. If it wasn't out of respect for the ladies, I'd come in there and drill you!

Energy. Give him the bum's rush.

1st Proton kicks Alfie off.

Mic. Voice. Calling Energy 235! This is the electron guard calling Energy! A flash neutron dame known as 'Chadwick's neutron', alias Lola the Smasher, has penetrated the outer ring and is heading for the nucleus. Signing off! Signing off!

Enter Lola. Wolf whistles from the protons.

Lola. Hallo, boys . . . swell set-up you got here.

1st Proton. Boy, oh boy, is she a dish or is she a dish?

2nd Proton. Why don't you come on in?

Energy. On your way, sister. This is my outfit.

Lola. Yeah?

Energy. Yeah!

Protons. But, boss . . .

Energy. Nobody's going to muscle in on my territory.

Lola. Scared of competition, eh?

Energy. I'm warning you . . . I don't know my own strength.

Lola. You're kinda cute . . . my, what big muscles you got!

1st Proton. I got muscles, too, sweetie-pie!

2nd Proton. Quiet, fishface!

Lola crosses the chalk line and is in the centre.

1st Neutron. Look, she's crossed the line!

2nd Neutron. Oh, gee, something terrible's going to happen!

Lola. These your floozies?

2nd Proton. Kind of.

Lola. Kind of negative, ain't they?

Energy. All right, I warned you . . . don't say I didn't warn you!

Lola. Say, what's eating you? Do you two guys have to listen to this big lummox beefing like this all the time? What are you, men or mice?

1st Proton. What do you mean?

Lola. Why don't you run gangs of your own? You're tough . . . you've got experience . . . why, a coupla big jerks like you ought to clean up!

1st Proton. Say, that ain't a bad idea.

2nd Proton. It ain't at that.

1st Proton. We could see the world.

2nd Proton. (*To 1st Neutron*) Baby, this is where we blow.

Energy. For the last time . . .

Both Protons. So long, boss . . . it's been a long time.

1st Proton. There ain't room for all of us.

2nd Proton. California, here I come!

1st Proton. From now on, call me boss of the Krypton Gang!

2nd Proton. And I'm the big shot of the Barium Gang!

They go off.

Energy. O.K., sister, O.K. I ain't got no ties no more, no responsibilities. Hold me down to earth, I feel my powers a-working. Stand back and give me room according to my strength. I'm a rip-tailed snorting child of the elements . . . I'm half fire, half light, with a punch that can knock holes in the moon. I ride to town with a team of comets harnessed with cosmic rays. My whip is the North Wind and twin stars the rowels of my spurs. When I'm hungry I eat time and wash it down with the Milky Way. Yippee! Yippee! Bow down and wait! When I smoke I use a volcano for a pipe and thunderbolts for matches. I'm the father of the oceans, the guy who put the curvature in space. Bow down and tremble! I scratch my head with lightning and purr myself to sleep with thunder. Yippee! Owooo! I'm the toughest, roughest, goldarned particle in the Universe!

He leaps into the air. Loud and sustained explosion. Blackout. When the lights go on again, the Puppet Master, his Secretary and Death are discovered on stage.

Puppet Master. The release of Energy! What a closing act it'll make!

Secretary. Wonderful!

Puppet Master. With a show like that we'll clear the board of competition. We'll be running the entire show before we're through.

Death makes to leave.

Not yet, sonny! I'll give your cue when the time comes. (*Addressing Secretary*) You're quite clear about the schedule?

Secretary. Perfectly clear. Act One, 1914. Rehearsal for Act Two, 1936. Act Two, 1939. Act Three . . .

Puppet Master. Leave Act Three for the moment. The exact time will depend on the audience. Get your coat, my dear. It's time we were on our way.

The light fades down a little as they exit upstage right. At the same moment an actor and actress enter downstage left.

Actor. Put out the light – and then, put out the light!

Actress. Well, we've looked at the atom – now perhaps we ought to take a look at ourselves.

Actor. You mean us, personally, as actors?

Actress. No, just people . . . you know, people as in people.

Actor. Oh – that kind of people!

In the following scene, all the searchers wear rather nondescript outdoor clothes. Raincoats would serve perfectly. The first searcher, a man, enters and addresses the actor.

1st Man. I appear to have lost my way.

A girl enters.

Actor. Maybe the young lady can direct you.

1st Man. Excuse me, miss. I wonder if you can help me. I'm looking for the road that leads to a good life.

1st Woman. Sorry, I'm a stranger here myself.

2nd Woman. Can you tell me where I am, please? I seem to have been misdirected. I'm looking for the road to happiness.

1st Man. Did you come by the crossroads?

2nd Woman. No, I took the short cut. I thought it looked easier.

1st Woman. I came that way too, but it doesn't seem to lead anywhere.

Enter two women.

3rd Woman. It's awfully dark.

4th Woman. I'm afraid we're lost. We must have taken the wrong turning.

Enter man and woman.

2nd Man. We're looking for Freedom's road. Could you tell us the way?

1st Man. Sorry, but we're lost, too. This is a cul-de-sac.

2nd Woman. Well, what do we do now?

1st Woman. I suppose we'd better go back and start all over again.

3rd Woman. But it's so dark!

Actor. Oh, come on, you know the way.

4th Woman. We're supposed to be acting.

Actor. Maybe we need a different script. One that deals with a different set of facts.

1st Man. What kind of facts?

Actor. Well, we could show how the actors responded to the rehearsal of Act Two.

2nd Woman. Rehearsal?

Actor. I'm referring to Spain. Remember?

Mic. Voice. This is Madrid calling! This is Madrid calling! Belchite calling! Guernica calling! Hello! Hello! Are you receiving me?

Light changes. A single overhead spot makes a pool of light centre stage. The searchers and the two actors stand in a semicircle at the upstage edge of the light. Each of them takes a newspaper from his pocket and reads it throughout following episode. At the same time, two of them hurl themselves into the centre of the pool of light. One of them lies wounded, the other crouches over him. The scene is interrupted by the intermittant crash of bombs.

Soldier. It's not much further now, Jimmy! Can't be more than a hundred yards at the outside. Don't worry, we'll make it!

Distant artillery barrage.

They got all the bleedin' artillery in the world out there! German, Italian, Spanish . . . Christ! If only . . . never mind, we'll show 'em. The way we did at Teruel. (*Singing*) Forward, you must remember! (*Speaking again*) Who could forget the smell of Badajos . . . or the stillness of Guernica when they'd finished with it? Butchers!

Member of Chorus. A hundred and forty-three for four wickets! Hutton's coming in to bat.

Drone of planes and crash of bombs.

Soldier. Madrid's getting it bad tonight . . . they'll never take Madrid, not with all the tanks and planes in the world. (*Singing*) Forward, you must remember, herein our strength does lie. Forward, you must remember, in hunger or in plenty . . . (*Speaking again*) Remember how we drove 'em back at Guadarrama? Rifles against tanks! And Belchite! The Thaelmann brigade on our left flank and the French on our right. They won't forget those days, Jimmy. Nobody will.

Bombs.

Member of Chorus. There's Larwood coming now!

Member of Chorus. Shouldn't allow bodyline bowling. Not cricket!

Soldier. It'll be quiet back home now. People'll be asleep in bed and the streets'll be quiet with the roofs of the houses shining like silver under the northern moon. There'll be no fear of bombing, that's for sure. Not yet, anyroad. (*Shouting*) Hey, you in bed back home! Wake up! Wake up! (*To his companion*) Sorry, kid. Forgot.

Member of Chorus. A hundred and eighty-six for four wickets!

Member of Chorus. A hundred and ninety! Verity coming in to bowl.

Member of Chorus. Two hundred and five for four wickets!

Member of Chorus. Boundary! Bravo!

Member of Chorus. He'll make his century, easy.

Member of Chorus. Two-twenty-four not out!

Member of Chorus. Two-seventy-six for six!

Gunfire very close.

Soldier. Shut up! Shut up, you rotten bastards! My mate's trying to sleep. Can't even get a kip without some noisy bleeder banging away with all he's got! Go on, shoot, shoot! You can't bloody well kill all of us . . . you fascist bastards!

Burst of machine-gun fire. He falls over the body of his mate.

Jimmy! Jimmy!

Mic. Voice. All right, soldier, you can get up now. This is only a play, an attempt to discover the location of the audience's conscience.

Soldier. (*Rising to his feet*) There were more than a million men and women in Spain who didn't get up.

Mic. Voice. The rehearsal. The stage was Spain, Austria, the Saar, Czechoslovakia. But the stage management was provided by Germany. Germany calling! Germany calling! The Germany of Guns-Before-Butter, the Germany which was defending Europe from the menace of Communism. The Germany of the blond hero and the concentration camp. The Germany of Adolf Hitler and the Anglo-German Naval Agreement.

Two men, members of the chorus, man-handle a third man in the centre of the light.

1st Gestapo. All right, Eisler, talk!

2nd Gestapo. You heard what he said.

1st Gestapo. You might as well talk, Eisler, We've been on to you for a long time.

Chorus. (*Whispering*) Long time. Long time. Long time.

2nd Gestapo. We want to know where you got the leaflet.

1st Gestapo. And no lies, Eisler. We know you're part of the cell at Siemen's. We want to know who number one is. Who issues the instructions? You've got sixty seconds to talk!

Chorus. Quiet! Quiet! Quiet! Quiet!

2nd Gestapo. (*Striking him*) Talk, you red bastard!

1st Gestapo. Maybe you'd like me to jog your memory.

He produces a rubber blackjack from his pocket.

You had a sister once, Eisler. Remember?

Chorus. Elsa. Elsa. Elsa. Elsa.

1st Gestapo. You never knew what happened to her, did you? But we know, Eisler. We were there. Isn't that right, Kurt?

2nd Gestapo. We were there, all right. And did we let her know it!

1st Gestapo. Took her a long time to die.

2nd Gestapo. Sit down and think it over.

He kicks him in the stomach.

1st Gestapo. Thirty seconds left.

Chorus. Thirty seconds! Thirty seconds! Thirty seconds!

1st Gestapo. That's all you got. Speak up! Who printed the leaflets? Who are the other members of the cell? Who issues the instructions? Talk, you ghet!

They begin to beat him up.

Chorus. This is it! This is it! This is it!

2nd Gestapo. Do we take him in?

1st Gestapo. Haven't the time. I promised to take the wife to the pictures.

2nd Gestapo. Better finish him, then.

He produces a pistol.

1st Gestapo. Not that way. Too noisy! The town's full of foreign visitors. Hold him up.

They break his neck and he falls to the ground.

Mic. Voice. This scene is called 'Strength Through Joy'.

The two Gestapo officers become actors again and help Eisler to his feet. All three rejoin the semicircle.

1st Gestapo. The scene ends and the actor rises to his feet. But there were hundreds of thousands of real actors who never rose again.

Mic. Voice. And there were the refugees: the writers, doctors, students, scientists.

A woman leaves the semi-circle and stands downstage, waiting.

Chorus. He's late! Late! Late! Late!

A man leaves the chorus and joins her.

Lisa Meidtner. Thank God!

Frisch. Have you been here long?

Meidtner. No, I just arrived.

Frisch. Sure you weren't followed?

Meidtner. I came a long way round. Is something wrong?

Frisch. I had visitors today.

Meidtner. The Gestapo?

Frisch. I . . . think so.

Meidtner. Listen, something very important has happened. I have a contact in Strassman's laboratory. His neutron bombardment of uranium has produced an isotope of barium.

Frisch. You are certain?

Meidtner. Positive! The nucleus split into equal parts releasing enormous amounts of energy.

Frisch. I take it you understand the implications of this news.

Meidtner. Of course. The laboratory is already on a war footing.

Frisch. We've got to get out of Germany immediately.

Meidtner. I've made all the arrangements. Can you get a travel permit?

Frisch. I . . . yes, I think I can.

Meidtner. I have an aunt who lives in Schleswig. If you could get that far, it should be easy to slip over the border into Denmark.

Frisch. Denmark, Copenhagen and Professor Nils Bohr!

Meidtner. If anything should happen . . .

Chorus. Watch out! Watch out!

Frisch suddenly embraces her. A man enters, pauses, lights a cigarette, then walks off.

Frisch. Sorry, Miss Meidtner. To have to play such games!

Meidtner. We'd better go. It's dangerous being out so late.

Frisch. See you in Copenhagen.

They shake hands.

Both. Good luck!

They resume their positions in the semicircle.

Meidtner. We did not have to make the perilous journey through a hostile land.

Frisch. But thousands of others did.

Member of Chorus. It isn't pleasant to remember such things. It is so easy to forget other people's sufferings. And yet our century has taught us that disaster may result from a defective memory.

Mic. Voice. Is there a mental specialist in the house? The world's gone mad again! September the third, 1939. WAR!

Sound of marching feet. Five scientists wearing white lab coats enter. They form two small groups and stand deep in conversation. The Puppet Master enters briskly.

Puppet Master. Fall in!

The scientists form a straight line. The entire scene is performed as bayonet-drill, with Puppet Master as sergeant.

Puppet Master. Squad 'shun! Left turn! Tem-po!

1st Scientist. MC squared equals E.

2nd Scientist. B equals bracket ZMp unbracket minus M.

3rd Scientist. K infinity equals 0.87.

4th Scientist. K infinity equals 0.98.

5th Scientist. Epsilon pf eta equals K infinity.

1st Scientist. K infinity equals 1.007.

Mic. Voice. The piping must have a high neutron absorption cross section. The highest are lead . . .

All. Water corrosion.

Mic. Voice. Bismuth.

All. Water corrosion.

Mic. Voice. Beryllium.

2nd Scientist. There is no beryllium tubing in the country.

Mic. Voice. Aluminium.

All. Doubtful.

Mic. Voice. Magnesium.

All. Water corrosion.

Mic. Voice. Zinc.

All. Water corrosion.

Mic. Voice. Tin.

All. Water corrosion.

Mic. Voice. Try aluminium.

All. It works!

3rd Scientist. For a separation producing 90 per cent uranium 235 from natural uranium, r must equal 1,260 but alpha equals root 352 over 349 which is only 1.0043.

4th Scientist. 92 uranium 238 by neutron gamma reaction to 92 uranium 239.

5th Scientist. 92 uranium 239.

Mic. Voice. Half-life twenty-three minutes.

5th Scientist. By beta emission to 93 neptunium 239.

Mic. Voice. Half-life 2.3 days.

5th Scientist. By beta-gamma emission to 94 plutonium 239.

4th Scientist. 94 plutonium 239 by alpha emission to 92 uranium 235.

There is a blinding flash and a loud, sustained explosion followed by a blackout. The light comes up again and discovers the Puppet Master, his Secretary and Death, leading Energy on a leash.

Puppet Master. Let us pause here.

Secretary. But the audience . . .!

Puppet Master. The audience?

Secretary. Is it wise to let them see so much of you?

Puppet Master. They will have forgotten me by the morning.

Secretary. Are you sure?

Puppet Master. I know my audience. In a few minutes they will leave this building imagining that a man can walk out of his own life. They don't realise that they are the main protagonists in the play. They will go out into the night sharing the same dream until the dream is shattered by a stream of petty circumstances. In fifteen minutes, only half the dream will remain. In thirty minutes only half of half the dream and in an hour nothing will be left but a blurred image on the retina of the mind's eye. For the last bus home tonight is more important than the hearse which bears one to a worm's banquet in twelve months' time. Let us be thankful, my dear, that people have such short memories.

Secretary. Last night I dreamed of my dead lovers. They looked at me out of the empty sockets of their eyes and spoke of their unborn children.

Puppet Master. I will find you new lovers.

Secretary. But they will die like all the others.

Puppet Master. Because you break them. You always break the toys I bring you.

Secretary. Now you are scolding me.

Puppet Master. I? Now, why would I scold you? There are plenty more toys. Soon there will be another generation of young men and you shall have them all.

Secretary. Soon?

Puppet Master. As soon as the chorus is ready for the next scene.

Secretary. The young men who talk with voices of caressing hands . . . the young men of the red hands and the smoke of battle in their hair . . . the young men whose bodies live like a flame which burns the night and dies with burning . . .

Energy and Death rise up.

Puppet Master. Not yet! The actors haven't recovered from the Second Act. Give them a sporting chance, I say, and the hunt will be the keener.

Secretary. Why can't the play go on and never stop?

Puppet Master. Let them repair the broken cities first. Let them breed again. Let them erect a superstructure on their lives and we four will destroy it.

Enter a woman.

Woman. I had a son,
A song in my veins,
A green shoot in my heart,
A flight of grace notes,
That was my son.

Secretary. Where is he now?

Puppet Master. Yes, where?

Woman. Where?
My heart is a barren field
Where withered nettles whisper dry laments,
Where the sun gives no warmth,
Where the broken stars are fallen on a rubbish heap.

Puppet Master. You should apply for a pension.

Woman. Yes, I will apply for a pension.
I will buy me an axe
And lop off the dead branches of the world.

Puppet Master. You can't do that without a permit.

Woman. I will search for a man
In whom there is no singing,
No warmth, no light, no music.
A man of shades and empty silence.

Secretary. I warned you. The audience!

Woman. I will find a man
Who tears the young plants out of the earth
And feeds his swine with roses;
The man with the woodman's axe
Who fells the striplings in spring
Before their leaves are born;
The smiler with the knife.
A man like you who talks of pensions
When the blade of anguish
Turns within the womb.

Puppet Master. Dear lady, you are distraught. I am not the man you seek, for like you, I too know parental love. Sleep is what you need, good lady.

Woman. Sleep!

Puppet Master. My friend here is a famous sleep practitioner. He will give you something which will help you to forget.

Death approaches her but stops as a soldier enters.

Soldier. Can he give me something that will take the smell of burning flesh out of my nostrils, something to make my ears forget a screaming soldier?

Puppet Master. He can do all that.

Soldier. Can he show me the man who makes of my death a mockery, the commander who never leaves the field of battle for fear that life should grow there? Can he show me him?

Woman. Young man, you have looked at the stars and stumbled in a grave.

Soldier. I was a young man
With eyes that looked to see things grow,
Corn from the seed,
Cities from the rock,
Wheels from the iron-ore.

Secretary. What are you now?

Soldier. I was a man
With hands that drew
The goodness out of metals,
The whirling shaft,
The lunging piston,
The hissing bar.

Woman. What do you do now?

Soldier. I plant corpses in a desert,
Because a man with a barren mind
Has forgotten what life is.
A man like you.

Puppet Master. Come, come, young man! My grey hairs deserve respect.

Enter two men wearing garb of concentration camp inmates.

1st Inmate. Do my grey hairs deserve respect?

2nd Inmate. Do mine?

Both. We were men once.

1st Inmate.
Hope, desire, pity, love,
We knew them once.

2nd Inmate.
Ambition, anger, laughter, tears,
Familiar things.

1st Inmate.
Familiar no more.
All gone, destroyed.

Both. Reduced to ashes in the ovens of Auschwitz.

Secretary. Send them away – they frighten me!

1st Inmate. We frighten ourselves.

Puppet Master. People want to forget.

2nd Inmate. Who will help *us* forget?

Puppet Master. (*Indicating Death*) I have a friend here who is a specialist.

1st Inmate. I know his face. I've seen him in the camp.

Soldier. I know him, too!

Several Voices. He is the Puppet Master's friend.

Puppet Master. All this is foolishness.

Enter the Scientist.

Puppet Master. There is the man you seek. He it is whose brain conceives the tools of death. If the graves are now prepared for other wars, then he's the man who is responsible.

All. The enemy!

Scientist. Wait! Let me speak.

Puppet Master. Your voice is cracked.

1st Inmate. Let him speak. We have known too much of death to welcome it.

2nd Inmate. Let him have the benefit of the trial we never had.

1st Inmate. You are accused of conspiring against the world, of betraying mankind to war and wretchedness, of using the brain to do the work of Death.

Woman. You are accused of conspiring against tomorrow's generations.

Soldier. You are accused of planning to destroy the very fabric of the world, of having released the forces of death in everything that lives.

All. You are accused of conspiring against the human race.

Scientist. The road that we have built across the wastes of ignorance is not a road which leads to Death except for fools who would throw themselves over the precipice. It is a good road which can lead to peace itself if only men will stop wearing blinkers on their eyes. It can lead to peace such as you have never known.

Puppet Master. An empty dream!

Scientist.

He is the man of the shades
The woodman with the axe,
The puppet-master who shapes the play
Of death. He is the enemy.

All. The enemy!

Puppet Master. Good people, please. I am an old man interested only in my son here. (*He indicates Energy*). The very apple of his father's eye.

Scientist. He is no child of yours. I accuse this man of having kidnapped Energy, the child of my own brain.

Puppet Master. He's mad.

Scientist. I accuse him of conspiring against the peace of the world, of debauching science's discoveries, perverting progress, and of gross distortion of the truth.

Puppet Master. He is my child.

Scientist. You lie!

Puppet Master. Come, I will do the sporting thing. (*He produces dice.*) Let us decide with the dice.

Soldier. Let me see them first. (*He takes the dice.*) The dice are loaded.

All. He is condemned.

1st Man. Let Energy speak. Who are your parents?

Energy. Albertus Magnus, Einstein, Democritus, da Vinci, Planck, Dalton, Rutherford, Paracelsus, Thomson, Mendeleyev, Curie, Bohr, Chadwick, Dirac, Heisenberg. The men and women of the whole earth and of all ages. I am their child.

1st Man. But you cannot go with them all.

Woman. Which way will you go?

Energy. I will go where you go. If you work for war I will work with you. If you work for peace I will work too. There are two roads.

Puppet Master. My road is the familiar one. You can walk it blindfold. Come with me.

Scientist. Mine is the new road, where a man walks with his eyes on the future. The road out of the night.

Energy. There are two roads. It is for you to choose and for me to follow.

The crowd hesitates.

Which is it to be?

All. Which way are you going? *[The End]*

NOTE

Following Theatre Workshop's practice of keeping the play up to date, the author has written a new ending, one more in accord with his present political position. After the Puppet Master's speech 'An empty dream' (p. 125), the play continues as follows:

The actress who has been playing the role of the mother suddenly abandons the role and becomes an actress again, talking to her workmates. The rest of the characters onstage follow her example.

Woman. You know, I think I agree with you.

Those onstage are put to a nonplus for a moment.

Puppet Master. That isn't in the script.

Woman. No, it isn't. At least, it isn't in the original script.

Soldier. Which original script? I understand there's half a dozen 'original' versions of the script.

1st Man. That's right – the original script was written in 1946 and played for just over an hour. Then a longer version was made in 1947 and then they kept altering it by subtracting scenes and adding others until about 1952.

2nd Man. And the final script is the one we've been performing tonight?

1st Man. Not exactly. A lot of it's from the original and the rest from some of the later versions.

Puppet Master. Confusing, to say the least?

Woman. (*To the audience*) Are you confused? Perhaps I should explain. What you have seen so far, is what the author wrote way back in the late forties and early fifties. At that time he believed, as many people did, in what Eisenhower called 'Atoms for Peace'. Indeed, he ended the play on a note of hope. 'We have the choice,' he said, 'between two roads: the road to war and the road to peace.'

Scientist. So?

Woman. Events have forced him to change his mind.

Scientist. Which events?

1st Man. The blow-out at Windscale in 1957 which released twenty thousand curies of radioactive iodine-131 into the atmosphere.

Soldier. The explosion of stored radioactive waste at Kyshtym in the Soviet Union in 1958, which resulted in more than a thousand square miles being contaminated by radioactive stronium-90 and caesium-137.

Secretary. The partial melt-down in the fast-breeder reactor at Detroit, Michigan, in 1966.

3rd Man. And similar accidents in West Germany, France, Switzerland, Japan – and of course, there was Three Mile Island.

Soldier. The U.S. Safety Information Center at Oak Ridge recently disclosed that of the two thousand incidents investigated in 1979, no fewer than thirty-two could have ended in a catastrophic melt-down of the core.

Scientist. That wasn't here in Britain, was it!

Soldier. No, that wasn't here in Britain. We don't know how many near catastrophies have occurred here as the British nuclear industry refuses to make its safety findings available to the public.

Secretary. What do you think they're trying to hide?

Scientist. Look, you talk as if there's some kind of conspiracy.

Woman. There is a conspiracy! A conspiracy to keep us in the dark, to keep us from knowing what they've got in store for us.

Scientist. This isn't some B-film about mad scientists intent on destroying civilisation.

Puppet Master. No? I think it *is*. And a bloody awful B-film at that! A cast of third-rate actors playing at politics.

Scientist. It's scientists we're talking about, not politicians.

Secretary. Are they any different?

Scientist. Of course they are! At least, their motivations are different.

1st Man. Grow up! Don't tell me you still believe all that nonsense about the scientist's pure motives, about his only interest being the furtherance of human knowledge.

Scientist. I don't think it is nonsense. There are scientists who . . .

Puppet Master. A minority. A small minority. Most of them are pretty much the same as everybody else.

Scientist. Exactly! So why suggest that they're all alike?

Soldier. You're the one who suggested that.

Scientist. I did nothing of the kind.

2nd Man. You implied it.

Puppet Master. Their motivations are different, you said. Well, perhaps that's true for a small handful of them but I'll bet that for every scientist who is a selfless seeker after knowledge there are a hundred or more who are as much on the make as any politician. Their motivations, as you call them, are ambition, the need to feel successful, to feel 'in the know', to have the symbols of success constantly in one's sight: the Mercedes, the modest estate, the fine house, the right school for one's children, a title possibly. And it's satisfying to be able to pontificate at high table or on TV or at conferences of experts. When you have achieved these things, you tend to put any doubts you may have about what you are doing into a locked drawer and forget about them.

Scientist. You're being cynical.

Puppet Master. Maybe. But not nearly as cynical as some of the people we're discussing who, in the course of their professional careers, have managed to put their conscience into a deep coma. They're clever people, yes! But the search for truth, knowledge, and all the other noble concepts . . . bilge! It's a bloody great fraud! They're con-artists! You'd better recognise the fact that a man or woman can be a brilliant nuclear physicist and yet be a third-rate human being.

Scientist. In which case, they're no different from the rest of us.

Woman. They *are* different. They're worse than the worst of us.

Scientist. How do you make that out?

Woman. They *know* what they're doing. They're not like someone who goes out and murders a child – some old man, sick in the head. Oh, no! We're talking about rational people: brilliant minds! People who're supposed to be more far-seeing than the rest of us. And what do these rational, brilliant, far-seeing people do with all that know-how? All that knowledge, that effort to understand the physical laws of the universe! What do they do with it? They turn to us, the stupid, gullible, easily impressed public and say: 'Here is a present for you, the wherewithal to destroy yourself and the world you live in. Our greatest achievement!'

Soldier. Isn't that something! Use a little of it to make a bomb, a small bomb just big enough to wipe out a town with maybe two hundred thousand inhabitants. With a slightly bigger bomb you could wipe out Liverpool or Edinburgh.

2nd Man. And with four or five such bombs you could eradicate London from the face of the earth. No more traffic problems, no housing problems . . .

Secretary. And no people problems. Period!

From now on, all the dialogue is directed straight to the audience.

Puppet Master. And if you want something really big, then there's the nuclear reactors dotted all over Britain, those old-fashioned Magnox reactors at Windscale and Hunterston, Chapel Cross and Dungeness. They are the time-bombs in the atomic nursery. And then there's the A.G.R.s at Hartlepool, Heysham and Hinkley Point, and the rapid breeder they propose to build at Dounreay. They'd really be effective at dealing with our problems, since there'd be nobody left to experience problems.

Woman. Each of those reactors is a weapon pointed at the heart of this nation.

Scientist. They produce power.

Woman. They only produce electricity and we've got more of that kind of power than we need. They produce radioactive substances which poison everything they touch – the land, the rivers, the seas, the air . . . they breed cancers in the bones and flesh of people like us. Man's greatest achievement! A device, a series of devices with which we can kill ourselves, our children, our families, our friends.

Scientist. You don't seem to understand . . .

Woman. And *you* don't seem to understand what is at stake. These people that you admire so much, these dedicated scientists are as venal, as corrupt as . . . you expect venality from business tycoons, you expect generals and professional hit-men to be ruthless but . . . you read about some old lady being beaten up by teenage thugs and we're all horrified! But these people plan the murder of cities, continents, millions of men, women and children! Even while we're talking, the reactors go on breeding more and more plutonium and more and more radioactive waste . . . plutonium has a half-life of twenty-four thousand years and it takes about ten half-lives for radioactive material to become harmless. That means plutonium has to be kept out of the environment for a quarter of a million to half a million years.

If at any time during that period it is released into the environment, land and water are poisoned forever. Forever! Forever! Who are the real vandals? The football gangs who tear up railway carriages or the glib engineering geniuses and men of science who are prepared to tear up the planet we live on? Why do they do it? Why? Why?

Scientist. (*Taking off his white coat*) It isn't so much a question of why they do it, it's why do we let them do it?

2nd Woman. Yes, why? Are we too lazy, too preoccupied with other things? Don't we care? What about those we love and those who love us? Are we prepared to stand back and do nothing to stop them from being murdered? What about our children? Do we really love them? Enough to save them from this horror?

Soldier. Yes, that is the question. And it isn't only human life that is threatened – it's all life. And it's forever.

All. (*Quietly*) Forever!

Woman. Have you decided where you're going on your holidays next year? Have you made your plans yet? Perhaps you shouldn't bother. There may not be any next year or next month for that matter, or next week . . . or tomorrow . . . forever is an awful long time.

3rd Woman. It really depends on us. On you, me, him, her, all of us. We're all responsible for what happens. This is one situation we can't opt out of. In any case, there's nowhere to opt out to.

Puppet Master. We can stop them, you know! It'll take courage, determination, nerve and the capacity to put up with a hell of a lot of double-talk.

1st Man. Of course, you may prefer to gamble, staking humankind's future against the slow burn or the big bang. It really depends on whether you think the world's worth saving.

Puppet Master. Do you think you might give it some thought? It's worth thinking about. And remember what's at stake: our future and our past, all two or three million years of it. Anyway, think it over.

Woman. Yes, think it over. But don't take too long. Please don't take too long.

A brief pause and the light begins to fade.

All. (*Quietly*) Remember – forever is an awful long time.

The stage is left in darkness and the theatre is filled with whispers . . . 'Forever . . . forever . . . forever . . .' *[The End]*

The beaten track is beaten frae the start
– Hugh MacDiarmid

The Other Animals

by Ewan MacColl

CENTRAL LIBRARY THEATRE
ST. PETER'S SQUARE · MANCHESTER
GENERAL MANAGER & LICENSEE
CHARLES NOWELL, M.A., F.L.A., CITY LIBRARIAN

JULY 5th to 24th Evenings at 7 Matinee: Saturday at 2-15 Box Office: CENtral 5972 (10-30 a.m.—7 p.m.)
House Manager, Peter Carpenter.

THEATRE WORKSHOP

presents

THE OTHER ANIMALS

Ewan MacColl's new play

Produced by

JOAN LITTLEWOOD

The Other Animals was presented by Theatre Workshop at The Library Theatre, Manchester, on 5 July 1948, with the following cast:

HANAU	Ewan MacColl
ROBERT	David Scase
DOCTOR GRAUBARD	Peter Varley
1st GUARD	John Blanshard
2nd GUARD	Denis Ford
MARIA	Julia Jones
ROLF	Howard Goorney
ANDERSON	Edmond Bennett
THE MOON	Jean Newlove
THE GIRL IN WHITE	Doreen Warburton
THE GIRL IN GREEN	Leila Greenwood
THE GIRL IN CRIMSON	Kristin Lind
A NURSE	Leila Greenwood
AN ARCHITECT	Edmond Bennett
A YOUNG LABOURER	Denis Ford
AN OLD MAN	Howard Goorney
A YOUNG WOMAN	Doreen Warburton
AN OLD WOMAN	Jean Newlove
FRANCISCO PIERA	Howard Goorney
CLEMENCE GAUDRY	Julia Jones
JAMES GUTHRIE	Edmond Bennett
A COMMERCIAL TRAVELLER	John Blanshard
BRAVE LITTLE WOMAN	Leila Greenwood
DEATH AS AN OLD WOMAN	Kristin Lind
MORNING AS A YOUNG GIRL	Jean Newlove

Directed by Joan Littlewood. Sets designed by Joan Littlewood. Costumes designed by Bernard O'Connell. Lighting by John Bury. Choreography by Jean Newlove.

[**PART ONE**] *The curtain rises on a stage draped in black. In the centre stands a circular steel cage, broad at the base, narrowing as it reaches up into the darkness. Left and right of the cage and as far back as possible are two platforms raised above stage level. At first there is little light on the stage, just one dim spotlight beam falling into the cage, which becomes brighter during the announcer's introduction.*

Announcer. (*Intimately*) The word 'cage' is a noun. 'Old French from Latin Cavea – cavity, from CAVUS – hollow. A box or enclosure wholly or partly of openwork for confining birds or other animals.'

1st Voice.

Thus, in our dictionary,
Simply and precisely,
Is defined
The penultimate abode
Of those marked down for death
By history's enemies.

Somewhere in the night a man screams.

Here in this purgatory
Set between two hells,
The hell of blindness
And the hell of seeing,
The species wages war
Upon the genus.

Phrase of music.

2nd Voice.

Both are the other animals,
Alike in external features as two peas,
Two spirochetes or two baboons,
And yet dissimilar as a thing
And its reflection in a mirror;
A difference measured
In the terms of dreams.

Phrase of music.

3rd Voice.

Both are the other animals.
One is the hawk, keen-sighted, solitary;
The other a jackdaw, noisy, gregarious.
One is the white, poised gull,
A visual song of infinite variation,
Counterpoised on wind and sky;
The other, the snot-green shag,
A stomach with wings, haunting its ichthyic past
In worlds of fishes' bones and coastal silt.
One is the eagle, rejecting the valley's scars

For the utmost pinnacle of vertiginous dream;
The other, the small, nocturnal owl
Avoiding abacination from the candle's gleam.
These are the other animals.

A metallic tapping becomes audible. A voice keeps pace with the tapping: 'They – are – bringing – him – back.' The echoes die away.

1st Voice.

They envied his keen sight,
His quick perception;
The perfection which lies
In co-ordination of mind and eye.
And he would not join their chorus.
And fearing his silence
And hating what they feared,
The jackdaws fell upon the lark,
Mobbed him,
Crowded his flight with clumsy jackdaw wings,
Tore at his silence with blunt jackdaw cries,
Robbed him of that fine co-ordination,
The essence of his being.
And his seeing eyes glazed over,
Leaving a lesser world
For jackdaws
And the other animals.

Music.

2nd Voice.

Shags opened the breast of the wheeling gull
As he rode the shifting currents of the air.
His perfect flight
Was a reminder,
Constantly before their eyes,
Of the gulf
Which lies between
Their world, half-fish, half-bird,
And his,
All bird,
Perfect.

Music.

3rd Voice.

Behind the walls of darkness,
Where he wields dominion over frogs and mice,
The captive owl conspires against the eagle:
Plans a regime where night
Will be perpetual and universal
And sight limited to those things
That avoid the light and love the darkness.

The tapping and the voice are heard again. 'They – are – coming. Pass – it – on.'

1st Voice.

Where there were eyes
Of suns and stars,
Gouging batrachian thumbs
Left only cavities,
Hollows of darkness
Where life festers
And cries out with iron voice,
In words of rust,
Inflicting ferrous wounds
Upon the silence.
That they can still be heard
Above the twittering, bat-voices of the dead,
Is a tribute
To the light behind the eyes,
The dream behind the fact,
Which characterise
That Individual.
(genus Homo, family Hominidae, class Mammalia)
Of the highest type of animal
Existing
Or known to have existed,
Differing from other high types of animals
Especially
In his extraordinary mental development.

All.

Man – the other animal.
Men – the other animals.

In the distance a steel door clangs. The tapping begins again accompanied by the voice. 'They – are – bringing – Number – Three – back.' The tapping and the voice increase in volume until it seems that every nook and cranny of this dark, sub-world is alive with hoarse, tearing echoes. The sounds reach a peak and then stop with sharp and terrific finality. Two guards enter, half carrying, half dragging the prisoner, Hanau, known to the other prisoners as Number Three. Though still in his early forties, weeks of captivity and torture have given him the appearance of an old man. His hair is streaked with grey and the stubble of his beard bloody from countless beatings. At the moment he is unconscious of his surroundings, the wide, staring eyes see only the phantoms which people his private world of delirium and pain.

1st Guard. Home again, brother! There's no place like home.

2nd Guard. Christ, how this place stinks!

1st Guard. You get used to it. A matter of time, that's all.

2nd Guard. Hope you're right.

1st Guard. With time you can get used to anything. Take me, now – I've seen the day my stomach was as queasy as a bitch's belly full of its first load. The slightest whiff of anything that disagreed with me and I'd be off my food for days. Now I could eat my dinner off the floor of a privy and not even notice. Habit, that's all!

2nd Guard. At the training centre we used to turn the hoses on the prisoners.

1st Guard. This is a prison not a bath-house.

2nd Guard. I still don't like the way the bastards smell.

1st Guard. Maybe you'd like some eau-de-cologne. If you want to make good in this world then you've got to be master of your own stomach. A rebellious belly is like a spoiled woman: both have to be tamed or they'll tame you.

Hanau. One . . . two . . . three . . . four. There's one too many.

2nd Guard. Shut up!

1st Guard. Here, hold him up while I unlock the door.

Hanau. All except the fourth. Anderson . . . Rolf . . . Maria . . . Maria . . .

1st Guard. Sure, Maria . . . we'll send her to you later.

Hanau. Was it safe to bring him here?

2nd Guard. You heard me, be quiet!

1st Guard. He can't hear you. As far as he's concerned you don't exist.

Hanau. There is a certain familiarity . . .

2nd Guard. If I had my way I'd talk to him with my boot.

Hanau. He looks as if he slept too much;
It leaves a mark, makes a man look
Like a blurred reproduction of himself.
Just stand aside a little! You see,
He has the sleeper's voluntary deafness.
And do the sleeping bedrooms hear
The statement of the streets,
The factual report of feet on pavements?
Sleep is a perpetual multiplication
Of dead tissue, a parasitic growth
Which feeds upon awareness,
Dulling the pitch and volume
Of infinite, stratose gradations
Of acquired perception.

1st Guard. All right, professor, the party's over. (*He stands by the open door of the cage.*) Right! Release the prisoner.

The 2nd Guard throws Hanau into the cage. He falls flat on his back and lies quite still.

He's tired. Wants to lie down.

2nd Guard. It beats me how the sod manages to go on living.

1st Guard. Habit, just habit!

2nd Guard. If the commandant would give me three minutes of the prisoner's time, I'd break him of all his habits.

1st Guard. And then Graubard would break you.

2nd Guard. What's Graubard got to do with it?

1st Guard. Why don't you ask him?

2nd Guard. I thought he was only the doctor here.

1st Guard. That's right, only the doctor. Listen, I'm going to give you some advice. Whether you take it or not is none of my business, but if you don't I'll guarantee you'll be in the front line within a week, and a front line which is always falling back is a very unhealthy place to be in.

2nd Guard. Well, what's your advice?

1st Guard. Just this: remember that it's Doctor Graubard who writes the prescriptions. The commandant is only the dispenser.

2nd Guard. But I don't see . . .

1st Guard. Think it over, just think it over. Let's go!

They make to leave, but stand back to allow Dr Graubard to enter. He is a man of about forty-five years of age, alert and vigorous, but possessing an air of detachment. In spite of holding the rank of a major, he consistently wears civilian clothes, conscious of the fact that this makes him conspicuous in a world where everyone wears a uniform.

Graubard. And how is my patient?

1st Guard. Still out, sir.

Graubard. Out? He appears to be very much 'in'.

1st Guard. Yes, sir. I meant he's still unconscious.

Graubard. Has he said anything since he had his treatment?

1st Guard. Only in delirium, sir. He spoke of sleep.

Graubard. Hallucinate, no doubt.

1st Guard. Sir?

Graubard. Did he appear to be seeing things?

1st Guard. Yes, sir. Definitely, sir!

Graubard. And he spoke of sleep?

1st Guard. Yes, sir.

Graubard crosses to the cage and stands looking down at Hanau.

Graubard. Beware of dreams, Hanau! Beware of dreams!

The 2nd Guard laughs obediently. Graubard comes back and stands facing him.

Do you have dreams?

2nd Guard. No, sir.

Graubard. Then why did you laugh?

2nd Guard. It was what you said, sir. It struck me as funny.

Graubard. It did? I see. So you think I'm a humorist.

The Guard is silent.

You're new here.

2nd Guard. Yes, sir.

Graubard. Where were you before?

2nd Guard. Training course, sir. Number Five Interrogation Centre.

Graubard. Did you volunteer?

2nd Guard. Yes, sir.

Graubard. Why?

2nd Guard. (*Flustered*) Why, sir?

Graubard. Yes, why did you volunteer? Do you like the work?

2nd Guard. Oh, yes sir!

Graubard. Why?

2nd Guard. (*Very confused*) I . . . I don't know, sir.

Graubard. Doesn't that strike you as strange?

2nd Guard. No, sir . . . I mean, yes sir.

Graubard. Make up your mind. Tell me, was the killing of prisoners part of your training?

2nd Guard. Yes, sir.

Graubard. And how did you react?

2nd Guard. I don't quite know what you mean, sir.

Graubard. Did you enjoy it?

2nd Guard. I . . . it was an order, sir.

Graubard. I know it was an order, and I'm asking you whether you enjoyed carrying out the order. What were your personal feelings towards the prisoners?

2nd Guard. I hated them!

Graubard walks slowly round the Guard, like an officer inspecting a private on parade.

Graubard. You're a neurotic. Did you know that?

2nd Guard. No, sir.

Graubard. Well, you know it now. (*To the 1st Guard*) See that he keeps away from Hanau. Understand?

1st Guard. Yes, sir.

Graubard. (*Speaking softly, but with great emphasis to the 2nd Guard*) Hanau is my masterpiece and I want no psychopathic scribblings on the canvas. This place is not an abattoir, remember that: it is a laboratory where I carry on my research. Is that clear?

2nd Guard. Yes, sir.

Graubard. Remember also, that the prisoners in this wing are necessary to my work. They are not brought here for the gratification of your neurotic impulses. Your experience in dealing with peddlers of badly written leaflets is, no doubt, extensive, but . . .

Hearing Hanau's voice, he stops abruptly.

Hanau. The decision was clear . . .
Cell nuclei composed
Of three and only three.
Three shadows in all the streets
Of all the cities, combining
To form the nervous system
Of October.

He falls silent again. Graubard crosses to the cage.

1st Guard. Do you need us, sir?

Graubard. No, you can go.

The Guards exit.

Hanau! Hanau!

Hanau. A trinity of shadows,
Answering to names
Assumed and thrown aside
At the dictation of events.
The struggle of the living nucleus
Against dead tissue.
That was it.

Graubard. Was, Hanau, was! The past tense.

Hanau. We plotted the course of unseen stars
Across a stinking wilderness.
Night was the enemy we fought
In groups of three.
Three who cheated death
By simulating death;
Three pairs of eyes
Concealing vision
Under the habits of the blind.
Three minds that still know how to think
Even when thought was outlawed.

He becomes silent again.

Graubard. Hanau, can you hear me?

Hanau. Rolf, will you vouch for him?
Will you, Maria?
Why was he brought here, then?

He sinks back and his speech becomes increasingly incoherent.

One . . . two . . . three . . .
The stable atom.
Rolf . . . Anderson . . . Maria . . .
One . . . two . . . three . . . four . . .

Four is the extra proton.
Seen his face but not
The recognition which
Is swift and yet
And yet seen somewhere . . .

His words are lost in a low muttering.

Graubard. Destroy the enemy's lines of communication. That is a classic axiom of war and the fact that this is a war of ideas fought on the battlefield of your mind makes it none the less relevant. Yes, Hanau, your defence was strong, perfectly co-ordinated, I'll grant you that, but it is broken now, and your fortress is a ruin haunted by shadows. Later, you will introduce me to these phantoms and we will interview them together. Later . . . when you have returned from that strange and fascinating region to which you have retreated. I shall be waiting for you at the border, on your side of the border, so that we can discuss your experiences while their impression is still vivid in your mind. The battle is almost finished, my friend; it only remains for us to take the citadel and the best time for storming the barricades is at the moment when night and morning are still joined. If it were possible, I would stay and follow all the stages of your journey, but my time is not my own. Today is the twenty-second of December, the Day of National Deliverance; a pompous title I agree, but then fools love pompousness and most people are such fools. Your refusal to realise that was the cause of your downfall. It was your greatest weakness, Hanau. Ah well, you won't have to listen to the Commandmant's speech, you have been spared that. You can rest assured, though, that our separation will not be prolonged. I'll be back before the applause has died away. Au revoir, and a safe return.

He goes out. The metallic tapping and the voice are heard again, quiet at first, but gathering volume and intensity.

Voice of the Prison. Number Three! Number Three! Are you all right? Are you all right? Answer, Number Three! Are you all right?

There is a pause. Hanau groans and attempts to drag himself up into a sitting position.

Why don't you answer? Number Three . . . hold out! Hold out! Hold out, Number Three! We are with you! Hold out! Hold out!

The voice has been joined by other voices filling the night with whispers. Hanau is seized with a sudden spasm of fury. He grasps the bars of his cage and tries to shake them.

Hanau. They have murdered light
And nothing is left
But a bloody butcher's axe!
There is a conspiracy of shadows
Plotting against the moon!
Send a warning through
The customary channels!
Notify all cadres that
Winter will not end this year.

Music, harsh and discordant. From out of the shadows behind the cage appear two men and a woman dancing in the rhythm of a slow march. Behind them appears a fourth dancer whose movements are more violent than the others. He attempts to confront the prisoner to whom he bears a strong resemblance, but is prevented by the trio. This sequence should have the quality of a dream, which indeed it is, the dancers being merely the creations of the prisoner's delirium. The fourth dancer, to whom, for the purpose of clarification we shall refer as Robert, is Hanau's projection of himself. The music ceases abruptly, leaving the dancers grouped in attitudes of antagonism to Robert, who makes a grotesque and mocking bow to the prisoner.

Maria!

The woman slowly turns to him without speaking.

No word of greeting?
Anderson? Rolf?

The two men turn and face him.

They said that you were dead!

Maria. They say that you are damned!

Rolf. Broken to the bit of treachery!

Anderson.
They say that from now on you'll tread
Only the beaten track, where you will stand,
Bareheaded,
With a yellow permit in your hand.

Rolf. One of the patient ranks
Of those who sell themselves
For the bare expenses
Of a counterfeit existence.

Hanau. Who says such things?

Anderson.
Voices in every street.

Rolf. The sentries who guard the ultimate defences.

Maria. Whispers resound like tolling bells
In every channel of the underground.

Hanau. No!

Maria. Is it true?

Hanau. Maria, you knew me well,
We were together in the March days
When the deluge was unleashed
And all our world was covered
By its foul waters.

Anderson.
Rolf (*together*)
Is it true?

Hanau. No! No!
Am I to be murdered in duplicate,
Once by my enemies and once by you?
Here are voices that will speak for me,
Mouths that will testify on my behalf.

He tears open his prison jacket, exposing wounds and burns upon his body.

Tell those who whisper my damnation
That you heard my flesh scream 'Liars! Liars!'
Tell them I am an exposed nerve
Throbbing in the world's teeth,
That my body is a field of flowering wounds
Or a tree that's twisted to a crooked cross
On which my dreams are crucified.
The croaking voices of my wounds
Have begged for nothing except nothingness

And in my extremity, my friends
Have handed me the sponge of slander.
Tell them I am no longer human
But a void, a loathsome pit
Where agony ferments
And poisons every heart-beat
With its rank exhalations.

Robert. Have you said everything?

Hanau. Is he another of my accusers?

Robert. I am an old friend of ours.

Hanau. (*To the others*) Do you know him?

Maria, Rolf and Anderson shake their heads.

Why are you here?

Robert. Exile has been tedious.
It was time that I came home.

Hanau. Riddles!

Robert. To which you know the answers.

He addresses the others.

I, too, have a message to deliver;
Tell them that two of us are here,
Hanau and Hanau's prisoner,
And that salvation is in short supply.
Say that there's only enough for one of us
And that the one who wins it, wins it all
And shifts the whole burden of damnation
On to the other's shoulders.
Tell them that!

The others slowly turn and begin to move towards the shadows from whence they came.

Hanau. Don't go! Maria! My friends!
There is no message but the one I gave you!

They look back and raise their arms in a sorrowful farewell.

Hanau. Stay, just a little! Wait!
This creature is no prisoner.
Look at his face!
His trade is written there on every feature.
He's an informer, a tame crow
That wears the stool bird's plumage.

They go; very softly, like a faint echo, is heard the noise of tapping and the prison's voice. 'Hold out! We are with you!'

Robert. No, Hanau!
They are not with us.
No one can follow us
Along the spiral staircase
Of our soul.

Hanau. Who sent you here?
Answer me!
Where are you from?

Robert. From the frontier
Which you dare not pass.

Hanau. I have crossed all the frontiers.

Robert. Think!

Hanau. I know them all.
May is the first frontier
With its banners of spring
And eager faces, and after May
July – the armoured wall
Which guards the boulevards
And the clearing-house in Père-Lachaise.

Robert. And beyond July?

Hanau. The eastward journey
To the last frontier,
October.

Robert. And there,
Each honest traveller
Renews his passport.
Looks around and checks
The details of his own identity.
Have you done that?

Hanau. I've paid full fare
For every mile I've travelled,
That is enough! The worms
Which guard the terminus
Will need no affidavits
To prove that I am theirs.

Robert. The terminus was not our destination.

Hanau. Our destination! Ours!

Robert. Ours! Yours and mine.

Hanau. So this is the line of attack
Decided on by Graubard!
I'm to have a fellow-traveller,

The Doctor's own creation,
One of his spare eyes,
An honest tradesman
Who, for a living wage,
Will undertake to make
A corpse yield information.
Tell me, does Graubard instruct all his spies
In metaphysics, or did you specialise,
Graduating first in simple murder?

Robert. Why are you so afraid?

Hanau. Afraid? Of what? Of you?

Robert. Yes, of me.
Not of what you wish to think I am
But rather of who I am.

Hanau. I am past all fear
Except the fear of fearing.

Robert. You are afraid of silence
Because the voice of silence
Constantly repeats a fundamental question
Which, if your life and death are to achieve
Even a momentary significance,
Demands a truthful answer.
And in the course of answering
You may be forced to deal
The death-blow at your dreams
And see yourself completely stripped
Of all illusions, all supports, to find
That you are just a hollow shell
Left in the wake of an incurious wave
Upon a rotting beach.
It is because you are afraid
That you attempt to fill the void
With noisy speech and clamour,
For silence may bring sudden recognition
And the discovery of my identity
Would raise the question of your own,
Of proving that you are yourself
And not just one who's taken refuge
In a crowded fantasy because
He was constitutionally unfitted
To live at the same time as himself.

Hanau. Who are you?

Robert. My name is Hanau, Robert Hanau!
I am yourself.

Phrase of music. Hanau begins to laugh. The tapping on the pipes is heard. Suddenly, Hanau stops laughing and begins to talk with exaggerated calm.

Hanau. This is a dream, a crazy dream,
The product of the madness prison breeds.
Dreams grow like fungi in the dark,
Needing no special season for their seeds.
You are myself, it's true, for I created you
And I can banish you again as easily.
I am myself and master of myself;
If I exert my reason, swim against the stream
Of my delirium, you'll disappear.

Robert. Fear is your stimulus, not reason.

Hanau. Would I myself preach treason to myself?
You are a symptom of confinement
Like sleeplessness or loss of appetite,
No more significant than that
Grey pallor which is common to us all.

Robert. There is a difference:
I have the power of speech.

Hanau. This is a world of voices,
Every minute is articulate,
Every shadow has its blabbing tongue,
Even the bars have mouths.
Since the first day I was buried here
I have kept a careful check upon the signs
Which mark the progress of decay.
At first there was the voice, sudden, remote,
Ceasing abruptly on the unformed word,
Leaving a hollow where the silence swirled
And eddied, drowning me, causing me to panic
In the unclean flux of fear and doubt,
A doubt inhibiting all other thought;
But I fought the doubt with reason,
Argued that speech is a necessary habit,
Part of the complex process
Of the mind's co-ordination;
And rationalisation of my doubt
Destroyed my fear. For if a man here
Continues to explain the causes
Of his minor aberrations,
Then that man's sanity is sound.
You are an aberration,
A phantom, inhabiting my brain,

Whose function is to play companion
On the journey out of pain
Which follows each interrogation.
It always happens.
It's a form of compensation,
An aspect of the subtle defence-mechanism
With which the mind protects itself
From what the body must endure.
Once, as they beat me on the genitals,
I found myself preoccupied with time,
Worried because I'd lost count of the days,
Obsessed with the thought that I couldn't be sure
Whether the day was Saturday or not.
As if it mattered! For pain is timeless.

He laughs and then continues.

It is all time
But not all space.
That is what they cannot realise.
For when my body lies broken in their hands
My mind escapes the foul abyss of pain
And stands and watches.
Even when my ears are full of screams
And each small cell erupts in agony
There is part of me which stands outside
And reasons . . . reasons! . . . reasons!

Robert. I am that part,
The divided self.

Hanau. You are a dream.
I am reality.

Robert. Where did you acquire the habit
Of making such fine distinctions?
Reality is what is,
Not just what we accept.
If I'm unreal because I am a dream
Then all your thinking is unreal too,
For dreams are just as real as thoughts
Conceived as they are in the same womb
And fathered by the same experience.

Hanau. Leave me! I am exhausted.
I can talk no more.

Robert. Then I will talk and you can listen.

Hanau. Why do you torture me?

Robert. Why have you condemned us both to death?

Hanau. The decision was not mine.

Robert. They offered an alternative.

Hanau. To live on their terms
Would be less than life
And more than death.
Every breath would be a knife
Hacking at my self-respect.
Better to die once and be forgotten
Than to die a thousand times a day,
Murdered by memories, perpetually
Wounded by men's eyes, a symbol
Of contempt and lies, a rank, dead weed
Whose dry, marcescent leaves deceived no one
But reminded all of how the root was poisoned.

Robert. My question is unanswered:
Why are we to die?
For what reason?

Hanau. Because of my belief in truth.

Robert. Men have been known to die
For faith even when the basis
Of faith had crumbled
And disappeared.
Such men are like snakes
That cannot shed their skin.
Belief is sometimes the result
Of empirical knowledge but often
It is a sign of mental cowardice
Or self-inflicted blindness.

Hanau. And yet men die for it.

Robert. Men die for many reasons,
Few of which are laudable.
They die for words – or rather for
The sound of words – hypnotic
Echoes of the voices of the dead
Which fill their ears with loud commands
To come and join the band.
Some die of laziness;
Living demands much effort and much skill;

It is easier to die, to kill and be killed,
Less painful than facing the final truth
About themselves. Vanity also
Claims a high percentage of the martyrs,
Those who sell their lives for approbation
And die because their friends expect them to,
Lacking the strength of mind to oppose
The wishes of the most casual acquaintance.

Hanau. Your wish to live at any cost
Makes you contemptible.
You would reduce all life
To such a mediocre level
That by comparison
The instinct to survive
Would assume the proportions
Of an act of heroism.

Robert. Is it less heroic than
The instinct to escape from life through death?

Hanau. Yes! Yes!

Robert. And that is the fine belief we die for!

Hanau. I believe in life.

Robert. Only when it's tamed and wearing harness.

Hanau. I believe in man.

Robert. But not in men.

Hanau. I believe in the free mind
With its infinite capacity
For extending life,
In the flowering consciousness
Which can encompass all reality.

Robert. The mind which puts your body in a cage?

Hanau. The mind which holds the seed
Of all potential energy;
The starting-point and field
Of endless chain-reactions which can make
All things possible, even rejection
Of a familiar world of social anarchy
For an unknown universe
Where the mind will have to leap
Instead of crawling as it now does.
I believe in man's ability
And his intention to create

A social mechanism which will be
So perfect and so unobtrusive that
Man will have time to achieve humanity;
And living will assume such complex and
Such varied forms that men who look back
Will see us as symbols of abortive growth,
Crude products of a crude machine.

Robert. That *was* your creed.

Hanau. That *is* my creed.

Robert. And has your life run parallel
To your beliefs?
Suppose, for the sake of argument,
Your death should merely contribute
To that appalling waste of life
To which you are opposed. Suppose
Your dreams were merely symptoms of
A terrible neurosis which
Produced an epinastic growth,
Distorting life. Suppose that those
Whom you describe as enemies
Were really the only healthy ones
And that the host was sick because
Bacteria was waging war
Within the blood. Can you be sure
That your refusal to accept
Life as it is is not a proof
Of some deficiency in you?

Hanau. The words are yours,
The arguments are Graubard's.

Robert. What difference does it make?
Is your acceptance of a truth
Conditioned by who speaks it?

Hanau. These apologetics are not truth.

Robert. Have you never felt doubts
Or questioned your beliefs,
Weighed your illusion on the scales,
Or measured faith against experience?
Fear of doubt is doubt
In its acutest form.
It cripples the mind,
Burdens it with guilt,
Implies that the fabric of belief
Has worn too thin to bear the weight of truth.

Hanau. I have settled with my doubts.
In the light of analysis they disappear.

Robert. And yet there are men of judgement,
Men of undisputed courage
Who, on looking inward, saw
Their solid faith evaporate
Like so much mist. They were your friends
And suffered what you suffered,
Fought where you fought, starved,
Knew exile, poverty, humiliation;
But now they stand opposed, hostile
To the cause for which they sacrificed.
Can you explain the reason?

Hanau. Every battle has its casualties.
Only the strongest can survive.

Robert. Oh, let us finish with these platitudes!
Can you not see that the battle is lost,
That it is always lost, that defeat is implicit
In the nature of the dream? Admit it, man!
Your dream is broken by reality,
Consign the fragments to the attic
Where they can lie forgotten,
Toys to instruct a childish fantasy.
Remove the bandage from your eyes,
Scrutinise your cause,
Look revolution in the face.
Is its beauty unimpaired?
Is that the same fair mistress
That seduced your youth?
Is what you see the subtle instrument
Of history, the alchemical device
For changing dreams into reality?
Or is it a primitive machine
Which dominates its engineers?
Yours is not the only cause
That men have died for,
And gone on dying for,
Long after the cause had lost its meaning.
Each age imagines that it has produced
The perfect solution of all the problems.
And yet life doesn't change,
In its essentials it remains the same.
The seasons come and go,
With a show of flowers and snow
And beneficial rains.
The seas accept the gifts

That rivers bring from plains
And dying mountains.
Nothing is changed.
Men live and procreate
And the wise ones take
The kisses which life offers
Without requiring proofs
Of her virginity.
Hanau, it's not too late
For us to salvage what remains
Of time and life.
One word to Graubard . . .

Hanau. No!
The price is too high.

Robert. The price of freedom cannot be too high.

Hanau. Freedom!

Robert. Yes, freedom! Not the illusion
But the thing itself.

Hanau. Freedom from what? From self-respect?

Robert. From all unnecessary thought,
From dogmas, duties, rules,
From self-imposed responsibility.
Just let the mind be free of such restraint
And it becomes as buoyant as a bird,
Choosing its element to suit its mood.

Hanau. More like a carrion crow that picks the eyes
Out of a murdered conscience.

Robert. All my life I have been led
By that relentless part of you
Which dreams an iron dream.
Now I am asking for my liberty.

Hanau. I am weary of this argument.

Robert. Do not cover your face with the shroud,
Nor close your eyes,
Nor seek the company of shadows.
We can trample upon death
As the swan tramples upon the water
Or the horse upon the plain.
I want to show you a life like a swallow's flight,
Effortless, full of grace.
There is no virtue in the renunciation
Of life and the taste of her mouth.
Help me to escape the heavy burden

Which you have put upon me
And my freedom will win peace for both of us.

Hanau. Why do I listen to this voice?
And yet – what if the dream were false?

Faint music.

Robert. (*Ecstatically*) Listen! (*He stands tense and expectant.*)

The earth sings.

The music becomes fuller.

Keen blade of music swings through silence.
The sleeping spring awakes,
Opens the shutters of the darkness,
Breaks the long winter.
This is resurrection!

Percussion, loud and triumphant. The light in the cage lessens. Pools of coloured light form in the region outside the cage. Three girls leap from behind the rim of the darkness. One wears a dress of white, another a green dress and the third a dress of crimson. Robert leaps towards them and dances from one to the other. The music changes, becomes lyrical. The Moon enters dancing, a flaxen-haired girl in a silver dress, a blue hyacinth in her hand. On seeing her, Robert becomes perfectly still. The stage is suffused with blue light.

Robert. She has broken the cloud's net.
My heart sings after her,
Not the brown gull is she,
Not the blue tern
But the white seal on the black wave.

He attempts to approach her but constantly finds himself confronted by the other dancers.

White Girl. (*Confronting him*)
She is not the glad song
Nor the heart's music,
But the lost echo of a dead voice.

They dance.

Green Girl. (*Confronting him*)
She is not the rose,
Nor the carnation,
But the wax-lily without odour.

They dance.

Crimson Girl. (*Confronting him*)
She is not the warm flesh,
Nor the quick blood,
But the bone the wind polished.

Robert. Let me pass!

He reaches her and they dance together, but without touching, in rapt concentration. The other three come together and dance as a group on a fixed spot, following the rhythm with the upper halves of their bodies.

Robert. What lies beyond the horizons of your eyes?

Chorus. No fire,
No gift,
No final landscape.
Only ashes,
And the promise unfulfilled,
Only the desolate night.

Robert. Teach me the words of the song you sing
When the year trembles on the edge of spring.

Chorus. No song,
No voice,
No whispered answer.
Only echoes
And the silence after
The last reverberation;
Only the question.

Robert. Must I go on alone upon the quest
Never knowing the taste of your mouth,
Forgetting the lustre of your hair,
And the milky cluster shining there,
And the jewel of Sirius lying on your breast?

Chorus. The quest is a journey between heart-beats,
A voyage on the river of the blood.
There is no goal, only the journey,
There is no end, only the means.
There is no answer, only perpetual renewal
Of the question and the one who questions.

Robert attempts to embrace the Moon but she eludes him.

Robert. Go then! Be chaste and barren.
No, not chaste! Merely indifferent.
I have regained my sight!
I see you clearly now, a white-faced whore
Who walks the beat of darkness
Soliciting men's dreams,
Sowing infection in the crystal night.
Leave me! I'll sleep no more,
Nor strive to scale the rock of shadows
With its inaccessible pinnacle of dream.

The Moon glides off and the light fades.

The time of preparation is behind me.

The music changes. A simple, childish theme is introduced but still in dance tempo, rather like the 'Henry Martin' theme in Mahler's First Symphony. The three girls dance towards Robert. He seizes the girl in white and dances with her.

Can you answer riddles?

White Girl. I can only ask them.

Robert. Tell me your name.

White Girl. I have no name.

Robert. What are you then?

White Girl. A voyager on the wave's crest.

Robert. You too?
Would my hands falter in their praise
If I touched your sleeping breasts?

White Girl. The web of your hands would bruise my heart.

Robert. You are trembling.

White Girl.
With joy, with fear!
Oh, what is this I feel?

Robert. Time vibrates like a plucked string.

White Girl.
It is shrill in the ears.

Robert. The earth opens.
Jump!

White Girl.
Not yet!
Let me sleep a little longer.
Your quest has just begun.

Robert. The quest!
You know about the quest?
Who told you?

White Girl.
I read it in your eyes.

Robert. And what is the object of my quest?

White Girl.
The song unsung,
The rose unopened.

Robert. Who am I? Can you tell me that?

White Girl.
The welcome thief,
The destroyer who heals by wounding.
You are the dream who comes when he is beckoned.

Robert suddenly backs away from her.

Robert. A dream?

White Girl. Yes?

Robert. Your dream?

White Girl. My dream, the prisoner of my sleep.

Robert. You're lying!
I have turned my back on sleep.
You are the thief, not I!
I am myself and master of myself!

Hanau laughs in delirium.

Hanau. Four paces and the bars.
Four paces and the cage
And between each pace the heartbeat.

He laughs again but the music swells up and covers the sound. The girl in white dances away from Robert. The other two dancers move towards him. He dances with the girl in green.

Robert. Who are you?

Green Girl. One who waits at the crossroads.

Robert. Why do you wait?

Green Girl. For a stranger who will pass this way.

Robert. Are you sure he will pass?

Green Girl. There is no other way.

Robert. What is your name?

Green Girl. Until the stranger comes I have no name. When he has passed, a child will christen me.

Robert. When will he come?

Green Girl. In the spring, when death renews itself.

Robert. And how will you recognise this stranger?

Green Girl. He will come bowed under a great burden.

Robert. I wonder if his burden will be as heavy as mine.

Green Girl. It is my burden, not his. He only carries it until I'm ready. I am ready now.

Robert. And you will carry it alone?

Green Girl. Life is too heavy to be borne alone.

Robert. And yet it must be borne.

Green Girl. But not by us, always by the one who comes after – always by him.

Robert stands silent for a moment, facing the girl.

Robert. Do you know who I am?

Green Girl. Yes, I know.

Robert. Who?

Green Girl. You are the father of my unborn child.

Robert thrusts her away from him.

Robert. No! I'll not relinquish my identity. Was I born to play porter to your needs?

Green Girl. You can be rid of the burden, you can rest.

Robert. So I'm to lie in your body's tomb and wait for death! I'm to abandon the quest before it has begun!

Green Girl. My body is the guarantee of the quest's continuity.

Robert. But I am more than your body's instrument. I am a man, not an abstraction – neither a young girl's dream nor a woman's appetite. I am a free traveller and my burden is my own.

Music. The girl in green retreats. The crimson girl comes forward and dances alone. Robert attempts to escape but is always drawn back to her, like a moth drawn to a candle's flame.

Robert.

Red is the colour of hunger.

Crimson Girl.

Red is the colour of the harvest moon.

Robert.

My hunger was born in the moon of mists,
The white moon of March put an edge on it,
Fashioned it into a keen, cold blade.

Crimson Girl.

Dead is the blade without blood on it.
Put a handle on the blade of hunger,
Let it swing through the corn.

Robert. Why?

Crimson Girl. I like to hear it sing.

They dance together. The white girl and the green girl dance on a fixed spot and speak in chorus.

Chorus. She will have flesh.
In the morning,
At noon,
In the whispered night.
The delicate loin,
The tender undercut
The bishop in the blue mitre.
She will have that.
She will have that.

Robert and the girl in the crimson dress dance off. The light outside the cage fades. The two remaining girls retreat into the shadows. Hanau groans and the interior of the cage is illuminated again. Very softly, at first, the metallic tapping begins, grows louder. Voices are heard, filling the world of Hanau's nightmare.

Voice of the Prison.
Hold out! Hold out!
You are sick but the night is dying.
Hold out! Hold out!

Music.

Can you hear? Can you hear?
It is the song of the wall
And the voice is the voice of history.

Hanau. History has no voice,
No eyes, no ears,
No memory,
No anything.
Only prisons and prisons and prisons
Without end.

Voice of the Prison.
Do not break
Nor reject the prize,
Nor forsake the ranks
Of those who walk behind us
With the sunlight in their eyes.

Hanau. (*Shrieking*) Hanau is dead!
They murdered him with voices!

Music.

Voice of the Prison.
Earth stirs and the wind sings.
Roses bloom in the barrels of the guns.

The faint sound of marching feet is heard behind the music.

Hanau. Stragglers stumble, fall –
The moving columns cannot wait.
I have fallen to the wolves.

Voice of the Prison.
Your body is theirs.
Your death belongs to us.

Hanau. Robert? Robert?
You dead man's shadow!
Why did I learn your language of the blood?

The metallic tapping fades out. The music changes. Simultaneously the light inside the cage is dimmed and the curtain concealing the raised plane on stage-right is drawn. Almost the entire area of the plane is occupied by a great bed over which is spread a shimmering black coverlet. The girl in crimson is discovered asleep, her arms outstretched. Robert stands by the bed looking down at her. When he moves it is with the slowness of a man in a dream. Far away, in the distance, a trumpet sounds. Robert raises his head and listens.

Robert. It has a familiar sound.

The trumpet sounds again, slightly nearer. Robert takes a step away from the bed and then stops.

No, I will not leave this room. The journey is finished . . . finished. Here, in a moment of forgetfulness, I found myself, knew, for one brief instant, death and immortality and the sweet pain of birth.

He looks at his hands as if seeing them for the first time.

Skin instead of feathers, flesh where there was light . . . and yet I learned to fly like any bird across a night of immeasurable distance. How pale and cold the sun is compared with the fiery beacon of the body's joy.

He approaches the sleeping girl.

Sleep robs me of her love – or is it my wakefulness that makes her so inaccesible?

He kisses her lightly.

My love.

Crimson Girl. The tide will carry us.

Robert. Open your eyes.

Crimson Girl. Yes . . .

Robert. It's morning.

Crimson Girl. Oh, not yet.

Robert. It scrapes at the window like a hungry cat.

Crimson Girl. Send it away.

Robert. Do you remember . . .

Crimson Girl. Put your arms round me.

The trumpet sounds again, nearer.

Robert. There it is again. Did you hear it?

Crimson Girl. I didn't hear anything.

Robert. A sound like a knife tearing through the fabric of a dream.

Crimson Girl. You imagined it. Come, lie by my side. Sleep. Rest.

Robert. Yes . . . yes . . . to sleep enfolded in your body's warmth. Only that is real. And yet . . .

Crimson Girl. You are troubled.

Robert. I feel as if there were a bird imprisoned in my breast and it was trying to escape. The beating of its wings is shaking me.

Crimson Girl. I will open the door of the cage.

Robert draws back quickly.

Robert. What did you say?

Crimson Girl. Love, what is it?

Robert. I thought . . .

Crimson Girl. You have awakened too early.

She kisses him.

Robert. If only . . .

Crimson Girl. If only what?

Robert. Tell me who you are.

Crimson Girl. But you know.

Robert. Last night I knew – or thought I knew – but now . . . Your beauty is a secret thing – it places you beyond my reach, makes you so complete, so perfect, so unapproachable.

Crimson Girl. Unapproachable? I?

Robert. If only I could see beyond the barrier of skin and flesh and tissue. No, to see is not enough. I want to be that little pulse which trembles in your throat.

Crimson Girl. Oh, my love!

Robert. Will the moment of recognition ever come again?

Crimson Girl. It is ours forever.

Robert. No, it comes like a flash of lightning, then it's gone. It passes on a tide of sleep. Oh, it was criminal to sleep.

Crimson Girl. It was beautiful, warm . . .

Robert. It's strange that you didn't ask my name.

Crimson Girl. There was no need to ask. The moment I saw you I recognised you.

Robert. You did?

Crimson Girl. Of course.

Robert. Why 'of course'?

Crimson Girl. I had been waiting for you.

Robert. Waiting for me? But . . . tell me, who do you think I am?

Crimson Girl. I don't think – I know.

Robert. Who am I?

Crimson Girl. You are mine.

Robert thrusts her from him.

Robert. No! You fool! You fool!

Crimson Girl. Oh, love . . .

Robert. You have murdered love! I belong to no one but myself.

Crimson Girl. But I only wanted . . .

Robert. You wanted to take me prisoner, put out my eyes and have me live in a cage. You wanted a tame bird who would sing at your command. But you've failed! The snare is empty. I am still free!

Crimson Girl. Oh, do not leave me!

The trumpet sounds, loud and clear.

Robert. I remember now! The quest!

Crimson Girl. Stay a little longer!

Robert. And lose my inheritance?

He leaps off the raised plane on to the stage. Music. The light fades on the crimson girl. The curtain falls across the plane. The Moon, the girl in white and the girl in green appear out of the shadows. They dance round Robert, hemming him in. This episode should have the quality of a children's singing game.

Chorus. You cannot escape.
The quest is a stage
In the journey between
The bars of the cage.

Music.

Twist and turn,
Round about,
The cage is sealed
You can't get out.

Music.

Twist and turn
Turn and spin,
The bars are strong
And you are in.

Music.

Spin and twist
Twist and turn,
Go from us
But you'll return.

The music which accompanies the above sequence cross-fades with a slow theme. The crimson girl enters dancing with Graubard. She is heavy with child. The chorus fall away from Robert and breathe a great sigh.

Aa . . . a . . . a . . . ah . . .
Our sister has crossed tomorrow morning.
Aa . . . a . . . a . . . ah.

Robert take a step towards the dancers, then recoils.

Robert. Ho! my bloodied mare of night,
Who rides thee now?
Who makes thee prance across the water?
Who touches thy flanks with spurs of ivory?
Who bridles thee with diamond bit?
Ho! my chestnut mare,
You carry a dead man in the saddle,
A bladder of wind.

Crimson Girl.
It could have been your child.

Graubard.
Come!

They dance off.

Robert. Does life consist of nothing but a choice between different forms of bondage? What am I searching for?

Chorus. For rest,
For peace,
Escape from the ceaseless quest.

Robert. Is there no blessed regime,
No fertile valley,
No green oasis,
Lying between
The stony ridge of living
And the gulf of sleep?

Chorus. There is a valley between the breasts
Where bliss is.
There is a healing well of kisses,
In the loved one's eyes
A blessed region lies,
In the arms' embraces
In the green oasis.

They approach him with gestures of supplication.

Robert. You sing with the voices of nightingales but your dreams are ravens on the wing for carrion.

White Girl. My lips are a cure for thirst.

Robert. They are camouflage for teeth: white, sharp teeth that would gnaw my soul to shreds.

Green Girl. My hands could teach your body how to sing.

Robert. They are tipped with iron claws.

The trumpet sounds, far away.

Chorus. Words bruise,
Love sighs,
The mind is blind,
The blood is wise.
Sleep is kind,
The spirit tries
In vain to gain
The world which lies
Beyond the bars.
The stars are far away
But love is near.

The music reaches a climax. Robert, retreating before the advancing chorus, finds himself against the cage. He covers his ears with his hands to shut out the intolerable sound of the shrill violins. The trumpet sounds again, nearer. Hanau begins to laugh. The music fades. The chorus avert their faces from the cage and slowly leave the stage.

Robert. Hanau!

The laughter ceases abruptly.

Hanau!

Hanau draws himself up into a sitting position.

Hanau. You!

Robert. Yes.

Hanau. Well?

Robert. You were laughing in your sleep.

Hanau. I was dreaming,
I thought that I was free
And you were in this cage.

Robert. A strange dream.

Hanau. Why have you returned?

Robert. To rest a little.

Hanau. Have you tired of freedom then?

Robert. I am tired of chasing its shadow.
I am sick of the weight of my body.

Hanau. This is rank blasphemy from you.

Robert. My body is a tethered goat,
An appetite with horns,
A slave condemned to tread
The dwindling circle of its own hot lust.
Round and round it goes
Until it stands, helpless at last,
Held fast against the post,
Incapable of any movement
Except the awkward turn
Which marks the repetition
Of the senseless journey.

Hanau laughs.

Hanau. And this is your great discovery!
You can trample upon death
As the swan tramples upon the water!
Or so you said, but instead
You have trampled upon life
And made as much impression
As the snail which tramples the bare stone.
You wanted freedom!
Not the illusion but the thing itself;
Freedom from dreams, from rules,
From self-imposed responsibility.

Robert. The quintessence of freedom.

Hanau. The quintessence of death.

Robert. I will find it yet.

Hanau. Only in the grave.

Robert. I will discard my body,
Forswear all action,
Except the action of the mind,
For the mind has neither weight nor mass,
Only motion.
I will go among the mountain peaks
Where the air is rarefied
And the blind lichens feed on time.
I will climb a pinnacle of abstract thought
And there on the summit
Build a laboratory where
I will distil pure Knowledge,
Reducing it until I find
A perfect crystal of reality.

Hanau. And how will you use this knowledge?

Robert. Use it? Why should I use it?
To possess it is enough.

Hanau. In isolation?

Robert. Why should I force a vintage wine
On men who are satisfied with water?

The trumpet sounds.

Hanau. There is not much time left.

Robert. Are you sending me away?

Hanau. Yes . . . yes . . .
There are doubts to be resolved,
Questions to be answered . . .
Is there another way out of the night . . .

His voice is drowned in a great surge of music. The curtain, concealing the raised plane stage-left of the cage is drawn, revealing Graubard seated on a glass throne. He wears white overalls patterned with eyes. In his right hand he holds a human skull and in the other a large hypodermic syringe. At his feet kneels a girl in the uniform of a nurse. The insane enter, dancing on the stage below. There are four men and two women and they wear grey, loosely fitting shirts and grey trousers or skirts. Their number includes an architect with delusions of grandeur, a young labourer with persecution mania, an old man with catatonic schizophrenia, an old woman with euphoria and a young woman with peace-mania. Suddenly, Graubard raps on the skull. The dancers freeze. He touches the nurse's head with the syringe as though knighting her.

Graubard. Arise, our best-beloved subject. Serve us well and see that none disturb the peace and quiet of our realm.

Nurse. Amen. (*She takes the syringe.*)

Graubard.

Bid the dawn approach.
We are ready to assume
The cares and burdens
Of our daily office.

Fanfare of trumpets.

Nurse. Yes, my lord.

Graubard. And the doors?

Nurse. All bolted, my lord.

Graubard (*To the architect*) Hey! Caitiff, varlet, rogue, vassel, serf, wretch, miscreant, scullion, rascal!

Architect. Who, me?

Graubard.

Aye, thee!
Hast had any dreams of late?

Architect.

Last night I dreamt the past was dead
And all the people of the world
Had gathered to attend the funeral.

Graubard. (*To the nurse*)

Be thou my scribe, my cunny thou,
And let the purport of the prisoner's words
Be taken down and used as evidence.

He hands her a notebook. Meanwhile the young labourer has begun to sway backwards and forwards like a man wrestling with invisible chains. Suddenly he takes a tremendous leap into the air.

Labourer. (*Triumphantly*) Pawn to King's square.

The nurse directs the nozzle of the syringe at him and sprays him with water. The tension leaves his body, he slowly sinks to the ground and assumes the foetal position. Graubard leaps to his feet and begins to rant like a barker in a side-show.

Graubard. A prize for the little lady! 'Ere y' are! 'Ere y' are! Four for six! Four for six! Hit 'em on the top to win. You can't afford to miss! (*He sits down again and addresses the architect.*) Dids't say a funeral?

Architect. A funeral.

Graubard. Thou art morbid.

Architect.

It was no melancholy spectacle:
Men sang for joy and women danced
As they accompanied the corpse
On its last journey through the streets
Of the perfect town which I had built.

Young Woman.

If it is lost forever,
Then I am lost.

She approaches the old man, who stands perfectly still, looking at the ground.

What have they done with peace?
Where have they hidden it?
You are old and must know many things.

Graubard.

Quiet, wench! Restrain thyself!
Curb thy depraved appetite.
Wouldst have bismuth?
Wouldst have insulin?

Young Woman. No . . . no . . . no . . .

She cowers away from the old man.

Graubard. (*To the architect*) Proceed!

Architect.

At last the cortège reached the city walls
Where, ready to receive the grisly corpse,
A tall, unfinished campanile stood
Still wrapped in scaffolding. And there
A score or so of masons were engaged
In carving figurines and bas-relief
To decorate the raised entablature.
An artist more proficient than the rest,
An old man, sick with memory, in whom
Imagination had become diseased
Fashioned a mask, the image of your face
To be the centre of a monstrous group
Of gargoyles.
But scarcely had he finished carving it
When the stone was seized with sudden nausea,
The walls began to vomit powdered quartz,
A spasm of convulsions rocked the tower
Which tossed upon the writhing pilasters,
The bending transoms parted from the walls,
Leapt into the air and in an instant
Nothing remained of the great catafalque
Except a heap of dust and rubble,

Which soon was scattered by the cleansing wind.
The past was dead and memory was dead
And in that moment, time was born again.

Graubard. By St Freud! Thou art a pert, persistent paranoic. But I'll cure thee yet! We are inured to men's ingratitude and heed it not.

Architect. Ingratitude? Why should I be grateful?

Graubard. Did we not offer sanctuary to thee when thou wast sore beset by cares and troubles? Did we not offer thee a quiet retreat from the clash and turmoil of an embattled world? Look around thee, caitiff, and see if thou wantest aught. Dost want for food or raiment, a bed to sleep in or a roof to shelter thee? Nay! Thou hast everything that most men toil for. Ay, and time to think, to ponder life's incalculable problems. Here, we have built for thee a private world with all the civilised amenities and none of life's responsibilities. Here thou canst live in idleness tended by fair damsels in a world without collision. And still thou art not satisfied. Thou needs must dream and share thy dreams.

Robert slowly approaches Graubard.

Robert. Excuse me . . .

The insane advance upon him eagerly.

Insane. What news? What news? What news?

Architect. Has the edifice collapsed?

Young Woman. What have they done with peace?

Labourer. Are the pieces threatened?

Old Man. What is the meaning of meaning?

Insane. What news of the sleepers?

Graubard. (*Jumping to his feet*) Avaunt! Avaunt, thou carrion, or by the blood of St Adler I'll stop thy sweet pudding at lunch.

The insane fall away from Robert, whimpering.

Now, sirrah, speak! What meanest thou by intruding on us thus?

Robert. I am looking for a refuge, A sanctuary for meditation.

Graubard. Art a sage? Art a philosophical fellow? Dost dream?

Robert. No, I have turned my back on dreams.

Graubard. Then this is no place for thee. None but dreamers are accommodated here. Thy place is in the city of the plain.

Robert. I have searched there
And all I found was shadows.

Graubard. What art thou searching for?

Robert. For freedom, truth.

Graubard. Freedom? Truth? Thou art obsessed. Oh, thou art sick . . . Dost alternate between despair and ecstasy?

Robert. I have known both.

Graubard. A schizophrenic! I'll take my oath on't! He hath a pale and hungry look. He feels too much. Such men are dangerous.

Nurse. My lord, we have expected the arrival of this man.

Robert. Expected me? Impossible!

Nurse. I have his case-history here.

Graubard. Read it.

The nurse reads from the notebook.

Nurse. Name: Robert Hanau. Sex: male. Profession: man. Condition: malcontent. Description: Head, one; torso, one; limbs, four. Blood, skin, bone-tissue, nervous system central, nervous system sympathetic, endocrine system, etcetera. Distinguishing marks: acromegalous reasoning powers. Prognosis: sudden death. Diagnosis: fragmented mind, schizophrenia, hebephrenia, psycho-neurosis, psychopathic condition, paranoia, erotomania, etcetera. Symptoms: mania, phobia, delusional, confusional, obsessional, hallucinate. Tendency towards violence. Very dangerous.

Graubard. Dost thou admit the charges?

Robert. I admit nothing.

Graubard. Put him to the question! Pentethol!

He claps his hands. The other patients leap upon Robert and drag him towards Graubard.

Insane. Forgive us. We know not what we do.

The nurse sprays Robert with the syringe. The insane fall away from him. Music. The light changes, becomes dimmer. Robert staggers about the stage. The insane huddle together and speak in chorus in rhythm with his footsteps.

One, two, three, four,
Four paces and the bars.
One, two, three, four,
Four paces and the cage.
One pace, one heartbeat,
One pace, one heartbeat,
One pace, one heartbeat.
Four paces, one breath,
Four paces, one breath,
Four paces, one breath.

One breath, one life.
One cage, one life,
One cage, one death.
One breath, one life,
One cage, one death.

Hanau. (*Screaming*) Robert!

The music stops. Robert comes to a halt and stands facing Graubard. The light has faded so that now only Robert and the skull in Graubard's hand are illuminated. The rest are just amorphous clots of shadows. A drum begins to beat in a slow, steady rhythm.

Nurse. Take a deep breath. Relax. This won't hurt.

Mic. Voice.
Deep breath. Deep breath. Deep breath. Deep breath.

Nurse. Aina, peina, para, peddera, pimp, ithy, mithy, owera, lowera, dig, ain-a-dig, pein-a-dig, par-a-dig, peddera-dig, bumfit, ain-a-bumfit, pein-a-bumfit, par-a-bumfit, peddera-bumfit, giggy . . . out.

Mic. Chorus. You're out! You're out! You're out. Out! Out! Out! Out! Out! Out! Out!

The insane hiss. Graubard raps on the skull.

Graubard. Wilt swore to spike the ruth, the bold ruth and butting but the ruth?

Robert. I will.

Graubard. Twelfth man and true-blue are near to steer the dead events.

Insane. Now is the tomb of all dead men so run to the blade of the party.

Graubard. Violence in port!

Mic. Chorus. Tick-tock! Tick-tock! Tick-tock! Tick-tock!

Graubard. Thou are abused of being a devoded man, of soaking to effect undesirable and fundamenial changes inter social larder. Beerover thoo hast pants-pressed the litter of the Beaverly lore which sues a subject of the state cannote fush for thrut in Static waters widoubt a spermit, farm, herstiffibate or lessence. Aleso, yow hast with Alice, a whore bought, maid sindray effords to Walter the moaning of ruality. Dost oddman the charges?

Robert. I do.

Graubard. Hast anything to pay differ I pronoun syntax against thee?

Robert. Nothing.

Graubard. Then thou art conflicted and condamned. I phoned thee guilty, double one double one.

Nurse. Allelulia!

The insane clap their hands three times. The light changes.

Graubard. Thou art now officially enrolled as a citizen of this secluded realm and here thou wilt reside until successive insulin assaults have breached thy madness.

Robert. I am not mad.

Insane. We are not mad.

Graubard. Oh, but thou *art*, infectiously and dangerously mad. All thought pursued beyond a certain limit is a form of madness. If thought were naught but what it seems, then it were nothing. If it were self-sufficient then 'twould be a toy to while away an idle hour, but no! Thought must needs extend itself in action and therefore must be dammed up at the source. Look round upon thy fellows and see if they are not mad. Observe that withered crone who stands behind thee. See how she smiles and smiles and smiles, her gaze intent upon her secret thoughts. What is it makes her smile? Some meditated crime against the state, some flaw in man that only she can see? I tell thee, whatsoever be the cause of her euphoria, the effect is dangerous, for that perpetual, mocking smile would destroy the basic *fear* on which all laws and institutions here are founded.

The young labourer leaps into the centre of the stage.

Labourer. The Knight is finished, taken en-passant!

Insane. Ah!

Graubard. This wretch hath persecution mania. He doth imagine he is a pawn and that I, his benefactor, have ordained that he should occupy an unimportant square upon the board. If this were the full extent of his strange malady, he would be harmless, but he must constantly incite the other pawns to clear the board of more important pieces.

The young labourer begins to march and countermarch across the stage.

Insane. One, two, three, four,
King's Pawn to King four.

Labourer. Advance, pawns! Double file!

Insane. Five, six, seven, eight,
Pawn queens. Checkmate!

The labourer jumps on to Graubard's plane. The nurse sprays him with water and he falls on to the stage.

Graubard. Could he but learn the rules of the game, he would be cured, just as yonder wench there would be cured if she'd accept her biological responsibilities. Hey, wench, approach and be acquainted with a friend!

The young woman backs away from Robert.

Young Woman.
I will not bear your child,
Nor any man's.
I will not carry the seed of death.
What have they done with peace?
Where have they hidden it?

She moves around, peering into the shadows.

So many dead in the world,
So many dying . . .
I'll breed no more,
My body is sealed.

Robert steps towards her.

No, do not touch me!
It is the sowing time
And I am fertile.
If you touch me
I will conceive murders,
Bear a litter of skulls.

Architect.
Golgotha was built of skulls,
Paris and Byzantium.
Colchis was built on a fever-swamp
And Nineveh was plagued by flies
That swarmed in Tigris River.
Bone and blood built Troy town,
But the blood was green
And men were poisoned
By the sewers of Babylon.
Give me a plot of ground,
A river and two hills
And a tenth part of the energy
Which is dissipated in a day of war
And I will build a city
Like a song. A place
Where nothing will offend the eye
And nothing will be hidden.

Graubard. Thou art dreaming again.

Architect.
If I cannot build a dream
Then I'll not repair a nightmare.
I will sit on my hands and listen.
I will hear it soon.

Robert. Hear what?

Architect.

The crack of doom,
The rumble of collapse
The world is breaking up
Like sheet-ice in the spring.

Insane. Crack! Crack! Crack!

Graubard groans.

Nurse. My lord, what is it?

Graubard.

Our belly doth complain.
Our privy councillor speaks.

The old man, who until now has stood without moving, suddenly begins to twitch his body. The spasm becomes acute. He takes a few quick steps towards the other patients and then stops.

Old Man. It means . . . it means . . .

Insane. Yes?

Old Man. Take away the stone.

Insane. Lazarus, come forth!

Nurse. My lord, the catatonic symptoms . . .

Graubard. Back, dotard, back! Get thee back into thy rigid self!

Graubard clasps his stomach and groans.

Old Man.

The trapped thought swings
In the body's cell,
Ricochets on taut nerves
Stretched on hollow worlds,
Ascends the spiral grooves,
Beats on a roof of skull.
Tries to fly beyond
The wall of muscle,
Atrophies and falls
In nothingness.
Eyes stare inwards,
Gaze at interior suns,
Glaze under creeping cataracts.
Ears fill with wax
Hear only muffled whispers of the blood.
Thought dies in this padded world,
Returns defeated to its source,
Lives only when the body responds
To the world beyond the body.

Where is the world now?
I will heal it and be healed.

Graubard groans and leaps to his feet.

Graubard. A stool! A stool! My kingdom for a stool!

He runs off, followed by the nurse. Music. The insane begin to dance.

Robert. Wait! There is not much time.

Architect. Time for what?

Robert. Time to revolt!

Insane. No, no! He'll stop the sweet pudding at lunch!

Robert jumps on to the raised plane, the better to address them.

Robert. They say that we are mad,
But is it mad to dream
When dreams are better than reality?

Old Man. What is reality?

Robert. There are enough of us assembled here
To overpower the doctor and the nurse.

Insane. It is against the law.

Robert. The law of the needle!
Freedom can end that law.
Freedom lies at your finger-tips!
Reach out and it's yours.

Architect. Freedom . . .

Robert. With freedom, you can build your perfect town.

Architect. Yes.

Robert. With freedom, the game is ended.

Labourer. Yes.

Robert. With freedom, peace will come again.

Young Woman. Yes.

Robert. With freedom, thought is not fettered in the brain.

Old Man. Yes.

Robert. Freedom is yours if you will take it!

Insane. Yes.

Graubard and the nurse enter.

Graubard. What is this, a mutiny?

Robert. An awakening of the dead.

Graubard. In this, our realm, the dead only awaken at meal-times. (*To the insane*) Hast thou forgotten the terrors of the outside world? Remember how the sane ones hunted thee like dogs?

Robert. Would you have freedom?

Graubard. Wouldst miss thy lunch?

Insane. No . . . no . . .

Robert. Remember your dreams.

Graubard. (*To the nurse*) Fetch thou some warmer raiment for our friend.

Exit nurse.

What, dost desert thy deliverer already?

The insane cower back.

It is well. It is a sign that thou all art cured. Thou, master architect, wilt be released this afternoon, and if thy mind hath not lost all its cunning thou shalt proceed upon an undertaking which shall bring thee fame and augmented rations. Tomorrow thou wilt proceed to build an annexe to this place and in return thou shalt have duff for breakfast, lunch and dinner every day. Art satisfied?

Architect. Yes.

Old Man. A sweet at every meal?

Graubard. At every meal, and thou shalt have it, too. For thou shalt teach the young how to sterilize thought.

Old Man. Yes.

Graubard. As for thee, my good Pawn, thou shalt become a Pawn of substance and teach the other Pawns the rules of our game.

Labourer. Yes.

Young Woman. And what of me?

Graubard. The seed will flourish in thy womb and in the time of harvest thou wilt bear fruit for thine own sustenance.

Young Woman. Yes.

Graubard. This is farewell. Go forth and multiply, and dream no more.

Insane. Yes.

They turn and file out like sleep-walkers. The nurse enters, carrying a strait-jacket.

Robert. No! No! It must not end like this!

The nurse and Graubard fall upon him and force him into the strait-jacket.

Graubard. This is for thine own safety.

Robert. Let me go!

The trumpet sounds.

Graubard. 'Tis time for lunch. Come.

He goes off, followed by the nurse. Robert stares at the strait-jacket in stunned bewilderment.

Hanau. Robert!

Robert's mouth moves spasmodically, but no words come.

Robert!

The metallic tapping is heard, grows in intensity.

Voice of the Prison. Are you all right? Are you all right?

Robert. There is no road back! We are lost . . . lost . . . lost . . .

The tapping reaches a peak of unendurable intensity. Music swells up, harsh and dissonant. The curtain falls *[End of Part One]*

[**PART TWO**] *An hour has elapsed. The cage apears to have increased its floor area and the shadows cast by the bars radiate over the stage like a great spider's web. To the left of the cage is a raised platform on which is built the interior of a railway carriage with a door at the back leading into a corridor. Hanau is seated in the cage staring straight in front of him. Robert, outside, leans against the bars, his back towards Hanau. Music is heard in the background, the slow march of an earlier sequence. A steel door clangs and the music stops.*

Hanau. And there is no retreat.

Robert. None.

Hanau. Nothing to do but wait.

Robert. Nothing.

Hanau. No manumission that would leave us whole.

Robert. No.

Hanau. No life without stigmata.

Robert. No.

Hanau. Only bars and silence.

Robert. Death and silence.

Hanau. The future and silence.

Robert. Yes.

Hanau. No company but the dying.

Robert. And the dead.

Hanau. Only brittle words,
Voices of hands on metal pipes.

Robert. Only that.

Hanau. We have come full circle.

Robert. Yes.

Hanau. You said . . .

Robert. I said what I was told to say.

Hanau. By whom?

Robert. By you.

Hanau. If you had been less inconsistent . . .

Robert. That was how you created me.

Hanau. Yes . . . in my own image . . .

Robert. Yes.

They are silent for a moment.

Hanau. Well?

Robert. (*Turning to him*) Well?

Hanau. Has anything been left unsaid?

Robert shakes his head.

We have lived dangerously.

Robert. We have lived.

Hanau. But to what purpose? If only one could be sure which was the credit side of one's accounts.

Robert. Death will dispose of all our doubts.

Hanau. But not resolve them. Oh, there should be rules for dying!

Robert. There is one rule: death should precede corruption.

Hanau. Yes . . . yes . . . but can a man repudiate his doubts and still be incorruptible?

Robert. What is life but a tight-rope stretched between two doubts? No one ever reaches the other side.

Hanau. And yet if one could see the other side clearly for just an instant, the ultimate fall would lose its terrors. These are difficult days for dying. Life is so confused – such a complex process.

Robert. And such a simple conclusion.

Hanau. Did the others doubt,
The ones who went before –
Those who fell at the shooting wall,
The fustian men in the hulks,
The dead at the Ebro River?

Robert. Theirs was a simple dream,
Remote as a star,
Convenient symbol of unrealised hope.

Hanau. But we have touched our dream,
Fondled it with bloody hands,
Lain with it through a long winter,
Fed it with bitterness and sour despair.
It was a seedling nurtured in the mind
But we transplanted it in stony soil.
Can it survive the climate of reality?

Robert. It has survived.

Hanau. Would the others recognise it now,
Or would they mourn its metamorphosis?

Robert. We will never know.

Hanau. Why not? You are still free.

The trumpet sounds.

Robert. Am I?

Hanau. It will be the last journey.

The trumpet sounds again.

Robert. What if they deny the dream?

Hanau. Then we die for nothing.

Music. Robert begins to go off.

Robert. I will tell them you are coming.

Exit Robert.

Hanau. They will not hear – or if they hear
They will not understand.

Music fades out.

Death is not curious
For it negates all questions
And takes, without selection,
What life discards,
Fragments of dreams,
Abandoned hopes
And bones of dead desires.

The metallic tapping is heard accompanied by whispering voices.

Voice of the Prison.
Do not despair,
Night will not last forever.

Hanau. How can there be night
When there is no morning?
Time has stopped!

Voice of the Prison.
Time stands on the rim of night
Armed with grenade of sun
And blade of morning.

Phrase of music.

Earth stirs in the trough of sleep.

Mic. Chorus.
It is the time of decision.

Voice of the Prison.
Deep fissures rend the darkness.

Mic. Chorus.
It is the time of decision.

Voice of the Prison.
Now the moon is struggling in an ambush of cloud.

Mic. Chorus.
It is the time of decision.

Voice of the Prison.
The stars open their eyes.

Mic. Chorus.
It is the time of decision.
The past dies,
The minute sings,
The night is full of wounds,
The hammer rings on the anvil.
The dead rise from their tombs.
The night is torn
On the rock of dawn.
Hope is born
In the disinherited.
Now is the time,
The reaping time,
For all good men,
When once again,
Then all good men –
Now is the time,
Now is the time,
Now is the time . . .

Behind the above chorus the sound of a railway train is heard, synchronising with the voices. It grows louder until the voices are no longer audible. The light in the cage is faded down and simultaneously the railway carriage is illuminated. Robert is discovered seated.

Hanau. Ask them how long the night will last.

The train gathers speed, the rattle of the wheels becomes louder.

Voice of the Prison.
Wind howls
And the wheels flash
On the strip of hypnotic parallel.
Plumes of sparks
Bloom for an instant's season.
Cities pass and seas and mountains
Centuries and dreams are left behind.
It's the Express History,
The dark comet across the universe!

From the corridor a man enters the railway carriage. He wears the semi-uniform of a Spanish dynamitero.

Mic. Voice. Francisco Piera, coal-miner: died in the siege of Oviedo, nineteen-thirty-seven.

Piera sits facing Robert. A woman enters. She is dressed in the costume of the National Guard adopted by the citizens of the Faubourg Montmartre in the Paris of 1871.

Mic. Voice. Clémence Gaudry: died in the commune of Paris, eighteen-seventy-one.

She sits facing Robert. A man enters wearing worker's attire of the period of 1840.

Mic. Voice. James Guthrie, weaver: died in the struggle for the Charter, eighteen-hundred-and-forty.

He sits facing Robert. The sound of the train is held at peak for a moment then faded down until it is scarcely audible.

Piera. Well?

Robert. Forgive me if I have disturbed your peace.

Gaudry. Is the struggle ended then?

Robert. It grows fiercer every day.

Gaudry. Then how can we know peace?

Robert. But surely for the dead . . .

Gaudry. Yes, we are dead,
Our bodies are broken.
The winds and rains have scattered us,
Washed us into the earth's mouth,

Left no residue of bone or hair.
We have fed woundwort and willow-herb,

Guthrie. An' the muckle fishes.

Piera. Yes, we are dead,
And yet we are more a part of life
Than the sleek-haired pistoleros
Who walk across our graves
Carrying death in their portfolios.

Gaudry. Our wounds are banners.

Guthrie. Our deiths are sangs.

Piera. And our deeds are dynamite,
Exploding in the living memory.

Robert. Yours was a time of hope –
You died whole.

Gaudry. I died on a grey morning
While the smoke erected twisted columns
Above the ruins of Belleville
And wrote the Commune's epitaph
In dirty smears across the sky.
You talk of hope!
But hope was murdered,
Butchered by the Versaillese.
It died a thousand deaths on every street,
And left its corpse at every barricade.
We who had lost a thousand battles
And survived to fight among the graves
In Père Lachaise and die before the wall
Were not sustained by hope but by despair.

Robert. You had grown accustomed to defeat,
Learned to embellish death with words,
Like 'justice', 'freedom', 'human dignity'.

Gaudry. And are the words forgotten?

Robert. Time has blurred their meaning.
They are like old shoes
Which anyone can wear.

Guthrie. The words were bleezin' suns
That lichtit the blackest corners
O' oor makeshift world.

Robert. But nothing has changed.

Guthrie. Ay, we were changed,
For we kent then wha we were
An' whit we were and whit we could become.

Robert. All because of a few tattered phrases?

Guthrie. We made the words oor ain
An' sent them singin' doon the sunless roads,
Whaur the shilpit collier-bairns crooched agin the rock.
They ris abune the stramach o' the looms
An' folk wha stuid perpetually stoopit
Straightened their shoulder an' minded they were men.

Robert. The words were abstractions!
What could they mean to you?

Guthrie. They pit a limit tae the time o' skaith.
They were comets i' the nicht
An' by their licht I fund a path
Which sprauchled heigh abune the wa's o' darkness.
The words were blyth an' but for them
Ma life had a' been mirk . . .
The weirdless agony o' birth,
The blin' years tint i' the mill stour,
An' deith claumin' at ma thrapple
I' the ugsome hold o' a transportation hulk.

Robert. Yes, it was different for you.

Gaudry. How was it different?

Robert. You never had to bear the burden of a victory.
You minted deathless phrases out of dreams.
Ours is the heavier task: we build a world.

Gaudry. It is a task for heroes.

Robert. The junk and debris of the ages
Is our inheritance.
We carry it upon our backs.

Gaudry. But you are strong.

Robert. There are times when even the strongest men
Are overcome with weariness and yearn
To bed down in the rubble of the world
And sleep . . . and sleep . . . and sleep.

Piera. We have slept too long.
The time of awakening is overdue.

Robert. Have you never doubted the moment of awakening?

Piera. We have doubted it and feared it,
For who is not vulnerable in sleep?
And yet on that brittle noon,
When the smoking guns
Were stuttering calumnies

Against tomorrow
And death ran howling
Through Oviedo's streets,
I knew a moment of reality
When history spoke,
Delivered its ultimatum:
Awake or perish!
And even as the sleepers murdered us,
I knew they were condemned,
For they were deaf and did not hear the voice.
And they were blind
And thought their dunghill was a mountain peak
Comparable with the highest ranges of tomorrow.

Robert. No one has seen tomorrow's peaks.

Piera. But we have seen the dunghill
And watched life decay.
If, out of all the riches of the earth
We cannot create conditions for survival
Then it is time that man was written off
As one of evolution's failures.

Gaudry. Ours was a time of hope, you said,
But yours is the time of labour;
History is brought to bed with child,
A new world struggles in the womb.

Robert. Suppose the child is born deformed?

Gaudry. Then you will know that history
Has done the act of darkness with the past.

There is a roar of wheels as the train enters a tunnel. The carriage is plunged in darkness. Hanau shrieks in delirium.

Hanau. Robert! Robert!

Voice of the Prison.
The lines branch
Left and right,
Route to the sun,
Road to the night.
There are no brakes,
There's a world behind,
Signals flash,
But the driver's blind.
Hands on levers,
Fumble, grope,
Without skill,
Without hope.

The train gathers speed. Suddenly it emerges from the tunnel. The carriage is illuminated again but Guthrie, Gaudry and Piera have disappeared and in their places sit three other passengers: Graubard, balancing a brief-case on his knees and looking like a prosperous man of business; the commercial traveller asleep in a corner; and the brave little woman asleep in the other corner. The sound of the wheels fades.

Robert. Where are they?

Graubard. I beg your pardon?

Robert. My friends . . . they've disappeared!

Graubard. Really!

Robert. They were dead.

Graubard. Ah! You were dreaming.

Robert. Was I? Then what am I doing here?

Graubard. You are travelling.

Robert. Yes, but where to? Where is this train going?

Graubard. Does it matter? Surely one should travel for the sake of travelling. Travel broadens the mind.

Robert. Your face . . . it seems familiar. I'm sure I've seen you somewhere.

Graubard. One of my many brothers, perhaps, or a distant cousin. We are a large family.

Robert peers through the window.

Robert. Darkness, nothing but darkness and a trail of sparks.

Graubard. One can easily dispose of the night.

He draws the blind down.

You see, it's very simple.

Robert. I've forgotten something . . . I have an appointment and yet I'm sure I shouldn't be here. Isn't there some way of stopping the train? I must get out of here! I can't breathe!

Graubard. Please! . . . please! You'll wake the other passengers. Why not try to sleep? Sleep is a wonderful thing.

The train rocks violently. Robert is thrown off balance. The sound of the wheels is heard for a moment as the train gathers speed.

Robert. Why are we travelling so fast if we aren't going anywhere?

Graubard. We are going downhill.

The sound of the train is faded up again, travelling still faster. Robert stands up in sudden panic.

Robert. There's something wrong. I feel it. We are leaving the rails.

Graubard. Nerves! Just nerves!

Robert. I tell you, this train is out of control. There's something wrong. Perhaps the engineer is ill!

Graubard. There is no engineer on this line.

Robert. No engineer? Then who drives the train?

Graubard. It drives itself.

Robert. But the risk!

Graubard. Exactly. That is what makes travel so fascinating.

Robert. But surely the passengers . . .

Graubard. The passengers have not complained about our administration.

Robert. Your administration!

Graubard. I am a director of the company which operates this line.

Robert. And yet you don't know where we're going?

Graubard. I do not.

Robert. But it's criminal!

Robert shakes the other two passengers.

Wake up! Wake up!

Commercial Traveller. Eh! Eh! What is it?

Robert. We're in danger. The engine's out of control.

Commercial Traveller. Out of control?

Robert. There's no driver on the train.

Commercial Traveller. Well, what do you expect me to do?

Robert. But we can't just sit here and wait for it to crash!

Commercial Traveller. Driving a train isn't in my line of business.

Graubard. As a director of the railway company . . .

Commercial Traveller. A director? Really, sir!

Graubard. Actually, I'm the managing director.

Commercial Traveller. Now, that's very interesting. I wonder if I can interest you in a little business proposition?

Robert. Are you crazy? We are all in peril!

Graubard. Please! May I ask, Mr . . . er . . .

Commercial Traveller. Christie's the name.

Graubard. What is your line of business?

Commercial Traveller. Loaves and fishes, sir, loaves and fishes.

He rises to his feet and opens his sample case.

Now here are one or two samples which may interest you.

He hands several small loaves and fishes around the carriage.

Food for the multitude. The staff of life. At the present market price and allowing for fluctuations due to wars, floods, earthquakes and political crises . . .

Robert. This is monstrous! The loaves are rotten, full of worms. Do you expect people to eat such filth?

Commercial Traveller. Eat them? You don't eat them! You sell them.

The sound of the wheels is heard again, the speed increasing.

Robert. It's going faster . . . faster . . . Lady, we're travelling with lunatics.

Brave Little Woman. Oh, surely not.

Robert. The train is heading for destruction.

Brave Little Woman. You must be mistaken. I've been travelling on this line for years.

Robert. But look out of the window!

Brave Little Woman. I'll do no such thing. I'm quite comfortable where I am. My father worked all his life for the railway company and when he was killed, the company paid the funeral expenses and sent a wreath of daffodils. They were so kind. It's the little kindnesses that count.

Graubard. Quite!

Brave Little Woman. I believe in minding my own business. No good comes of interfering in things which don't concern us.

Robert. Doesn't your life concern you?

Brave Little Woman. Life has given me everything I've asked for. I'm quite content to sit in my little corner and dream. George – that's my husband – I have his picture here . . .

She produces several snapshots.

Graubard. Hmm!

Brave Little Woman. We've only a little camera. That's my little boy and that's my little house standing in my little garden. The gladioli won a prize this year, a little silver cup . . .

Robert. Will nothing wake you up?

Commercial Traveller. Be quiet!

Robert. If you won't do something then I must try alone.

Graubard. Can you drive a train?

Robert. I can try – and that's better than sitting here waiting to be killed.

He makes for the door leading into the corridor.

Graubard. One moment!

He produces a pistol from his brief-case.

I must ask you not to interfere in the company's affairs.

Robert. My life is my affair.

Graubard. Not while you travel on this line.

Robert. I am going to stop this train or learn to drive it.

Graubard. I'm sorry, but it's against the regulations.

Robert. Then damn the regulations!

He opens the door.

Graubard. You leave me no alternative.

He shoots Robert.

Your pardon, madam.

The brave little woman, however, is asleep.

These little contretemps occur from time to time.

Commercial Traveller. About my proposition . . .

Graubard. Later. Some other time.

Commercial Traveller. Later, then. I think I'll have a nap.

He sleeps. Graubard stands up.

Graubard. Yes, sleep. It passes the time. Perhaps there is an element of danger. Fortunately the company provides an armoured coach for its directors. Good-bye, young man. If you had learned to sleep on journeys, this would never have happened.

Exits via the corridor. The sound of the train fades up, a deafening clatter. There is a loud explosion and a blinding flash. Robert is hurled towards the cage and the railway carriage is blacked out. The light in the cage increases.

Hanau. Always the same ending.

Robert rises to his feet.

Robert. And what now?

Hanau. We will wait for the morning
To lend a little light for death.
We will look her in the eyes.

Robert. The sun cannot penetrate
These barriers of darkness.

Hanau. It can and will.
Soon it will climb to its meridian.

Robert. Strange to think the sun still shines.

Hanau. We have lived through a long night
But now the sun stands poised and ready
On the furthest ridge of Capricorn.

Robert. Then we can rest.

Hanau. Yes.
It has been an uncomfortable journey.
And we have not slept.

Robert. Have we accomplished anything?

Hanau. We have travelled.
We have looked over the horizon.

Robert. And the body pays for the mind's excursion.

Hanau. It is a fair exchange.

Robert. And doubt?

Hanau. Our doubts are growing pains,
Symptoms of the nascent mind
Extending its sphere of operations.
We doubt tomorrow only because
We have not escaped from yesterday.

Robert. So the journey is ended!

Hanau. Our journey is ended,
But there are other travellers.

Music, quiet and intimate, in which a cello takes the solo part, singing of man's hope. Suddenly the mood is broken by a distant pistol shot. The music stops. More pistol shots are heard. The metallic tapping begins.

Voice of the Prison. Number Three! Number Three! Can you hear? Answer, Number Three! Can you hear? Number Three! They are coming! Number . . .

There is a shot, loud and hollow, then silence.

Hanau. The journey is ended.

Robert slowly backs away from the cage, moving towards the shadows beyond.

Robert!

Robert. The shadows beckon.

Hanau. Do not go yet.
Share this long night-watch.

Robert. The night is spent.

Hanau. Your image slips away, dissolves
Into the cloudy mirror of the darkness.
Face blurrs, featureless.
Body thins to shadow
Without edge or substance.
Circumference of life contracts.
Too far to see, to concentrate . . .
Remember feeling often known,
Room full of shadows,
Discreet agony of darkness.
Stay! Stay!
Will not resolve itself
Until the cold sweat of dawn.

Graubard has entered. He is dressed as on his first appearance and is slightly drunk. Robert stands back in the shadows unseen by Graubard.

Graubard.
Still fighting shadows?
Not at the frontier yet?

Hanau. (*To Robert*) Stay and we will talk about the morning.

Graubard.
Do they leave you, then?
Have they deserted you?
Dreams are poor companions.

Hanau. Come, there is a song . . .
We will forget our wounds.

Graubard.
There is a long forgetfulness.
It will soon be yours.

Hanau. That bleary eye of light
Is not the sun.
What have they done to my hands?

Graubard. Hanau! Hanau!

Hanau. (*Slowly turns his head*) Yes.

Graubard. So you can hear?

Hanau. Yes.

Graubard. Do you recognise me?

Hanau. You are death.

Graubard.
No, my friend, not death,
Merely a humble employee.

Hanau. There is a void behind your eyes.

Graubard.
A slight myopia, that's all.
We had an appointment.
You and I. Remember?

Hanau. Will you teach me the language of the worms?

Graubard. You will learn it soon enough.

Hanau. I remember now. Graubard . . .

Graubard.
I would have joined you earlier
But I was detained.
The Commandant was big with speech
And needed a midwife for his wind.
His relations with the spoken word
Are most unsatisfactory.
Fortunately, he provides
His audience with brandy.
Do you remember the taste of brandy,
The way it evaporates upon the tongue
And tenderly ascends into the brain
In warm caressing spirals?
But how could you?
You have forgotten everything except a dream
And soon you will have forgotten that.

There is a distant volley of shots.

Do you hear, Hanau?
Spring cleaning has begun.
Your friends are being moved
Into a permanent habitation
And when we leave . . .

Hanau. Leave?

Graubard.
Of course, you didn't know.
We're abandoning the camp.

The sound of firing is heard, nearer.

There's not much time, Hanau,
If you would save yourself.
A few words on the radio,
An announcement to your followers
That you accept the inevitable.

Hanau. I do accept the inevitable,
That is why I'm here.

Graubard.
What is it makes you take upon yourself
The burdens of this shoddy world?
Don't tell me that you still believe in man,
In the inherent goodness of the species.
Surely you are cured of that illusion!
They are louts, Hanau, louts!
When they're not stupefied with fear
They're drunk with ignorance.
Examine them under the microscope
And beneath the accretions of the ages
You will find a clumsy ape
Who dreams of nothing but his past.
And you would make him dream about his future!
I tell you, he has no future!
One or two individuals have a future,
Those who can see themselves objectively,
The deviations from the type;
The rest are quite content to move
Backwards and forwards, emulating
The shuttle in its groove.
Man is content if he acquires
His little stock of superstitions
And his book of rules.
Examine him coldly, without sentiment
And tell me honestly if what you see
Is worth the expenditure of a single thought.
How does he differ from his ancestors,
This snivelling, shiftless clown?
He has less hair, it's true, and smaller teeth;
His patella is more flexible and compensates
For the loss of that shambling stoop
By allowing him to assume
The posture of permanent genuflexion.
He doesn't want your future, or your dreams.
He'd rather wallow in his filthy rut,
Lost in a state of fugue.
For him the highest point of life is reached
When some hungry female of his kind
Offers the sweaty pit of her body
For his immolation.
And you would die for him!
Why? Why? What is this quality
Which defies my understanding
And eludes all definition?

Hanau. The quality of life, Graubard.

Graubard.
Do you talk of life to me,
You who have lived with death these last three years?
I have looked life squarely in the face,
Accepted it for what it is,
As one accepts a woman for one's pleasure.

Hanau. You have looked in a sewer
And seen your own reflection.
The image has aborted thought.
Your eyes are clouded over
With the malice of emasculation.

Graubard. I am drunk and therefore tolerant.
Believe me, Hanau, if I envied you
Or coveted your precious fantasy
I'd tear it out of you as easily
As one removes the filling
From a dead man's tooth.

Hanau. Once, Graubard, I thought that you,
And what you represent, might dam the course
Of history for a thousand years.
That was before I knew you,
Before I realised that your hatred
Of all life developed beyond the termite stage
Springs from a terrible fear.
Your mind is crippled, twisted horribly;
It approaches life with a clumsy, crab-like gait
And looks at everything through bloodshot eyes.

Graubard. Have you finished?

Hanau. You hate us because you envy us,
You envy us because we walk upright
And constantly remind you
Of your own mis-shapenness.
How does it feel to know
That life has cast you off?

Graubard. You have too much breath, Hanau.

He produces a pistol from his pocket.

I will give you an injection
Which will make you sleep.

Hanau. Your contribution to social medicine.

Graubard. An instrument to rid you of delusions.

Hanau. Will it cure your deformity?

Graubard. Stand up!

Hanau. What, are we to stand on ceremony?

Graubard. I want to see you fall.

Hanau. Must I teach you to die?

Graubard. Get up!

Hanau pulls himself up. Music fades up. Hanau turns, listening intently.

What is it now?

Hanau. Music. I can hear music.

Graubard.
A choir of worms, most likely,
Singing for their supper.

Robert slowly advances to the cage.

Hanau. Yes, it's time that we were joined.
We will die whole.

Robert slips between the bars into the cage.

We will trample upon death
As the swan tramples upon the water,
Or the horse upon the plain.

Graubard.
Hanau, come back!
You cannot escape again!

Hanau. I can smell the dawn, Robert.

Maria enters behind Graubard and stands in the shadows.

Hanau. Maria!
Did you tell them?

She nods in the affirmative.

Graubard.
No, I'll not shoot
While you're anaesthetised with dreams.
You must be lucid
For that final interview.
When death comes
I want to look into your eyes
And see the endless vista of despair.
I want you to be conscious of
The full extent of your defeat.

Piera and Anderson enter and stand in the shadows.

Hanau. Guthrie.

Graubard. More phantoms?

Hanau. The spectres that haunt Europe,
Those who call from the high hills
Across the arid years. The deathless ones
Who cannot be silenced.
These are your judges, Graubard.
And all your loud-mouthed threats,
Your thunderous denunciations,
Your chorus of sonorous guns
With their emphatic statements of defence,
Cannot delay the verdict
Nor postpone your execution.
Your world is dying, Graubard.
It totters in the final stages of decrepitude.
It is incapable of all activity
Except the activity of decay.
Do you think you can outlive it
Or halt the process of senility
By prescribing a diet of blood?
Can you disguise its atrabilious stench?
The sulphurous reek of cannon,
The acrid stink of fire-raped towns,
The flowers of infamous harvest
And all the perfumes of synthetic victory
Will not eradicate
The hellish odour of putrefaction.

Graubard. My world will survive you, Hanau.

Hanau. Yes, but it will not survive
The new world that is being born.

Graubard.
And who will sire this precious infant?
Not you, my friend! Who, then?
One of the barren shadows of the dead?

Music which dies away on a flourish of trumpets.

What was that?

Hanau. The cock crew.

Graubard. Nonsense! It isn't morning yet.

Hanau. And yet the cock crew.

Graubard.
Strange! I could have sworn there were two of you.
Stand still. Stand still!
What! Have you multiplied?
The atmosphere of your apartment

Combining with the Commandant's liquor
Has given me the doubtful pleasure
Of seeing you in duplicate.
I have four eyes with which to watch you die
And by killing both of you
I'll double the measure of my satisfaction.

The trumpet sounds again.

There it is again.

Hanau. The second summons.

Graubard.
Some cock with a full crop
Impatient for the tread.

Robert. It stands on the roof of night.

Hanau. It sees the dawn.

Chorus of the dead. Tick-tock, tock-tock.

Robert. The minutes fall like dead leaves.

Chorus of the dead. Tick-tock, tick-tock.

Hanau. The world dies in a bed of mould.

Chorus of the dead. Tick-tock, tick-tock, tick-tock, tick-tock.

Graubard.
My ears are practising an imposture
Upon my reason.
There's no clock here, no voices,
Only the dry scampering of rat's feet.

Robert. And the heart tolling its own funeral.

Chorus of the dead.
Tick-tock, tick-tock,
Another beat nearer death,
Tick-tock, tick-tock,
A minute lost, a lost breath.
Tick-tock, tick-tock, tick-tock, tick-tock.

Graubard. Stop!

Voice of the prison. Stop! Stop! Stop!

Graubard. Sleep too little . . . can't sleep . . .

Voice of the prison. Can't sleep. Can't sleep. Can't sleep.

Graubard.
Thoughts go on echoing inside my skull
Long after formulation.
Am I breaking up?

Voice of the prison. Breaking up!

Graubard. Something moved in the shadows!

Hanau
Robert. (*together*) Look round, Graubard!

Voice of the prison. Look round!

Chorus of the dead. Look round!

Graubard. What is there to see but shadows?

Chorus of the dead.
The shadows fly before the rush of light.
The sun destroys the ambush of the night.

Voice of the prison.
The past dies, the minute sings.
The dead arise, the earth swings
Into a new constellation.

Graubard.
Delirium is not infectious
And yet in some strange way . . .
No, that's impossible!
I need rest, that's all, rest!

Chorus of the dead.
You cannot hide from tomorrow's eye,
You cannot escape a universal dream
Or silence tomorrow's hope.

Graubard.
I have an antidote for dreams,
A prophylactic against hope.
Here, Hanau, take it!

He shoots Hanau, who, for a moment, stands swaying against the bars and then slowly sinks to the ground. Music in the rhythm of a slow march. Enter Death as an old woman and the Morning as a girl in a gold dress patterned with red suns. They dance towards the cage. From out of the shadows behind the cage appear Gaudry and the dead Chartist.

Now the stillness moves.
The cock grows in my head.
Oh, I am sick! sick!

Robert. You are dying.

Graubard. What, do you still stand?

He shoots at Robert. The music stops. The air is full of whispers.

Robert. You have planted banners in the hungry soil.

Chorus of the Dead.

Red like anger
Like the disc of sun in the mist of morning.

Graubard. This place is full of echoes.

Voice of the Prison. His voice is an infinity of echoes.

Graubard.

His voice is lost in silence,
Withered away.

The Morning. It is time.

Music. Robert slips out of the cage and dances off with the Morning. Graubard attempts to follow but is restrained by Death.

Death. You cannot go after him.

Graubard. You have not paid me for your lodging, Hanau!

Death. I will pay you, son.

Graubard.

The light behind your eyes was mine.
The instrument which made that fine-spun dream
Is my inheritance. Where has it gone?
Is this unyielding clay, this grey silence
The sum and total of my legacy?
You have left me nothing, Hanau,
But a worn-out body and a cage.

Voice of the Prison.

Five paces and the bars,
Five paces and the cage.

The Dead begin to advance slowly upon Graubard. The light on the stage lessens.

Graubard. I am beset by hostile shadows.

Death. Come to me, my son. Come home.

Graubard. Back, old woman.

Death. Do not shrink from your mother, child.

Graubard. Where has Hanau gone?

Death. He is there, son.

Graubard. That is not Hanau. What am I doing in this cage?

He rattles the bars furiously.

Hanau! Hanau! Let me out! Let me out, Hanau!

There is a great crescendo of music. Graubard continues to shout as the curtain falls.

[The End]

Epilogue

Though all theatre is, in a broad sense 'political', the term 'political theatre' has been accepted as defining a left-wing theatre, critical of the capitalist system and expressing in its work the need for radical change.

The first organised political theatre in this country was the Workers' Theatre Movement, which spanned the period from 1928 to 1938. 1968 saw the upsurge of Alternative Theatre and the formation of several socialist theatre groups. Linking these two movements was the pre-war work of Theatre Union in Manchester and the post-war work of Theatre Workshop.

The Workers' Theatre Movement of the thirties, as important a cultural and political manifestation in its own time as the Alternative movement of the seventies, has been almost completely ignored in the main stream of writing on theatre history, and such information as is available is limited, in the main, to specialist journals such as *History Workshop*.

The third edition of the *Oxford Companion to the Theatre*, though it claims 'an effort has been made to provide information on every aspect of the theatre up to the end of 1964' has nothing to say on the subject. *The Illustrated Encyclopedia of World Theatre*, published by Thames and Hudson in 1977, deals solely, in seventy words, with agitational theatre in the U.S.S.R. and Germany before the Second World War, though Theatre Union does get a brief mention under 'Littlewood'. Methuen's *Encyclopedia of World Drama*, published in 1970, and the Penguin *Dictionary of Theatre* have no entry under Street Theatre, Agit-Prop or Political Theatre. Surprisingly, even David Edgar wrote in the *Theatre Quarterly* of winter 1979, 'there are two reasons why 1968 can be taken as the starting date of political theatre in Britain'.

Political theatre goes back even earlier than the start of the Workers' Theatre Movement in 1928, but that year marks the beginning of an attempt to organise left-wing theatre on a comparatively widespread scale. It was directly agitational, rejecting completely all the theatrical conventions of the time, embracing the class-struggle and identifying itself closely with the Communist Party. The revolutionary nature of its work was unable to survive the formation of the Popular Front in 1936 – the alliance between the Communist Party, the I.L.P. and the left wing of the Labour Party. Also, unemployment had declined, industrial strife was easing and progressive forces felt that the urgent need was to unite against what was then seen as the main danger – the rise of Fascism all over Europe. To alert a broader section of the people to this new threat, the direct, simple sketches of street agit-prop had to give way to indoor theatre, full-length plays and, consequently, the need to improve the artistic and technical levels of performance. Joan Littlewood and Ewan MacColl had led the way with Theatre of Action in Manchester as early as 1934, culminating in the production of *Last Edition* in 1940, paving the way for the even more complex requirements of plays like *Uranium 235* in the post-war years.

Though little has been documented of the many groups that made up the Workers' Theatre Movement a great deal is known about the present-day Alternative Theatre. Unlike the Workers' Theatre Movement it is an accepted part of the theatrical scene. Until recently public subsidy has been available to many of them on the basis of their merit. Now, in the political climate of the 1980s, these are being withdrawn from the more radical groups such as 7:84 and they are now fighting for their survival. Many of its writers are established 'names' and their plays are published. Some of these, like John Arden, David Mercer, John McGrath, had been writing since the fifties, but 1968 marked the beginning of the upsurge of left-wing theatre groups in this country, alongside other theatre groups with no specific political commitment.

It is significant that the formation in 1928 of the Workers' Theatre Movement and the rise of political theatre in the late sixties both had, as their springboard, a rejection of orthodox Labour politics and the need to seek out a more radical solution to the injustices of Capitalism though the differences in the economic conditions of the two periods was considerable. 1928 was a time of depression, high unemployment and poverty, and the Workers' Theatre Movement, born out of discontent and struggle, was an integral part of the political movement of the working class. 1968 on the other hand, was a time of comparative prosperity, unemployment was low and the recession had not yet hit the Consumer Society. Nevertheless, the Labour government that had come to power in 1964 had failed to effect any of the expected radical changes. From the resulting disillusionment and the political awareness of students, intellectuals and young theatre workers, some of whom were from the working class, sprang the theatre of protest. Some groups adopted agit-prop techniques, taking their theatre to non-theatrical venues: halls, clubs, pubs, community centres, places of work and out on to the streets, in much the same way as the Workers' Theatre Movement had done.

It may be that Harold Hobson was overstating the case when he said 'I doubt if there would have been any Fringe without Theatre Workshop and Joan Littlewood', but the influence on the work of some of the pioneers of the political theatre in the late sixties has been acknowledged, not least in their appreciation of the need to develop the physical skills of the actors, the value of the use of common speech in the theatre and the advantages resulting from group work. Albert Hunt has said that these were just some of the elements in Theatre Workshop productions he saw over the years that inspired his subsequent work with the Bradford College of Art group. His memorable large-scale piece of street theatre *The Russian Revolution* and drama documentaries like *John Ford's Cuban Missile Crisis* in turn influenced much of the political theatre of the seventies, including the work of groups like General Will and Welfare State. John McGrath has also acknowledged the influence of Theatre Workshop on his work with 7:84 Company and their commitment to create a popular working-class theatre. How this can best be achieved has exercised the minds of everyone engaged in political theatre since the twenties. The agit-prop theatre of those years took their sketches to those directly concerned with specific issues – at their places of work, into clubs or out into the streets; and since the late sixties this form of theatre has been developed by groups like North-West Spanner, Belt and Braces and Red Ladder. Agit-prop certainly ensures that your message gets to the intended audience, and its impact is immediate, but it has obvious limitations. It is unable to cope with the complex historical progression of events, or with rapid transitions of time and place, essential to a play like *Uranium 235*. To effect this and to create the right atmosphere for each scene the help of music and lighting is needed and a flexible form of staging to break up the stage area for the movements of the actors. So a certain amount of technical equipment is necessary, but provided a group is prepared to load and unload this on to a vehicle and rig and de-rig stages, plays of this kind are mobile and can reach working-class audiences in their own clubs and halls.

All this was done in the one-night-stand tours of Theatre Workshop from 1945 to 1952, which included the South Wales mining villages, the miners' halls of the North-East and the Scottish coalfields. We didn't always play to good houses, but we knew that whoever turned up was almost bound to be working class – there were very few others around. A notable success in our search for working-class audiences was the five performances of *Uranium 235* which we played at Butlin's Holiday Camp at Filey in May 1946. Each episode was applauded as though it was an item on a variety bill, and the enthusiasm shown for what must have been, for most of the audience, a novel theatrical experience, confirmed our belief that there was no need to compromise or 'play down' to working people.

There were no recognised venues or touring circuits in the forties and fifties as there are now, and every hall had to be sought out and booked. We were the only political theatre touring at this time. We had no subsidy, and playing six one-night stands a week for months at a time was very hard work. Notable amongst the many groups now touring the country is John McGrath's 7:84 Company, whose work with popular theatre forms, song, dance and documentary drama has attracted new audiences to the theatre in Scotland and England. David Scase, a founder-member of Theatre Workshop, directed *Johnny Noble* for the 7:84 Company in 1983. At the time of writing this company, as might be expected, has lost its subsidy. Perhaps they should follow Lord Gowrie's advice and seek commercial sponsorship!

An important stimulus to this creation of new audiences has been the setting-up of local community theatres all over the country, usually in non-theatre locations – though occasionally conventional theatres have been put to good use. A feature of the work of Peter Cheeseman (who was also influenced by Theatre Workshop), at the Victoria Theatre, Stoke-on-Trent, has been to extend the Living Newspaper form into historical documentaries of local interest, using idiomatic speech and researched by his own group of actors. The Everyman Theatre, Liverpool, also attracted a largely working-class audience, particularly when John McGrath worked there in 1971 and 1972.

Unfortunately much of socialist theatre tends to play to the converted, thereby restricting its audience to the politically aware, and is thus unable to extend the boundaries of theatre to the apolitical majority. The attraction of a ready made, sympathetic response is understandable, but it is the 'unknown quantity' in an audience that provides the challenge to new ideas and stimulating theatre. It also needs to be accessible to working people, which cannot be said of cultural institutions like the National Theatre, the Royal Shakespeare Company or even the Royal Court. That is not to say that socialist writers like Howard Brenton, David Edgar, David Hare, Edward

Bond and others should not be writing for these theatres any more than that socialist actors shouldn't act there. They have to make a living, and the mainly middle-class audiences can only benefit from being exposed to some of the harsher realities of life through some of the plays of these writers. David Edgar wrote a few years ago: 'the most potent, rich and in many ways politically acute theatrical statements of the past ten years have been made in custom-built buildings patronised almost exclusively by the middle class'. He quotes scenes from the plays of Edward Bond, Barry Keeffe and Howard Barker to illustrate this point. Many of those working in socialist theatre would disagree, but in any case, however exciting they may be in theatrical terms, the impact of these political statements is largely negated if they are inaccessible to those most directly concerned – the working class. David Edgar goes on to assert that the form and language of these plays requires, for their understanding, a cultural or academic background denied to the vast majority of people, thus rendering them even more inaccessible. It is possible to write 'up' as well as 'down'! It is a concept of theatre that differs substantially from that which motivated the work of Theatre Workshop and the pre-war Manchester groups that preceded it. From the early thirties political theatre set out to identify, in its work, with the lives and language of the industrial working class. The aim was for a theatre that was widely understood while still able to deal with complex subjects though a wide variety of theatrical styles. This was epitomised in plays like *Uranium 235* which reached out to a wide variety of audiences – from the Comedy Theatre in London's West End to the holiday-makers at Butlin's Camp in Filey.

While plays written for the 'prestige' theatres cannot be said to contribute to the building of a popular theatre, these writers have of course also written extensively for socialists groups, and their contribution in this area has been considerable.

My concern is that the theatre should play a part in enriching the lives of many more people. I believe that the Theatre Workshop Manifesto of 1945 still holds good as the basic foundation for a People's Theatre, and that our first production, *Johnny Noble*, embodied, to a large extent, our conception of theatre:

> The great theatres of all times have been popular theatres which reflected the dreams and struggles of the people. The theatre of Aeschylus and Sophocles, of Shakespeare and Ben Jonson, of the Commedia dell'-Arte and Molière derived their inspiration, their language, their art from the people.
>
> We want a theatre with a living language, a theatre which is not afraid of

> its own voice and which will comment as fearlessly on Society as did Ben Jonson and Aristophanes.
>
> Theatre Workshop is an organisation of artists, technicians and actors who are experimenting in stage-craft. Its purpose is to create a flexible theatre-art, as swift moving and plastic as the cinema, by applying the recent technical advances in light and sound, and introducing music and the 'dance theatre' style of production.

A popular theatre cannot be built solely on the basis of contemporary plays concerned with the political or social ills of our society. The plays inherited from the great theatres of the past, the Greeks, the Elizabethans, the Commedia dell'arte and the Spanish theatre of Lope de Vega, are the heritage of all people and must not remain, as at present, the privilege of the few. These playwrights wrote for a popular theatre of their own time and many of their themes are still relevant today. Who has matched Ben Jonson's exposure of greed and corruption in *Volpone* and *The Alchemist* or the tyranny of power in Lope de Vega's *The Sheepwell*? The Théâtre National Populaire of Roger Planchon and the political theatre of Erwin Piscator in Weimar Germany, both succeeded in creating a popular theatre on the basis of a wide repertoire of plays including the classics. To their names could be added that of Joan Littlewood.

It was no doubt easier in those optimistic days of 1945 to take a long-term view of the function of the theatre and how it could play its full part in the better times we were certain lay ahead. After all, we had a Labour government with a massive majority ready to lead us to the millennium. Our friendship with the Soviet Union had been cemented in war, never to be broken. Fascism had been defeated, a secure future lay ahead for all mankind, and we were determined to build a theatre worthy of that future. It could be said that the political reality turned out to be a lot less worthy than our theatre; and in the 1980's we see MacMillan's phrase 'the unacceptable face of Capitalism' translated into grim reality. The forces of reaction have never been stronger, and the political and industrial strength of the working class is divided and ineffective in the fight against the evils of our society and the ultimate horror – the threat of nuclear extinction. The miners were defeated by the disunity within their own ranks and the lack of organised workers' support rather than by the government and the N.C.B.

The cutting of Arts subsidies following on the abolition of the G.L.C. and the Metropolitan Boroughs threatens the existence of many groups in the Alternative Theatre movement. No effective proposals have been made by Central government to replace the funding previously provided by local government. The disbanding of theatre groups with a social commitment can only be welcomed by a government antagonistic to all progressive institutions. It is part and parcel of the attack on the quality of life and those who strive to enhance it. If we accept that the legacy of man's achievements in our art galleries and museums must be accessible to all, then, equally, the great plays of the past must be made available, not only on paper in libraries but in performance. They are our allies in the struggle for a more civilised society.

The capacity for theatre to stimulate man's critical awareness and question the accepted tenets of our society makes it a danger to conformism. Rather a 'mass' culture based on Bingo, the Generation Game and soap opera, which serves as an opiate, and whose very triviality ensures that it does not impinge on the workings of society or those who live in it. The concept that Art generally, including theatre, exists to enrich our spirit, to inform and extend our horizons is quite alien to those who are content to see it as a form of relaxation for a largely middle-class minority. The Alternative Theatre movement is not only fighting for its own survival but also, hopefully, for this concept of theatre. In the words of Bertold Brecht:

> How can the theatre be entertaining and instructive at the same time? How can it be taken out of the hands of intellectual drug traffic and become a place offering real experiences rather than illusions? How can the unliberated and unknowing man of our century with his thirst for knowledge and freedom, the tortured and heroic, misused and inventive man of our terrible and great century, himself changeable and yet able to change the world, how can he be given a theatre which will help him to be master of his world?

ANGELA CARTER was born in 1940 and died at the age of 51 in February 1992. 'With Angela's death English literature has lost its high sorceress, its benevolent witch queen, a burlesque artist of genius and antic grace', wrote Salman Rushdie.

Before she died, Angela Carter completed *The Second Virago Book of Fairy Tales* – a collection which reflects her long-standing passion for the art of the fairy tale. One of Britain's most original writers, she was highly acclaimed for her novels, short stories and journalism. She translated the fairy tales of Charles Perrault and adapted two of her works for film, *The Company of Wolves* and *The Magic Toyshop*. Angela Carter's last novel was the much-lauded *Wise Children*, published in 1991.

CORINNA SARGOOD, one of Angela Carter's oldest friends, is the author and illustrator of *Journey to the Jungle: An Artist in Peru*. Her work includes print-making, illustrating books, film animation, furniture decoration, puppet shows, painting and etching. She illustrated this book while living in Mexico.

The Second VIRAGO BOOK *of* FAIRY TALES

edited by
ANGELA CARTER

illustrated by CORINNA SARGOOD

Published by VIRAGO PRESS Limited 1993
20–23 Mandela Street, Camden Town, London NW1 0HQ

First published in hardback by Virago Press 1992

A CIP catalogue record for this book is available from the British Library

Typeset by Goodfellow & Egan
Printed and bound in Great Britain by
Cox & Wyman Ltd, Reading, Berkshire

Designed by Lone Morton

Contents

Acknowledgements

Permission to reproduce these fairy tales is gratefully acknowledged to the following: Pantheon Books, a division of Random House, Inc. for 'The Old Woman Against the Stream' from *Norwegian Folktales* by Christen Asbjornsen and Jorgen Moe and 'A Fable of a Bird and Her Chicks' from *Yiddish Folktales* by Beatrice Silverman Wienreich; Constable Publishers for 'The Werefox' and 'The Mirror' from *Chinese Ghouls and Goblins* by G. Willoughby-Mead, copyright © 1924; The American Folklore Society for 'Old Foster', from *Journal of American Folklore* XXXVIII (1925) and 'The Untrue Wife's Song from *Journal of American Folklore* XLVII (1934); The University Press of Kentucky for 'The Telltale Lilac Bush' from *The Telltale Lilac Bush and Other West Virginian Ghost Tales* by Ruth Ann Musick, copyright © 1965; University of Chicago Press for 'Pretty Maid Ibronka', 'The Witches' Piper, 'The Midwife and the Frog' and 'A Stroke of Luck' from *Folktales of Hungary* by Degh © 1956 by University of Chicago; 'The Greenish Bird' from *Folktales of Mexico* by Paredes © 1970 by University of Chicago; 'Resaon to Beat your Wife' from *Folktales of Egypt* by El Shamy © 1980 by University of Chicago; 'The Witchball', 'Father and Mother Both "Fast" ' and 'The Beans in the Quart Jar' from *Buying the Wind* by Dorson © 1964 by University of Chicago; Jonathan Cape and Basic Books for 'The Height of Purple Passion' from *The Rationale of Dirty Jokes*; Stanford University Press for 'The Three Lovers'; Columbia University Press, New York, for 'The Sleeping Prince', 'The Letter Trick' and 'Spreading the Fingers' from *Suriname Folklore*, by Melville J. Herskovits and Frances S. Herskovits, © 1936 and C. W. Daniel Company for 'Vasilissa the Fair', 'Enchanter and Enchantress', 'The Little Old Woman with Five Cows', 'Story of a Bird Woman', 'The Crafty Woman', 'The Dog's Snout People' from *Siberian and Other Folktales: Primitive Literature of the Empire of the Tsars*, collected and translated by C. Fillingham Coxwell © 1925; University of Calfornia Press for 'Šāhīn', 'Tănjur, Tănjur', 'The Woman Who Married Her Son' and 'The Seven Leavenings' from *Speak Bird, Speak Again: Palestinian Arab Folktales* collected and edited by Ibrahim Muhawi and Sharif Kanann, copyright © 1988 The Regents of the University of California; Oxford University Press for 'The Frog Maiden' from *Burmese Folktales* by Maun Htin Aung, Calcutta, 1948; Holmes and Meier publishers for 'Diirawic and her Incestuous Brother', 'Achol and her Wild Mother', 'Achol and her Adoptive Lioness-Mother', 'Duang and his Wild Wife' from *Dinka Folktales, African Stories from Sudan* by Francis Mading Deng, (New York, Africana publishing Company, a division of Holmes & Meier, 1974), copyright © 1974 by Francis Mading Deng; Pantheon Books, a division of Random House, Inc. for 'Salt, Sauce and Spice, Onion Leaves, Pepper and Drippings' and 'Tale of an Old Woman, from *African Folktales* by Roger D. Abrahams copyright © 1983 Roger D. Abrahams; Popular Publications for 'The Orphan' from *Tales of Old Malawi*, edited by E. Singano & A.A. Roscoe, 1977, 1986.

Every effort has been made to trace the copyright holders in all copyright material in this book. The publisher regrets if there has been any oversight and suggests that Virago be contacted in any such event.

Introduction

Italo Calvino, the Italian writer and fabulist and collector of fairy tales believed strongly in the connection between fantasy and reality: 'I am accustomed to consider literature a search for knowledge,' he wrote. 'Faced with [the] precarious existence of tribal life, the shaman responded by ridding his body of weight and flying to another world, another level of perception, where he could find the strength to change the face of reality.'[1] Angela Carter wouldn't have made the same wish with quite such a straight face, but her combination of fantasy and revolutionary longings corresponds to the flight of Calvino's shaman. She possessed the enchanter's lightness of mind and wit – it's interesting that she explored, in her last two novels, images of winged women. Fevvers, her aërialiste heroine of *Nights at the Circus*, may have hatched like a bird, and in *Wise Children*, the twin Chance sisters play various fairies or feathered creatures, from their first foot on the stage as child stars to their dalliance in Hollywood for a spectacular extravaganza of *A Midsummer Night's Dream*.

Fairy tales also offered her a means of flying – of finding and telling an alternative story, of shifting something in the mind, just as so many fairy tale characters shift something in their shape. She wrote her own – the dazzling, erotic variations on Perrault's Mother Goose Tales and other familiar stories in *The Bloody Chamber* – where she lifted Beauty and Red Riding Hood and Bluebeard's last wife out of the pastel nursery into the labyrinth of female desire. She had always read very widely in folklore from all over the world, and compiled her first collection, *The Virago Book of Fairy Tales*, two years ago; this second volume is being published after her death, in February 1992, from cancer.

She found the stories in sources ranging from Siberia to Suriname, and she arranged them into sections in a sequence that runs from one tale of female heroic endeavour to another about generosity rewarded. There are few fairies, in the sense of sprites, but the stories move in fairyland, not the prettified, kitschified, Victorians' elfland, but the darker, dream realm of spirits and tricks, magical, talking animals, riddles and spells. In 'The Twelve Wild Ducks', the opening tale, the heroine vows not to speak or to laugh or to cry until she has rescued her brothers from their enchanted animal forms. The issue of women's speech, of women's noise, of their/our clamour and laughter and weeping and shouting and hooting runs through all Angela Carter's writings, and informed her love of the folk tale. In *The Magic Toyshop* the lovely Aunt Margaret cannot speak because she is strangled by the silver torque which the malign puppetmaster her husband has made her as a bridal gift. Folklore, on the other hand, speaks volumes about women's experience, and women are often the storytellers, as in one of the dashingly comic and highly Carteresque tales in this collection ('Reason to Beat Your Wife').

Angela Carter's partisan feeling for women, which burns in all her work, never led her to any conventional form of feminism; but she continues here one of her original and effective strategies, snatching out of the jaws of misogyny itself, 'useful stories' for women. Her essay 'The Sadeian Woman' (1979) found in Sade a liberating teacher of the male–female status quo and made him illuminate the far reaches of women's polymorphous desires; here she turns topsy-turvy some cautionary folk tales and shakes out the fear and dislike of women they once expressed to create a new set of values, about strong, outspoken, zestful, sexual women who can't be kept down (see 'The Old Woman Against the Stream'; 'The Letter Trick'). In *Wise Children,* she created a heroine, Dora Chance, who's a showgirl, a soubrette, a vaudeville dancer, one of the low, the despised, the invisible poor, an old woman who's illegitimate and never married (born the wrong side of the blanket, the wrong side of the tracks), and each of these stigmas is taken up with exuberant relish and scattered in the air like so much wedding confetti.

The last story here, 'Spreading the Fingers', a tough morality tale from Suriname about sharing what one has been given with others, also discloses the high value Angela Carter placed on generosity. She gave herself – her ideas, her wit, her incisive, no-bullshit mind – with open but never sentimental prodigality. Her favourite fairy tale in the first *Virago Book* was a Russian riddle story 'The Wise Little Girl', in which the tsar asks her heroine for the impossible, and she delivers it without batting an eyelid. Angela liked it because it was as satisfying as 'The Emperor's New Clothes', but 'no one was humiliated and everybody gets the prizes'. The story comes in the section called 'Clever Women, Resourceful Girls and Desperate Stratagems', and its heroine is an essential Carter figure, never abashed, nothing daunted, sharp-eared as a vixen and possessed of dry good sense. It's entirely characteristic of Angela's spirit that she should delight in the tsar's confounding, and yet not want him to be humiliated.

She did not have the strength, before she died, to write the introduction she had planned to this volume, but she left four cryptic notes among her papers:

'every real story contains something useful, says Walter Benjamin

the *unperplexedness* of the story

"No one dies so poor that he does not leave something behind," said Pascal.

fairy tales – cunning and high spirits'.

Fragmentary as they are, these phrases convey the Carter philosophy. She was scathing about the contempt the 'educated' can show, when two-thirds of the literature of the world – perhaps more – has been created by the illiterate. She liked the solid common sense of folk tales, the straightforward aims of their protagonists, the simple moral distinctions, and the wily stratagems they suggest. They're tales of the underdog, about cunning and high spirits winning through in the end; they're practical, and they're not high-flown. For a fantasist with wings, Angela kept her eyes on the ground, with reality firmly in her sights. She once remarked, 'A fairy tale is a story where one king goes to another king to borrow a cup of sugar.'

Feminist critics of the genre – especially in the 1970s – jibbed at the socially conventional 'happy endings' of so many stories (for example, 'When she grew up he married her and she became the tsarina'). But Angela knew about satisfaction and pleasure; and at the same time she believed that the goal of fairy tales wasn't 'a conservative one, but a utopian one, indeed a form of heroic optimism – as if to say: One day, we might be happy, even if it won't last.' Her own heroic optimism never failed her – like the spirited heroine of one of her tales, she was resourceful and brave and even funny during the illness which brought about her death. Few writers possess the best qualities of their work; she did, in spades.

Her imagination was dazzling, and through her daring, vertiginous plots, her precise yet wild imagery, her gallery of wonderful bad-good girls, beasts, rogues and other creatures, she causes readers to hold their breath as a mood of heroic optimism forms against the odds. She had the true writer's gift of remaking the world for her readers.

She was a wise child herself, with a mobile face, a mouth which sometimes pursed with irony, and, behind the glasses, a wryness, at times a twinkle, at times a certain dreaminess; with her long, silvery hair and ethereal delivery, she had something of the Faerie Queene about her, except that she was never wispy or fey. And though the narcissism of youth was one of the great themes in her early fiction, she was herself exceptionally un-narcissistic. Her voice was soft, with a storyteller's confidingness, and lively with humour; she spoke with a certain syncopation, as she stopped to think – her thoughts made her the most exhilarating companion, a wonderful talker, who wore her learning and wide reading with lightness, who could express a mischievous insight or a tough judgement with scalpel precision and produce new ideas by the dozen without effort, weaving allusion, quotation, parody and original invention, in a way that echoed her prose style. 'I've got a theory that . . .' she'd say, self-deprecatorily, and then would follow something that no one else had thought of, some sally, some rich paradox that would encapsulate a trend, a moment. She could be Wildean in her quickness and the glancing drollery of her wit. And then she would pass on, sometimes leaving her listeners astonished and stumbling.

Angela Carter was born in May 1940, the daughter of Hugh Stalker, a journalist for the Press Association, who was a Highlander by birth, had served the whole term of the First World War, and had come south to Balham to work. He used to take her to the cinema, to the Tooting Granada, where the glamour of the building (Alhambra-style) and of the movie stars (Jean Simmons in *The Blue Lagoon*) made an impression which lasted – she has written some of the most gaudy, stylish, sexy passages about seduction and female beauty on record; 'snappy' and 'glamorous' are key words of pleasure and praise in her vocabulary. Her mother was from South Yorkshire, on her own mother's side; this grandmother was tremendously important to Angela: 'every word and gesture of hers displayed a natural dominance, a native savagery, and I am very grateful for all that, now, though the core of steel was a bit inconvenient when I was looking for boyfriends in the South'. Angela's mother was a scholarship girl, and 'liked things to be nice'; she worked as a cashier in Selfridge's in the 1920s, and had passed exams and wanted the same for her daughter. Angela went to Streatham grammar school, and for a time entertained a fancy of becoming an Egyptologist, but left school to take up an apprenticeship on the *Croydon Advertiser* arranged by her father.

As a reporter on the news desk, she had trouble with her imagination (she used to like the Russian storyteller's formula, 'The story is over, I can't lie any more') and switched to writing a record column as well as features. She got married for the first time when she was twenty-one, to a chemistry teacher at Bristol technical college, and began studying English at Bristol University in the same year, choosing to concentrate on medieval literature, which was then definitely uncanonical. Its forms – from allegory to tales – as well as its heterogeneity of tone – from bawdy to romance – can be found everywhere in her own *oeuvre*; Chaucer and Boccaccio remained among her favourite writers. She also remembered those days, in a recent interview with her great friend Susannah Clapp, for the talking in cafés 'to situationists and anarchists . . . It was the Sixties . . . I was very very unhappy but I was perfectly happy at the same time.'

During this period, she first began developing her interest in folklore, discovering with her husband the folk and jazz music scenes of the 1960s. (At a more recent, staid, meeting of the Folklore Society, she fondly recalled those counter-cultural days when a member would attend with a pet raven on one shoulder.) She began writing fiction: in her twenties she published four novels (*Shadow Dance*, 1966; *The Magic Toyshop*, 1967; *Several Perceptions*, 1968; *Heroes and Villains*, 1969; as well as a story for children, *Miss Z, the Dark Young Lady*, 1970). She was heaped with praise and prizes; one of them – the Somerset Maugham – stipulated travel, and she obeyed, using the money to run away from her husband ('I think Maugham would have approved'). She chose Japan, because she revered the films of Kurosawa.

Japan marks an important transition; she stayed for two years, from 1971. Her fiction till then, including the ferocious, taut elegy *Love* (1971; revised 1987), showed her baroque powers of invention, and her fearless confrontation of erotic violence, of female as well as male sexuality: she marked out her territory early, and men and women clash on it, often bloodily, and the humour is mostly of the gallows variety. From the beginning, her prose was magnificently rich, intoxicated with words – a vivid and sensual lexicon of bodily attributes, minerals, flora and fauna – and she dealt in strangeness. But Japan gave her a way of looking at her own culture which intensified her capacity to conjure strangeness out of the familiar. She also deepened her contact with the Surrealist movement at this time, through French exiles from *les évènements* of '68 who had fetched up in Japan. On her return, she examined various English sacred cows as well as the style of the times (from scarlet lipstick to stockings in D.H. Lawrence) in her wonderfully pungent series of articles for *New Society* (collected as *Nothing Sacred* in 1982).

Two novels arose from her time in Japan, though they do not deal with Japan directly: *The Infernal Desire Machines of Doctor Hoffman* (1972) and *The Passion of New Eve* (1977), in which contemporary conflicts are transmuted into bizarre, multiple, picaresque allegories. Though she never won the bestseller fortunes of some of her contemporaries (she would reflect ruefully that it was still a Boys' Club out there, and did not really mind much), and was never selected for one of the major prizes, she enjoyed greater international esteem: her name tells from Denmark to Australia, and she was repeatedly invited to teach – accepting invitations from Sheffield (1976–78), Brown University, Providence (1980–81), the University of Adelaide (1984), and the University of East Anglia (1984–87). She helped change the course of postwar writing in English – her influence reaches from Salman Rushdie to Jeanette Winterson to American fabulists like Robert Coover.

Distance from England helped her lay bare women's collusion with their own subjection. In the new collection of her criticism, *Expletives Deleted*, she remembers, 'I spent a good many years being told what I ought to think, and how I ought to behave . . . because I was a woman . . . but then I stopped listening to them [men] and . . . I started answering back.'[2] Angela was never someone to offer an easy answer, and in her frankness she was important to the feminist movement: she liked to quote, semi-ironically, 'Dirty work – but someone has to do it' when talking about facing hard truths, and she would say of someone, in a spirit of approval 's/he doesn't temper the wind to the new-shorn lamb'. Her publisher and friend Carmen Callil published her in Virago and her presence here since the start of the house helped establish a woman's voice in literature as special, as *parti pris*, as a crucial instrument in the forging of an identity for post-imperial, hypocritical, fossilised Britain. For in spite of her keen-eyed, even cynical grasp of reality, Angela Carter has always believed in change: she'd refer to her 'naive leftie-ism', but she never let go of it.

The American critic Susan Suleiman has celebrated Angela Carter's fiction as truly breaking new ground for women by occupying the male voice of narrative authority and at the same time impersonating it to the point of parody, so that the rules are changed and the dreams become unruly, transformed, open to 'the multiplication of narrative possibilities', themselves a promise of a possibly different future; the novels also 'expand our notions of what it is possible to dream in the domain of sexuality, criticizing all dreams that are too narrow'.[3] Angela's favourite icon of the feminine was Lulu, in Wedekind's play, and her favourite star was Louise Brooks who played her in *Pandora's Box*; Louise/Lulu was hardly someone who rejected traditional femaleness, but rather took it to such extremes that its nature was transformed. 'Lulu's character is very attractive to me,' she would say dryly, and she borrowed from it to create her wanton, ribald and feisty heroines of the boards in *Wise Children*. Lulu never ingratiated herself, never sought fame, or fortune, and suffered neither guilt nor remorse. According to Angela, 'her particular quality is, she makes being polymorphously perverse look like the only way to be'. If she had had a daughter, she once said, she would have called her Lulu.

She liked to refer to her opinions as 'classic GLC' but in spite of these demurrals she was an original and committed political thinker too. *Wise Children* (1989) was born out of her democratic and socialist utopianism, her affirmation of 'low' culture, of the rude health of popular language and humour as a long-lasting, effective means of survival: her Shakespeare (the novel contains almost all his characters and their plots in one form or another) isn't a poet for the élite, but an imagination springing out of folklore, with energy and know-how.

She found happiness with Mark Pearce, who was training to become a primary schoolteacher when she became ill. She often spoke of the radiance of children, their unutterable beauty and their love; their son Alexander was born in 1983.

Sometimes, in the case of a great writer, it's easy to lose sight of the pleasure they give, as critics search for meaning and value, influence and importance; Angela Carter loved cinema and vaudeville and songs and the circus, and she herself could entertain like no other. She included a story from Kenya in *The Virago Book of Fairy Tales* about a sultana who is withering away while a poor man's wife is kept happy because her husband feeds her 'meat of the tongue' – stories, jokes, ballads. These are what make women thrive, the story says; they are also what Angela Carter gave so generously to make others thrive. *Wise Children* ends with the words, 'What a joy it is to dance and sing!' That she should not have thrived herself is sad beyond words.

Since her death, tributes have filled the papers and the airwaves. She would have been astonished by the attention, and pleased. It did not come to her in her lifetime, not with such whole-heartedness. It's partly a tribute to her potency that while she was alive people felt discomfited by her, that her wit and witchiness and subversiveness made her hard to handle, like some wonderful beast of the kind she enjoyed in fairy tales. Her friends were lucky knowing her, and her readers too. We have been left a feast and she laid it out with 'spread fingers' for us to share.

Marina Warner, 1992

1. Italo Calvino, *Six Memos for the Next Millennium*, trans. William Weaver (London, 1992), p. 26.
2. Angela Carter, *Expletives Deleted* (London, 1992), p. 5.
3. Susan Rubin Suleiman, *Subversive Intent: Gender, Politics and the Avant-Garde* (Harvard, 1990), pp. 136–40.

This introduction contains material from Marina Warner's obituary of Angela Carter which appeared in the Independent *18 February 1992.*

Part One

STRONG MINDS AND LOW CUNNING

The Twelve Wild Ducks

(Norwegian)

NCE on a time there was a queen who was out driving, when there had been a new fall of snow in the winter; but when she had gone a little way, she began to bleed at the nose, and had to get out of her sledge. And so, as she stood there, leaning against the fence, and saw the red blood on the white snow, she fell a-thinking how she had twelve sons and no daughter, and she said to herself –

'If I only had a daughter as white as snow and as red as blood, I shouldn't care what became of all my sons.'

But the words were scarce out of her mouth before an old witch of the Trolls came up to her.

'A daughter you shall have,' she said, 'and she shall be as white as snow, and as red as blood; and your sons shall be mine, but you may keep them till the babe is christened.'

So when the time came the queen had a daughter, and she was as white as snow, and as red as blood, just as the Troll had promised, and so they called her 'Snow-white and Rosy-red'. Well, there was great joy at the king's court, and the queen was as glad as glad could be; but when what she had promised to the old witch came into her mind, she sent for a silversmith, and bade him make twelve silver spoons, one for each prince, and after that she bade him make one more, and that she gave to Snow-white and Rosy-red. But as soon as ever the princess was christened, the princes were turned into twelve wild ducks, and flew away. They never saw them again – away they went, and away they stayed.

So the princess grew up, and she was both tall and fair, but she was often so strange and sorrowful, and no one could understand what it was that ailed her. But one evening the queen was also sorrowful, for she had many strange thoughts when she thought of her sons. She said to Snow-white and Rosy-red, 'Why are you so sorrowful, my daughter? Is there anything you want? If so, only say the word, and you shall have it.'

'Oh, it seems so dull and lonely here,' said Snow-white and Rosy-red; 'everyone else has brothers and sisters, but I am all alone; I have none; and that's why I'm so sorrowful.'

'But you *had* brothers, my daughter,' said the queen; 'I had twelve sons who were your brothers, but I gave them all away to get you'; and so she told her the whole story.

So when the princess heard that, she had no rest; for, in spite of all the queen could say or do, and all she wept and prayed, the lassie would set off to seek her brothers, for she thought it was all her fault; and at last she got leave to go away from the palace. On and on she walked into the wide world, so far, you would never have thought a young lady could have strength to walk so far.

So, once, when she was walking through a great, great wood, one day she felt tired, and sat down on a mossy tuft and fell asleep. Then she dreamt that she went deeper and deeper into the wood, till she came to a little wooden hut, and there she found her brothers. Just then she woke, and straight before her she saw a worn path in the green moss, and this path went deeper into the wood; so she followed it, and after a long time she came to just such a little wooden house as that she had seen in her dream.

Now, when she went into the room there was no one at home, but there stood twelve beds, and twelve chairs, and twelve spoons – a dozen of everything, in short. So when she saw that she was so glad, she hadn't been so glad for many a long year, for she could guess at once that her brothers lived here, and that they owned the beds, and chairs and spoons. So she began to make up the fire, and sweep the room, and make the beds, and cook the dinner, and to make the house as tidy as she could; and when she had done all the cooking and work, she ate her own dinner, and crept under her youngest brother's bed, and lay down there, but she forgot her spoon upon the table.

So she had scarcely laid herself down before she heard

something flapping and whirring in the air, and so all the twelve wild ducks came sweeping in; but as soon as ever they crossed the threshold they became princes.

'Oh, how nice and warm it is in here,' they said. 'Heaven bless him who made up the fire, and cooked such a good dinner for us.'

And so each took up his silver spoon and was going to eat. But when each had taken his own, there was one still left lying on the table, and it was so like the rest that they couldn't tell it from them.

'This is our sister's spoon,' they said; 'and if her spoon be here, she can't be very far off herself.'

'If this be our sister's spoon, and she be here,' said the eldest, 'she shall be killed, for she is to blame for all the ill we suffer.'

And this she lay under the bed and listened to.

'No,' said the youngest, ''twere a shame to kill her for that. She has nothing to do with our suffering ill; for if anyone's to blame, it's our own mother.'

So they set to work hunting for her both high and low, and at last they looked under all the beds, and so when they came to the youngest prince's bed, they found her, and dragged her out. Then the eldest prince wished again to have her killed, but she begged and prayed so prettily for herself.

'Oh! gracious goodness! don't kill me, for I've gone about seeking you these three years, and if I could only set you free, I'd willingly lose my life.'

'Well!' said they, 'if you will set us free, you may keep your life; for you can if you choose.'

'Yes; only tell me,' said the princess, 'how it can be done, and I'll do it, whatever it be.'

'You must pick thistledown,' said the princes, 'and you must card it, and spin it and weave it; and after you have done that, you must cut out and make twelve coats, and twelve shirts and twelve neckerchiefs, one for each of us, and while you do that, you must neither talk, nor laugh nor weep. If you can do that, we are free.'

'But where shall I ever get thistledown enough for so many

neckerchiefs, and shirts, and coats?' asked Snow-white and Rosy-red.

'We'll soon show you,' said the princes; and so they took her with them to a great wide moor, where there stood such a crop of thistles, all nodding and nodding in the breeze, and the down all floating and glistening like gossamers through the air in the sunbeams. The princess had never seen such a quantity of thistledown in her life, and she began to pluck and gather it as fast and as well as she could; and when she got home at night she set to work carding and spinning yarn from the down. So she went on a long long time, picking, and carding and spinning, and all the while keeping the princes' house, cooking, and making their beds. At evening home they came, flapping and whirring like wild ducks, and all night they were princes, but in the morning off they flew again, and were wild ducks the whole day.

But now it happened once, when she was out on the moor to pick thistledown – and if I don't mistake, it was the very last time she was to go thither – it happened that the young king who ruled that land was out hunting, and came riding across the moor, and saw her. So he stopped there and wondered who the lovely lady could be that walked along the moor picking thistledown, and he asked her her name, and when he could get no answer he was still more astonished; and at last he liked her so much, that nothing would do but he must take her home to his castle and marry her. So he ordered his servants to take her and put her up on his horse. Snow-white and Rosy-red wrung her hands, and made signs to them, and pointed to the bags in which her work was, and when the king saw she wished to have them with her, he told his men to take up the bags behind them. When they had done that the princess came to herself, little by little, for the king was both a wise man and a handsome man too, and he was as soft and kind to her as a doctor. But when they got home to the palace, and the old queen, who was his stepmother, set eyes on Snow-white and Rosy-red, she got so cross and jealous of her because she was so lovely, that she said to the king, 'Can't you see now, that this thing whom you have picked up, and whom you are going to marry, is a witch? Why, she can't either talk, or laugh or weep!'

But the king didn't care a pin for what she said, but held on with the wedding, and married Snow-white and Rosy-red, and they lived in great joy and glory; but she didn't forget to go on sewing at her shirts.

So when the year was almost out, Snow-white and Rosy-red brought a prince into the world, and then the old queen was more spiteful and jealous than ever. At dead of night she stole in to Snow-white and Rosy-red, while she slept, and took away her babe, and threw it into a pit full of snakes. After that she cut Snow-white and Rosy-red in her finger, and smeared the blood over her mouth, and went straight to the king.

'Now come and see,' she said, 'what sort of a thing you have taken for your queen; here she has eaten up her own babe.'

Then the king was so downcast, he almost burst into tears, and said, 'Yes, it must be true, since I see it with my own eyes; but she'll not do it again, I'm sure, and so this time I'll spare her life.'

So before the next year was out she had another son, and the same thing happened. The king's stepmother got more and more jealous and spiteful. She stole in to the young queen at night while she slept, took away the babe, and threw it into a pit full of snakes, cut the young queen's finger, and smeared the blood over her mouth, and then went and told the king she had eaten up her own child. Then the king was so sorrowful, you can't think how sorry he was, and he said, 'Yes, it must be true, since I see it with my own eyes, but she'll not do it again, I'm sure, and so this time too I'll spare her life.'

Well, before the next year was out, Snow-white and Rosy-red brought a daughter into the world, and her, too, the old queen took and threw into the pit full of snakes, while the young queen slept. Then she cut her finger, smeared the blood over her mouth, and went again to the king and said, 'Now you may come and see if it isn't as I say; she's a wicked, wicked witch, for here she has gone and eaten up her third babe too.'

Then the king was so sad, there was no end to it, for now he couldn't spare her any longer but had to order her to be burnt alive on a pile of wood. But just when the pile was all ablaze, and they were going to put her on it, she made signs to them to take twelve boards and lay them round the pile, and on these she laid the neckerchiefs, and the shirts and the coats for her brothers, but the youngest brother's shirt wanted its left arm, for she hadn't had time to finish it. And as soon as ever she had done that, they heard such a flapping and whirring in the air, and down came twelve wild ducks flying over the forest, and each of them snapped up his clothes in his bill and flew off with them.

'See now!' said the old queen to the king, 'wasn't I right when I told you she was a witch; but make haste and burn her before the pile burns low.'

'Oh!' said the king, 'we've wood enough and to spare, and so I'll wait a bit, for I have a mind to see what the end of all this will be.'

As he spoke, up came the twelve princes riding along as handsome well-grown lads as you'd wish to see; but the youngest prince had a wild duck's wing instead of his left arm.

'What's all this about?' asked the princes.

'My queen is to be burnt,' said the king, 'because she's a witch, and because she has eaten up her own babes.'

'She hasn't eaten them at all,' said the princes. 'Speak now, sister; you have set us free and saved us, now save yourself.'

Then Snow-white and Rosy-red spoke, and told the whole story; how every time she was brought to bed, the old queen, the king's stepmother, had stolen in to her at night, had taken her babes away, and cut her little finger, and smeared the blood over her mouth; and then the princes took the king, and showed him the snake-pit where three babes lay playing with adders and toads, and lovelier children you never saw.

So the king had them taken out at once, and went to his stepmother, and asked her what punishment she thought that woman deserved who could find it in her heart to betray a guiltless queen and three such blessed little babes.

'She deserves to be fast bound between twelve unbroken steeds, so that each may take his share of her,' said the old queen.

'You have spoken your own doom,' said the king, 'and you

shall suffer it at once.'

So the wicked old queen was fast bound between twelve unbroken steeds, and each got his share of her. But the king took Snow-white and Rosy-red, and their three children, and the twelve princes, and so they all went home to their father and mother and told all that had befallen them, and there was joy and gladness over the whole kingdom, because the princess was saved and set free, and because she had set free her twelve brothers.

Old Foster

(Hillbilly, USA)

HEY use to be an old man, he lived way over in the forest by hisself, and all he lived on was he caught women and boiled 'em in front of the fire and eat 'em. Now the way my mother told me, he'd go into the villages and tell 'em this and that and get 'em to come out and catch 'em and jest boil they breasts. That's what she told me, and then I've heard hit that he jest eat 'em. Well, they was a beautiful stout woman, he liked 'em the best (he'd a been right atter me un your mother) so every day he'd come over to this woman's house and he'd tell her to please come over to see his house. 'Why, Mr Foster, I can't find the way.' 'Yes, you can. I'll take a spool of red silk thread out of my pocket and I'll start windin' hit on the bushes and it'll carry ye straight to my house.' So she promised him one day she'd come.

So she got her dinner over one day and she started. So she follered the red silk thread and went on over to his house. When she got there, there was a poor little old boy sittin' over the fire a boilin' meat. And he says, 'Laws, Aunt' – she was his aunt – 'what er you doin' here? Foster kills every woman that comes here. You leave here jest as quick as you can.'

She started to jump out the door and she saw Foster a comin' with two young women, one under each arm. So she run back and says, 'Jack, honey, what'll I do, I see him a comin'?' 'Jump in that old closet under the stair and I'll lock you in,' says Jack.

So she jumped in and Jack locked her in. So Foster come in and he was jest talkin' and a laughin' with those two girls and tellin' the most tales, and he was goin' to taken 'em over to a corn shuckin' next day. Foster says, 'Come on in and have supper with me.' So Jack put up some boiled meat and water. That's all they had. As soon as the girls stepped in and seed the circumstance and seed their time had come their countenance fell. Foster says, 'You better come in and eat, maybe the last chanct you'll ever have.' Girls both jumped up and started to run. Foster jumps up and ketched 'em, and gets his tomihawk and starts upstairs with 'em. Stairs was shackly and rattly, and as they went up one of the girls retched her hand back and caught hold of a step and Foster jest tuck his tomihawk and hacked her hand off. It drapped into whar my mother was. She laid on in there until next day atter Foster went, then Jack let her out.

She jest bird worked over to where the corn shuckin' was. When she got there Foster was there. She didn't know how to git Foster destroyed. The people thought these people got out in the forest and the wild animals ud ketch 'em. So she says, 'I dreamt an awful dream last night. I dreamed I lived close to Foster's house and he was always a-wantin' me to come to his house.'

Foster says, 'Well, that ain't so, and it shan't be so, and God forbid it ever should be so.'

She went right on, 'And I dreamt he put out a red thread and I follered hit to his house and there uz Jack broilin' women's breasts in front of the fire.'

Foster says, 'Well, that ain't so, and it shan't be so, and God forbid it ever should be so.'

She went right on, 'And he says, "What er you doin' here! Foster kills every woman uz comes here." '

Foster says, 'Well, that ain't so, and it shan't be so, and God forbid it ever should be so.'

She went right on, 'And I seed Foster a-comin' with two girls. And when they git thar the girls their hearts failed 'em and Foster ketched 'em and gets his tomihawk and starts up stairs with 'em.'

Foster says, 'Well, that ain't so, and it shan't be so, and God forbid it ever should be so.'

She went right on, 'The stairs was shackly and rattly and as they went up, one of the girls retched her hand back and caught hold of a step and Foster jest tuk his tomihawk and hacked her hand off.'

Foster says, 'Well, that ain't so, and it shan't be so, and God forbid it ever should be so.'

She says, 'Hit is so, and it shall be so and here I've got the hand to show.'

And they knowed the two girls was missin' and they knowed it was so, so they lynched Foster and then they went and got Jack and bound him out.

Šāhīn

(Palestinian Arab)

NCE there was a king (and there is no kingship except that which belongs to Allah, may He be praised and exalted!) and he had an only daughter. He had no other children, and he was proud of her. One day, as she was lounging about, the daughter of the vizier came to visit her. They sat together, feeling bored.

'We're sitting around here feeling bored,' said the daughter of the vizier. 'What do you say to going out and having a good time?'

'Yes,' said the other.

Sending for the daughters of the ministers and dignitaries of state, the king's daughter gathered them all together, and they went into her father's orchard to take the air, each going her own way.

As the vizier's daughter was sauntering about, she stepped on an iron ring. Taking hold of it, she pulled, and behold! it opened the door to an underground hallway, and she descended into it. The other girls, meanwhile, were distracted, amusing themselves. Going into the hallway, the vizier's daughter came upon a young man with his sleeves rolled up. And what! there were deer, partridges, and rabbits in front of him, and he was busy plucking and skinning.

Before he was aware of it, she had already saluted him. 'Peace to you!'

'And to you, peace!' he responded, taken aback. 'What do you happen to be, sister, human or jinn?'

'Human,' she answered, 'and the choicest of the race. What are you doing here?'

'By Allah,' he said, 'we are forty young men, all brothers.

Every day my brothers go out to hunt in the morning and come home toward evening. I stay home and prepare their food.'

'That's fine,' she chimed in. 'You're forty young men, and we're forty young ladies. I'll be your wife, the king's daughter is for your eldest brother, and all the other girls are for all your other brothers.' She matched the girls with the men.

Oh! How delighted he was to hear this!

'What's your name?'

'Šāhīn,' he answered.

'Welcome, Šāhīn.'

He went and fetched a chair, and set it in front of her. She sat next to him, and they started chatting. He roasted some meat, gave it to her, and she ate. She kept him busy until the food he was cooking was ready.

'Šāhīn,' she said when the food was ready, 'you don't happen to have some seeds and nuts in the house, do you?'

'Yes, by Allah, we do.'

'Why don't you get us some. It'll help pass away the time.'

In their house, the seeds and nuts were stored on a high shelf. He got up, brought a ladder, and climbed up to the shelf. Having filled his handkerchief with seeds and nuts, he was about to come down when she said, 'Here, let me take it from you. Hand it over!' Taking the handkerchief from him, she pulled the ladder away and threw it to the ground, leaving him stranded on the shelf.

She then brought out large bowls, prepared a huge platter, piled all the food on it, and headed straight out of there, taking the food with her and closing the door of the tunnel behind her. Putting the food under a tree, she called to the girls, 'Come eat, girls!'

'Eh! Where did this come from?' they asked, gathering around.

'Just eat and be quiet,' she replied. 'What more do you want? Just eat!'

The food was prepared for forty lads, and here were forty lasses. They set to and ate it all.

'Go on along now!' commanded the vizier's daughter. 'Each one back where she came from. Disperse!'

She dispersed them, and they went their way. Waiting until

they were all busy, she took the platter back, placing it where it was before and coming back out again. In time the girls all went home.

Now we go back. To whom? To Šāhīn. When his brothers came home in the evening, they could not find him.

'Oh Šāhīn,' they called. 'Šāhīn!'

And behold! he answered them from the shelf.

'Hey! What are you doing up there?' asked the eldest brother.

'By Allah, brother,' Šāhīn answered, 'I set up the ladder after the food was ready and came to get some seeds and nuts for passing away the time. The ladder slipped, and I was stranded up here.'

'Very well,' they said, and set up the ladder for him. When he came down, the eldest brother said, 'Now, go bring the food so we can have dinner.' Gathering up the game they had hunted that day, they put it all in one place and sat down.

Šāhīn went to fetch the food from the kitchen, but he could not find a single bite.

'Brother,' he said, coming back, 'the cats must have eaten it.'

'All right,' said the eldest. 'Come, prepare us whatever you can.'

Taking the organs of the hunted animals, from this and that he made dinner and they ate. Then they laid their heads down and went to sleep.

The next morning they woke up and set out for the hunt. 'Now brother,' they mocked him, 'be sure to let us go without dinner another evening. Let the cats eat it all!'

'No, brothers,' he said. 'Don't worry.'

No sooner did they leave than he rolled up his sleeves and set to skinning and plucking the gazelles, rabbits and partridges. On time, the vizier's daughter showed up. Having gone to the king's daughter and gathered all the other girls, she waited till they were amusing themselves with something and then dropped in on him.

'Salaam!'

'And to you, peace!' he answered. 'Welcome to the one who took the food and left me stranded on the shelf, making me look ridiculous to my brothers!'

'What you say is true,' she responded. 'And yet I'm likely to do even more than that to the one I love.'

'And as for me,' he murmured, 'your deeds are sweeter than honey.'

Fetching a chair, he set it down for her, and then he brought some seeds and nuts. They sat down to entertain themselves, and she kept him amused until she realised the food was ready.

'Šāhīn,' she said, 'isn't there a bathroom in your house?'

'Yes, there is,' he replied.

'I'm pressed, and must go to the bathroom. Where is it?'

'It's over there,' he answered.

'Well, come and show it to me.'

'This is it, here,' he said, showing it to her.

She went in and, so the story goes, made as if she did not know how to use it.

'Come and show me how to use this thing,' she called.

I don't know what else she said, but he came to show her, you might say, how to sit on the toilet. Taking hold of him, she pushed him inside like this, and he ended up with his head down and his feet up. She closed the door on him and left. Going into the kitchen, she served up the food on to a platter and headed out of there. She put the food under a tree and called to her friends, 'Come eat!'

'And where did you get all this?'

'All you have to do is eat,' she answered.

They ate and scattered, each going her way. And she stole away and returned the platter.

At the end of the day the brothers came home, and there was no sign of their brother. 'Šāhīn, Šāhīn!' they called out. 'O Šāhīn!' But no answer came. They searched the shelf, they searched here, and they searched there. But it was no use.

'You know,' said the eldest, 'I say there's something odd about Šāhīn's behaviour. I suspect he has a girlfriend. Anyway, some of you go into the kitchen, find the food, and bring it so we can eat. I'm sure Šāhīn will show up any moment.'

Going into the kitchen, they found nothing. 'There's no food,' they reported. 'It's all gone! We're now sure that Šāhīn has a girlfriend, and he gives her all the food. Let's go ahead and fix whatever there is at hand so we can eat.'

Having prepared a quick meal, they ate dinner and were

content. They prepared for sleep, but one of them (All respect to the listeners!) was pressed and needed to relieve himself. He went to the bathroom, and lo! there was Šāhīn, upside down.

'Hey, brothers!' he shouted. 'Here's Šāhīn, and he's fallen into the toilet!'

They rushed over and lifted him out. What a condition he was in! They gave him a bath.

'Tell me,' said the eldest, 'what's going on?'

'By Allah, brother,' replied Šāhīn, 'after I cooked dinner I went to relieve myself, and I slipped.'

'Very well,' returned the eldest. 'But the food, where is it?'

'By Allah, as far as I know it's in the kitchen, but how should I know if the cats haven't eaten it?'

'Well, all right!' they said, and went back to sleep.

The next morning, as they were setting out, they mocked him again. 'Why don't you leave us without dinner another night?'

'No, brothers!' he said. 'Don't worry.'

Pulling themselves together, they departed. Now, on time, the daughter of the vizier came to see the king's daughter, gathered the others, and they came down to the orchard and spread out. Waiting until they were all caught up with something, she slipped away to him, and listen, brothers! she found him at home.

'Salaam!'

'And to you, peace!' he retorted. 'Welcome! On the shelf the first day, and you made away with the food; and the second day you threw me into the toilet and stole the food, blackening my face in front of my brothers!'

'As for me,' she said, 'I'll do even more than that to the one I love.'

'And to me, it's sweeter than honey,' he responded, bringing her a chair. She sat down, he brought seeds and nuts, and they passed away the time entertaining themselves. She kept chatting with him, until she knew the food was ready.

'Šāhīn,' she said.

'Yes.'

'Don't you have some drinks for us to enjoy ourselves? There's meat here, and seeds and nuts. We could eat and have something to drink.'

'Yes,' he replied, 'we do.'

'Why don't you bring some out, then?' she urged him.

Bringing a bottle, he set it in front of her. She poured drinks and handed them to him. 'This one's to my health,' she egged him on, 'and this one's also for my sake,' until he fell over, as if no one were there. She then went and took some sugar, put it on to boil, and made a preparation for removing body hair. She used it on him to perfection, and, brother, she made him look like the most beautiful of girls. Bringing a woman's dress, she put it on him. Then, bringing a scarf, she wrapped it around his head and laid him down to sleep in bed. She powdered his face, wrapped the scarf well around his head, put the bed covers over him, and left. Then into the kitchen she went, loaded the food, and departed. The girls ate, and the platter was replaced.

When the brothers returned in the evening, they did not find Šāhīn at home.

'O Šāhīn! Šāhīn! Šāhīn!'

No answer. 'Let's search the bathroom,' they said among themselves. But they did not find him there. They searched the shelf, and still no sign of him.

'Didn't I tell you Šāhīn has a girlfriend?' the eldest declared. 'I'd say Šāhīn has a girlfriend and goes out with her. Some of you, go and see if the food's still there.' They did, and found nothing.

Again they resorted to a quick meal of organ meat. When it was time to sleep, each went to his bed. In his bed, the eldest found our well-contented friend stretched out in it. Back to his brothers he ran. 'I told you Šāhīn has a girlfriend, but you didn't believe me. Come and take a look! Here's Šāhīn's bride! Come and see! Come and see!'

He called his brothers, and they all came, clamouring, 'Šāhīn's bride!' Removing his scarf, they looked at him carefully. Eh! A man's features are hard to miss. They recognised him. 'Eh! This is Šāhīn!' they shouted. Bringing water, they splashed his face till he woke up. Looking himself over, what did he find? They fetched a mirror. He looked at himself, and what a sight he was – all rouged, powdered and beautified.

'And now,' they asked him, 'what do you have to say for yourself?'

'By Allah, brother,' answered Šāhīn, 'listen and I'll tell you the truth. Every day, around noon, a girl with such and such features comes to see me. She says, "We're forty young ladies. The king's daughter is for your eldest brother, I am yours, and all the other girls are for all your other brothers." She's the one who's been doing these things to me every day.'

'Is that so?'

'Yes, it is.'

'Fine. All of you go to the hunt tomorrow,' suggested the eldest, 'and I'll stay behind with Šāhīn. I'll take care of her!'

Pulling out his sword (so the story goes), he sat waiting in readiness. By Allah, brothers, in due time she came. She had gathered the girls as usual, and they had come down to the orchard. Waiting until their attention was caught, she slipped away to him. Before he was even aware of her, she had already saluted him.

'Salaam!'

'And to you, peace!' he answered. 'The first item on the shelf, and I said all right; the second time in the bathroom, and I said all right; but the third time you put make-up on me and turned me into a bride!'

'And yet I'm likely to do even more than that to the one I love.'

No sooner had she said that than up rose the eldest brother and rushed over to her, his sword at the ready.

'Listen,' she reasoned with him. 'You are forty, and we are forty. The king's daughter is to be your wife, and I, Šāhīn's; and so and so among us is for so and so among you, and so on.' She calmed him down.

'Is it true, what you're saying?' he asked.

'Of course it's true,' she replied.

'And who can speak for these girls?'

'I can.'

'You're the one who can speak for them?'

'Yes.'

(Šāhīn, meanwhile, was listening, and since he was already experienced, he mused to himself that his brother had been taken in already.)

'Agreed,' said the eldest brother. 'Come over here and let me pay you the bridewealth for the forty girls. Where are we to meet you?'

'First pay me the bridewealth,' she answered, 'and tomorrow, go and reserve a certain public bath for us at your expense. Stand guard at the gate, and as we go in you yourself can count us one by one – all forty of us. We'll go into the baths and bathe, and after we come out each of you will take his bride home by the hand.'

'Just like that?' he wondered.

'Of course,' she assured him.

He brought out a blanket, she spread it, and – count, count, count – he counted one hundred Ottoman gold coins for each girl. When he had finished counting out the money, she took it and went straight out. Calling her friends over, she said, 'Sit here! Sit under this tree! Each of you open your hand and receive your bridewealth.'

'Eh!' they protested, 'You so and so! Did you ruin your reputation?'

'No one's to say anything,' she responded. 'Each of you will take her bridewealth without making a sound.' Giving each of them her money, she said, 'Come. Let's go home.'

After she had left their place, Šāhīn said to his brother, 'Brother, she tricked me and took only the food. But she tricked you and got away with our money.'

'Who, me?' the brother declared, 'Trick me? Tomorrow you'll see.'

The next day the brothers stayed at home. They went and reserved the baths at their own expense, and the eldest stood watch at the door, waiting for the girls to arrive. Meanwhile, the vizier's daughter had got up the next day, gathered all the girls, the king's daughter among them, and, leading them in front of her, headed for the bath with them. And behold! there was our *effendi* guarding the door. As they were going in, he counted them one by one. Count, count, he counted them all – exactly forty.

Going into the baths, the girls bathed and enjoyed themselves. But after they had finished bathing and put on their clothes, she, the clever one, gave them this advice: 'Each of you is to shit in the tub she has bathed in, and let's line the tubs up all in a row.' Each of them shat in her tub, and they arranged them neatly in a row, all forty of them. Now, the baths had another door, away from the entrance. 'Follow me this way,' urged the vizier's daughter, and they all hurried out.

The eldest brother waited an hour, two, three, then four, but the girls did not emerge. 'Eh!' he said. 'They're taking a long time about it.'

'Brother,' said Šāhīn, 'they're gone.'

'But listen!' he replied, 'where could she have gone? They all went inside the bath-house together.'

'All right,' said Šāhīn, 'let's go in and see.'

Going into the bath-house, brother, they found the owner inside.

'Where did the girls who came into the bath-house go?'

'O uncle!' replied the owner, 'they've been gone a long time.'

'And how could they have left?' asked the eldest brother.

'They left by that door,' he replied.

Now, Šāhīn, who was experienced, looked in the bathing place and saw the tubs all lined up.

'Brother!' he called out.

'Yes. What is it?'

'Come here and take a look,' he answered. 'Here are the forty! Take a good look! See how she had them arranged so neatly?'

Finally the brothers went back home, wondering to themselves, 'And now, what are we going to do?'

'Leave them to me!' volunteered Šāhīn. 'I'll take care of them.'

The next day Šāhīn disguised himself as an old lady. Wearing an old woman's dress, he put a beaded rosary around his neck and headed for the city. The daughter of the vizier, meanwhile, had gathered the girls, and she was sitting with them in a room above the street. As he was coming from afar, she saw and recognised him. She winked to her friends, saying, 'I'll go call him, and you chime in with, "Here's our aunt! Welcome to our aunt!" ' As soon as she saw him draw near, she opened the door and came out running. 'Welcome, welcome, welcome to our aunty! Welcome, aunty!' And, taking him by the hand, she pulled him inside to where they were. 'Welcome to our aunty!' they clamoured, locking the door. 'Welcome to our aunty!'

'Now, girls, take off your clothes,' urged the vizier's daughter. 'Take off your clothes. It's been a long time since we've had our clothes washed by our aunty's own hands. Let her wash our clothes!'

'By Allah, I'm tired,' protested Šāhīn. 'By Allah, I can't do it.'

'By Allah, you must do it, aunty,' they insisted. 'It's been such a long time since we've had our clothes washed by our aunty's hands.'

She made all forty girls take off their clothes, each of them leaving on only enough to cover her modesty, and she handed the clothes to him. He washed clothes till noon.

'Come girls,' said the vizier's daughter. 'By Allah, it's been such a long time since our aunty has bathed us with her own hands. Let her bathe us!'

Each of them put on a wrap and sat down, and he went around bathing them in turn. By the time he had finished bathing them all, what a condition he was in! He was exhausted.

When he had finished with one, she would get up and put on her clothes. The vizier's daughter would then wink at her and whisper that she should take the wrap she was wearing, fold it over, twist it, and tie a knot at one end so that it was like a whip.

When all forty girls had finished bathing, the leader spoke out, 'Eh, aunty! Hey girls, she has just bathed us, and we must bathe her in return.'

'No, niece!' he protested. 'I don't need a bath! For the sake of . . .'

'Impossible, aunty!' insisted the vizier's daughter. 'By Allah, this can't be. Eh! You bathe and bathe all of us, and we don't even bathe you in return. Come, girls!'

At a wink from her, they set on him against his will. They were forty. What could he do? They took hold of him and removed his clothes, and lo and behold! he was a man.

'Eh!' they exclaimed. 'This isn't our aunty. It's a man! Have at him, girls!'

And with their whips, each of them having braided her robe and tied knots in it, they put Šāhīn in the middle and descended on his naked body. Hit him from here, turn him around there, and beat him again on the other side! All the while he was jumping among them and shouting at the top of his voice. When she thought he had had enough, she winked at them to clear a path. As soon as he saw his way open, he opened the door and dashed out running, wearing only the skin the Lord had given him.

His brothers were at home, and before they were even aware of it, he showed up, naked. And what a condition he was in! Up they sprang, as if possessed. 'Hey! What happened to you?' they asked. 'Come! Come! What hit you?'

'Wait a minute,' he answered. 'Such and such happened to me.'

'And now,' they asked among themselves, 'what can we do?'

'Now, by Allah,' answered Šāhīn, 'we have no recourse but for each of us to ask for the hand of his bride from her father. As for me, I'm going to ask for her hand. But as soon as she arrives here, I'm going to kill her. No other punishment will do. I'll show her!'

They all agreed, each going to ask for his bride's hand from her father, and the fathers gave their consent.

Now, the daughter of the minister was something of a devil. She asked her father, if anyone should come asking for her hand, not to give his consent before letting her know. When Šāhīn came to propose, the father said, 'Not until I consult with my daughter first.' The father went to consult with his daughter, and she said, 'All right, give your consent, but on condition that there be a waiting period of one month so that the bridegroom can have enough time to buy the wedding clothes and take care of all the other details.'

After the asking for her hand was completed, the minister's daughter waited until her father had left the house. She then went and put on one of his suits, wrapped a scarf around the lower part of her face, and, taking a whip with her, headed for the carpenter's workshop.

'Carpenter!'

'Yes, Your Excellency!'

'In a while I'll be sending you a concubine. You will observe her height and make a box to fit her. I want it ready by tomorrow. Otherwise, I'll have your head cut off. And don't hold her here for two hours!'

'No, sir. I won't.'

She lashed him twice and left, going directly – where? To the halva maker's shop.

'Halva maker!'

'Yes.'

'I'm going to be sending you a concubine momentarily. You will observe her. See her shape and her height. You must make me a halva doll that looks exactly like her. And don't you keep her here for a couple of hours or I'll shorten your life!'

'Your order, O minister,' said the man, 'will be obeyed.'

She lashed him twice with the whip and left. She went and changed, putting on her ordinary clothes, then went to the carpenter's shop and stayed a while. After that she went and stood by the halva maker's shop for a while. Then she went straight home. Changing back into her father's suit, she took the whip with her and went to the carpenter.

'Carpenter!'

'Yes, my lord minister!'

'An ostrich shorten your life!' responded the girl. 'I send you the concubine, and you hold her here for two hours!'

She descended on him with the whip, beating him all over.

'Please, sir!' he pleaded, 'it was only because I wanted to make sure the box was an exact fit.'

Leaving him alone, she headed for the halva maker's. Him too, she whipped several times, and then she returned home.

The next day she sent for her slave and said to him, 'Go bring the wooden box from the carpenter's shop to the halva maker's. Put the halva doll in it, lock it, and bring it to me here.'

'Yes, I'll do it,' he answered.

When the box was brought, she took it in and said to her mother, 'Listen, mother! I'm going to leave this box with you in trust. When the time comes to take me out of the house and to load up and bring along my trousseau, you must have this box brought with the trousseau and placed in the same room where I will be.'

'But, dear daughter!' protested the mother, 'what will people say? The minister's daughter is bringing a wooden box with her trousseau! You will become a laughing-stock.' I don't know what else she said but it was no use.

'This is not your concern,' insisted the daughter. 'That's how I want it.'

When the bridegroom's family came to take the bride out of

her father's house, she was made ready, and the wooden box was brought along with her trousseau. They took the wooden box and, as she had told them, placed it in the same room where she was to be. As soon as she came into the room and the box was brought in, she threw out all the women. 'Go away!' she said. 'Each of you must go home now.'

After she had made everyone leave, she locked the door. Then, dear ones, she took the doll out of the box. Taking off her clothes, she put them on the doll, and she placed her gold around its neck. She then set the doll in her own place on the bridal seat, tied a string around its neck, and went and hid under the bed, having first unlocked the door.

Her husband, meanwhile, was taking his time. He stayed away an hour or two before he came in. What kind of mood do you think he was in when he arrived? He was in a foul humour, his sword in hand, ready to kill her, as if he did not want to marry her in the first place. As soon as he passed over the doorstep, he looked in and saw her on the bridal seat.

'Yes, yes!' he reproached her. 'The first time you abandoned me on the shelf and took the food, I said to myself it was all right. The second time you threw me into the toilet and took the food, and I said all right. The third time you removed my body hair and made me look like a bride, taking the food with you, and even then I said to myself it was all right. After all that, you still weren't satisfied. You tricked us all and took the bridewealth for the forty girls, leaving each of us a turd in the washtub.'

Meanwhile, as he finished each accusation, she would pull the string and nod the doll's head.

'As if all that weren't enough for you,' he went on, 'you had to top it all with your aunty act. "Welcome, welcome, aunty! It's been a long time since we've seen our aunty. It's been such a long time since aunty has washed our clothes!" And you kept me washing clothes all day. And after all that, you insisted, "We must bathe aunty." By Allah, I'm going to burn the hearts of all your paternal and maternal aunties!'

Seeing her nod her head in agreement, he yelled, 'You mean you're not afraid? And you're not going to apologise?' Taking hold of his sword, he struck her a blow that made her head roll. A piece of halva (if the teller is not lying!) flew into his mouth.

Turning it around in his mouth, he found it sweet.

'Alas, cousin!' he cried out. 'If in death you're so sweet, what would it have been like if you were still alive?'

As soon as she heard this, she jumped up from under the bed and rushed over to him, hugging him from behind.

'O cousin! Here I am!' she exclaimed. 'I'm alive!'

They consummated their marriage, and lived together happily.

This is my tale, I've told it; and in your hands I leave it.

The Dog's Snout People
(Lettish)

ONG ago there lived in a forest country two peoples: people with dogs' snouts and good people. The former were hunters, and the latter tilled the soil. Once the dog's snout people, while hunting, caught a girl belonging to the good people; she did not come from an adjacent settlement, but from a distant village. The people with dogs' snouts took the girl home and fed her on nuts and sweet milk; then after a while, wishing to judge of her condition, they took a long needle and drove it into her forehead. They licked up the blood, as a bear licks honey from a hive. They fed the girl, till at last she seemed to be suitable for their purpose. 'She will be a delicious morsel!' they said, telling their mother to roast the girl while they were away hunting in the forest. The oven had already been heating for two days. The men's mother now sent the girl to a neighbouring farm for a shovel, upon which the victim could be thrown into the oven, but by chance the girl went for the shovel to a farm belonging to the good people. She arrived and said to their mother, 'Little mother, lend our woman with the dog's snout a shovel.' 'Why does she require a shovel?' 'I do not know.' 'You are a stupid girl,' said the mother of the good people. 'Do you not know that the oven is being heated for you? In carrying the shovel you will be assisting your own death, but I will instruct you, little daughter. Take the shovel with you, and when the woman with the dog's snout says, "Lie upon the shovel!" then lie upon it crossways; and when she says, "Lie more conveniently" beg her to show you how to take your position. As soon as she has lain down lengthways on the shovel throw her as quickly as possible into the oven, and shut the door so tight that she cannot open it. When you have done this strew around you some ashes, and taking off your bast shoes, put them on reversed, so that the front shall become the back and the back shall become the front; then run away with all your might; they will not find you by your traces! Take care that you do not fall into the hands of the dog's snout people, or there will be an end of you!'

The girl took the shovel and returned with it, and the dog's snout woman said to her, 'Lie down upon the shovel!' The girl lay crossways. Then the dog's snout woman said, 'Lie down lengthways; it will be better.' 'I do not understand,' said the girl; 'show me.' They disputed a long while, until the dog's snout woman lay down upon the shovel. The girl immediately seized it, thrust the woman rapidly into the oven and shut the door tight. Then she shod herself, as the mother of the good people had instructed her, and ran away. The dog's snout men came home and looked for their mother unsuccessfully. One said to another, 'Perhaps she has gone on a visit to her neighbours; let us see if the roast meat is ready!'

The Old Woman Against the Stream
(Norwegian)

HERE was once a man who had an old wife, and she was so cross and contrary that she was hard to get along with. The man, in fact, didn't get along with her at all. Whatever *he* wanted, she always wanted the very opposite.

Now one Sunday in late summer it happened that the man and the wife went out to see how the crop was getting along. When they came to a field on the other side of the river, the man said, 'Well, now it's ripe. Tomorrow we'll have to start reaping.'

'Yes, tomorrow we can start to clip it,' said the old woman.

'What's that? Shall we clip? Aren't we going to be allowed to reap either, now?' said the man.

No, clip it they should, the old woman insisted.

'There's nothing worse than knowing too little,' said the man, 'but this time you certainly must have lost what little wits you had. Have you ever seen anyone *clip* the crop?'

'Little do I know, and little do I care to know,' said the old woman, 'but this I know to be sure: the crop is going to be clipped and not reaped!' There was nothing more to be said. Clip it they should, and that was that.

So they walked back, wrangling and quarrelling, until they came to a bridge over the river, just by a deep pool.

'It's an old saying,' said the man, 'that good tools do good work. But I dare say *that'll* be a queer harvest which they clip with sheepshears!' he said. 'Shan't we be allowed to reap the crop at all, now?'

'Nay, nay! – Clip, clip, clip!' shrieked the old woman, hopping up and down, and snipping at the man's nose with her fingers. But in her fury she didn't look where she was going, and she tripped over the end of a post in the bridge and tumbled into the river.

'Old ways are hard to mend,' thought the man, 'but it'd be nice if I were right for once – me too.'

He waded out in the pool and caught hold of the old woman's topknot, just when her head was barely above the water. 'Well, are we going to reap the field?' he said.

'Clip, clip, clip!' shrieked the old woman.

'I'll teach you to clip, I will,' thought the man, and ducked her under. But it didn't help. They were going to clip, she said, when he let her up again.

'I can only believe that the old woman is mad!' said the man to himself. 'Many people are mad and don't know it; many have sense and don't show it. But now I'll have to try once more, all the same,' he said. But hardly had he pushed her under before she thrust her hand up out of the water, and started clipping with her fingers as with a pair of scissors.

Then the man flew into a rage, and ducked her both good and long. But all at once her hand sank down below the surface of the water, and the old woman suddenly became so heavy that he had to let go his hold.

'If you want to drag me down into the pool with you now, you can just lie there, you Troll!' said the man. And so there the old woman stayed.

But after a little while, the man thought it a pity that she should lie there and not have a Christian burial. So he went down along the river, and started looking and searching for her. But for all he looked and for all he searched, he couldn't find her. He took with him folk from the farm, and other folk from the neighbourhood, and they all started digging and dragging down along the whole river. But for all they looked, no old woman did they find.

'No,' said the man. 'That's no use at all. This old woman had a mind of her own,' he said. 'She was so contrary while she was alive that she can't very well be otherwise now. We'll have to start searching upstream, and try above the falls. Maybe she's floated herself upstream.'

Well, they went upstream, and looked and searched above the

falls. There lay the old woman!

She was *the old woman against the stream*, she was!

The Letter Trick

(Surinamese)

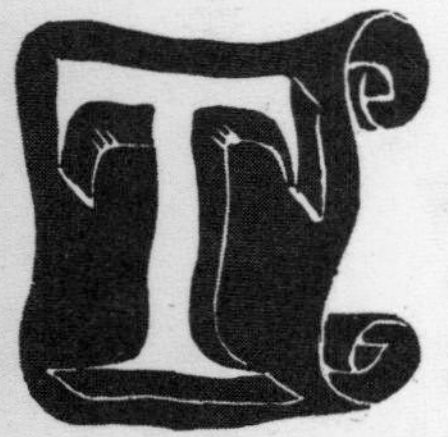

HERE was a woman who had a husband. Well, then her husband was in the bush, and she had another man. But when her husband went to the city, then the other man said to her, said 'If you love me, you must let me come sleep in your house.' Then she said to the man, said, 'All right. My husband is in the city, I will let you come. I am going to dress you in one of my skirts and blouses, and I am going to tell my husband that you are my sister from the plantation.' Then when she dressed him in the dress, then that night he came there. And the woman told her husband this was her sister.

Then at night they went to sleep. But in the morning the woman went to the market because she sold things. Then the man lay down upstairs. But when the woman's husband saw she did not come down, then he went to look, and he saw a man. Then the man was angry. He took a stick and came running to the market towards the woman. But when the woman saw him coming, then the woman took a piece of paper, then she read and cried. Then, when the man came he said, 'What are you doing?' Then she made up a speech. 'Hm! I just received a letter that all my sisters on the plantation have changed into men.' Then the man said, 'They do not lie, because the one who came to sleep with you last night, that one, too, changed into a man.' But the man did not know how to read. That is why the woman deceived him with such a trick.

Rolando and Brunilde

(Italy, Tuscan)

MOTHER and her daughter lived in a village. The daughter was happy because she was engaged to a boy who lived in the same village, a woodcutter, and they were to be married within a few weeks. So she passed all her time helping her mother a little, working in the fields a little, gathering wood a little; and then in her free time she sat at the window and sang . . . as she spun. She spun and she sang, waiting for her fiancé to return from the forest.

One day, a magician passed through town, and he heard singing; she had a pretty voice. He turned around and saw this girl at the window. Seeing her and falling in love with her was one and the same for the magician. And so he sent . . . he sent someone to ask if she would marry him. This prin . . . this girl said, 'No, because I am already engaged to be married. I have a fiancé and I am very fond of him,' she replied, 'and in a few weeks we are getting married,' she said, 'so I don't need a magician or these riches,' because he had told her that he would make her a rich lady because she was poor.

Then the magician, who had become indignant at her refusal, sent an eagle to kidnap the girl, who was called Brunilde, and it carried her to his castle where he showed her all his riches, all his castles, all his gold, all his money, but she didn't care about any of it. She said, 'I will marry Rolando and I want Rolando.' The magician then told her, 'If you don't marry me then you will never leave this castle.' And in fact he locked her up . . . he locked her in a room near his bedroom. Since the magician slept very soundly during the night and snored, for fear that someone would steal her he had an effigy made of himself as big as he was and then he had bells put on it, a thousand tiny bells, so that if anyone bumped into this effigy he would wake up.

Now, her mother and Rolando were worried because the girl didn't come home, and her fiancé wanted to go and kill the magician. But her mother said, 'No, wait, let's wait a little.' She said, 'If not, he could hurt you, too; let's wait a bit.' And they tried one night to get into the garden, but the magician had had a wall built that surrounded the garden and it was so tall that it was impossible to enter. And the girl's mother sat all day and cried.

Finally, one day when she was in the forest she came upon a fairy in the form of an old lady who said to her, 'Tell me, why are you crying so?' And the girl's mother told the old woman about her Brunilde and how she had been carried off. 'Listen,' the fairy said, 'listen, I don't have much power in this case because the magician is much more powerful than I. I can't do anything,' she said. 'However, I can help you,' and she told her that he had closed the girl in a room and that he had had an effigy made of himself. So she said, 'You can't go there because if one of those bells should ring, he'll wake up.' She said: 'Listen to what you should do. This is the season when the cotton falls from the trees. You should go every day and fill a bag with cotton. In the evening when Rolando comes home from the forest, you have him take the cotton to the castle and I'll help you crawl through a hole.' She said: 'I get the bag into the garden and you'll get inside the palace . . . into the castle. In the castle you must stuff a few bells each night with cotton. Until you have stuffed them all, so that they will not ring any more, then we'll see what we can do.' And, in fact, this poor woman said: 'Of course, I'll do it. It will take time but I'll do it gladly.'

So they talked to the young man. During the day the mother gathered the cotton while he went to work, and in the evening they took the bag of cotton to the castle, and the mother stuffed the bells. Until one night the bells had finally all been stuffed. She went back to the old woman in the forest and told her that the last bell had been stuffed that same evening. Then the old woman said, 'Take Rolando with you.' And so the young man was made to enter through the same door that was used to stuff the bells, and the old woman gave him a sword and told him that when they were near enough he should cut off the left ear of the magician. All the power of the magician lies in his left ear, she said . . . In fact they entered the castle and went to get the girl. And the young man went to cut off the magician's ear. After he cut off the ear, the left ear where all his power lay, the entire castle crumbled, everything crumbled. The young couple took all the gold, the silver, and everything that belonged to the magician. They became rich, they got married, and they lived happily ever after.

The Greenish Bird
(Mexican)

HERE were three girls who were orphaned, and Luisa did much sewing. The other two said that they didn't like Luisa's kind of life. They would rather go to bars and such things. Well, that kind of women – gay women. So Luisa stayed home. She kept a jar of water on the window sill, and she sewed and sewed and sewed.

So then he came, the Greenish Bird that was an enchanted prince. And of course he liked Luisa a lot, so he would light there on the window sill and say, 'Luisa, raise your eyes to mine, and your troubles will be over.' But she wouldn't.

On another night he came and said, 'Luisa, give me a drink of water from your little jar.' But she wouldn't look to see if he was a bird or a man or anything. Except she didn't know whether he drank or not, but then she saw he was a man. She gave him some water. So then he came again and proposed to her, and they fell in love. And the bird would come inside; he would lie in her bed. There on the headboard. And he set up a garden for her, with many fruit trees and other things, and a messenger and a maid; so the girl was living in grand style.

What should happen but that her sisters found out. 'Just look at Luisa, how high she has gone overnight. And us,' one of the sisters says, 'just look at us the way we are. Let's spy on her and see who it is that goes in there.' They went and spied on her and saw it was a bird, so they bought plenty of knives. And they put them on the window sill. When the little bird came out, he was wounded all over.

He said, 'Luisa, if you want to follow me, I live in crystal towers on the plains of Merlin. I'm badly wounded,' he said.

So she bought a pair of iron shoes, Luisa did, and she took

some clothes with her – what she could carry walking – and a guitar she had. And she went off after him. She came to the house where the Sun's mother lived. She was a blonde, blonde old woman. Very ugly. So she got there and knocked on the door and it opened. The old woman said, 'What are you doing here? If my son the Sun sees you, he'll devour you,' she said.

'I'm searching for the Greenish Bird,' she said.

'He was here. Look, he's badly wounded. He left a pool of blood there, and he just left a moment ago.'

She said, 'All right, then, I'm going.'

'No,' she said, 'hide and let's see if my son can tell you something. He shines on all the world,' she said.

So he came in, very angry:

Whoo! Whoo!
I smell human flesh. Whoo-whoo!
If I can't have it, I'll eat you.

He said this to his mother.

'What do you want me to do, son? There's nobody here.' She calmed him down and gave him food. Then she told him, little by little.

He said, 'Where's the girl,' he said. 'Let her come out so I can see her.' So Luisa came out and asked him about the Greenish Bird. He said, 'Me, I don't know. I haven't heard of him. I don't know where to find him. I haven't seen anything like that, either. It could be that the Moon's mother, or the Moon herself, would know,' he said.

Well then, 'All right, I'm going now.' Without tasting a bite of food. So then the Sun told her to eat first and then go. And so then they gave her something to eat, and she left.

All right, so she got to the house where the Moon's mother lived. And so, 'What are you doing here? If my daughter the Moon sees you, she will devour you.' And I don't know how many other things the old woman said to her.

'Well then, I'll go. I just wanted to ask her if she hadn't seen the Greenish Bird pass by here.'

'He was here. Look, there's the blood; he's very badly wounded,' she said.

All right, so she started to go away, but the Moon said,

'*Hombre*, don't go. Come eat first, and then you can go.' So they also gave her a bite to eat. As soon as they gave her something, she left. 'Why don't you go where the mother of the Wind lives and wait for the Wind to come home? The Wind goes into every nook and cranny; there isn't a place he doesn't visit.'

The mother of the Wind said, 'All right,' so she hid. She said, 'But you'll have to hide, because if my son the Wind sees you, Heaven help us.'

'All right,' she said.

The Wind came home, all vapoury and very angry, and his mother told him to behave, to take a seat, to sit down and have something to eat. So he quieted down. And then the girl told him that she was looking for the Greenish Bird.

But no. 'I can't tell you anything about that. I've never seen anything,' he said.

Well, so the girl went out again, but they gave her breakfast first and all that. The thing is that by the time she did find out, she had worn out the iron shoes she was wearing. It happened that there was an old hermit way out there, who tended to all the birds. He would call them by blowing on a whistle, and they would all come, and all kinds of animals, too. So she went there, too. And he asked her what she was doing out there, in those lonely wilds, and this and that. So she told the hermit, 'I'm in search of the Greenish Bird. Don't you know where he lives?'

'No,' he said. 'What I do know is that he was here. And he's badly wounded. But let me call my birds, and it may be that they know or have heard where he is, or something.'

Well, no. All the birds were called, but the old eagle was missing. The old eagle was right in the middle of it, eating tripe. The prince was to be married, but he had prayed to God that he would get leprosy, something like sores, and he was ill with sores. He was hoping Luisa would get there. But they were getting ready to marry him. The bride was a princess and very rich, but even so he didn't love her. He wanted to wait for his Luisa. Well then, so the old eagle was missing. The old man, the hermit, began blowing and blowing on his whistle until she came.

'What do you want, *hombre*? There I was, peacefully eating tripe, and you have to carry on like that, with all that blowing.'

'Wait, don't be mean,' he said. 'There's a poor girl here

looking for the Greenish Bird. She says she's his sweetheart and is going to marry him.'

'She's looking for the Greenish Bird? The Greenish Bird is about to get married. The only reason he hasn't married yet is that he's very sick of some sores. Hmm, yes. But the wedding feast is going on, and the bride's mother is there and everything. But, anyway, if she wants to go, it's all right. I just came from there. I was there eating tripe and guts and all that stuff they throw away. If she wants to go, all she has to do is butcher me a cow, and we'll go.'

The girl heard, and she was very happy, even if he was getting married and all that. The hermit called her, and she came out, and she saw all kinds of birds. And he said, 'The old eagle says that if you butcher a cow, she will take you all the way to the very palace.'

All right, she said she would. For she had plenty of money with her. The bird had made her well off from the beginning. He would have married her then and there, if it hadn't been for those bratty sisters of hers. So all right, so they did go. She slaughtered the cow, and the eagle took her and the cow on her back. She would fly high, high, high; and then she would start coming down.

'Give me a leg,' she would say. And she would eat the meat. That's why we say a person is 'an old eagle' when they ask for meat. She would give her meat. And, 'What do you see?'

'Nothing,' she would say. 'You can't see anything yet. It's a very pretty palace made of nothing but glass. It will shine in the sun,' the eagle would say. 'I don't see anything yet.' And she would keep on going, straight, straight ahead, who knows how far. And then she would fly up, and up, and up.

'What do you see?'

'Well, something like a peak that shines. But it's very far away.'

'Yes, it's very far.'

So the cow was all eaten up, and still they didn't get there. And she said she wanted more meat. Luisa said, 'Here, take the knife.' She told the eagle that. 'Cut off one of my legs, or I'll cut it off myself,' Luisa told the eagle. But she didn't say it wholeheartedly, of course. Not a chance.

Anyway the eagle said, 'No, no. I only said it to test you. I'm going to leave you just outside because there are many cops around – or something like that – guarding the doors. You ask permission to go in from one of them. Tell them to let the ladies know you are coming in to cook. Don't ask for anything else,' she said. 'Get a job as a cook and then, well, we'll see how things go for you.'

All right, so she left Luisa just outside the yard. It was a great big yard made of pure gold or God knows what. As beautiful as could be. She asked the guard to let her in. 'And what is your reason for going in? What are you going to do?'

She said, 'Well, I'm very poor, and I've come from a long way off. And I'm looking for work. Anything I can do to eat, no matter if it is working in the kitchen.' And her carrying a golden comb, and all that the Greenish Bird had given her. And the guitar.

'Let me go ask the mistress,' he said, 'to see if they want to hire some kitchen help.' So he went and told her, 'A woman is looking for work.' And who knows what else.

'What kind of woman is she?'

'Well, she is like this, and this way, and that way.'

'All right, tell her to come in, and have her go around that way, so she won't come in through here in the palace,' she said. She didn't want her to go through the house.

So she went over there. And everybody was very kind to her. Meanwhile the Greenish Bird was a person now, but he was all leprous and very sick. There was a little old woman who had raised him. She was the one who took care of him. They had her there as a servant. First she had raised the boy, when she worked for his parents. Then she had moved over here, to the bride's house. She was no bride when the old woman first came there, but the girl had fallen in love with him. But he loved his Luisa.

And well, the wedding feast was in full swing, you might say, and he began to feel much better, for he heard a guitar being played, and he asked the old woman why they hadn't told him there were strangers in the house.

And when he heard the guitar, he told the woman who was taking care of him, who came to see him when he was sick, 'Who is singing and playing the guitar?'

'Oh, I had forgotten to tell you. A lady came wearing a pair of worn-out iron shoes, and she also has a guitar and a comb.'

'Is there anything on the comb?'

'Well, I don't know.' She couldn't read any more than I can.

'I don't know what's on it. They look like little wreaths or letters or I don't know what.'

'Ask her to lend it to you and bring it here.' And once he heard about the guitar, once he heard the guitar playing and all, he began to get well. He got much better. But neither the mother and father of the girl nor anybody else came to see him there.

He was all alone with the woman who took care of him. Because he looked very ugly. But then the woman went and told the princess who was going to be his mother-in-law, 'You should see how much better the prince is, the Greenish Bird. He is quite well now.'

So they all came to see him. And that made him angrier yet, because they came to see him now that he was well. The girl was very rich and a princess and all that, and Luisa was a poor little thing. But he said, 'Go ask her to lend you her comb and bring it to me.'

The old woman went and asked for the comb as if she wanted to comb her hair, and she went back where he was. He didn't say anything; he just looked at it.

'What do you say?'

'No, nothing,' he said. 'Tomorrow, or this afternoon, when they bring me food, have her bring it to me. She's working here, after all,' he said.

So when it was time to take him his dinner, she said, 'Listen, Luisa, go take the prince his dinner. I'm very tired now. I'm getting old.' Luisa didn't want to go; she was putting on. She hung back and she hung back, but at last she went.

Well, they greeted each other and saw each other and everything. And she said, 'Well, so you are already engaged and are going to get married,' Luisa said. 'And one cannot refuse anything to kings and princes.'

'But I have an idea, ever since I heard the guitar,' said the boy.

'What is it?'

'Everybody is going to make chocolate, and the cup I drink, I'll marry the one who made it.'

And she says, 'But I don't even know how to make chocolate!'

The old woman said she would make it for her, the woman who was taking care of him. Because Luisa went and told her about it. 'Just imagine what the prince wants. For all of us to come in, cooks and no cooks and absolutely all the women here, princesses and all. And each one of us must make a cup of chocolate, and the cup he drinks, he'll marry the woman who made it.' And she said, 'I don't know how . . .'

'Now, now,' said the old woman, 'don't worry about that. I'll make it for you. And you can take it to him.'

Well, the first to come in were all the big shots, as is always the case. First the bride, then the mother-in-law, the father-in-law, sisters-in-law, and everybody. And all he said was, 'I don't like it. I don't like it.'

The mother-in-law said, 'Now, I wonder who he wants to marry?' And, 'I wonder who he wants to marry?'

Well . . . nobody. So then the old woman who took care of him came. Neither. Then the other cook went in. And Luisa was the last one. He told them that she was the one he wanted to marry. That she had come searching for him from very far away, and that he would marry her. And he drank all of Luisa's cup of chocolate. Bitter or not, he didn't care. And he married her. And *colorin* so red, the story is finished.

The Crafty Woman

(Lithuanian)

MAN and his young wife, who had settled down to life in a village, agreed so well that neither of them pronounced a single unpleasant word, they only caressed and kissed each other. For fully six months the Devil did his best to make the pair quarrel, but, at last, irritated by continued failure, he expressed his rage by making a disagreeable noise in his throat and made ready to depart. However, an old woman who was roaming about met him and said, 'Why are you annoyed?' The Devil explained, and the woman, on the understanding that she would receive some new bast shoes and a pair of boots, endeavoured to make the young couple disagree. She went to the wife while the husband was at work in the fields and, having begged for alms, said, 'Ah, my dear! how pretty and good you are! Your husband ought to love you from the depths of his soul. I know you live more amicably than any other couple in the world, but, my daughter! I will teach you to be yet happier. Upon your husband's head, at the very summit, are a few grey hairs, you must cut them off, taking care that he does not notice what you are about.'

'But how shall I do that?'

'When you have given your husband his dinner, tell him to lie down and rest his head upon your lap, then as soon as he goes to sleep, whip a razor out of your pocket and remove the grey hairs.' The young wife thanked her adviser and gave her a present.

The old woman went immediately to the field and warned the husband that a misfortune threatened him, since his amiable wife not only had betrayed him, but intended that afternoon to kill him and later to marry someone richer than himself. When at midday, the wife arrived and, after his meal, placed her husband's head upon her knees, he pretended to be asleep and she took a razor from her pocket in order to remove the grey hairs. Instantly the exasperated man jumped on to his feet and, seizing his wife by the hair, began to abuse and strike her. The Devil saw all and could not believe his eyes; soon he took a long pole, attached loosely to one end of it the promised bast shoes and boots, and without coming close, passed them to the old woman. 'I will not on any account approach nearer to you,' he said, 'lest you should in some way impose upon me, for you really are more crafty and cunning than I am!' Having delivered the boots and bast shoes, the Devil vanished as quickly as if he had been shot from a gun.

Part Two

UP TO SOMETHING – BLACK ARTS AND DIRTY TRICKS

Pretty Maid Ibronka

(Hungarian)

HERE was a pretty girl in the village. That is why she was called by the name of Pretty Maid Ibronka. But what of it, if all the other girls – and what a bevy of them used to gather to do their spinning together – had a lover to themselves, and she alone had none? For quite a while she waited patiently, pondering over her chances, but then the thought took hold of her mind: 'I wish God would give me a sweetheart, even if one of the devils he were.'

That evening, when the young were together in the spinning room, in walks a young lad in a sheepskin cape and a hat graced with the feather of a crane. Greeting the others, he takes a seat by the side of Pretty Maid Ibronka.

Well, as is the custom of the young, they start up a conversation, talking about this and that, exchanging news. Then it happened that the spindle slipped from Ibronka's hand. At once she reached down for it and her sweetheart was also bending for it, but as her groping hand touched his foot, she felt it was a cloven hoof. Well, great was her amazement as she picked up her spindle.

Ibronka went to see them out, as on that evening the spinning had been done at her place. Before separating they had a few words together, and then they bid each other goodbye. As is the custom of the young they parted with an embrace. It was then that she felt her hand go into his side, straight through his flesh. That made her recoil with even greater amazement.

There was an old woman in the village. To that woman she went and said, 'Oh mother, put me wise about this. As you may know, for long they have been wagging their tongues in the village, saying that of all the village girls, only Pretty Maid Ibronka is without a sweetheart. And I was waiting and waiting for one, when the wish took hold of my mind that God would give me a sweetheart, even if one of the devils he were. And on that very same evening a young man appeared, in a sheepskin cape and a hat graced with a crane feather. Straight up to me he walked and took a seat by my side. Well, we started up a conversation, as is the custom of the young, talking about this and that. I must have become heedless of my work and let the spindle slip from my hand. At once I reached down to pick it up, and so did he, but as my groping hand chanced to touch his foot, I felt it was a cloven hoof. This was so queer it made me shudder. Now put me wise, mother, what should I be doing now?'

'Well,' she said, 'go and do the spinning at some other place, changing from here to there, so you can see if he will find you.'

She did so and tried every spinning room there was in the village, but wherever she went, he came after her. Again she went to see the old woman. 'Oh mother, didn't he come to every single place I went? I see I shall never get rid of him this way, and I dare not think of what is going to come of all this. I do not know who he is, nor from where he came. And I find it awkward to ask him.'

'Well, here's a piece of advice to you. There are little girls in the village who are just learning to spin, and they find it good practice to wind the thread into balls. Get yourself such a ball, and when they gather again at your place for the spinning, see them out when they leave, and while you are talking to each other before parting, fuss about until you can get the end of the thread tied in a knot round a tuft in his sheepskin cape. When he takes leave and goes his way, let the thread unwind from the ball. When you feel that there is no more to come, make it into a ball again, following the track of the unwound thread.'

Well, they came to her place to do the spinning. The ball of thread she kept in readiness. Her sweetheart was keeping her waiting. The others began teasing her: 'Your sweetheart is going to let you down, Ibronka!'

'To be sure, he won't. He will come; only some business is now keeping him away.'

They hear the door open. They stop in silence and expectation: who is going to open the door? It is Ibronka's sweetheart. He greets them all and takes a seat at her side. And as is the custom of the young, they make conversation, each having something to tell the other. Amid such talk the time passes.

'Let's be going home, it must be close to midnight.'

And they did not tarry long, but quickly rose to their feet and gathered their belongings.

'Good night to you all!'

And they file off and leave the room, one after the other. Outside the house a final goodbye was said, and each went his way and was soon bound homeward.

And the pair drew closer to each other and were talking about this and that. And she was manipulating the thread until she got the end knotted round a tuft of wool in his sheepskin cape. Well, they did not make long with their conversation as they began to feel the chill of the night. 'You better go in now, my dear,' he said to Ibronka, 'or you'll catch cold. When the weather turns mild we may converse at greater leisure.'

And they embraced. 'Good night,' he said.

'Good night,' she said to him.

And he went his way. And she began to unwind the ball as he was walking away. Fast did the thread unwind from the ball. And she began to speculate how much more there would be still to come, but no sooner than this thought came into her head, than it stopped. For a while she kept waiting. But no more thread came off the ball. Then she started to rewind it. And bravely she followed the track of the thread as she went winding it into a ball again. Rapidly the ball was growing in her hand. And she was thinking to herself that she would not have to go very much farther. But where would the thread be leading her? It led her straight to the church.

'Well,' she thought, 'he must have passed this way.'

But the thread led her further on, straight to the churchyard. And she walked over to the door. And through the keyhole the light shone from the inside. And she bent down and peeped through the keyhole. And whom does she behold there? Her own sweetheart. She keeps her eye on him to find out what he was doing. Well, he was busy sawing the head of a dead man in two. She saw him separate the two parts, just the same way we cut a melon in two. And then she saw him feasting on the brains from the halved head. Seeing that, she grew even more horrified. She broke the thread, and in great haste made her way back to the house.

But her sweetheart must have caught sight of her and briskly set out after her. No sooner had she reached home in great weariness and bolted the door safely on the inside, than her sweetheart was calling to her through the window, 'Pretty Maid Ibronka, what did you see looking through the keyhole?'

She answered, 'Nothing did I see.'

'You must tell me what you saw, or your sister shall die.'

'Nothing did I see. If she dies, we'll bury her.'

Then her sweetheart went away.

First thing in the morning she went to the old woman. In great agitation did she appeal to her, as her sister had died. 'Oh mother, I need your advice.'

'What about?'

'Well, I did what you advised me to do.'

'What happened then?'

Oh, just imagine where I was led in following the thread. Straight to the churchyard.'

'Well, what was his business there?'

'Oh, just imagine, he was sawing a dead man's head in two, just the same way we'd go about cutting up a melon. And there I stayed and kept my eye on him, to see what he'd be doing next. And he set to feasting on the brains from the severed head. I was so horrified that I broke the thread and in great haste made my way back home. But he must have caught sight of me, because as soon as I had the door safely bolted on the inside, he was calling to me through the window, "Pretty Maid Ibronka, what did you see looking through the keyhole?" "Nothing did I see." "You must tell me what you saw, or your sister shall die." I said then, "If she dies, we will bury her, but nothing did I see through the keyhole."'

'Now listen,' the old woman said, 'take my advice and put your dead sister in the outhouse.'

Next evening she did not dare to go spinning with her friends, but her sweetheart was calling again through her window, 'Pretty Maid Ibronka, what did you see through the keyhole?'

'Nothing did I see.'

'You must tell me what you saw,' he said, 'or your mother shall die.'

'If she dies, we will bury her, but nothing did I see looking through the keyhole.'

He turned away from the window and was off. Ibronka was preparing for a night's rest. When she rose in the morning, she found her mother dead. She went to the old woman. 'Oh, mother, what will all this lead to? My mother too – she's dead.'

'Do not worry about it, but put her corpse in the outhouse.'

In the evening her sweetheart came again. He was calling her through the window, 'Pretty Maid Ibronka, tell me, what did you see looking through the keyhole?'

'Nothing did I see.'

'You must tell me what you saw,' he said, 'or your father shall die.'

'If he dies, we will bury him, but nothing did I see looking through the keyhole.'

Her sweetheart turned away from the window and was off, and she retired for the night. But she could not help musing over her lot; what would come of all this? And she went on speculating until she felt sleepy and more at ease. But she could not rest for long. Soon she lay wide awake and was pondering over her fate. 'I wonder what the future keeps in store for me?' And when the day broke she found her father dead. 'Now I am left alone.'

She took the corpse of her father into the outhouse, and then she went as fast as she could to the old woman again. 'Oh, mother, mother! I need your comfort in my distress. What is going to happen to me?'

'You know what's going to happen to you? I may tell you. You are going to die. Now go and ask your friends to be there when you die. And when you die, because die you will for certain, they must not take out the coffin either through the door or the window when they carry it to the churchyard.'

'How then?'

'They must cut a hole through the wall and must push the coffin through that hole. But they should not carry it along the road but cut across through the gardens and the bypaths. And they should not bury it in the burial ground but in the ditch of the churchyard.'

Well, she went home. Then she sent word to her friends, the girls in the village, and they appeared at her call.

In the evening her sweetheart came to the window. 'Pretty Maid Ibronka, what did you see looking through the keyhole?'

'Nothing did I see.'

'You must tell me at once,' he said, 'or you shall die.'

'If I die, they will bury me, but nothing did I see through the keyhole.'

He turned away from the window and took off.

Well, for a while she and her friends kept up their conversation. They were only half inclined to believe that she would die. When they grew tired they went to sleep. But when they awoke, they found Ibronka dead. They were not long in bringing a coffin and cutting a hole through the wall. They dug a grave for her in the ditch of the churchyard. They pushed the coffin through the hole in the wall and went off with it. They did not follow the road, but went cross-country, cutting through the gardens and the bypaths. When they came to the churchyard they buried her. Then they returned to the house and filled in the hole they had cut through the wall. It so happened that before she died, Ibronka enjoined them to take care of the house until further events took place.

Before long, a beautiful rose grew out of Ibronka's grave. The grave was not far from the road, and a prince, driving past in his coach, saw it. So much was he taken by its beauty that he stopped the coachman at once. 'Hey! Rein in the horses and get me that rose from the grave. Be quick about it!'

At once the coachman came to a halt. He jumps from the coach and goes to fetch the rose. But when he wants to break it off, the rose will not yield. He is pulling harder now, but still it does not yield. He is pulling the rose with all his might, but all in vain.

'Oh, what a dummy you are! Haven't you got the brains to pick a rose? Come on here, get back on the coach and let me go and get the flower.'

The coachman got back on to his seat, and the prince gave him the reins, which he had been holding while the other went for the rose. The prince then jumped down from the coach and went to the grave. No sooner had he grasped the rose, than it came off at once and he was holding it in his hand.

'Look here, you idiot, with all your tearing and pulling you could not get me this rose, and hardly did I touch it and off it came into my hand.'

Well, they took off, driving back home at great speed. The prince pinned the rose on his breast. At home, he found a place for it in front of the dining-room mirror so that he should be able to look at it even while he was having his meals.

There the rose stayed. One evening some leftovers remained on the table after supper. The prince left them there. 'I may eat them some other time.'

This happened every now and again. Once the servant asked the prince, 'Did your majesty eat the leftovers?'

'Not I,' said the prince. 'I guessed it was you who finished off what was left.'

'No, I did not,' he says.

'Well, there's something fishy about it.'

Says the servant, 'I am going to find out who's in this – the cat, or whoever.'

Neither the prince nor the servant would have guessed that the rose was eating the remains.

'Well,' said the prince, 'we must leave some more food on the table. And you will lie in wait and see who's going to eat it up.'

They left plenty of food on the table. And the servant was lying in wait, but never for a moment did he suspect the rose.

And the rose alighted from her place by the mirror, and shook itself, and at once it turned into such a beautiful maiden that you could not find a second to her, not in all Hungary, not in all the wide world. Well, she sat down on a chair at the table and supped well off the dishes. She even found a glass of water to finish off her supper. Then she shook herself a little and back again she was in her place in front of the mirror, in the shape of a rose.

Well, the servant was impatiently waiting for day to break. Then he went to the prince and reported, 'I've found it out, your royal majesty, it was the rose.'

'This evening you must lay the table properly and leave plenty of food on it. I am going to see for myself whether you are telling me the truth.'

And as they were lying in wait, the prince and the servant, they saw the rose alight from her place. She made a slight movement, then shook herself and at once turned into a fine and beautiful maiden. She takes a chair, sits down at the table, and sups well on the dishes. The prince was watching her as he sat under the mirror. And when she finished her supper and poured herself a glass of water and was about to shake herself into a rose again, the prince clasped his arms round her and took her into his lap.

'My beautiful and beloved sweetheart. You are mine, and I am yours for ever, and nothing but death can us part.'

'Oh, it cannot be so,' said Ibronka.

'To be sure, it can be,' he says. 'And why not?'

'There is more to it than you think.'

Well, I just remember a slip I have made in the story. Here goes then. On the day she was buried, her sweetheart appeared at her window as usual. He called in to her. But no answer came. He goes to the door and kicks it open. 'Tell me, you door, was it through you they took out Ibronka's coffin?'

'No, it was not.'

He goes then to the window. 'Tell me, you window, was it through you they took the coffin out?'

'No, it was not.'

He takes himself off to the road. 'Tell me, you road, was it this way they took the coffin?'

'No, it was not.'

He goes to the churchyard. 'Tell me, you churchyard, was it in your ground they buried Pretty Maid Ibronka?'

'No, it was not.'

Well, that is the missing part.

Fervently the prince is now wooing her and tries to win her consent to their marriage. But she resorts to evasion. And finally she made her condition, 'I will marry you only if you never compel me to go to church.'

Said the prince, 'Well then, we could get along without you going to church. Even if I sometimes go myself. I shall never compel you to come with me.'

Here is another part of the story I missed telling in its proper order. As he did not get any the wiser from the answer of the road, and the churchyard either, her sweetheart said to himself, 'Well, I see I must get myself a pair of iron moccasins and an iron staff and then I shall not stop until I find you, Pretty Maid Ibronka, even if I have to wear them away to naught.'

The time comes when Ibronka is expecting a child. The couple are living happily, only she never goes along with him to church. Day follows day, the years slip by. Again she is with child. They have already two children, and they are no longer babes, but a boy of five and six years of age. And it is their father who takes them to church. True enough, he himself had found it strange enough that only his children went with him while all other folks appeared together with their wives. And he knew that they rebuked him for it and said, 'Why does not your majesty bring along the queen?'

He says, 'Well, that is the custom with us.'

But all the same he felt embarrassed after this rebuke, and next Sunday, when he was getting ready with the boys to go to church, he said to his wife, 'Look here, missus, why won't you come with us too?'

She answered, 'Look here, husband, don't you remember your promise?'

'How then? Must we stick to it for ever and aye? I've been hearing their scorn long enough. And how could I give up going to church when the kids want me to go with them? Whatever we were saying then, let us forget about it.'

'All right, let it be as you wish, but it will give rise to trouble between us two. However, as I see you've set your mind on it, I am willing to go with you. Now let me go and dress for church.'

So they went, and it made the people rejoice to see them together. 'That is the right thing, your majesty,' they said, 'coming to church with your wife.'

The mass is drawing to a close, and when it ends, a man is walking up to the couple wearing a pair of iron moccasins worn to holes, and with an iron staff in his hand. He calls out loudly, 'I pledged myself, Ibronka, that I would put on a pair of iron moccasins and take an iron staff, and go out looking for you, even if I should wear them to naught. But before I had worn them quite away, I found you. Tonight I shall come to you.'

And he disappeared. On their way home the king asked his wife, 'What did that man mean by threatening you?'

'Just wait and see, and you will learn what will come of it.'

So both were anxiously waiting for the evening to come. The day was drawing to a close. Suddenly there was someone calling through the window, 'Pretty Maid Ibronka, what did you see through the keyhole?'

Pretty Maid Ibronka then began her speech: 'I was the prettiest girl in the village, but to a dead and not a living soul am I speaking – and all the other girls had a sweetheart – but to a dead and not to a living soul am I speaking. Once I let it out, I wish God would give me one, even if one of the devils he were. There must have been something in the way I said it, because that evening, when we gathered to do our spinning, there appeared a young lad in a sheepskin cape, and a hat graced with a feather of a crane. He greets us and takes a seat at my side and we are conversing, as is the custom of the young. And then it so happened – but to a dead and not to a living soul am I speaking – that my spindle slipped from my hand. I bent to pick it up and so did my sweetheart, but as my groping hand touched his foot, I felt at once – but to a dead and not to a living soul am I speaking – that it was a cloven hoof. And I recoiled in horror that God had given me a devil for a sweetheart – but to a dead and not to a living soul am I speaking.'

And he is shouting at the top of his voice through the window. 'Pretty Maid Ibronka, what did you see looking through the keyhole?'

'But when at the parting, as is the custom with the young, we embraced, my hand went straight through his flesh. At that I grew even more horrified. There was a woman in the village, and I went to ask for her advice. And she put me wise – but to a dead and not to a living soul am I speaking.'

And he kept shouting through the window, 'Pretty Maid Ibronka, what did you see looking through the keyhole?'

'And then my sweetheart took leave and went away. And I wished he would never come again – but to a dead and not to a living soul am I speaking. The woman said, I was to try to do the spinning at some other place, once here, once there, so that he might not find me. But wherever I went, there he came. And again I went for advice to the woman – but to a dead and not to a living soul am I speaking.'

And he was shouting through the window, 'Pretty Maid Ibronka, what did you see looking through the keyhole?'

'Then the woman advised me to get myself a ball of thread, which I was to fasten on to his sheepskin cape. And when he asked me and I said "Nothing did I see", he said, "Tell me at once, or your sister shall die," "If she dies, we will bury her, but nothing did I see looking through the keyhole." And he came again next evening and asked me what I had seen through the keyhole – but to a dead and not to a living soul am I speaking.'

And all the while he never stops shouting through the window.

'And my sister died. And the next evening he came again and was calling to me through the window – but to a dead and not to a living soul am I speaking. "Tell me what you saw, or your mother shall die." "If she dies, we will bury her." Next evening he is calling to me again, "Pretty Maid Ibronka, what did you see looking through the keyhole?" – but to a dead and not to a living soul am I speaking. "Tell me what you saw, or your father shall die." "If he dies, we will bury him, but nothing did I see looking through the keyhole." On that day I sent word to my friends, and they came and it was arranged that when I died they would not take my coffin either through the door or the window. Nor were they to take me along the road or bury me in the churchyard.'

And he went on shouting through the window, 'Pretty Maid Ibronka, what did you see looking through the keyhole?'

'And my friends cut a hole through the wall and went along the road when they took me to the churchyard where they buried me in the ditch – but to a dead and not to a living soul am I speaking.'

And then he collapsed under the window. He uttered a shout which shook the castle to its bottom, and it was he who died then. Her mother and her father and her sister rose from their long sleep. And that is the end of it.

Enchanter and Enchantress

(Mordvin)

MAN who was a magician took a girl-magician as his wife. The man went to the bazaar, whereupon his wife, who had a lover, called him, and they drank and ate together. In the evening the husband returned late from the bazaar and, looking through the window, saw his wife and her lover drinking and eating. The lover caught a glimpse of the husband and said to the woman, 'Who peered through the window just now?'

'I know,' said the woman; she took a small whip, and going out, struck her husband with the whip and said, 'Be no more a man; become a yellow dog!' The peasant became a yellow dog. It grew day, and the other dogs seeing the yellow dog, began to tear him. The yellow dog galloped along the road; bounded and leapt; he saw some shepherds feeding their flock, and he went to them. Pleased that the yellow dog had joined them, the shepherds fed him and gave him water. The dog looked after the flock so well that there was nothing left for the shepherds to do. As they saw that the dog acted efficiently they began to stay away from the field.

Once, when the dog was guarding the flock, the shepherds were in the tavern. A merchant entered this tavern and said, 'A thief is pestering me; he comes every night.' 'You should have our dog!' said the shepherds, and they related the dog's services. The merchant made an offer for the dog, and though the shepherds did not wish to sell him, they were overcome by the thought of the money. The merchant bought the dog and led him home. Night came, and with it the magician-wife of the yellow dog arrived to commit a theft. The woman entered the merchant's house and began to remove his money chest. The yellow dog threw himself upon his wife, took away the money chest and lay down upon it. In the morning the merchant rose and saw that the chest was gone; pushing the yellow dog, he said, 'I bought a dog to no purpose, for thieves have got hold of my money.' No sooner had the merchant pushed the dog, than he saw his coffer. The yellow dog slept three nights at the merchant's, and each night deprived his wife of the merchant's money. The wife ceased to visit the merchant for the purpose of theft.

The queen bore two sons, but both disappeared in the night; the wife of the yellow dog had stolen them. When the queen was again about to give birth to a child the king, who had heard of the yellow dog, went to the merchant and asked for him. The queen bore a son, but the wife of the yellow dog came by night and tried to steal him. However, no sooner had the wife of the yellow dog entered the royal dwelling and seized the third little prince, than the yellow dog rushed up and snatched the infant from her. In the morning the child was found safe and protected by the dog in the middle of a field. The king took his son and said to the yellow dog, 'If you were a man I would give you half my kingdom.'

The yellow dog lived well now at the king's house; nevertheless, he longed for his wife. He left the king and galloped to his own home, where he looked in at the window and found his wife again drinking with her lover. The lover saw the yellow dog and said, 'Someone looked through the window.' 'I know him,' answered the woman. She went out and struck the yellow dog with a whip, and he became a sparrow. For a long time he flew about as a sparrow.

Then the wife began to long for her husband. She went into the forest and, having made a cage, threw into it some millet seeds and hoped to effect a capture. The husband was roaming about in the form of a sparrow and was very hungry. He flew into the forest, found the cage, and, stepping in to peck at the grains, was caught. The wife came and took the cage, dragged her husband out of it, made him once more a man, and said, 'Return home, take the king's two first children from the cellar, and restore them to him.' The peasant accompanied his wife home, and, having taken the king's children from the cellar, carried them to the king. When the king saw his eldest sons his delight knew no bounds, and he loaded the peasant with gifts.

The peasant took the money and went home and said, 'Well, woman, we have enough money now!' 'Come old man,' his wife replied, 'let us build a stone house and sell the square logs.' But the peasant had not forgotten the tortures inflicted on him by his wife, and he said, 'Woman, become a chestnut mare; I will use you to transport both stones and logs.' The peasant-magician had scarcely spoken when his wife became a chestnut mare, and by harnessing her and setting her to transport stones he was enabled to erect a stone house. When it was completed he harnessed the chestnut, and transported the logs, a great number of them. The yard was now filled with the timber, and the old man said, 'Wife, change again to a woman.' Immediately the mare became a woman. The woman had taught the peasant and the peasant had taught the woman. Now she is always baking pancakes and feeding her husband, and he sells logs and they live very well.

The Telltale Lilac Bush

(USA, Hillbilly)

N OLD MAN and woman once lived by themselves along the Tygart Valley River. There had been trouble between them for many years. Few people visited them, and it was not immediately noticed that the wife had unaccountably disappeared. People suspected that the old man had killed her, but her body could not be found, and the question was dropped.

The old man lived a gay life after his wife's disappearance, until one night when a group of young men were sitting on his porch, talking of all the parties which the old man was giving. While they were talking, a large lilac bush growing nearby began beating on the window pane and beckoning towards them as though it were trying to tell them something. No one would have thought anything of this if the wind had been blowing. But there was no wind – not even a small breeze.

Paying no attention to the old man's protests, the young men dug up the lilac bush. They were stunned when the roots were found to be growing from the palm of a woman's hand.

The old man screamed and ran down the hill towards the river, never to be seen again.

Tatterhood

(Norwegian)

NCE on a time there was a king and a queen who had no children, and that gave the queen much grief; she scarce had one happy hour. She was always bewailing and bemoaning herself, and saying how dull and lonesome it was in the palace.

'If we had children there'd be life enough,' she said.

Wherever she went in all her realm she found God's blessing in children, even in the vilest hut; and wherever she came she heard the Goodies scolding the bairns, and saying how they had done that and that wrong. All this the queen heard, and thought it would be so nice to do as other women did. At last the king and queen took into their palace a stranger lassie to rear up, that they might have her always with them, to love her if she did well, and scold her if she did wrong, like their own child.

So one day the little lassie whom they had taken as their own, ran down into the palace-yard, and was playing with a gold apple. Just then an old beggar wife came by, who had a little girl with her, and it wasn't long before the little lassie and the beggar's bairn were great friends, and began to play together, and to toss the gold apple about between them. When the queen saw this, as she sat at a window in the palace, she tapped on the pane for her foster-daughter to come up. She went at once, but the beggar girl went up too; and as they went into the queen's bower, each held the other by the hand. Then the queen began to scold the little lady, and to say, 'You ought to be above running about and playing with a tattered beggar's brat.' And so she wanted to drive the lassie downstairs.

'If the queen only knew my mother's power, she'd not drive

me out,' said the little lassie; and when the queen asked what she meant more plainly, she told her how her mother could get her children if she chose. The queen wouldn't believe it, but the lassie held her own, and said every word of it was true, and bade the queen only to try and make her mother do it. So the queen sent the lassie down to fetch up her mother.

'Do you know what your daughter says?' asked the queen of the old woman, as soon as ever she came into the room.

No; the beggar wife knew nothing about it.

'Well, she says you can get me children if you will,' answered the queen.

'Queens shouldn't listen to beggar lassies' silly stories,' said the old wife, and strode out of the room.

Then the queen got angry, and wanted again to drive out the little lassie; but she declared it was true every word that she had said.

'Let the queen only give my mother a drop to drink,' said the lassie. 'When she gets merry she'll soon find out a way to help you.'

The queen was ready to try this; so the beggar wife was fetched up again once more, and treated both with wine and mead as much as she chose; and so it was not long before her tongue began to wag. Then the queen came out again with the same question she had asked before.

'One way to help you perhaps I know,' said the beggar wife. 'Your Majesty must make them bring in two pails of water some evening before you go to bed. In each of them you must wash yourself, and afterwards throw away the water under the bed. When you look under the bed next morning, two flowers will have sprung up, one fair and one ugly. The fair one you must eat, the ugly one you must let stand; but mind you don't forget the last.'

That was what the beggar wife said.

Yes; the queen did what the beggar wife advised her to do. She had the water brought up in two pails, washed herself in them, and emptied them under the bed; and lo! when she looked under the bed next morning, there stood two flowers. One was ugly and foul, and had black leaves; but the other was so bright and fair, and lovely, she had never seen its like; so she ate it up at once. But the pretty flower tasted so sweet, that she couldn't help herself. She ate the other up too, for, she thought, 'It can't hurt or help one much either way, I'll be bound.'

Well, sure enough, after a while the queen was brought to bed. First of all, she had a girl who had a wooden spoon in her hand, and rode upon a goat; loathly and ugly she was, and the very moment she came into the world she bawled out 'Mamma.'

'If I'm your mamma,' said the queen, 'God give me grace to mend my ways.'

'Oh, don't be sorry,' said the girl, who rode on the goat, 'for one will soon come after me who is better looking.'

So, after a while, the queen had another girl, who was so fair and sweet, no one had ever set eyes on such a lovely child, and with her you may fancy the queen was very well pleased. The elder twin they called 'Tatterhood', because she was always so ugly and ragged, and because she had a hood which hung about her ears in tatters. The queen could scarce bear to look at her, and the nurses tried to shut her up in a room by herself, but it was all no good; where the younger twin was, there she must also be, and no one could ever keep them apart.

Well, one Christmas eve, when they were half grown up, there rose such a frightful noise and clatter in the gallery outside the queen's bower. So Tatterhood asked what it was that dashed and crashed so out in the passage.

'Oh!' said the queen, 'it isn't worth asking about.'

But Tatterhood wouldn't give over till she found out all about it; and so the queen told her it was a pack of Trolls and witches who had come there to keep Christmas. So Tatterhood said she'd just go out and drive them away, and in spite of all they could say, and however much they begged and prayed her to let the Trolls alone, she must and would go out to drive the witches off; but she begged the queen to mind and keep all the doors close shut, so that not one of them came so much as the least bit ajar. Having said this, off she went with her wooden spoon, and began to hunt and sweep away the hags; and all this while there was such a pother out in the gallery, the like of it was never heard. The whole palace creaked and groaned as if every joint and beam were going to be torn out of its place.

Now, how it was, I'm sure I can't tell; but somehow or other one door did get the least bit ajar. Then her twin sister just peeped out to see how things were going with Tatterhood, and put her head a tiny bit through the opening. But, POP! up came an old witch, and whipped off her head, and stuck a calf's head on her shoulders instead; and so the princess ran back into the room on all fours, and began to 'moo' like a calf. When Tatterhood came back and saw her sister, she scolded them all round, and was very angry because they hadn't kept better watch, and asked them what they thought of their heedlessness now, when her sister was turned into a calf.

'But still I'll see if I can't set her free,' she said.

Then she asked the king for a ship in full trim, and well fitted with stores; but captain and sailors she wouldn't have. No, she would sail away with her sister all alone; and as there was no holding her back, at last they let her have her own way.

Then Tatterhood sailed off, and steered her ship right under the land where the witches dwelt, and when she came to the landing place, she told her sister to stay quite still on board the ship; but she herself rode on her goat up to the witches' castle. When she got there, one of the windows in the gallery was open, and there she saw her sister's head hung up on the window frame; so she leapt her goat through the window into the gallery, snapped up the head, and set off with it. After her came the witches to try to get the head again, and they flocked about her as thick as a swarm of bees or a nest of ants; but the goat snorted and puffed, and butted with his horns, and Tatterhood beat and banged them about with her wooden spoon; and so the pack of witches had to give it up. So Tatterhood got back to her ship, took the calf's head off her sister, and put her own on again, and then she became a girl as she had been before. After that she sailed a long, long way, to a strange king's realm.

Now the king of that land was a widower, and had an only son. So when he saw the strange sail, he sent messengers down to the strand to find out whence it came, and who owned it; but when the king's men came down there, they saw never a living soul on board but Tatterhood, and there she was, riding round and round the deck on her goat at full speed, till her elf locks streamed again in the wind. The folk from the palace were all amazed at this sight, and asked were there not more on board. Yes, there were; she had a sister with her, said Tatterhood. Her, too, they wanted to see, but Tatterhood said 'No.'

'No one shall see her, unless the king comes himself,' she said, and so she began to gallop about on her goat till the deck thundered again.

So when the servants got back to the palace, and told what they had seen and heard down at the ship, the king was for setting out at once, that he might see the lassie that rode on the goat. When he got down, Tatterhood led out her sister, and she was so fair and gentle, the king fell over head and ears in love with her as he stood. He brought them both back with him to the palace, and wanted to have the sister for his queen; but Tatterhood said 'No': the king couldn't have her in any way, unless the king's son chose to have Tatterhood. That you may fancy the prince was very loath to do, such an ugly hussy as Tatterhood was; but at last the king and all the others in the palace talked him over, and he yielded, giving his word to take her for his queen; but it went sore against the grain, and he was a doleful man.

Now they set about the wedding, both with brewing and baking, and when all was ready they were to go to church; but the prince thought it the weariest churching he had ever had in all his life. First, the king drove off with his bride, and she was so lovely and so grand, all the people stopped to look after her all along the road, and they stared at her till she was out of sight. After them came the prince on horseback by the side of Tatterhood, who trotted along on her goat with her wooden spoon in her fist, and to look at him, it was more like going to a burial than a wedding, and that his own; so sorrowful he seemed, and with never a word to say.

'Why don't you talk?' asked Tatterhood, when they had ridden a bit.

'Why, what should I talk about?' answered the prince.

'Well, you might at least ask me why I ride upon this ugly goat,' said Tatterhood.

'Why do you ride on that ugly goat?' asked the prince.

'Is it an ugly goat? why, it's the grandest horse a bride ever rode on,' answered Tatterhood; and in a trice the goat became a horse, and that the finest the prince had ever set eyes on.

Then they rode on again a bit, but the prince was just as woeful as before, and couldn't get a word out. So Tatterhood asked him again why he didn't talk, and when the prince answered, he didn't know what to talk about, she said, 'You can at least ask me why I ride with this ugly spoon in my fist.'

'Why do you ride with that ugly spoon?' asked the prince.

'Is it an ugly spoon? why, it's the loveliest silver wand a bride ever bore,' said Tatterhood; and in a trice it became a silver wand, so dazzling bright, the sunbeams glistened from it.

So they rode on another bit, but the prince was just as sorrowful, and said never a word. In a little while Tatterhood asked him again why he didn't talk, and bade him ask why she wore that ugly grey hood on her head.

'Why do you wear that ugly grey hood on your head?' asked the prince.

'Is it an ugly hood? why, it's the brightest golden crown a bride ever wore,' answered Tatterhood, and it became a crown on the spot.

Now they rode on a long while again, and the prince was so woeful that he sat without sound or speech, just as before. So his bride asked him again why he didn't talk and bade him ask now why her face was so ugly and ashen-grey?

'Ah!' asked the prince, 'why is your face so ugly and ashen-grey?'

'I ugly?' said the bride. 'You think my sister pretty, but I am ten times prettier'; and lo! when the prince looked at her, she was so lovely he thought there never was so lovely a woman in all the world. After that, I shouldn't wonder if the prince found his tongue, and no longer rode along hanging down his head.

So they drank the bridal cup both deep and long, and, after

that, both prince and king set out with their brides to the princess's father's palace, and there they had another bridal feast, and drank anew, both deep and long. There was no end to the fun; and, if you make haste and run to the king's palace, I dare say you'll find there's still a drop of the bridal ale left for you.

The Witchball

(USA Hillbilly)

NCE there was a poor boy who wanted to marry a girl, but her folks didn't want him. His grandma was a witch, an' she said she'd fix it up. She made a horsehair witchball, an' put it under the girl's doorstep. The girl come outside, passin' over the witchball, an' went back in the house. She started to say somethin' to her mother, an' ripped out, an' every time she spoke a word, she'd rip out. Her mother told her to stop that or she'd lick her. Then the mother went out for somethin', an' when she came back in, she broke wind, too, every time she spoke. The father come in an' he did the same thing.

He thought somethin' was the matter, so he called the doctor, an' when the doctor come in over the doorstep, he started to poop with every word he said, and they were all atalkin' an' apoopin' when the ole witch come in, an' told 'em God had probably sent that on them as a curse because they wouldn' allow their daughter to marry the poor boy. They told her to run an' git the boy, 'cause he could marry their girl right away, if God would only take that curse offa them. The ole witch went an' got the boy, an' on her way out, she slipped the witchball out from under the doorstep. The boy an' girl got married an' lived happy ever after.

The Werefox

(Chinese)

ANY years ago, a Buddhist monk, named Chi Hsüan, led a very holy and mortified life. He never wore silk, tramped from town to town on foot, and slept in the open. One moonlight night, he was preparing to sleep in a copse adjoining a grave, ten miles from a city in Shan Si. By the light of the moon he saw a wild fox place on its head a skull and some withered bones, go through several mysterious movements, and then deck itself out with grass and leaves. Presently the fox assumed the form of a beautiful woman, very quietly and plainly dressed, and in this guise it wandered out of the copse on to the adjoining high road. As the trampling of a horseman's mount became audible, coming from the north-west, the woman began to weep and wail, her attitude and gestures showing extreme grief. A man on horseback approached, pulled his horse up, and alighted.

'Lady,' he cried, 'what brings you here, alone, in the night? Can I help you?'

The woman stopped crying and told her tale. 'I am the window of So-and-so. My husband died suddenly last year, leaving me penniless; my parents live a long way off. I do not know the way, and there is no one I can turn to, to help me to get back to my home.'

When he heard where her parents lived, the horseman said, 'I come from that place, and I am now on my way home again. If you do not mind rough travelling, you may ride my horse, and I will walk beside it.'

The woman accepted gratefully, and vowed she would never forget the horseman's kindness. She was just on the point of mounting, when the monk, Chi Hsüan, came out of the copse, crying to the horseman, 'Beware! She is not human; she is a werefox. If you do not believe me, wait a few moments and I will make her resume her true shape.'

So he made a sign, or mudra, with his fingers, uttered a *dhârani* (or spell) and cried in a loud voice, 'Why do you not return at once to your original form?'

The woman immediately fell down, turned into an old fox, and expired. Her flesh and blood flowed away like a stream, and nothing remained but the dead fox, a skull, a few dry bones and some leaves and blades of grass.

The cavalier, quite convinced, prostrated himself several times before the priest, and went away full of astonishment.

The Witches' Piper

(Hungarian)

MY elder brother was piping for some people at a certain place, while another fellow, a man from Etes, was playing for the children at the same house. It must have been on a day before Ash Wednesday. At eleven o'clock or so, the children were taken home. The man who had been playing for them, Uncle Matyi, was paid for his piping. He took leave of my brother and left for home.

On his way home, three women stepped up to him and said, 'Come along, Uncle Matyi! We want you to play for us. Let's go to that house over there, at the end of the street. And have no fear, we're going to pay for your piping.'

When he went in, they took him by the arms (by the way, the man is still living in the village) and made him stand on the bench near the wall. And there he was piping for them. Money came in showers at his feet. 'Gee, I'm not doing badly at all!' he said to himself.

At about midnight, there came a terrible crash, and in a wink he found himself standing right in the top of the white poplar, at the end of the village.

'Damn it! How the dickens can I get down from this tree?'

Suddenly a cart came up the road. When it reached the tree, he called down, 'Oh, brother, do help me!' But the man drove on, taking no heed of Uncle Matyi. Before long another cart drove up towards the tree. On the cart was Péter Barta, a fellow from Karancsság. 'I say, brother, stop your horses and help me get down.' The man brought his horses to a halt and said, 'Is that you, Uncle Matyi?'

'Damn it, to be sure it's me.'

'What on earth are you doing up there?'

'Well, brother, three women stopped me on my way home. They asked me to follow them to a house at the end of the street. When I went in, they made me stand on a bench and there I was to pipe for them. And they've given me a lot of money for it.'

When the man got him down from the tree, Uncle Matyi began looking for the money he had tucked into the hem of his cloak. But there was no money. There was only a lot of broken crockery and little chips of glass.

Such strange things sometimes still happen.

Vasilissa the Fair

(Russian)

MERCHANT and his wife living in a certain country had an only daughter, the beautiful Vasilissa. When the child was eight years old the mother was seized with a fatal illness, but before she died she called Vasilissa to her side and, giving her a little doll, said, 'Listen, dear daughter! remember my last words. I am dying, and bequeath to you now, together with a parent's blessing, this doll. Keep it always beside you, but show it to nobody; if at any time you are in trouble, give the doll some food and ask its advice.' Then the mother kissed her daughter, sighed deeply and died.

After his wife's death the merchant grieved for a long time, and next began to think whether he should not wed again. He was handsome and would have no difficulty in finding a bride; moreover, he was especially pleased with a certain little widow, no longer young, who possessed two daughters of about the same age as Vasilissa.

The widow was famous as both a good housekeeper and a good mother to her daughters, but when the merchant married her he quickly found she was unkind to his daughter. Vasilissa, being the chief beauty in the village, was on that account envied by her stepmother and stepsisters. They found fault with her on every occasion, and tormented her with impossible tasks; thus, the poor girl suffered from the severity of her work and grew dark from exposure to wind and sun. Vasilissa endured all and became every day more beautiful; but the stepmother and her daughters who sat idle with folded hands, grew thin and almost lost their minds from spite. What supported Vasilissa? This. She received assistance from her doll; otherwise she could not have surmounted her daily difficulties.

Vasilissa, as a rule, kept a dainty morsel for her doll, and in the evening when everyone had gone to bed she would steal to her closet and regale her doll and say, 'Now, dear, eat and listen to my grief! Though I am living in my father's house, my life is joyless; a wicked stepmother makes me wretched; please direct my life and tell me what to do.'

The doll tasted the food, and gave advice to the sorrowing child, and in the morning performed her work, so that Vasilissa could rest in the shade or pluck flowers; already the beds had been weeded, and the cabbages watered, and the water carried, and the stove heated. It was nice for Vasilissa to live with her doll.

Several years passed. Vasilissa grew up, and the young men in the town sought her hand in marriage; but they never looked at the stepsisters. Growing more angry than ever, the stepmother answered Vasilissa's suitors thus: 'I will not let you have my youngest daughter before her sisters.' She dismissed the suitors and vented her spite on Vasilissa with harsh words and blows.

But it happened that the merchant was obliged to visit a neighbouring country, where he had business; and in the meanwhile the stepmother went to live in a house situated close to a thick forest. In the forest was a glade, in which stood a cottage, and in the cottage lived Baba-Yaga, who admitted nobody to her cottage, and devoured people as if they were chickens. Having moved to the new house, the merchant's wife continually, on some pretext or other, sent the hated Vasilissa into the forest, but the girl always returned home safe and unharmed, because the doll directed her and took care she did not enter Baba-Yaga's cottage.

Spring arrived, and the stepmother assigned to each of the three girls an evening task; thus, she set one to make lace, a second to knit stockings, and Vasilissa to spin. One evening, having extinguished all the lights in the house except one candle in the room where the girls sat at work, the stepmother went to bed. In a little while the candle needed attention, and one of the stepmother's daughters took the snuffers and, beginning to cut the wick, as if by accident, put out the light.

'What are we to do now?' said the girls. 'There is no light in the whole house, and our tasks are unfinished; someone must run for a light to Baba-Yaga.'

'I can see my pins,' said the daughter who was making lace. 'I shall not go.'

'Neither shall I,' said the daughter who was knitting stockings; 'my needles are bright.'

'You must run for a light. Go to Baba-Yaga's,' they both cried, pushing Vasilissa from the room.

Vasilissa went to her closet, placed some supper ready for the doll, and said, 'Now, little doll, have something to eat and hear my trouble. They have sent me to Baba-Yaga's for a light, and she will eat me.'

'Do not be afraid!' answered the doll. 'Go on your errand, but take me with you. No harm will befall you while I am present.' Vasilissa placed the doll in her pocket, crossed herself and entered the thick forest, but she trembled.

Suddenly a horseman galloped past; he was white and dressed in white, his steed was white and had a white saddle and bridle. The morning light was appearing.

The girl went further and another horseman rode past; he was red and dressed in red and his steed was red. The sun rose.

Vasilissa walked all night and all day, but on the following evening she came out in a glade, where stood Baba-Yaga's cottage. The fence around the cottage was made of human bones, and on the fence there were fixed human skulls with eyes. Instead of doorposts at the gates there were human legs; instead of bolts there were hands, instead of a lock there was a mouth with sharp teeth. Vasilissa grew pale from terror and stood as if transfixed. Suddenly another horseman rode up; he was black and dressed in black and upon a black horse; he sprang through Baba-Yaga's gates and vanished, as if he had been hurled into the earth. Night came on. But the darkness did not last long; the eyes in all the skulls on the fence lighted up, and at once it became as light throughout the glade as if it were midday. Vasilissa trembled from fear, and not knowing whither to run, she remained motionless.

Suddenly she heard a terrible noise. The trees cracked, the dry leaves rustled, and out of the forest Baba-Yaga appeared, riding in a mortar which she drove with a pestle, while she swept away traces of her progress with a broom. She came up to the gates and stopped; then sniffing about her, cried, 'Phoo, phoo, I smell a Russian! Who is here?'

Vasilissa approached the old woman timidly and gave her a low bow; then she said, 'It is I, granny! My stepsisters have sent me to you for a light.'

'Very well,' said Baba-Yaga, 'I know them. If you first of all live with me and do some work, then I will give you a light. If you refuse, I will eat you.' Then she turned to the gates and exclaimed, 'Strong bolts, unlock; wide gates, open!' The gates opened, and Baba-Yaga went out whistling. Vasilissa followed, and all again closed.

Having entered the room, the witch stretched herself and said to Vasilissa, 'Hand me everything in the oven; I am hungry.' Vasilissa lit a torch from the skulls upon the fence and, drawing the food from the oven, handed it to the witch. The meal would have been sufficient for ten men. Moreover, Vasilissa brought up from the cellar kvass, and honey, and beer and wine. The old woman ate and drank almost everything. She left nothing for Vasilissa but some fragments, end-crusts of bread and tiny morsels of sucking pig. Baba-Yaga lay down to sleep and said, 'When I go away tomorrow, take care that you clean the yard, sweep out the cottage, cook the dinner and get ready the linen. Then go to the cornbin, take a quarter of the wheat and cleanse it from impurities. See that all is done! otherwise I shall eat you.'

After giving these injunctions Baba-Yaga began to snore. But Vasilissa placed the remains of the old woman's meal before her doll and, bursting into tears, said, 'Now, little doll, take some food and hear my grief. Baba-Yaga has set me a terrible task, and has threatened to eat me if I fail in any way; help me!'

The doll answered, 'Have no fear, beautiful Vasilissa! Eat your supper, say your prayers and lie down to sleep; morning is wiser than evening.'

It was early when Vasilissa woke, but Baba-Yaga, who had

already risen, was looking out of the window. Suddenly the light from the eyes in the skulls was extinguished; then a pale horseman flashed by, and it was altogether daylight. Baba-Yaga went out and whistled; a mortar appeared before her with a pestle and a hearth broom. A red horseman flashed by, and the sun rose. Then Baba-Yaga took her place in the mortar and went forth, driving herself with the pestle and sweeping away traces of her progress with the broom.

Vasilissa remained alone and, eyeing Baba-Yaga's house, wondered at her wealth. The girl did not know which task to begin with. But when she looked she found that the work was already done: the doll had separated from the wheat the last grains of impurity.

'Oh, my dear liberator,' said Vasilissa to the doll, 'you have rescued me from misfortune!'

'You have only to cook the dinner,' said the doll, climbing into Vasilissa's pocket. 'God help you to prepare it; then rest in peace!'

Towards evening Vasilissa laid the table and awaited Baba-Yaga's return. It became dusk, and a black horseman flashed by the gates; it had grown altogether dark. But the eyes in the skulls shone and the trees cracked and the leaves rustled. Baba-Yaga came. Vasilissa met her. 'Is all done?' asked the witch. 'Look for yourself, granny!'

Baba-Yaga examined everything and, vexed that she had no cause for anger, said, 'My true servants, my bosom friends, grind my wheat!' Three pairs of hands appeared, seized the wheat and bore it from sight.

Baba-Yaga ate to repletion, prepared for sleep, and again gave an order to Vasilissa. 'Tomorrow repeat your task of today; in addition remove the poppies from the cornbin and cleanse them from earth, seed by seed; you see, someone has maliciously mixed earth with them!' Having spoken, the old woman turned to the wall and snored.

Vasilissa began to feed her doll, who said, as on the previous day, 'Pray to God and go to sleep; morning is wiser than evening; all will be done, dear Vasilissa!'

In the morning Baba-Yaga departed again in her mortar, and immediately Vasilissa and the doll set to work at their tasks. The old woman returned, observed everything and cried out, 'My faithful servants, my close friends, squeeze the oil from the poppies!' Three pairs of hands seized the poppies and bore them from sight. Baba-Yaga sat down to dine, and Vasilissa stood silent.

'Why do you say nothing?' remarked the witch. 'You stand as if you were dumb.'

Timidly Vasilissa replied, 'If you would permit me, I should like to ask you a question.'

'Ask, but remember, not every question leads to good. You will learn much; you will soon grow old.'

'I only wish to ask you,' said the girl, 'about what I have seen. When I came to you a pale horseman dressed in white on a white horse overtook me. Who was he?'

'He is my clear day,' answered Baba-Yaga.

'Then another horseman, who was red and dressed in red, and who rode a red horse, overtook me. Who was he?'

'He was my little red sun!' was the answer.

'But who was the black horseman who passed me at the gate granny?'

'He was my dark night; all three are my faithful servants.'

Vasilissa recalled the three pairs of hands, but was silent. 'Have you nothing more to ask?' said Baba-Yaga.

'I have, but you said, granny, that I shall learn much as I grow older.'

'It is well,' answered the witch, 'that you have enquired only about things outside and not about anything here! I do not like my rubbish to be carried away, and I eat over-inquisitve people! Now I will ask you something. How did you succeed in performing the tasks which I set you?'

'My mother's blessing assisted me,' answered Vasilissa.

'Depart, favoured daughter! I do not require people who have been blessed.' Baba-Yaga dragged Vasilissa out of the room and pushed her beyond the gate, took down from the fence a skull with burning eyes and, putting it on a stick, gave it to the girl and said, 'Take this light to your stepsisters; they sent you here for it.'

Vasilissa ran off, the skull giving her light, which only went out in the morning; and at last, on the evening of the second day, she reached home. As she approached the gates, she was on the point of throwing away the skull, for she thought that there would no longer be any need for a light at home. Then suddenly a hollow voice from the skull was heard to say, 'Do not cast me aside, but carry me to your stepmother.' Glancing at the house, and not seeing a light in any of the windows, she decided to enter with the skull.

At first her stepmother and stepsisters met her with caresses, telling her that they had been without a light from the moment of her departure; they could not strike a light in any way, and if anybody brought one from the neighbours, it went out directly it was carried into the room. 'Perhaps your light will last,' said the stepmother. When they carried the skull into the room its eyes shone brightly and looked continually at the stepmother and her daughters. All their efforts to hide themselves were vain; wherever they rushed they were ceaselessly pursued by the eyes, and before dawn had been burnt to ashes, though Vasilissa was unharmed.

In the morning the girl buried the skull in the ground, locked up the house and visited the town, where she asked admission into the home of a certain old woman who was without kindred. Here she lived quietly and awaited her father. But one day she said to the old woman, 'It tires me to sit idle, granny! Go off and buy me some of the best flax; I will busy myself with spinning.'

The old woman purchased the flax and Vasilissa sat down to spin. The work proceeded rapidly, and the thread when spun was as smooth and fine as a small hair. The thread lay in heaps, and it was time to begin weaving, but a weaver's comb could not be found to suit Vasilissa's thread, and nobody would undertake to make one. Then the girl had recourse to her doll, who said, 'Bring me an old comb that has belonged to a weaver, and an old shuttle, and a horse's mane, and I will do everything for you.' Vasilissa obtained everything necessary, and lay down to sleep. The doll, in a single night, made a first-rate loom. Towards the end of winter linen had been woven of so fine a texture that it could be drawn through the needle where the thread should pass.

In spring the linen was bleached, and Vasilissa said to the old woman, 'Sell this linen, granny, and keep the money for yourself.'

The old woman glanced at the work and said with a sigh, 'Ah! my child, nobody but a tsar would wear such linen. I will take it to the palace.'

She went to the royal dwelling, and walked up and down in front of the windows. When the tsar saw her he said, 'What do you desire, old woman?'

'Your Majesty,' she answered, 'I have brought some wonderful material, and will show it to nobody but yourself.'

The tsar ordered that she should be admitted, and marvelled when he saw the linen. 'How much do you ask for it?' he enquired.

'It is not for sale, Tsar and Father! I have brought it as a gift.' The tsar thanked her, and sent her away with some presents.

Some shirts for the tsar were cut out from this linen, but a seamstress could nowhere be found to complete them. At last the tsar summoned the old woman and said to her, 'You were able to spin and weave this linen, so you will be able to sew together some shirts from it.'

'Tsar, it was not I who spun and wove the linen; it is the work of a beautiful maiden.'

'Well, let her sew them!'

The old woman returned home and related everything to Vasilissa. The girl said in reply, 'I knew that this work would not pass out of my hands.' She shut herself in her room and began the undertaking; soon without resting her hands, she had completed a dozen shirts.

The old woman bore them to the tsar, while Vasilissa washed herself and combed her hair, dressed and then took a seat at the window, and there awaited events. She saw a royal servant come to the old woman's house. He entered the room and said, 'The Tsar-Emperor desires to see the skilful worker who made his shirts, and to reward her out of his royal hands.'

Vasilissa presented herself before the tsar. So much did she please him that he said, 'I cannot bear to separate from you; become my wife!' The tsar took her by her white hands, placed her beside himself, and the wedding was celebrated.

Vasilissa's father quickly returned to rejoice at his daughter's good fortune and to live with her. Vasilissa took the old woman into the palace, and never separated from the little doll, which she kept in her pocket.

The Midwife and the Frog

(Hungarian)

Y grandmother's mother was a midwife – the queen's midwife, as we used to say, because she drew her pay from the parish, which in our eyes meant the whole country.

One night she was called away to assist at a childbirth. It was about midnight. It was pitch dark on the road and it was raining. When the woman was delivered of her babe – God let her have a good one – my great-grandmother started off homeward. On the road she came across a big frog. It was hopping along right in front of her. My great-grandmother had always had a holy fear of frogs, and she cried out in terror, 'Get out of my way, you hideous creature! Why on earth are you hopping around me? Is it a midwife you may be wanting?'

And thus she was conversing with the frog as she proceeded on her way, and the frog jumped closer and closer to her. Once it got right under her feet, and she stepped on it. It gave such a shriek that my great-grandmother almost jumped out of her shoes. Well, she went home leaving the frog on the road, and the frog hopped off to some place, wherever it had its abode.

Back at home, my great-grandmother went to bed. Suddenly she heard a cart driving into the yard. She thought there was another childbirth where her assistance would be needed. Soon she saw the door open. Two men came in; both were very dark-skinned. They were both spindleshanks; their legs looked like a pair of pipestems, and their heads were as big as a bushel. They greeted her with, 'Good evening,' and then said, 'We want to take you along, mother; you must come and help with a birth.'

She said, 'Who is it?' as it is the custom of a midwife to enquire where her assistance is wanted.

One of the men said, 'On the road you promised my wife to

help her with the child when her time came.'

And this gave my great-grandmother something to think of, because she had not met a single soul on her way back, except the frog. 'It's true' she thought to herself, 'I asked her by way of a joke "Is it a midwife you're looking for? I might come and help you too."'

The two men said to her, 'Do not tarry, mother.'

But she said to them, 'I'm not going with you because I've met no human creature and I've promised nothing.'

But they were so insistent that she should keep her promise that finally she said, 'Well, as you are so keen on taking me along, I'll go with you.'

She thought to herself that in any case she'd take her rosary with her, and that if she would pray, God would not forsake her, wherever she'd be taken by the two men. And then the men left her alone, and she began to dress. She dressed herself quite neatly, and when she was ready she asked the men, 'Is it a long journey? Shall I put on more warm clothes?'

'We aren't going far. It will take us an hour and a half or so to get back. But hurry up, mother, because my wife was in a bad state when I left her.'

Then she finished dressing and went out with the two men. They put her in their black coach and soon were driving up a big mountain. It was Magyarós Mountain, not far from the banks of the Szucsáva. As they were driving along, suddenly the mountain opened up before them, and they drove straight through the split, right into the centre of the mountain. They pulled up before a house and one of the men opened the door for her.

'Well, you go in to her,' he said. 'You'll find my wife there. She's lying on the floor.'

And as she stepped through the door, she beheld a small woman lying on the floor. She, too, had a head as big as a bushel. She looked ill and was groaning terribly.

My great-grandmother said to her, 'You're in a bad state, daughter, aren't you? But have no fear, God will deliver you of your burden, and then you'll feel well again.'

The woman then said to my great-grandmother, 'Don't say that God will help me. My husband must not hear you saying it.'

The midwife asked, 'What else could I say?'

'Say the *gyivák* [a type of devil] will help you.'

Then my great-grandmother – we had it from her own mouth – felt as if the words had frozen on her lips, so alarmed did she grow at the thought of what place she had been brought to. No sooner had she thought about it than the child was born, a spindleshanks, with legs as thin as pipestems and a head as big as a stewpot. My great-grandmother thought to herself, 'Well, I was brought here, but how am I to get back? So she turned to the woman. 'Well, your men have brought me to your place, but how can I get back? It's pitch dark outside. I couldn't find my way back home alone.'

The sick woman then said, 'Do not worry about that. My husband will take you back to the same place he brought you from.' And then she asked my great-grandmother, 'Well, mother, do you know who I am?'

'I couldn't say I do. I've asked your husband a few questions about you, but he didn't tell me a thing. He said I should go with them and I'd learn in time who you were.'

'Well, you know who I am? I am the frog you kicked about on the road and trod under your feet. Now, this should serve as a lesson that if you happen to come across some creature like me at about midnight or an hour past it, do not speak to it, nor take heed of what you see. Just pass along on your way. You see, you stopped to talk to me and made a promise to me. So you had to be brought here, because I was that frog you met on the road.'

Then my great-grandmother said, 'I've done my job here; now get me back to my home.'

Then the man came in and asked her, 'Well, what would you want me to pay for your troubles?'

Then the old midwife said, 'I don't want you to pay me anything. Get me right back to the place you brought me from.'

The man said, 'Do not worry. We still have half an hour or so to get you back. But now let me take you to our larder so that you may see for yourself that we are doing well. You needn't fear that we haven't the wherewithal to pay for your services.'

And my great-grandmother followed him to the larder. In the larder she beheld all sorts of food heaped on the shelves: flour and bacon and firkins of lard here, and loaves of bread and cream there and a lot of other things, all arranged in neat order, to say nothing of veritable mounds of gold and silver.

'Now you can see for yourself what plenty there is. Whatever the rich men and the wealthy farmers deny to the poor in their greed becomes ours and goes into our storeroom.' And he turned to my great-grandmother and said, 'Well, mother, let's get along. There isn't much time left for us to get you back to your home. Take of this gold an apronful, as I see you have on your Sunday apron.'

And he insisted on her taking an apronful of gold. He wouldn't let her leave the larder until she had filled her apron with it.

When she had put the gold in her apron, she was taken to the top of Magyarós Mountain by the same coach in which she had first come. But dawn was already coming on, and soon the cock uttered its first crow. Then the men pushed her from the black coach – though they were still near the top – and said to her, 'Trot along, mother, you can find your way home from here.'

And when she took a look at her apron to make sure that she had the gold, there was nothing whatever in her apron; that heap of gold had vanished into thin air.

And that is all there is to the story; you can take it from me.

Part Three

BEAUTIFUL PEOPLE

Fair, Brown and Trembling

(Irish)

KING Aedh Cúrucha lived in Tir Conal, and he had three daughters, whose names were Fair, Brown, and Trembling.

Fair and Brown had new dresses, and went to church every Sunday. Trembling was kept at home to do the cooking and work. They would not let her go out of the house at all; for she was more beautiful than the other two, and they were in dread she might marry before themselves.

They carried on in this way for seven years. At the end of seven years the son of the king of Omanya fell in love with the eldest sister.

One Sunday morning, after the other two had gone to church, the old henwife came into the kitchen to Trembling, and said, 'It's at church you ought to be this day, instead of working here at home.'

'How could I go?' said Trembling. 'I have no clothes good enough to wear at church. And if my sisters were to see me there, they'd kill me for going out of the house.'

'I'll give you,' said the henwife, 'a finer dress than either of them has ever seen. And now tell me what dress will you have?'

'I'll have,' said Trembling, 'a dress as white as snow, and green shoes for my feet.'

Then the henwife put on the cloak of darkness, clipped a piece from the old clothes the young woman had on, and asked for the whitest robes in the world and the most beautiful that could be found, and a pair of green shoes.

That moment she had the robe and the shoes, and she brought them to Trembling, who put them on. When Trembling was dressed and ready, the henwife said, 'I have a honey-bird here to sit on your right shoulder, and a honey-finger to put on your left. At the door stands a milk-white mare, with a golden saddle for you to sit on, and a golden bridle to hold in your hand.'

Trembling sat on the golden saddle. And when she was ready to start, the henwife said, 'You must not go inside the door of the church, and the minute the people rise up at the end of mass, do you make off, and ride home as fast as the mare will carry you.'

When Trembling came to the door of the church there was no one inside who could get a glimpse of her but was striving to know who she was; and when they saw her hurrying away at the end of mass, they ran out to overtake her. But no use in their running; she was away before any man could come near her. From the minute she left the church till she got home, she overtook the wind before her, and outstripped the wind behind.

She came down at the door, went in, and found the henwife had dinner ready. She put off the white robes, and had on her old dress in a twinkling.

When the two sisters came home the henwife asked, 'Have you any news today from the church?'

'We have great news,' said they. 'We saw a wonderful, grand lady at the church door. The like of the robes she had we have never seen on woman before. It's little that was thought of our dresses beside what she had on. And there wasn't a man at the church, from the king to the beggar, but was trying to look at her and know who she was.'

The sisters would give no peace till they had two dresses like the robes of the strange lady; but honey-birds and honey-fingers were not to be found.

Next Sunday the two sisters went to church again, and left the youngest at home to cook the dinner.

After they had gone, the henwife came in and asked, 'Will you go to church today?'

'I would go,' said Trembling, 'if I could get the going.'

'What robe will you wear?' asked the henwife.

'The finest black satin that can be found, and red shoes for my feet.'

'What colour do you want the mare to be?'

'I want her to be so black and so glossy that I can see myself in her body.'

The henwife put on the cloak of darkness, and asked for the robes and the mare. That moment she had them. When Trembling was dressed, the henwife put the honey-bird on her right shoulder and the honey-finger on her left. The saddle on the mare was silver, and so was the bridle.

When Trembling sat in the saddle and was going away, the henwife ordered her strictly not to go inside the door of the church, but to rush away as soon as the people rose at the end of mass, and hurry home on the mare before any man could stop her.

That Sunday the people were more astonished than ever, and gazed at her more than the first time, and all they were thinking of was to know who she was. But they had no chance, for the moment the people rose at the end of mass she slipped from the church, was in the silver saddle, and home before a man could stop her or talk to her.

The henwife had the dinner ready. Trembling took off her satin robe, and had on her old clothes before her sisters got home.

'What news have you today?' asked the henwife of the sisters when they came from the church.

'Oh, we saw the grand strange lady again! And it's little that any man could think of our dresses after looking at the robes of satin that she had on! And all at church, from high to low, had their mouths open, gazing at her, and no man was looking at us.'

The two sisters gave neither rest nor peace till they got dresses as nearly like the strange lady's robes as they could find. Of course they were not so good, for the like of those robes could not be found in Erin.

When the third Sunday came, Fair and Brown went to church dressed in black satin. They left Trembling at home to work in the kitchen, and told her to be sure and have dinner ready when they came back.

After they had gone and were out of sight, the henwife came to the kitchen and said, 'Well, my dear, are you for church today?'

'I would go if I had a new dress to wear.'

'I'll get you any dress you ask for. What dress would you like?' asked the henwife.

'A dress red as a rose from the waist down, and white as snow from the waist up; a cape of green on my shoulders; and a hat on my head with a red, a white, and a green feather in it; and shoes for my feet with the toes red, the middle white, and the backs and heels green.'

The henwife put on the cloak of darkness, wished for all these things, and had them. When Trembling was dressed, the henwife put the honey-bird on her right shoulder and the honey-finger on her left, and placing the hat on her head, clipped a few hairs from one lock and a few from another with her scissors, and that moment the most beautiful golden hair was flowing down over the girl's shoulders. Then the henwife asked what kind of a mare she would ride. She said white, with blue and gold-coloured diamond-shaped spots all over her body, on her back a saddle of gold, and on her head a golden bridle.

The mare stood there before the door, and a bird sitting between her ears, which began to sing as soon as Trembling was in the saddle, and never stopped till she came home from the church.

The fame of the beautiful strange lady had gone out through the world, and all the princes and great men that were in it came to church that Sunday, each one hoping that it was himself would have her home with him after mass.

The son of the king of Omanya forgot all about the eldest sister, and remained outside the church, so as to catch the strange lady before she could hurry away.

The church was more crowded than ever before, and there were three times as many outside. There was such a throng before the church that Trembling could only come inside the gate.

As soon as the people were rising at the end of mass, the lady slipped out through the gate, was in the golden saddle in an instant, and sweeping away ahead of the wind. But if she was, the prince of Omanya was at her side, and seizing her by the foot, he ran with the mare for thirty perches, and never let go of the beautiful lady till the shoe was pulled from her foot, and he was left behind with it in his hand. She came home as fast as the mare could carry her, and was thinking all the time that the henwife would kill her for losing the shoe.

Seeing her so vexed and so changed in the face, the old woman asked, 'What's the trouble that's on you now?'

'Oh! I've lost one of the shoes off my feet,' said Trembling.

'Don't mind that; don't be vexed,' said the henwife. 'Maybe it's the best thing that ever happened to you.'

Then Trembling gave up all the things she had to the henwife, put on her old clothes, and went to work in the kitchen. When the sisters came home, the henwife asked, 'Have you any news from the church?'

'We have indeed,' said they; 'for we saw the grandest sight today. The strange lady came again, in grander array than before. On herself and the horse she rode were the finest colours of the world, and between the ears of the horse was a bird which never stopped singing from the time she came till she went away. The lady herself is the most beautiful woman ever seen by man in Erin.'

After Trembling had disappeared from the church, the son of the king of Omanya said to the other kings' sons, 'I will have that lady for my own.'

They all said, 'You didn't win her just by taking the shoe off her foot, you'll have to win her by the point of the sword. You'll have to fight for her with us before you can call her your own.'

'Well,' said the son of the king of Omanya, 'when I find the lady that shoe will fit, I'll fight for her, never fear, before I leave her to any of you.'

Then all the kings' sons were uneasy, and anxious to know who was she that lost the shoe; and they began to travel all over Erin to know could they find her. The prince of Omanya and all the others went in a great company together, and made the round of Erin. They went everywhere – north, south, east and west. They visited every place where a woman was to be found, and left not a house in the kingdom they did not search, to know could they find the woman the shoe would fit, not caring whether she was rich or poor, of high or low degree.

The prince of Omanya always kept the shoe. And when the young women saw it they had great hopes, for it was of proper size, neither large nor small, and it would beat any man to know of what material it was made. One thought it would fit her if she cut a little from her great toe; and another, with too short a foot, put something in the tip of her stocking. But no use, they only spoiled their feet, and were curing them for months afterwards.

The two sisters, Fair and Brown, heard that the princes of the world were looking all over Erin for the woman that could wear the shoe, and every day they were talking of trying it on. And one day Trembling spoke up and said, 'Maybe it's my foot that the shoe will fit.'

'Oh, the breaking of the dog's foot on you! Why say so when you were at home every Sunday?'

They were that way waiting, and scolding the younger sister, till the princes were near the place. The day they were to come, the sisters put Trembling in a closet, and locked the door on her. When the company came to the house, the prince of Omanya gave the shoe to the sisters. But though they tried and tried, it would fit neither of them.

'Is there any other young woman in the house?' asked the prince.

'There is,' said Trembling, speaking up in the closet. 'I'm here.'

'Oh! we have her for nothing but to put out the ashes,' said the sisters.

But the prince and the others wouldn't leave the house till they had seen her. So the two sisters had to open the door. When Trembling came out, the shoe was given to her, and it fitted exactly.

The prince of Omanya looked at her and said, 'You are the woman the shoe fits, and you are the woman I took the shoe from.'

Then Trembling spoke up, and said, 'Do you stay here till I return.'

Then she went to the henwife's house. The old woman put on the cloak of darkness, got everything for her she had the first Sunday at church, and put her on the white mare in the same fashion. Then Trembling rode along the highway to the front of the house. All who saw her the first time said, 'This is the lady we saw at church.'

Then she went away a second time, and a second time came back on the black mare in the second dress which the henwife gave her. All who saw her the second Sunday said, 'That is the lady we saw at church.'

A third time she asked for a short absence, and soon came back on the third mare and in the third dress. All who saw her the third time said, 'That is the lady we saw at church.' Every man was satisfied, and knew that she was the woman.

Then all the princes and great men spoke up, and said to the son of the king of Omanya, 'You'll have to fight now for her before we let her go with you.'

'I'm here before you, ready for combat,' answered the prince.

Then the son of the king of Lochlin stepped forth. The struggle began, and a terrible struggle it was. They fought for nine hours. And then the son of the king of Lochlin stopped, gave up his claim, and left the field. Next day the son of the king of Spain fought six hours, and yielded his claim. On the third day the son of the king of Nyerfói fought eight hours, and stopped. The fourth day the son of the king of Greece fought six hours, and stopped. On the fifth day no more strange princes wanted to fight. And all the sons of kings in Erin said they would not fight with a man of their own land, that the strangers had had their chance, and as no others came to claim the woman, she belonged of right to the son of the king of Omanya.

The marriage day was fixed, and the invitations were sent out. The wedding lasted for a year and a day. When the wedding was over, the king's son brought home the bride, and when the time came a son was born. The young woman sent for her eldest sister, Fair, to be with her and care for her. One day, when Trembling was well, and when her husband was away hunting, the two sisters went out to walk. And when they came to the seaside, the eldest pushed the youngest sister in. A great whale came and swallowed her.

The eldest sister came home alone, and the husband asked, 'Where is your sister?'

'She has gone home to her father in Ballyshannon. Now that I am well, I don't need her.'

'Well,' said the husband, looking at her, 'I'm in dread it's my wife that has gone.'

'Oh! no,' said she. 'It's my sister Fair that's gone.'

Since the sisters were very much alike, the prince was in doubt. That night he put his sword between them, and said, 'If you are my wife, this sword will get warm; if not, it will stay cold.'

In the morning when he rose up, the sword was as cold as when he put it there.

It happened when the two sisters were walking by the seashore that a little cowboy was down by the water minding cattle, and saw Fair push Trembling into the sea; and next day, when the tide came in, he saw the whale swim up and throw her out on the sand. When she was on the sand she said to the cowboy, 'When you go home in the evening with the cows, tell the master that my sister Fair pushed me into the sea yesterday; that a whale swallowed me, and then threw me out, but will come again and swallow me with the coming of the next tide; then he'll go out with the tide, and come again with tomorrow's tide, and throw me again on the strand. The whale will cast me out three times. I'm under the enchantment of this whale, and cannot leave the beach or escape myself. Unless my husband saves me before I'm swallowed a fourth time, I shall be lost. He must come and shoot the whale with a silver bullet when he turns on the broad of his back. Under the breast-fin of the whale is a reddish-brown spot. My husband must hit him in that spot, for it is the only place in which he can be killed.'

When the cowboy got home, the eldest sister gave him a draught of oblivion, and he did not tell.

Next day he went again to the sea. The whale came and cast Trembling on shore again. She asked the boy, 'Did you tell the master what I told you to tell him?'

'I did not,' said he. 'I forgot.'

'How did you forget?' asked she.

'The woman of the house gave me a drink that made me forget.'

'Well, don't forget telling him this night. And if she gives you a drink, don't take it from her.'

As soon as the cowboy came home, the eldest sister offered him a drink. He refused to take it till he had delivered his message and told all to the master. The third day the prince went down with his gun and a silver bullet in it. He was not long down when the whale came and threw Trembling upon the beach as the two days before. She had no power to speak to her husband till he had killed the whale. Then the whale went out, turned over once on the broad of his back, and showed the spot for a moment only. That moment the prince fired. He had but the one chance, and a short one at that. But he took it, and hit the spot, and the whale, mad with pain, made the sea all around red with blood, and died.

That minute Trembling was able to speak, and went home with her husband, who sent word to her father what the eldest sister had done. The father came, and told him any death he chose to give her to give it. The prince told the father he would leave her life and death with himself. The father had her put out then on the sea in a barrel, with provisions in it for seven years.

In time Trembling had a second child, a daughter. The prince and she sent the cowboy to school, and trained him up as one of their own children, and said, 'If the little girl that is born to us now lives, no other man in the world will get her but him.'

The cowboy and the prince's daughter lived on till they were married. The mother said to her husband, 'You could not have saved me from the whale but for the little cowboy. On that account I don't grudge him my daughter.'

The son of the king of Omanya and Trembling had fourteen children, and they lived happily till the two died of old age.

Diirawic and Her Incestuous Brother

(Sudan, Dinka)

GIRL called Diirawic was extremely beautiful. All the girls of the tribe listened to her words. Old women all listened to her words. Small children all listened to her words. Even old men all listened to her words. A man called Teeng wanted to marry her, but her brother, who was also called Teeng, refused. Many people each offered a hundred cows for her bridewealth, but her brother refused. One day Teeng spoke to his mother and said, 'I would like to marry my sister Diirawic.'

His mother said, 'I have never heard of such a thing. You should go and ask your father.'

He went to his father and said, 'Father, I would like to marry my sister.'

His father said, 'My son, I have never heard of such a thing. A man marrying his sister is something I cannot even speak about. You had better go and ask your mother's brother.'

He went to his mother's brother and said, 'Uncle, I would like to marry my sister.'

His maternal uncle exclaimed, 'My goodness! Has anybody ever married his sister? Is that why you have always opposed her marriage? Was it because you had it in your heart to marry her yourself? I have never heard of such a thing! But what did your mother say about this?'

'My mother told me to ask my father. I agreed and went to my father. My father said he had never heard such a thing and told me to come to you.'

'If you want my opinion,' said his uncle, 'I think you should ask your father's sister.'

He went around to all his relatives that way. Each one

expressed surprise and suggested that he should ask another. Then he came to his mother's sister and said, 'Aunt, I would like to marry my sister.'

She said, 'My child, if you prevented your sister from being married because you wanted her, what can I say! Marry her if that is your wish. She is your sister.'

Diirawic did not know about this. One day she called all the girls and said, 'Girls, let us go fishing.' Her words were always listened to by everyone, and when she asked for anything, everyone obeyed. So all the girls went, including little children. They went and fished.

In the mean time, her brother Teeng took out his favourite ox, Mijok, and slaughtered it for a feast. He was very happy that he was allowed to marry his sister. All the people came to the feast.

Although Diirawic did not know her brother's plans, her little sister had overheard the conversation and knew what was happening. But she kept silent; she did not say anything.

A kite flew down and grabbed up the tail of Teeng's ox, Mijok. Then it flew to the river where Diirawic was fishing and dropped it in her lap. She looked at the tail and recognised it. 'This looks like the tail of my brother's ox, Mijok,' she said. 'What has killed him? I left him tethered and alive!'

The girls tried to console her, saying, 'Diirawic, tails are all the same. But if it is the tail of Mijok, then perhaps some important guests have arrived. It may be that they are people wanting to marry you. Teeng may have decided to honour them with his favourite ox. Nothing bad has happened.'

Diirawic was still troubled. She stopped the fishing and suggested that they return to find out what had happened to her brother's ox.

They went back. As they arrived, the little sister of Diirawic came running to her and embraced her, saying, 'My dear sister Diirawic, do you know what has happened?'

'I don't know,' said Diirawic.

'Then I will tell you a secret,' continued her sister, 'but please don't mention it to anyone, not even to our mother.'

'Come on, sister, tell me,' said Diirawic.

'Teeng has been preventing you from being married because *he* wants to marry you,' her sister said. 'He has slaughtered his ox, Mijok, to celebrate his engagement to you. Mijok is dead.'

Diirawic cried and said, 'So that is why God made the kite fly with Mijok's tail and drop it in my lap. So be it. There is nothing I can do.'

'Sister,' said her little sister, 'let me continue with what I have to tell you. When your brother bedevils you and forgets that you are his sister, what do you do? I found a knife for you. He will want you to sleep with him in the hut. Hide the knife near the bed. And at night when he is fast asleep, cut off his testicles. He will die. And he will not be able to do anything to you.'

'Sister,' said Diirawic, 'you have given me good advice.'

Diirawic kept the secret and did not tell the girls what had occurred. But she cried whenever she was alone.

She went and milked the cows. People drank the milk. But when Teeng was given milk, he refused. And when he was given food, he refused. His heart was on his sister. That is where his heart was.

At bedtime, he said, 'I would like to sleep in that hut, Diirawic, sister, let us share the hut.'

Diirawic said, 'Nothing is bad, my brother. We can share the hut.'

They did. Their little sister also insisted on sleeping with them in the hut. So she slept on the other side of the hut. In the middle of the night, Teeng got up and moved the way men do! At that moment, a lizard spoke and said, 'Come, Teeng, have you really become an imbecile? How can you behave like that towards your sister?

He felt ashamed and lay down. He waited for a while and then got up again. And when he tried to do what men do, the grass on the thatching spoke and said, 'What an imbecile! How can you forget that she is your sister?'

He felt ashamed and cooled down. This time, he waited much longer. Then his desire rose and he got up. The rafters spoke and said, 'O, the man has really become an idiot! How can your heart be on your mother's daughter's body? Have you become a hopeless imbecile?'

He cooled down. This time he remained quiet for a very long time, but then his mind returned to it again.

This went on until very close to dawn. Then he reached that point when a man's heart fails him. The walls spoke and said, 'You monkey of a human being, what are you doing?' The utensils rebuked him. The rats in the hut laughed at him. Everything started shouting at him, 'Teeng, imbecile, what are you doing to your sister?'

At that moment, he fell back ashamed and exhausted and fell into a deep sleep.

The little girl got up and woke her older sister, saying, 'You fool, don't you see he is now sleeping? This is the time to cut off his testicles.'

Diirawic got up and cut them off. Teeng died.

Then the two girls got up and beat the drums in a way that told everybody that there was an exclusive dance for girls. No men could attend that dance. Nor could married women and children. So all the girls came out running from their huts and went to the dance.

Diirawic then spoke to them and said, 'Sisters, I called you to say that I am going into the wilderness.' She then went on to explain to them the whole story and ended, 'I did not want to leave you in secret. So I wanted a chance to bid you farewell before leaving.'

All the girls decided they would not remain behind.

'If your brother did it to you,' they argued, 'what is the guarantee that our brothers will not do it to us? We must all leave together!'

So all the girls of the tribe decided to go. Only very small girls remained. As they left, the little sister of Diirawic said, 'I want to go with you.'

But they would not let her. 'You are too young,' they said. 'You must stay.'

'In that case,' she said, 'I will cry out loud and tell everyone your plan!' And she started to cry out.

'Hush, hush,' said the girls. Then turning to Diirawic they said, 'Let her come with us. She is a girl with a heart. She has already taken our side. If we die, we die together with her!'

Diirawic accepted and they went. They walked; they walked and walked and walked, until they came to the borders between the human territory and the lion world. They carried their axes and their spears; they had everything they might need.

They divided the work among themselves. Some cut the timber for rafters and poles. Others cut the grass for thatching. And they built for themselves an enormouse house – a house far larger even than a cattle-byre. The number of girls was tremendous. They built many beds for themselves inside the hut and made a very strong door to make sure of their safety.

Their only problem was that they had no food. But they found a large anthill, full of dried meat, grain, and all the other foodstuffs that they needed. They wondered where all this could have come from. But Diirawic explained to them. 'Sisters, we are women and it is the woman who bears the human race. Perhaps God has seen our plight, and not wanting us to perish, has provided us with all this. Let us take it in good grace!'

They did. Some went for firewood. Others fetched water. They cooked and ate. Every day they would dance the women's dance in great happiness and then sleep.

One evening a lion came in search of insects and found them dancing. But seeing such a large number of girls, he became frightened and left. Their number was such as would frighten anyone.

It then occurred to the lion to turn into a dog and go into their compound. He did. He went there looking for droppings of food. Some girls hit him and chased him away. Others said, 'Don't kill him. He is a dog and dogs are friends!'

But the sceptical ones said, 'What kind of dog would be in this isolated world? Where do you think he came from?'

Other girls said, 'Perhaps he came all the way from the cattle camp, following us! Perhaps he thought the whole camp was moving and so he ran after us!'

Diirawic's sister was afraid of the dog. She had not seen a dog following them. And the distance was so great that the dog could not have travelled all the way alone. She worried but said nothing. Yet she could not sleep; she stayed awake while all the others slept.

One night the lion came and knocked at the door. He had overheard the names of the older girls, one of them, Diirawic. After knocking at the door he said, 'Diirawic, please open the door for me.' The little girl who was awake answered, chanting:

'Achol is asleep,
Adau is asleep,
Nyankiir is asleep,
Diirawic is asleep,
The girls are asleep!'

The lion heard her and said, 'Little girl, what is the matter with you, staying up so late?'

She answered him, saying, 'My dear man, it is thirst. I am suffering from a dreadful thirst.'

'Why?' asked the lion. 'Don't the girls fetch water from the river?'

'Yes,' answered the little girl, 'they do. But since I was born, I do not drink water from a pot or a gourd. I drink only from a container made of reeds.'

'And don't they bring you water in such a container?' asked the lion.

'No,' she said. 'They only bring water in pots and gourds, even though there is a container of reeds in the house.'

'Where is that container?' asked the lion.

'It is outside there on the platform!' she answered.

So he took it and left to fetch water for her.

The container of reeds would not hold water. The lion spent much time trying to fix it with clay. But when he filled it, the water washed the clay away. The lion kept on trying until dawn. Then he returned with the container of reeds and put it back where it was. He then rushed back to the bush before the girls got up.

This went on for many nights. The little girl slept only during the daytime. The girls rebuked her for this, saying, 'Why do you sleep in the daytime? Can't you sleep at night? Where do you go at night?'

She did not tell them anything. But she worried. She lost so much weight that she became very bony.

One day Diirawic spoke to her sister and said, 'Nyanaguek, my mother's daughter, what is making you so lean? I told you to remain at home. This is too much for a child your age! Is it your mother you are missing? I will not allow you to make the other girls miserable. If necessary, daughter of my mother, I will kill you.'

But Diirawic's sister would not reveal the truth. The girls went on rebuking her but she would not tell them what she knew.

One day, she broke down and cried, and then said, 'My dear sister, Diirawic, I eat, as you see. In fact, I get plenty of food, so much that I do not finish what I receive. But even if I did not receive enough food, I have an enduring heart. Perhaps I am able to endure more than any one of you here. What I am suffering from is something none of you has seen. Every night a lion gives me great trouble. It is just that I am a person who does not speak. That animal you thought to be a dog is a lion. I remain awake at night to protect us all and then sleep in the daytime. He comes and knocks at the door. Then he asks for you by name to open the door. I sing back to him and tell him that you are all asleep. When he wonders why I am awake, I tell him it is because I am thirsty. I explain that I only drink out of a container made of reeds and that the girls bring water only in pots and gourds. Then he goes to fetch water for me. And seeing that he cannot stop the water from flowing out of the container, he returns towards dawn and disappears, only to be back the following night. So that is what is destroying me, my dear sister. You blame me in vain.'

'I have one thing to tell you,' said Diirawic. 'Just be calm and when he comes, do not answer. I will remain awake with you.'

They agreed. Diirawic took a large spear that they had inherited from their ancestors and remained awake, close to the door. The lion came at his usual hour. He came to the door, but somehow he became afraid and jumped away without knocking. He had a feeling that something was going on.

So he left and stayed away for some time. Then he returned to the door towards dawn. He said, 'Diirawic, open the door for me!' There was only silence. He repeated his request. Still there was only silence. He said, 'Well! The little girl who always answered me is at last dead!'

He started to break through the door, and when he succeeded in pushing his head in, Diirawic attacked him with the large spear, forcing him back into the courtyard.

'Please, Diirawic,' he pleased, 'do not kill me.'

'Why not?' asked Diirawic. 'What brought you here?'

'I only came in search of a sleeping place!'

'Well, I am killing you for that,' said Diirawic.

'Please allow me to be your brother,' the lion continued to plead. 'I will never attempt to hurt anyone again. I will go away if you don't want me here. Please!'

So Diirawic let him go. He went. But before he had gone a long way, he returned and said to the girls then gathered outside, 'I am going, but I will be back in two days with all my horned cattle.'

Then he disappeared. After two days, he came back with all his horned cattle, as he had promised. Then he addressed the girls, saying, 'Here I have come. It is true that I am a lion. I want you to kill that big bull in the herd. Use its meat for taming me. If I live with you untamed, I might become wild at night and attack you. And that would be bad. So kill the bull and tame me by teasing me with the meat.'

They agreed. So they fell on him and beat him so much that his fur made a storm on his back as it fell off.

They killed the bull and roasted the meat. They would bring a fat piece of meat close to his mouth, then pull it away. A puppy dog would jump out of the saliva which dripped from the lion's mouth. They would give the puppy a fatal blow on the head. Then they would beat the lion again. Another piece of fat meat would be held close to his mouth, then pulled away, and another puppy would jump out of the falling saliva. They would give it a blow on the head and beat the lion some more. Four puppies emerged, and all four were killed.

Yet the lion's mouth streamed with a wild saliva. So they took a large quantity of steaming hot broth and poured it down his throat, clearing it of all the remaining saliva. His mouth remained wide open and sore. He could no longer eat anything. He was fed only milk, poured down his throat. He was then released. For four months, he was nursed as a sick person. His throat continued to hurt for all this time. Then he recovered.

The girls remained for another year. It was now five years since they had left home.

The lion asked the girls why they had left their home. The girls asked him to address his questions to Diirawic, as she was their leader. So he turned to Diirawic and asked the same question.

'My brother wanted to make me his wife,' explained Diirawic. 'I killed him for that. I did not want to remain in a place where I had killed my own brother. So I left. I did not care about my life. I expected such dangers as finding you. If you had eaten me, it would have been no more than I expected.'

'Well, I have now become a brother to you all,' said the lion. 'As an older brother, I think I should take you all back home. My cattle have since multiplied. They are yours. If you find that your land has lost its herds, these will replace them. Otherwise they will increase the cattle already there, because I have become a member of your family. Since your only brother is dead, let me be in the place of Teeng, your brother. Cool your heart and return home.'

He pleaded with Diirawic for about three months. Finally she agreed, but cried a great deal. When the girls saw her cry, they all cried. They cried and cried because their leader, Diirawic, had cried.

The lion slaughtered a bull to dry their tears. They ate the meat. Then he said to them, 'Let us wait for three more days, and then leave!'

They slaughtered many bulls in sacrifice to bless the territory they crossed as they returned, throwing meat away everywhere they passed. As they did so, they prayed, 'This is for the animals and the birds that have helped keep us healthy for all this time without death or illness in our midst. May God direct you to share in this meat.'

They had put one bull into their big house and locked the house praying, 'Our dear house, we give you this bull. And you bull, if you should break the rope and get out of the house, that will be a sign of grace from the hut. If you should remain inside, then we bequeath you this hut as we leave.' And they left.

All this time the people at home were in mourning. Diirawic's father never shaved his head. He left the ungroomed hair of mourning on his head and did not care about his appearance. Her mother, too, was in the same condition. She covered herself with ashes so that she looked grey. The rest of the parents mourned, but everyone mourned especially for Diirawic. They did not care as much for their own daughters as they did for Diirawic.

The many men who had wanted to marry Diirawic also neglected themselves in mourning. Young men and girls wore only two beads. But older people and children wore no beads at all.

All the girls came and tethered their herds a distance from the village. They all looked beautiful. Those who had been immature had grown into maturity. The older ones had now reached the peak of youth and beauty. They had blossomed and had also become wiser and adept with words.

The little boy who was Diirawic's youngest brother had now grown up. Diirawic resembled her mother, who had been an extremely beautiful girl. Even in her old age, she still retained her beauty and her resemblance to her daughter still showed.

The little boy had never really known his sister, as he was too young when the girls left. But when he saw Diirawic in the newly arrived cattle camp, he saw a clear resemblance to his mother. He knew that his two sisters and the other girls of the camp had disappeared. So he came and said, 'Mother, I saw a girl in the cattle camp who looks like she could be my sister, even though I do not remember my sisters.'

'Child, don't you feel shame? How can you recognise people who left soon after you were born? How can you recall people long dead? This is evil magic! This is the work of an evil spirit!' She started to cry, and all the women joined her in crying.

Age-sets came running from different camps to show her sympathy. They all cried, even as they tried to console her with words.

Then came Diirawic with the girls and said, 'My dear woman, permit us to shave off your mourning hair. And all of you, let us shave off your mourning hair!'

Surprised by her words, they said, 'What has happened that we should shave off our mourning hair?'

Then Diirawic asked them why they were in mourning. The old woman started to cry as Diirawic spoke, and said, 'My dear girl, I lost a girl like you. She died five years ago, and five years is a long time. If she had died only two or even three years ago, I might have dared to say you are my daughter. As it is, I can't. But seeing you, my dear daughter, has cooled my heart.'

Diirawic spoke again, saying, 'Dear Mother, every child is a daughter. As I stand in front of you, I feel as though I were your daughter. So please listen to what I say as though I were your own daughter. We have all heard of you and your famed name. We have come from a very far-off place because of you. Please allow us to shave your head. I offer five cows as a token of my request.'

'Daughter,' said the woman, 'I shall honour your request, but not because of the cows – I have no use for cattle. Night and day, I think of nothing but my lost Diirawic. Even this child you see means nothing to me compared to my lost child, Diirawic. What grieves me is that God has refused to answer my prayers. I have called upon our clan spirits and I have called upon my ancestors, and they do not listen. This I resent. I will listen to your words, my daughter. The fact that God has brought you along and put these words into your mouth is enough to convince me.'

So she was shaved. Diirawic gave the woman beautiful leather skirts made from skins of animals they killed on the way. They were not from the hides of cattle, sheep or goats. She decorated the edges of the skirts with beautiful beads and made bead designs of cattle figures on the skirts. On the bottom of the skirts she left the beautiful natural furs of the animals.

The woman cried and Diirawic pleaded with her to wear them. She and the girls went and brought milk from their own cattle and made a feast. Diirawic's father welcomed the end of mourning. But her mother continued to cry as she saw all the festivities.

So Diirawic came to her and said, 'Mother, cool your heart. I am Diirawic.'

Then she shrieked with cries of joy. Everyone began to cry – old women, small girls, everyone. Even blind women dragged themselves out of their huts, feeling their way with sticks, and cried. Some people died as they cried. Drums were taken out and for seven days, people danced with joy. Men came from distant villages, each with seven bulls to sacrifice for Diirawic. The other girls were almost abandoned. All were concerned with Diirawic.

People danced and danced. They said, 'Diirawic, if God has brought you, then nothing is bad. That is what we wanted.'

Then Diirawic said, 'I have come back. But I have come with this man to take the place of my brother Teeng.'

'Very well,' agreed the people. 'Now there is nothing to worry about.'

There were two other Teengs. Both were sons of chiefs. Each one came forward, asking to marry Diirawic. It was decided that they should compete. Two large kraals were to be made. Each man was to fill his kraal with cattle. The kraals were built. The men began to fill them with cattle. One Teeng failed to fill his kraal. The other Teeng succeeded so well that some cattle even remained outside.

Diirawic said, 'I will not marry anyone until my new brother is given four girls to be his wives. Only then shall I accept the man my people want.'

People listened to her words. Then they asked her how the man became her brother. So she told the whole story from its beginning to its end.

The people agreed with her and picked four of the finest girls for her new brother. Diirawic then accepted the man who had won the competition. She was given to her husband and she continued to treat the lion-man as her full brother. She gave birth first to a son and then to a daughter. She bore twelve children. But when the thirteenth child was born, he had the characteristics of a lion. Her lion-brother had brought his family to her village and was living there when the child was born. The fields of Diirawic and her brother were next to each other. Their children played together. As they played, the small lion-child, then still a baby, would put on leather skirts and sing. When Diirawic returned, the children told her, but she dismissed what they said. 'You are liars. How can such a small child do these things?'

They would explain to her that he pinched them and dug his nails into their skins and would suck blood from the wounds. Their mother simply dismissed their complaints as lies.

But the lion-brother began to wonder about the child. He said, 'Does a newly born human being behave the way this child behaves?' Diirawic tried to dispel his doubts.

But one day her brother hid and saw the child dancing and singing in a way that convinced him that the child was a lion and not a human being. So he went to his sister and said, 'What you bore was a lion! What shall we do?'

The woman said, 'What do you mean? He is my child and should be treated as such.'

'I think we should kill him,' said the lion-brother.

'That is impossible,' she said. 'How can I allow my child to be killed? He will get used to human ways and will cease to be aggressive.'

'No,' continued the lion. 'Let us kill him by poison if you want to be gentle with him.'

'What are you talking about?' retorted his sister. 'Have you forgotten that you yourself were a lion and were then tamed into a human being? Is it true that old people lose their memory?'

The boy grew up with the children. But when he reached the age of herding, he would go and bleed the children by turn and suck blood from their bodies. He would tell them not to speak, and that if they said anything to their elders, he would kill them and eat them. The children would come home with wounds, and when asked, would say their wounds were from thorny trees.

But the lion did not believe them. He would tell them to stop lying and tell the truth, but they would not.

One day he went ahead of them and hid on top of the tree under which they usually spent the day. He saw the lion-child bleed the children and suck their blood. Right there, he speared him. The child died.

He then turned to the children and asked why they had hidden the truth for so long. The children explained how they had been threatened by the lion-child. Then he went and explained to his sister, Diirawic, what he had done.

The Mirror

(Japanese)

HERE is a pretty Japanese tale of a small farmer who bought his young wife a mirror. She was surprised and delighted to know that it reflected her face, and cherished her mirror above all her possessions. She gave birth to one daughter, and died young; and the farmer put the mirror away in a press, where it lay for long years.

The daughter grew up the very image of her mother; and one day, when she was almost a woman, her father took her aside, and told her of her mother, and of the mirror which had reflected her beauty. The girl was devoured with curiosity, unearthed the mirror from the old press, and looked into it.

'Father!' she cried, 'See! Here is mother's face!'

It was her own face she saw; but her father said nothing.

The tears were streaming down his cheeks, and the words would not come.

The Frog Maiden

(Burmese)

N old couple was childless, and the husband and the wife longed for a child. So when the wife found that she was with child, they were overjoyed; but to their great disappointment, the wife gave birth not to a human child, but to a little she-frog. However, as the little frog spoke and behaved as a human child, not only the parents but also the neighbours came to love her and called her affectionately 'Little Miss Frog'.

Some years later the woman died, and the man decided to marry again. The woman he chose was a widow with two ugly daughters and they were very jealous of Little Miss Frog's popularity with the neighbours. All three took a delight in ill-treating Little Miss Frog.

One day the youngest of the king's four sons announced that he would perform the hair-washing ceremony on a certain date and he invited all young ladies to join in the ceremony, as he would choose at the end of the ceremony one of them to be his princess.

On the morning of the appointed day the two ugly sisters dressed themselves in fine raiment, and with great hopes of being chosen by the prince they started for the palace. Little Miss Frog ran after them, and pleaded, 'Sisters, please let me come with you.'

The sisters laughed and said mockingly, 'What, the little frog wants to come? The invitation is to young ladies and not to young frogs.' Little Miss Frog walked along with them towards the palace, pleading for permission to come. But the sisters were adamant, and so at the palace gates she was left behind. However, she spoke so sweetly to the guards that they allowed her to go in. Little Miss Frog found hundreds of young ladies gathered round the pool full of lilies in the palace grounds; and she took her place among them and waited for the prince.

The prince now appeared, and washed his hair in the pool. The ladies also let down their hair and joined in the ceremony. At the end of the ceremony, the prince declared that as the ladies were all beautiful, he did not know whom to choose and so he would throw a posy of jasmines into the air; and the lady on whose head the posy fell would be his princess. The prince then threw the posy into the air, and all the ladies present looked up expectantly. The posy, however, fell on Little Miss Frog's head, to the great annoyance of the ladies, especially the two stepsisters. The prince also was disappointed, but he felt that he should keep his word. So Little Miss Frog was married to the prince, and she became Little Princess Frog.

Some time later, the old king called his four sons to him and said, 'My sons, I am now too old to rule the country, and I want to retire to the forest and become a hermit. So I must appoint one of you as my successor. As I love you all alike, I will give you a task to perform, and he who performs it successfully shall be king in my place. The task is, bring me a golden deer at sunrise on the seventh day from now.'

The youngest prince went home to Little Princess Frog and told her about the task. 'What, only a golden deer!' exclaimed Princess Frog. 'Eat as usual, my prince, and on the appointed day I will give you a golden deer.'

So the youngest prince stayed at home, while the three elder princes went into the forest in search of the deer.

On the seventh day before sunrise, Little Princess Frog woke up her husband and said, 'Go to the palace, prince, and here is your golden deer.'

The young prince looked, then rubbed his eyes, and looked again. There was no mistake about it; the deer which Little Princess Frog was holding by a lead was really of pure gold. So he went to the palace, and to the great annoyance of the elder princes who brought ordinary deers, he was declared to be the heir by the king. The elder princes, however, pleaded for a second chance, and the king reluctantly agreed.

'Then perform this second task,' said the king. 'On the seventh day from now at sunrise, you must bring me the rice that never becomes stale, and the meat that is ever fresh.'

The youngest prince went home and told Princess Frog about the new task. 'Don't you worry, sweet prince,' said Princess Frog. 'Eat as usual, sleep as usual, and on the appointed day I will give you the rice and meat.'

So the youngest prince stayed at home, while the three elder princes went in search of the rice and meat.

On the seventh day at sunrise, Little Princess Frog woke up her husband and said, 'My Lord, go to the palace now, and here is your rice and meat.'

The youngest prince took the rice and meat, and went to the palace, and to the great annoyance of the elder princes who brought only well-cooked rice and meat, he was again declared to be the heir. But the two elder princes again pleaded for one more chance, and the king said, 'This is positively the last task. On the seventh day from now at sunrise, bring me the most beautiful woman on this earth.'

'Ho, ho!' said the three elder princes to themselves in great joy. 'Our wives are very beautiful, and we will bring them. One of us is sure to be declared heir, and our good-for-nothing brother will be nowhere this time.'

The youngest prince overheard their remark, and felt sad, for his wife was a frog and ugly. When he reached home, he said to his wife, 'Dear Princess, I must go and look for the most beautiful woman on this earth. My brothers will bring their wives, for they are really beautiful, but I will find someone who is more beautiful.'

'Don't you fret, my prince,' replied Princess Frog. 'Eat as usual, sleep as usual, and you can take me to the palace on the appointed day; surely I shall be declared to be the most beautiful woman.'

The youngest prince looked at the princess in surprise; but he did not want to hurt her feelings, and he said gently, 'All right, Princess, I will take you with me on the appointed day.'

On the seventh day at dawn, Little Princess Frog woke up the prince and said, 'My Lord, I must make myself beautiful. So please wait outside and call me when it is nearly time to go.' The prince left the room as requested. After some moments, the prince shouted from outside, 'Princess, it is time for us to go.'

'Please wait, my Lord,' replied the princess, 'I am just powdering my face.'

After some moments the prince shouted, 'Princess, we must go now.'

'All right, my Lord,' replied the princess, 'please open the door for me.'

The prince thought to himself, 'Perhaps, just as she was able to obtain the golden deer and the wonderful rice and meat, she is able to make herself beautiful', and he expectantly opened the door, but he was disappointed to see Little Princess Frog still a frog and as ugly as ever. However, so as not to hurt her feelings, the prince said nothing and took her along to the palace. When the prince entered the audience chamber with his Frog Princess the three elder princes with their wives were already there. The king looked at the prince in surprise and said, 'Where is your beautiful maiden?'

'I will answer for the prince, my king,' said the Frog Princess. 'I am his beautiful maiden.' She then took off her frog skin and stood a beautiful maiden dressed in silk and satin. The king declared her to be the most beautiful maiden in the world, and selected the prince as his successor on the throne.

The prince asked his princess never to put on the ugly frog skin again, and the Frog Princess, to accede to his request, threw the skin into the fire.

The Sleeping Prince
(Surinamese)

FATHER had a daughter, but the child loved nothing so much as the field of grass which her father had planted. Only that she loved. Every morning her nurse took her to look at the grass. One morning when they went, the horses were feeding on the grass. Then they fought, and fought, and blood fell on the grass. The girl said, 'My nurse, look how the horses are eating my grass till they fight. But look how nice the red is on the earth.'

At once a voice answered her, it said, 'Look how nice the red is on top of the earth. Well, if you were to see the Sleeping Prince! But the one who said the thing must come before eight days are up, and she will see the Sleeping Prince. And she will see a fan, and she should fan the prince until the prince shall awaken. Then she should kiss the prince. And she will see a bottle of water, and she shall sprinkle all the sticks which she sees.'

But, when she went she took her clothes, and she had a black doll and a broken razor. Then she took them and carried them there, too. Then she saw the prince, and she took the fan and began to fan the prince. She fanned so till . . . an old woman sat by at the side. She was a witch. Then she asked her, she said, if she was not tired of fanning? But she said, 'No, no.'

Not long after, the old woman came back, and she asked her, she said, 'Don't you want to go and urinate?' And so at once she got up to go and urinate.

The old woman took up the fan and began to fan. And so, before the girl came back, the prince awakened, and the old woman kissed the prince. And so the old woman had to marry the prince, because the law was that the one who kissed the prince should be the one to marry him.

But when they were already married, then the woman made

her look after the fowls. She was very sad, because in her father's country she was a princess, and here she had to look after the fowls. They built a nice little house for her to live in. Then at night when she returned from her work, she put on her fine clothes, and she played a singing box. But when she finished playing, then she took up the black doll and the razor, and she asked it, she said, 'My black doll, my black doll, tell me if that is justice, or I will cut off your neck.' Then she put them back and she went to sleep.

But a soldier passed one night. Then he heard how sweetly the singing box played. He hid at the side of the house, and he heard everything the girl asked the black doll. And so he went and told the king that the girl who looked after the chickens did thus.

The selfsame night the king went to listen. Just as the woman asked the black doll if that was justice, the king knocked on the door that she open the door at once. As the door opened the king saw the woman and at once he fainted, because he did not know that this woman was a princess. She was wearing her fine clothes. And when the king came to himself, he called the woman and said he would call a big audience, and she must explain what made her ask that of the black doll.

When they came to the audience, she said before all the important people, 'Yes, in my father's country I was a princess, and here I must look after the fowls.' And she related everything that had happened between her and the old woman, and she had acted towards her, to cause her (the witch) to marry the prince. And so they found her in the right, and they killed the old woman.

From her bones they made a stepladder to climb to the top of her bed. And from the skin of the old woman she made a carpet to spread on the ground. And from the head she made a wash-basin in which to wash her face.

And so she came to marry the prince later. It was her destiny.

The Orphan
(African, Malawi)

A LONG time ago a certain man married. His wife gave birth to a baby girl whom they named Diminga. When Diminga's mother died, her father married again, and his new wife bore him several more children.

Although her husband asked her to care for Diminga, the stepmother cursed the child and would not treat her as her own. She would not bathe her, she fed her only husks, and made her sleep in a kraal. So Diminga looked a dirty miserable little girl, a skeleton dressed in rags. All she longed for was to die so that she might join her real mother.

One night Diminga dreamed that her mother was calling her: 'Diminga! Diminga my child! You need not starve,' said the voice. 'Tomorrow at noon, when you are grazing the cattle, take your big cow Chincheya and tell her to do what I have asked.'

The next day Diminga took her cattle into the fields as usual. When midday came and her hunger was at its worst, she remembered her dream. She went to Chincheya, patted her back, and said, 'Chincheya. Do what my mother told you.'

No sooner had she said this than many plates of food appeared before her. There was rice, beef, chicken, tea and much more. Diminga ate until she was full – and still there was food left over. She made the surplus disappear, and returned home that day so satisfied that she surprised her stepmother by refusing to eat the husks which were offered for her supper. 'Have them yourself,' she said.

Now this happened many times as each day Chincheya produced food for Diminga when they were alone in the fields. As Diminga grew fatter, her stepmother grew more suspicious, asking, 'Why are you growing fat even though you refuse to eat at home? What do you eat?'

But Diminga would not tell her secret and at last the stepmother insisted that her own daughter must accompany Diminga when she grazed her cattle the next day. Diminga was reluctant to take the girl, but she had no choice. When the time came for the midday meal, she told her stepsister to say nothing of what she was about to see.

The girl watched as Diminga took Chincheya aside and spoke to her. She was amazed when suddenly there was food everywhere. Her mouth watered; she tasted all the dishes, then she hid a bit of each under her fingernails before Diminga made the remains vanish.

That night after Diminga had gone to sleep, the girl told her mother to fetch plates, and when these were brought she heaped upon them all the food that she had hidden, saying, 'This food comes from that cow, Chincheya. Abundant and delicious food appears when Diminga speaks to her.'

The old woman was thunderstruck. She gobbled up the food and set about making plans to get all the rest that was still inside the cow. A few days later, she told her husband that she was feeling unwell. Now, for this reason a traditional dance was held and during this dance the stepmother seemed to fall into a trance. She cried out, 'The spirits demand the sacrifice of the cow Chincheya.'

Diminga was furious. She refused to allow the killing. Her stepmother pleaded with her husband, 'Should I die because of your daughter's infatuation with a cow?'

And her husband pleaded with his daughter, but Diminga was determined that Chincheya should not be killed. Then as she slept, one night she heard her mother's voice again. It said, 'My daughter Diminga, let them slaughter Chincheya. But do not eat the meat yourself. Take the stomach. Bury it on an island. You will see what will happen.'

So Diminga allowed the sacrifice to take place. The stepmother was sadly disappointed to find not even a single grain of rice inside the cow, indeed the meat itself was tasteless. Diminga wept at Chincheya's death; but she followed her mother's instructions and planted the cow's stomach on an island.

Where the stomach was planted a golden tree grew. Its leaves were pound notes and its fruits were coins: pennies, shillings, sixpences and florins. The tree glittered and dazzled the eyes of anyone who dared to look at it.

One day a ship passed the island. When the owner saw the golden tree he ordered his men to go ashore and collect the money. They shook the tree and tried to pick off the money, but they could not move it. The owner asked the local chief to shake the tree, then each of his villagers in turn to do the same. Still no one was successful in harvesting the money.

Then the ship's owner, who was a European, asked the chief, 'Is there anyone who has not tried to shake the tree? Go and search your village in case you have left anyone behind.'

The search took place, and the one remaining person who had not tried to shake the tree was found – a ragged dirty girl with sad eyes. It was Diminga. Everyone laughed when she was taken to the tree. 'Can this miserable girl succeed when we have failed!'

'Let her try,' said the European.

The tree swayed as Diminga approached. As she touched it, the tree began to shake, and when she held it, coins and notes showered to the ground in great piles, enough to fill several bags.

Instant marriage was arranged between Diminga and the European, and they went to live at his house. When she had bathed, dressed in new clothes and perfumed herself, Diminga was unrecognisably beautiful. And she was happy with her new life.

After some time Diminga visited her home, taking with her servants, carrying cases of clothes, food and money for her family. They welcomed her warmly, especially when they saw her gifts. And her father was glad that his daughter's troubles were now finished.

But her stepmother was full of envy and began planning once more to get the better of Diminga. Thus it happened that, when Diminga was sitting with her family, her one-eyed stepsister came to her with a needle in her hands, saying, 'Let me find lice in your hair, sister.'

'I have no lice,' said Diminga.

But her stepmother insisted and the girl began her search. Then suddenly, she drove the needle into Diminga's head. Diminga jerked, and was transformed into a bird, which flew away.

The old woman dressed her daughter in Diminga's clothes and veiled her face. She told Diminga's servants that their mistress was sick. They took 'Diminga' home, and told their master of his wife's illness. Whenever he tried to remove the veil, his 'wife' said, 'You must leave it for I am not well.'

One day his servant Guao went to the river to wash clothes and saw a small, bright beautiful bird perched on a tree. It began to sing:

Guao, Guao, Guao
Is Manuel at home
With one eyed-wife
This terrible one-eyed wife?

Guao listened, enchanted by the music and his curiosity was aroused. Each day he saw the little bird and heard the song, then finally he took his master to witness the strange event. The master trapped the bird and took it home, where he made a pet of it. Whenever he touched the bird's head, he noticed, it trembled. He looked closely and saw a needle. When he pulled out the needle the bird was transformed into a beautiful girl – Diminga, his wife.

When Diminga told him of her sufferings her husband ran and unveiled the 'sick wife' – and shot her. He ordered his servants to cut the body into pieces, which were dried then mixed with rice and put into bags. The bags of food were sent to Diminga's stepmother with the message, 'Diminga has arrived safely and sends you this gift.'

The old woman was satisfied to hear the news and shared the food amongst her family. It was only when she looked into the last bag of meat that she realised that she had been truly punished. Inside the bag was a human head, with its one eye fixed upon her in a terrible gaze.

Part Four

MOTHERS AND DAUGHTERS

Achol and Her Wild Mother

(Sudan, Dinka)

ACHOL, Lanchichor (The Blind Beast) and Adhalchingeeny (The Exceedingly Brave One) were living with their mother. Their mother would go to fetch firewood. She gathered many pieces of wood and then put her hands behind her back and said, 'O dear, who will help me lift this heavy load?'

A lion came passing by and said, 'If I help you lift the load, what will you give me?'

'I will give you one hand,' she said.

She gave him a hand; he helped her lift the load and she went home. Her daughter, Achol, said, 'Mother, why is your hand like that?'

'My daughter, it is nothing,' she answered.

Then she left again to fetch firewood. She gathered many pieces of wood and then put her hand behind her back and said, 'O dear, who will now help me lift this heavy load?'

The lion came and said, 'If I help you lift the load, what will you give me?'

'I will give you my other hand!' And she gave him the other hand. He lifted the load on to her head and she went home without a hand.

Her daughter saw her and said, 'Mother, what has happened to your hands? You should not go to fetch firewood again! You must stop!'

But she insisted that there was nothing wrong and went to fetch firewood. Again she collected many pieces of firewood, put her arms behind her back and said, 'Who will now help me lift this heavy load?'

Again the lion came and said, 'If I help you lift the load, what will you give me?'

She said, 'I will give you one foot!'

She gave him her foot; he helped her, and she went home.

Her daughter said, 'Mother, this time, I insist that you do not go for the firewood! Why is all this happening? Why are your hands and your foot like this?'

'My daughter, it is nothing to worry about,' she said. 'It is my nature.'

She went back to the forest another time and collected many pieces of firewood. Then she put her arms behind her back and said, 'Who will now help me lift this load?'

The lion came and said, 'What will you now give me?'

She said, 'I will give you my other foot!'

So she gave him the other foot; he helped her, and she went home.

This time she became wild and turned into a lioness. She would not eat cooked meat; she would only have raw meat.

Achol's brothers went to the cattle camp with their mother's relatives. So only Achol remained at home with her mother. When her mother turned wild, she went into the forest, leaving Achol alone. She would only return for a short time in the evening to look for food. Achol would prepare something for her and put it on the platform in the courtyard. Her mother would come at night and sing in a dialogue with Achol.

'Achol, Achol, where is your father?'
'My father is still in the cattle camp!'
'And where is Lanchichor?'
'Lanchichor is still in the cattle camp!'
'And where is Adhalchingeeny?'
'Adhalchingeeny is still in the cattle camp!'
'And where is the food?'
'Mother, scrape the insides of our ancient gourds.'

She would eat and leave. The following night, she would return and sing. Achol would reply; her mother would eat and return to the forest. This went on for a long time.

Meanwhile, Lanchichor came from the cattle camp to visit his mother and sister. When he arrived home, he found his mother absent. He also found a large pot over the cooking fire. He wondered about these things and asked Achol, 'Where is Mother gone, and why are you cooking in such a big pot?'

She replied, 'I am cooking in this big pot because our mother has turned wild and is in the forest, but she comes at night for food.'

'Take that pot off the fire,' he said.

'I cannot,' she replied. 'I must cook for her.'

He let her. She cooked and put the food on the platform before they went to bed. Their mother came at night and sang. Achol replied as usual. Her mother ate and left. Achol's brother got very frightened. He emptied his bowels and left the next morning.

When he was asked in the cattle camp about the people at home, he was too embarrassed to tell the truth; so he said they were well.

Then Achol's father decided to come home to visit his wife and his daughter. He found the big pot on the fire and his wife away. When he asked Achol, she explained everything to him. He also told her to take the pot off the fire, but she would not. She put the food on the platform, and they went to bed. Achol's father told her to let him take care of the situation. Achol agreed. Her mother came and sang as usual. Achol replied. Then her mother ate. But her father was so frightened that he returned to the camp.

Then came Adhalchingeeny (The Exceedingly Brave One) and brought with him a very strong rope. He came and found Achol cooking with the large pot, and when Achol explained to him their mother's condition, he told her to take the pot off the fire, but she would not give in. He let her proceed with her usual plan. He placed the rope near the food in a way that would trap his mother when she took the food. He tied the other end to his foot.

Their mother came and sang as usual. Achol replied. As their mother went towards the food, Adhalchingeeny pulled the rope, gagged her and tied her to a pole. He then went and beat her with part of the heavy rope. He beat her and beat her and beat her. Then he gave her a piece of raw meat, and when she ate it, he beat her again. He beat her and beat her and beat her. Then he gave her two pieces of meat, one raw and one roasted. She refused the raw one and took the roasted one, saying, 'My son, I have now become human, so please stop beating me.'

They then reunited and lived happily.

Tunjur, Tunjur
(Palestinian Arab)

TELLER: *Testify that God is One!*
AUDIENCE: *There is no god but God.*

HERE was once a woman who could not get pregnant and have children. Once upon a day she had an urge; she wanted babies. 'O Lord!' she cried out, 'why of all women am I like this? Would that I could get pregnant and have a baby, and may Allah grant me a girl even if she is only a cooking pot!'

One day she became pregnant. A day came and a day went, and behold! she was ready to deliver. She went into labour and delivered, giving birth to a cooking pot. What was the poor woman to do? She washed it, cleaning it well, put the lid on it, and placed it on the shelf.

One day the pot started to talk. 'Mother,' she said, 'take me down from this shelf!'

'Alas, daughter!' replied the mother, 'where am I going to put you?'

'What do you care?' said the daughter. 'Just bring me down, and I will make you rich for generations to come.'

The mother brought her down. 'Now put my lid on,' said the pot, 'and leave me outside the door.' Putting the lid on, the mother took her outside the door.

The pot started to roll, singing as she went, 'Tunjur, tunjur, clink, clink, O my mama!' She rolled until she came to a place where people usually gather. In a while people were passing by. A man came and found the pot all settled in its place. 'Eh!' he exclaimed, 'who has put this pot in the middle of the path? I'll be damned! What a beautiful pot! It's probably made of silver.' He looked it over well. 'Hey, people!' he called, 'whose pot is this? Who put it here?' No one claimed it. 'By Allah,' he said, 'I'm going to take it home with me.'

On his way home, he went by the honey vendor. He had the

pot filled with honey and brought it home to his wife. 'Look, wife,' he said, 'how beautiful is this pot!' The whole family was greatly pleased with it.

In two or three days they had guests, and they wanted to offer them some honey. The woman of the house brought the pot down from the shelf. Push and pull on the lid, but the pot would not open! She called her husband over. Pull and push, but open it he could not. His guests pitched in. Lifting the pot and dropping it, the man tried to break it open with hammer and chisel. He tried everything, but it was no use.

They sent for the blacksmith, and he tried and tried, to no avail. What was the man to do?

'Damn your owners!' he cursed the pot, 'Did you think you were going to make us wealthy?' And, taking it up, he threw it out the window.

When they turned their back and could no longer see it, she started to roll, saying as she went.

'Tunjur, tunjur, O my mama.
In my mouth I brought the honey.
Clink, clink, O my mama.
In my mouth I brought the honey.'

'Bring me up the stairs!' she said to her mother when she reached home.

'Yee!' exclaimed the mother. 'I thought you had disappeared, that someone had taken you.'

'Pick me up!' said the daughter.

Picking her up, my little darlings, the mother took the lid off and found the pot full of honey. Oh! How pleased she was!

'Empty me!' said the pot.

The mother emptied the honey into a jar, and put the pot back on the shelf.

'Mother,' said the daughter the next day, 'take me down!'

The mother brought her down from the shelf.

'Mother, put me outside the door!'

The mother placed her outside the door, and she started rolling – tunjur, tunjur, clink, clink – until she reached a place where people were gathered, and then she stopped. A man passing by found her.

'Eh!' he thought, 'what kind of a pot is this?' He looked it over. How beautiful he found it! 'To whom does this belong?' he asked. 'Hey, people! Who are the owners of this pot?' He waited, but no one said, 'It's mine.' Then he said, 'By Allah, I'm going to take it.'

He took it, and on his way home stopped by the butcher and had it filled with meat. Bringing it home to his wife, he said, 'Look, wife, how beautiful is this pot I've found! By Allah, I found it so pleasing I bought meat and filled it and brought it home.'

'Yee!' they all cheered, 'how lucky we are! What a beautiful pot!' They put it away.

Towards evening they wanted to cook the meat. Push and pull on the pot, it would not open! What was the woman to do? She called her husband over and her children. Lift, drop, strike – no use. They took it to the blacksmith, but with no result.

The husband became angry. 'God damn your owners!' he cursed it. 'What in the world are you?' And he threw it as far as his arm would reach.

As soon as he turned his back, she started rolling, and singing:

'Tunjur, tunjur. O my mama,
In my mouth I brought the meat.
Tunjur, tunjur, O my mama,
In my mouth I brought the meat.'

She kept repeating that till she reached home.

'Lift me up!' she said to her mother. The mother lifted her up, took the meat, washed the pot, and put it away on the shelf.

'Bring me out of the house!' said the daughter the next day. The mother brought her out, and she said, 'Tunjur, tunjur, clink, clink' as she was rolling until she reached a spot close by the king's house, where she came to a stop. In the morning, it is said, the son of the king was on his way out, and behold! there was the pot settled in its place.

'Eh! What's this? Whose pot is it?' No one answered. 'By Allah,' he said, 'I'm going to take it.' He took it inside and called his wife over.

'Wife,' he said, 'take this pot! I brought it home for you. It's the most beautiful pot!'

The wife took the pot. 'Yee! How beautiful it is! By Allah, I'm going to put my jewellery in it.' Taking the pot with her, she gathered all her jewellery, even that which she was wearing, and put it in the pot. She also brought all their gold and money and stuffed them in the pot till it was full to the brim, then she covered it and put it away in the wardrobe.

Two or three days went by, and it was time for the wedding of her brother. She put on her velvet dress and brought the pot out so that she could wear her jewellery. Push and pull, but the pot would not open. She called to her husband, and he could not open it either. All the people who were there tried to open it, lifting and dropping. They took it to the blacksmith, and he tried but could not open it.

The husband felt defeated, 'God damn your owners!' he cursed it, 'what use are you to us?' Taking it up, he threw it out the window. Of course he was not all that anxious to let it go, so he went to catch it from the side of the house. No sooner did he turn around than she started to run:

'Tunjur, tunjur, O my mama,
In my mouth I brought the treasure.
Tunjur, tunjur, O my mama,
In my mouth I brought this treasure.'

'Lift me up!' she said to her mother when she reached home. Lifting her up, the mother removed the lid.

'Yee! May your reputation be blackened!' she cried out. 'Wherever did you get this? What in the world is it?' The mother was now rich. She became very, very happy.

'It's enough now,' she said to her daughter, taking away the treasure. 'You shouldn't go out any more. People will recognise you.'

'No, no!' begged the daughter. 'Let me go out just one last time.'

The next day, my darlings, she went out, saying 'Tunjur, tunjur, O my mama.' The man who found her the first time saw her again.

'Eh! What in the world is this thing?' he exclaimed. 'It must have some magic in it, since it's always tricking people. God damn its owners! By Allah the Great, I'm going to sit and shit in it.' He went ahead, my darlings, and shat right in it. Closing the lid on him,' she rolled along:

'Tunjur, tunjur, O my mama
In my mouth I brought the caca.
Tunjur, tunjur, O my mama,
In my mouth I brought the caca.'

'Lift me up!' she said to her mother when she reached home. The mother lifted her up.

'You naughty thing, you!' said the mother. 'I told you not to go out again, that people would recognise you. Don't you think it's enough now?'

The mother then washed the pot with soap, put perfume on it, and placed it on the shelf.

This is my story, I've told it, and in your hands I leave it.

The Little Old Woman with Five Cows

(Yakut)

ONE morning a little old woman got up and went to the field containing her five cows. She took from the earth a herb with five sprouts and, without breaking either root or branch, carried it home and wrapped it in a blanket and placed it on her pillow.

Then she went out again and sat down to milk her cows. Suddenly she heard tambourine bells jingle and scissors fall, on account of which noise she upset the milk. Having run home and looked, she found that the plant was uninjured. Again she issued forth to milk the cows, and again thought she heard the tambourine bells jingle and scissors fall, and once more she spilt her milk. Returning to the house, she looked into the bedchamber. There sat a maiden with eyes of chalcedony and lips of dark stone, with a face of light-coloured stone and with eyebrows like two dark sables stretching their forefeet towards each other; her body was visible through her dress; her bones were visible through her body; her nerves spreading this way and that, like mercury, were visible through her bones. The plant had become this maiden of indescribable beauty.

Soon afterwards Kharjit-Bergen, son of the meritorious Khan Kara, went into the dark forest. He saw a grey squirrel sitting on a curved twig, near the house of the little old woman with five cows, and he began to shoot, but as the light was bad, for the sun was already setting, he did not at once succeed in his purpose. At this time one of his arrows fell into the chimney.

'Old woman! take the arrow and bring it me!' he cried, but received no answer. His cheeks and forehead grew flushed and he became angry; a wave of arrogance sprang from the back of his neck, and he rushed into the house.

When he entered and saw the maiden he lost consciousness. But he revived and fell in love. Then he went out and, jumping on his horse, raced home at full gallop. 'Parents!' said he, 'there is such a beautiful maiden at the house of a little old woman with five cows! Get hold of this maiden and give her to me!'

The father sent nine servants on horseback, and they galloped at full speed to the house of the little old woman with five cows. All the servants became unconscious when they beheld the maiden's beauty. However, they recovered, and all went away except the best one of them.

'Little old woman!' said he, 'give this girl to the son of the meritorious Khan Khara!'

'I will give her,' was the answer.

They spoke to the maiden. 'I will go,' she announced.

'Now, as the bridegroom's wedding gift,' said the old woman, 'drive up cattle, and fill my open fields with horses and horned stock!'

Immediately the request was uttered and before the agreement was concluded the man gave an order to collect and drive up the animals as the bridegroom's gift.

'Take the maiden and depart!' said the little old woman, when the stock of horses and cattle had been given as arranged.

The maiden was quickly adorned, and a finely speckled horse that spoke like a human being was led up to her skilfully. They put on it a silver halter, saddled it with a silver saddle, which was placed over an upper silver saddle-cloth and a lower silver saddle-cloth, and they attached a little silver whip. Then the son-in-law led the bride from the mother's side by the whip, mounted his horse and took the bride home.

They went along the road, and the young man said, 'In the depth of the forest there is a trap for foxes; I will go there. Proceed along this road! It divides into two paths. On the road leading to the east is hanging a sable skin. But on the road leading to the west there should be the skin of a male bear with the paws and head and with white fur at the neck. Go on the path where the sable skin is hanging.' He pointed out the road and went away.

The girl made her way to the fork in the road, but on coming to it forgot the directions. Going along the path where the bear skin was hanging, she reached a small iron hut. Suddenly out of the hut came a devil's daughter, dressed in an iron garment above the knee. She had only one leg, and that was twisted; a single bent hand projected from below her breast, and her single furious eye was situated in the middle of her forehead. Having shot forth a fifty-foot iron tongue on to her breast, she pulled the girl from the horse, dropped her to the ground and tore all the skin from her face and threw it on her own face. She dragged off all the girl's finery and put it on herself. Then mounting, the devil's daughter rode away.

The husband met the devil's daughter when she arrived at the house of the meritorious Khan Khara. Nine youths came to take her horse by the halter; eight maidens did likewise. It is said that the bride wrongly fastened her horse to the willow tree where the old widow from Semyaksin used to tether her spotted ox. The greater part of those who thus received the bride became sorely depressed and the remainder were disenchanted; sorrow fell on them.

All who met the bride abominated her. Even the red weasels ran away from her, thus showing she was repugnant to them. Grass had been strewn on the pathway up to her hut, and on this grass she was led by the hand. Having entered, she replenished the fire with the tops of three young larch trees. Then they concealed her behind a curtain, while they themselves also drank and played and laughed and made merry.

But the marriage feast came to an end, and there was a return to ordinary life. The little old woman with five cows, on going into open country to seek her cows, found that the plant with five sprouts was growing better than usual. She dug it up with its roots and, carrying it home, wrapped it up and placed it on her pillow. Then she went back and began to milk the cows, but the tambourine with the bells began to tinkle, and the scissors fell with a noise. Going back to the house, the old woman found the lovely maiden seated and looking more lovely than ever.

'Mother,' she said, 'my husband took me away from here. My dear husband said, "I must go away on some business," but before he went he said, "Walk along the path where the sable's skin is hanging, and do not go where the bear's skin is hanging." I forgot and went along the second path to a little iron house. A devil's daughter tore the skin from my face and put it on her own face; she dragged off all my fine things and put them on; and next this devil's daughter mounted my horse and set out. She threw away skin and bones and a grey dog seized my lungs and heart with his teeth and carried them to open country. I grew here as a plant, for it was decreed that I should not die altogether. Perhaps it has been settled that later I shall bear children. The devil's daughter has affected my fate, for she has married my husband and contaminated his flesh and blood; she has absorbed his flesh and blood. When shall I see him?'

The meritorious Khan Khara came to the field belonging to the little old woman with five cows. The speckled white horse, who was endowed with human speech, knew that his mistress had revived, and he began to speak.

He complained to Khan Khara thus: 'The devil's daughter has killed my mistress, torn all the skin from her face and covered her own face with it; she has dragged away my mistress's finery and clothed herself in it. The devil's daughter has gone to live with Khan Khara's son and become his bride. But my mistress has revived and now lives. If your son does not take this fair girl as his bride, then I will complain to the white Lord God on his seat of white stone, by the lake that has silver waves and golden floating ice, and blocks of silver and black ice; and I will shatter your house and your fire, and will leave you no means of living. A divine man must not take a devil's daughter. Fasten this devil's-daughter bride to the legs of a wild horse. Let a stream of rushing water fall on your son and cleanse him during thirty days; and let the worms and reptiles suck away his contaminated blood. Afterwards draw him from the water and expose him to the wind on the top of a tree for thirty nights, so that breezes from the north and from the south may penetrate his heart and liver, and purify his contaminated flesh and blood. When he is cleansed let him persuade and retake his wife!'

The khan heard and understood the horse's words. It is said he threw aside tears from both eyes; then he galloped home. On seeing him the bride changed countenance.

'Son!' said Khan Khara, 'whence and from whom did you take your wife?'

'She is the daughter of the little old woman with five cows.'

'What was the appearance of the horse on which you brought her? What kind of woman did you bring? Do you know her origin?'

To these questions the son answered, 'Beyond the third heaven, in the upper region which has the white stone seat is the white God; his younger brother collected migratory birds and united them into one society. Seven maidens, his daughters in the form of seven cranes, came to earth and feasted and entered a round field and danced; and an instructress descended to them. She took the best of the seven cranes and said, "Your mission is to go out to people; to be a Yakut on this middle land; you must not dislike this impure middle land! You are appointed worthy of the son of the meritorious Khan Khara and are to wear a skin made of eight sables. On account of him you will become human and bear children, and bring them up." After speaking she cut off the end of the crane's wings. The maiden wept. "Turn into a mare's tail-grass, and grow!" said the instructress; "A little old woman with five cows will find the herb and turn it into a maiden and give her in marriage to Khan Khara's son." I took her according to this direction and as she was described to me; but I accepted a strange being; in reality, as appears to me, I took nothing!'

After his son's reply the khan said, 'Having seen and heard, I have come. The speckled horse with the human voice has complained to me. When you bore away your wife you spoke to her of a forked road. You said, "On the eastern path there is hanging a sable's skin and on the western path a bear's skin." You said, "Do not go on the path with the bear's skin, but go along the path showing a sable skin!" But she forgot, and passed along the path which had a bear's skin. She reached the iron house and then a devil's daughter jumped out to meet her, dragged her from her horse and threw her down, tore the whole of the skin from her face and placed it on her own face. The devil's daughter dressed herself in the girl's finery and silver ornaments and rode hither as a bride. She fastened the horse to the old willow; it is already a mark. "Attach the devil's daughter to the feet of a wild stallion!" said the horse to me, "and wash your son in a swift stream for a whole month of thirty nights; let worms and reptiles suck away his contaminated body and blood.

Carry him away and expose him to the breeze on the top of a tree during a month of thirty nights. Let the breezes search him from the north and from the south; let it blow through his heart and liver!" said the horse to me. "Let him go and persuade his wife and take her! But away with this woman! Do not show her! She will devour people and cattle. If you do not get rid of her," said the horse, "I will complain to the white God."

On hearing this the son became much ashamed, and a workman called Boloruk seized the bride, who was sitting behind a curtain, and, dragging her by the foot, fastened her on the legs of a wild horse. The horse kicked the devil's daughter to pieces and to death. Her body and blood were attacked on the ground by worms and reptiles, and became worms and reptiles moving about till the present time. After being placed in a stream of rushing water the khan's son was placed on a tree, so that the spring breezes coming from the north and from the south blew through him. Thus his contaminated body and blood were purified and, when he was brought home, dried up and scarcely breathing, only his skin and bones remained.

He rode to the region of the wedding gift as before and, having picketed his horse, dismounted at his mother-in-law's house. The little old woman who owned the five cows fluttered out joyfully; she rejoiced as if the dead had come to life and the lost had been found. From the picketing spot to the tent she strewed green grass and spread on the front bed a white horse-skin with hoofs. She killed a milch cow and a large-breasted mare and made a wedding feast.

The girl approached her husband with tears. 'Why have you come to me?' she asked. 'You spilt my dark blood, you cut my skin deeply. You gave me up as food for dogs and ducks. You gave me to the daughter of an eight-legged devil. After that, how can you seek a wife here? Girls are more numerous than perch, and women than grayling; my heart is wounded and my mind is agitated! I will not come!'

'I did not send you to the daughter of an eight-legged devil and when I went away on an important matter I pointed out your path. I did not knowingly direct you to a perilous place and I did not know what would happen when I said to you "Go and meet your fate!" The lady-instructress and protectress, the creatress, chose you and appointed you for me; therefore you revived and are alive,' he said; 'and whatever may happen, good or ill, I shall unfailingly take you!'

The little old woman with five cows wiped aways tears from both eyes and sat down between these two children. 'How is it that, having met, you do not rejoice when you have returned to life after death, and been found after having been lost? Neither of you must oppose my will!'

The maiden gave her word, but said 'Agreed!' unwillingly. Then the young man sprang up and danced and jumped and embraced and kissed and drew in his breath. The couple played the best games and burst into loud laughter and talked unceasingly. Outside they fastened the speckled horse that spoke like a human being, laid on him the silver saddle-cloth, saddled him with the silver saddle, bridled him with the silver bridle, hung on him the silver saddle bags and attached to him the little silver whip.

When the maiden had been dressed and all was complete on her she was sent off. She and her husband knew as they went along that it was winter by the fine snow that was falling; they knew it was summer by the rain; they knew it was autumn by the fog.

The servants from the nine houses of Khan Khara, the house servants from eight houses and the room attendants from seven houses, and nine lords' sons who came out like nine cranes thought, 'How will the bride arrive? Will she march out or will she saunter? And will sables arise from her footsteps?'

Thinking thus, they prepared arrows so vigorously that the skin came off their fingers; they attended so closely to their work that their sight became dull. Seven grown-up daughters like seven cranes, born at one time, twisted threads so that the skin came from their knees, and said, 'If, when the bride comes, she blows her nose loudly, dear little kings will be plentiful.'

The son arrived with his bride, and two maidens took their horses by the bridle at the picket rope. The son and his bride dismounted and she blew her nose; therefore dear little kings would come! Instantly the women began to weave garments. Sables ran along the place from which the bride stepped forward, and some of the young men hastened into the dark forest to shoot them.

From the foot of the picketing post to the tent the way had been spread with green grass. On arriving, the bride kindled the fire with three branches of larch. Then they hid her behind a curtain. They stretched a strap in nine portions and tied to it ninety white speckled foals. On the right side of the house they thrust into the ground nine posts and fastened to them nine white foals and put on the foals nine friendly sorcerers who drank kumyss. On the left side of the house they set up eight posts.

Wedding festivities were begun in honour of the bride's entry into the home. Warriors collected and experts came together. It is said that nine ancestral spirits came from a higher place and twelve ancestral spirits rose from the ground. It is said that nine tribes came from under the ground and, using whips of dry wood, trotted badly. Those having iron stirrups crowded together and those having copper stirrups went unsteadily.

All had collected from the foreign tribes and from the tents of the nomad villages; there were singers, there were dancers, there were storytellers; there were those who jumped on one foot and there were leapers; there were crowds possessing five-kopeck pieces, there were saunterers. Then the dwellers-on-high flew upwards; those dwelling in the lower regions sank into the earth; and inhabitants of the middle region, the earth, separated and walked away. The litter remained till the third day; but before the morrow most of the fragments had been collected, all animals had been enclosed and children were sporting in the place. Their descendants are said to be alive today.

Achol and Her Adoptive Lioness-Mother

(Sudan, Dinka)

ACHIENG gave birth to two children, Maper and Achol. They had three paternal half-brothers. Achol was betrothed to a man called Kwol. The family moved to the lion territory. As Achol was still small, her brother carried her.

Their half-brothers were jealous of Achol's good fortune in being betrothed so young. They agreed on a plan to abandon Achol and her brother Maper in the wilderness. One evening, they secretly put some medicine in their milk. Achol and Maper fell into a heavy sleep. That night, a gourd full of milk was placed near them, and the cattle camp moved on, leaving them behind.

Achol was the first to wake up the next morning. When she saw that they had been left behind, she cried and woke her brother up. 'Maper, son of my mother, the camp has gone and we have been left behind!'

Maper woke up, looked around and said, 'So our own brothers have left us! Never mind, drink your milk.'

They drank some milk and then moved into a ditch made by an elephant. This provided them with shelter and protection. There they slept.

Along came a lioness looking for remains in the camp. When she saw the ditch, she looked into it and saw the children. They cried, 'O, Father, we are dead – we are eaten!'

The lioness spoke and said, 'My children, do not cry. I will not eat you. Are you children of human beings?'

'Yes,' they said.

'Why are you here?' she asked.

'We were abandoned by our half-brothers,' said Maper.

'Come along with me,' said the lioness. 'I will look after you as my own children; I have no children of my own.'

They agreed and went with her. On the way, Maper escaped and returned home. Achol remained with the lioness. They went to the lioness's house, and she looked after Achol and raised her until she became a big girl.

In the mean time, Achol's relatives were mourning her loss. The half-brothers denied having played a foul trick. But Maper explained that he and his sister were left behind and found by a lioness, from whom he had escaped.

Some years later, the camp again moved to the lion territory. By this time Maper had become a grown man. One day as he and his age-mates were herding, they came to the home of the lioness. Maper did not recognise the village. The lioness had gone to hunt. Achol was there. But Maper did not recognise her.

One of the age-mates spoke to Achol, saying 'Girl, will you please give us water to drink?'

Achol said, 'This is not a house where people ask for water. I see you are human beings; this place is dangerous for you!'

'We are very thirsty,' they explained. 'Please, let us drink.'

She brought them water, and they drank. Then they left. Achol's mother, the lioness, returned, carrying an animal she had killed. She threw the animal down and sang:

'Achol, Achol,
Come out of the hut,
My daughter whom I raised in plenty
When people were gathering wild grain.
My daughter was never vexed;
Daughter, come out, I am here.
My little one who was left behind,
My little one whom I found unhurt,
My little one whom I raised,
Achol, my beloved one,
Come, meet me my daughter.'

They met and embraced, and then cooked for themselves and ate. Achol's mother told her, 'Daughter, if human beings come, do not run away from them; be nice to them. That is how you will get married.'

Maper was attracted to Achol, and that same evening he returned with a friend to court her. Achol's mother gave her a separate hut in which to entertain her age-mates. So when Maper came with his friend and asked to be accommodated, she let them into that hut. She made their beds on one side of the hut, while she herself slept on the other side.

At night, Maper's desire for Achol increased and he wanted to move over to her side of the hut. But whenever he tried to move, a lizard on the wall spoke, saying, 'The man is about to violate his own sister!' So he stopped. Then he tried to move again, and a rafter on the ceiling spoke and said, 'The man is about to violate his sister!' When he tried again, the grass said the same.

Maper's friend woke up and said, 'Who is speaking? What are they saying?' Maper said, 'I do not know and I do not understand what they mean by "sister".'

So they asked the girl to tell them more about who she was. Achol then told them the story of how she and her brother had been abandoned and how the lioness had found them.

'Really?' said Maper with excitement.

'Yes,' said Achol.

'Then, let us leave for home. You are my sister.'

Achol embraced him and cried and cried. When she became calm she told Maper and his friend that she could not leave the lioness, for the lioness had taken very good care of her. But they persuaded her to leave with them. Their camp moved on the next morning to avoid meeting the lioness.

That morning, the lioness left very early to hunt. When she returned in the evening, she sang to Achol as usual, but Achol did not reply. She repeated the song several times, and Achol did not answer. She went inside the hut and found that Achol was gone. She cried and cried and cried: 'Where has my daughter gone? Has a lion eaten her or have the human beings taken her away from me?'

Then she ran, following the cattle camp. She ran and ran and ran.

The cattle camp arrived at the village, and Achol was hidden.

The lioness continued to run and run and run until she reached the village. She stopped outside the village and began to sing her usual song.

As soon as Achol heard her voice, she jumped out of her hiding place. They ran towards one another and embraced.

Achol's father took out a bull and slaughtered it in hospitality for the lioness. The lioness said she would not go back to the forest but would rather stay among the human beings with her daughter, Achol.

Achol was married and was given to her husband. Her mother, the lioness, moved with her to her marital home. And they all lived happily together.

Part Five

MARRIED WOMEN

Story of a Bird Woman

(Siberian tribal, Chukchi)

LAD went to a lake in the open country. There he saw many birds, of which some were geese and some were gulls, but both geese and gulls left their garments on the shore. The youth seized their clothing, whereupon all the geese and gulls said, 'Restore it.'

He gave back the stolen things of all the goose-girls, but kept the clothes of one gull-maiden and took her for himself. She bore him two children, real human children. When the women went to collect leaves the gull-wife went with them into the fields, but as she gathered grasses badly, her mother-in-law scolded her. All the birds were flying away, and the wife, who pined to return to her own land, went with her children behind the tent as the geese passed by.

'How would it be,' she said, 'for me to carry away my children?' The geese plucked their wings and stuck feathers on the children's sleeves, and the wife and her children flew away together.

When the husband came he could not find his wife, for she was gone. He could learn nothing about her, so he said to his mother, 'Make me ten pairs of very good boots.' Then he departed to the birds' country and saw an eagle who said to him, 'Go to the seashore; there you will find an old man cutting down wood; he is making firewood. He is of a monstrous aspect behind, so do not draw near to him from that direction; he would swallow you. Approach him face to face.'

The old man said, 'Whence have you come, and whither are you going?'

The lad answered, 'I married a gull-maiden, who bore me two children, but she has now disappeared with them. I am looking for her.'

'How will you travel?'

'I have ten pairs of boots,' was the reply.

The old man said, 'I will make you a canoe.' He made a beautiful canoe, with a cover like a snuff-box. The young man took his place in it, and the old one said, 'If you desire to go to the right, say to the canoe, "Wok, wok", and move your right foot. A little later, if you wish to go to the left, you will say, "Wok, wok!" and move your left foot.'

The canoe was swift as a bird. The old man continued, 'When you reach the shore and wish to land, say "Kay!" and push the cover with your hand!'

The young man approached the shore, pressed the cover, and the canoe grounded. He saw many bird-children at play on the ground. It was bird-land. He found his children and they recognised their father. 'Father has come!'

He said, 'Tell your mother I have arrived.'

They soon returned, and with them came the wife's brother, who approached the young man and said, 'Your wife has been taken as the wife of our chief, a great sea-bird.'

The man entered his wife's house. The chief bird kissed her on the cheek, and said to the young man, 'Why have you come? I will not restore your wife to you.'

The brother-in-law sat down in the tent. The husband and the great bird grappled with one another, and the young man, seizing his opponent by the neck, thrust him out. The chief bird departed to his country and was loud in complaint, whereupon many birds flew hither, and many gulls of various kinds.

While the young man was sleeping with his wife she called out, 'Countless warriors have come, wake up quickly!'

But he remained asleep and, as there were cries and noise around the house, she grew alarmed. Soon the birds drew feathers and poised them like arrows, but the young man went out and, seizing a stick, waved it in various directions; he struck one bird's wing, another's neck and another's back. Then all the birds fled, but on the morrow there came twice as many; they seemed as numerous as a swarm of gnats. But the young man filled a flat vessel with water and sprinkled the birds with it. Afterwards they could not fly, being frozen to the spot, and no more came.

The young man now bore his wife and children home to his own people. Taking his seat in the canoe, he covered it over as before, and coming to the shore, found the little old man.

'Well?' said the latter.

'I have brought them!' was the reply.

'Then depart! Here are your boots, take them and set off.'

When, in time, they forsook the canoe, they found the eagle in the old place. They were exhausted. The eagle said, 'Put on my clothing.' The young man attired himself in the eagle's clothing and flew home. The eagle had said to him, 'You will assume my attire, but do not take it into the house; leave it a little way off in a field!'

So the young man left the garment on the ground, and it flew back to the eagle. They arrived home. The youth now pushed some fallen wood with his foot, and it became a great herd. He drove the herd before him, then anointed his wife with blood and married her. Ceasing to be a bird, she became human and dressed herself as a woman.

Father and Mother Both 'Fast'

(USA, Hillbilly)

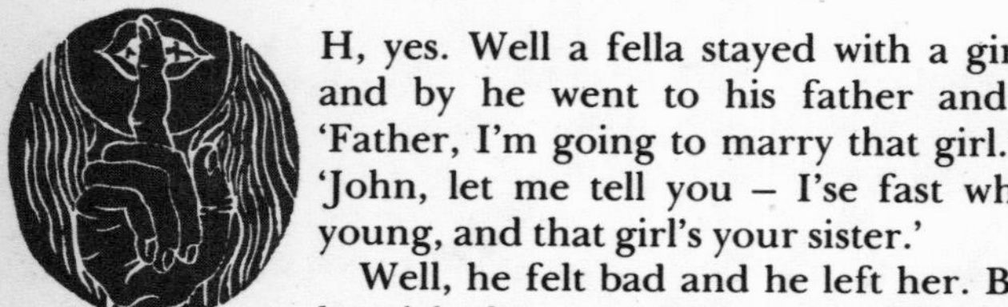

H, yes. Well a fella stayed with a girl, and by and by he went to his father and he said, 'Father, I'm going to marry that girl.' He says, 'John, let me tell you – I'se fast when I was young, and that girl's your sister.'

Well, he felt bad and he left her. By and by, he picked up another one, and he stayed with her for a while, and he went to his father and he said, 'Father, I'm going to marry that girl.' He said, 'Johnny, I was fast when I was young – that girl's your sister.'

Felt awful bad, and so one day he's setting up by the stove with his head hung down, and his mother said, 'What's the trouble, John?' 'No nothing.' She says, 'There's something, and I want to know what it is. Why did you leave that girl, the first one you stayed with, and you left your second one?' 'Well,' he said, 'Father told me he was fast when he was young, and they's both my sisters.' Says, 'Johnny, I want to tell you something, I was fast when I'se young, and your father ain't your father at all.'

Reason to Beat Your Wife

(Egyptian)

WO friends met. The first said to the second, 'How are you, So-and-so? We have not met for a long time. Those were the days. How are things going for you now?'

The second answered, 'Well, by God, I got married, and my wife is the "daughter of good people". Just as one wishes a wife to be.'

The first asked, 'Have you beaten her yet or not?'

'No, by God, there is no reason to beat her. She does everything as I wish.'

'She has to get at least one beating, just so that she may know who the master of the house is!'

'By God, yes! You are right.'

A week passed, and they met again. The first asked the second, 'Hey, what did you do? Did you beat her?'

'No! I just can't find a reason!'

'I will give you a reason. Buy fish, plenty of it, and take it to her and say, "Cook it, because we will have a guest for dinner", and leave the house. When you go home later, whatever she has cooked, say that you wanted it some other way!'

The man said, 'Fine.' He bought some catfish and went home. At the door, he shoved the fish at his wife and said, 'Cook it, for we will have guests', and he flew outside.

The woman said to herself, 'My girl, what are you going to do with all this fish? He didn't tell you how to fix it.' She thought and thought and finally said, 'I will fry some, bake some, and make some in a casserole with onions and tomatoes.'

She cleaned the house and prepared everything. As dinner time approached, her infant son made a mess on the floor right next to the table where they sit cross-legged on the floor to eat. As she went to get something to clean it, she heard her husband

and his friend knocking at the door. She ran to the door, and in order not to leave the mess like that, she covered it with a dish which happened to be in her hand.

They walked in and sat down on the floor at the table and said to her, 'Bring the food, mother of So-and-so.'

First she took out the fried fish. He said, 'Fried! I want it baked!' Immediately she took out the baked fish. He shouted, 'Not baked; I mean in a casserole!' Immediately she took out the casserole. He became frustrated and confused. He said, 'I want – I want –'

She asked, 'What?'

He replied in bafflement, 'I want shit!'

She immediately said, lifting the dish off the floor, 'Here it is!'

The Three Lovers

(USA, New Mexico)

NCE there was a woman who lived in a city and was married to a man named José Pomuceno. This man owned sheep. He was obliged to look after his business in the country. And whenever he would go out of the city, his wife never missed a chance to betray him. So it was that things got so bad that she had three lovers.

It so happened that one night when the husband wasn't at home the three were going to come the same night. That's the way this woman had things arranged when the first one came. Then the second one arrived. He knocked at the door. The wife said to the first one who was there, 'My husband.'

'Where shall I hide?'

'Hide in that wardrobe.'

The man hid in the wardrobe. The other man entered. A little while later the third one arrived and knocked at the door. The woman says to the second one, 'My husband.'

'No,' he says. 'If it is your husband, let him kill me. I'll do as I please. I am sure that it isn't your husband. You are giving several of us the run-around.'

When the woman saw that he didn't believe that it could be her husband, she tried to drive the other one off, telling him to go away, that everything was off, that he should return some other time.

Then this fellow said to her from outside, 'Since you can't do anything else, why don't you at least give me a kiss?'

'Yes' the one who is with her tells her. 'It's all right. Tell him to come to the window.'

The one outside comes to the window and the other one holds up his rump for him there, and the fellow outside kisses it.

When the latter saw that he had kissed the other's posterior, he felt rather bad and tried to get even some way; so he again called to him that he liked it, and for him to come back again. The second time that he appeared at the window he didn't try to kiss as he had done the first time, but struck a match and set fire to him.

When the one inside felt the flame, he came away from there yelling and leaping through the room, 'Fire! Fire! Fire!'

Then the one who was shut up in the wardrobe answered, 'Throw your furniture outside, lady.'

So ends the story of the wife of José Pomuceno.

The Seven Leavenings
(Palestinian Arab)

THERE was once in times past an old woman who lived in a hut all by herself. She had no one at all. One day when the weather was beautiful she said, 'Ah, yes! By Allah, today it's sunny and beautiful, and I'm going to take the air by the seashore. But let me first knead this dough.'

When she had finished kneading the dough, having added the yeast, she put on her best clothes, saying, 'By Allah, I just have to go and take the air by the seashore.' Arriving at the seashore, she sat down to rest, and lo! there was a boat, and it was already filling with people.

'Hey, uncle!' she said to the man, the owner of the boat. 'Where in Allah's safekeeping might you be going?'

'By Allah, we're heading for Beirut.'

'All right, brother. Take me with you.'

'Leave me alone, old woman,' he said. 'The boat's already full, and there's no place for you.'

'Fine,' she said. 'Go. But if you don't take me with you, may your boat get stuck and sink!'

No one paid her any attention, and they set off. But their boat had not gone twenty metres when it started to sink. 'Eh!' they exclaimed, 'It looks as if that old woman's curse has been heard.' Turning back, they called the old woman over and took her with them.

In Beirut, she did not know anybody or anything. It was just before sunset. The passengers went ashore, and she too came down and sat a while, leaning against a wall. What else could she have done? People were passing by, coming and going, and it was getting very late. In a while a man passed by. Everyone was already at home, and here was this woman sitting against the wall.

'What are you doing here, sister?' he asked.

'By Allah, brother,' she answered, 'I'm not doing anything. I'm a stranger in town, with no one to turn to. I kneaded my dough and leavened it, and came out for pleasure until it rises, when I'll have to go back.'

'Fine,' he said. 'Come home with me then.'

He took her home with him. There was no one there except him and his wife. They brought food, laughed and played – you should have seen them enjoying themselves. After they had finished, lo! the man brought a bundle of sticks this big and set to it – Where's the side that hurts most? – until he had broken them on his wife's sides.

'Why are you doing this, grandson?' the old woman asked, approaching in order to block his way.

'Get back!' he said. 'You don't know what her sin is. Better stay out of the way!' He kept beating his wife until he had broken the whole bundle.

'You poor woman!' exclaimed the old lady when the man had stopped. 'What's your sin, you sad one?'

'By Allah,' replied the wife, 'I've done nothing, and it hadn't even occurred to me. He says it's because I can't get pregnant and have children.'

'Is that all?' asked the old woman. 'This one's easy. Listen, and let me tell you. Tomorrow, when he comes to beat you, tell him you're pregnant.'

The next day, as usual, the husband came home, bringing with him the needed household goods and a bundle of sticks. After dinner, he came to beat his wife, but he had not hit her with the first stick when she cried out, 'Hold your hand! I'm pregnant!'

'Is it true?'

'Yes, by Allah!'

From that day on, he stopped beating her. She was pampered, her husband not letting her get up to do any of the housework. Whatever she desired was brought to her side.

Every day after that the wife came to the old woman and said, 'What am I going to do, grandmother? What if he should find out?'

'No matter,' the old woman would answer. 'Sleep easy. The burning coals of evening turn to ashes in the morning.' Daily the old woman stuffed the wife's belly with rags to make it look bigger and said, 'Just keep on telling him you're pregnant, and leave it to me. The evening's embers are the morning's ashes.'

Now, this man happened to be the sultan, and people heard what was said: 'The sultan's wife is pregnant! The sultan's wife is pregnant!' When her time to deliver had come, the wife went to the baker and said, 'I want you to bake me a doll in the shape of a baby boy.'

'All right,' he agreed, and baked her a doll which she wrapped and brought home without her husband seeing her. Then people said, 'The sultan's wife is in labour, she's ready to deliver.'

The old woman came forth. 'Back in my country, I'm a midwife,' she said. 'She got pregnant as a result of my efforts, and I should be the one to deliver her. I don't want anyone but me to be around.'

'Fine,' people agreed. In a while, word went out: 'She gave birth! She gave birth!'

'And what did she give birth to?'

'She gave birth to a boy.'

Wrapping the doll up, the wife placed it in the crib. People were saying, 'She gave birth to a boy!' They went up to the sultan and said she had given birth to a boy. The crier made his rounds, announcing to the townspeople that it was forbidden to eat or drink except at the sultan's house for the next week.

Now, the old woman made it known that no one was permitted to see the baby until seven days had passed. On the seventh day it was announced that the sultan's wife and the baby were going to the public baths. Meanwhile, every day the wife asked the old woman, 'What am I going to do, grandmother? What if my husband should find out?' And the old woman would reply, 'Rest easy, my dear! The evening's coals are the morning's ashes.'

On the seventh day the baths were reserved for the sultan's wife. Taking fresh clothes with them, the women went, accompanied by a servant. The sultan's wife went into the bath, and the women set the servant in front of the doll, saying to her, 'Take care of the boy! Watch out that some dog doesn't stray in and snatch him away!'

In a while the servant's attention wandered, and a dog came, grabbed the doll, and ran away with it. After him ran the servant, shouting, 'Shame on you! Leave the son of my master alone!' But the dog just kept running, munching on the doll.

It is said that there was a man in that city who was suffering from extreme depression. He had been that way for seven years, and no one could cure him. Now, the moment he saw a dog running with a servant fast behind him shouting, 'Leave the son of my master alone!' he started to laugh. And he laughed and laughed till his heartsickness melted away and he was well again. Rushing out, he asked her, 'What's your story? I see you running behind a dog who has snatched away a doll, and you're shouting at him to leave the son of your master alone. What's going on?'

'Such and such is the story,' she answered.

This man had a sister who had just given birth to twin boys seven days before. Sending for her, he said, 'Sister, won't you put one of your boys at my disposal?'

'Yes,' she said, giving him one of her babies.

The sultan's wife took him and went home. People came to congratulate her. How happy she was!

After some time the old woman said, 'You know, grandchildren, I think my dough must have risen, and I want to go home and bake the bread.'

'Why don't you stay?' they begged her. 'You brought blessings with you.' I don't know what else they said, but she answered, 'No. The land is longing for its people. I want to go home.'

They put her on a boat, filling it with gifts, and said, 'Go in Allah's safekeeping!'

When she came home, she put her gifts away and rested for a day or two. Then she checked her dough. 'Yee, by Allah!' she exclaimed. 'My dough hasn't risen yet. I'm going to the seashore for a good time.' At the shore she sat for a while, and lo! there was a boat.

'Where are you going, uncle?'

'By Allah, we're going to Aleppo,' they answered.

'Take me with you.'

'Leave me alone, old woman. The boat's full and there's no room.'

'If you don't take me with you, may your boat get stuck and sink in the sea!'

They set out, but in a while the boat was about to sink. They returned and called the old lady over, taking her with them. Being a stranger, where was she to go? She sat down by a wall, with people coming and going until late in the evening. After everybody had gone home for the night, a man passed by.

'What are you doing here?'

'By Allah, I'm a stranger in town. I don't know anyone, and here I am, sitting by this wall.'

'Is it right you should be sitting here in the street? Come, get up and go home with me.'

Getting up, she went with him. Again, there was only he and his wife. They had no children or anybody else. They ate and enjoyed themselves, and everything was fine, but when time came for sleep he fetched a bundle of sticks and beat his wife until he had broken the sticks on her sides. The second day the same thing happened. On the third day the old woman said, 'By Allah, I want to find out why this man beats his wife like this.'

She asked her, and the wife replied, 'By Allah, there's nothing the matter with me, except that once my husband brought home a bunch of black grapes. I put them on a bone-white platter and brought them in. "Yee!" I said, "How beautiful is the black on the white!" Then he sprang up and said, "So! May so-and-so of yours be damned! You've been keeping a black slave for a lover behind my back!" I protested that I had only meant the grapes, but he wouldn't believe me. Every day he brings a bundle of sticks and beats me.'

'I'll save you,' said the old woman. 'Go and buy some black grapes and put them on a bone-white platter.'

In the evening, after he had had his dinner, the wife brought the grapes and served them. The old woman then jumped in and said, 'Yee! You see, son. By Allah, there's nothing more beautiful than the black on the white!'

'So!' he exclaimed, shaking his head. 'It's not only my wife who says this! You're an old lady and say the same thing. It turns out my wife hasn't done anything, and I've been treating her like this!'

'Don't tell me you've been beating her just for that!' exclaimed the old woman. 'What! Have you lost your mind? Look here! Don't you see how beautiful are these black grapes on this white plate?'

It is said they became good friends, and the husband stopped beating his wife. Having stayed with them a few more months, the old woman said, 'The land has been longing for its people. Maybe my dough has risen by now. I want to go home.'

'Stay, old lady!' they said. 'You brought us blessings.'

'No,' she answered. 'I want to go home.'

They prepared a boat for her and filled it with food and other provisions. She gathered herself together and went home. There, in her own house, after she had sat down, rested, and put her things away, she checked the dough. 'By Allah,' she said, 'it has just begun to rise, and I might as well take it to the baker.' She took it to the baker, who baked her bread.

This is my tale, I've told it, and in your hands I leave it.

The Untrue Wife's Song

(USA, North Carolina)

NCE a man an' his wife were ridin' on a ship. One day the man was talkin' to the captain, an' they got to talkin' about women. The captain said he'd never seen a virtuous woman. The man said his wife was virtuous, and the captain bet the ship's cargo against the man's fiddle that he could seduce the man's wife within three hours. The man sent his wife up to the captain's cabin. After waiting for two hours the man became a little uneasy, so he walked by the captain's cabin, an' played on his fiddle an' sang:

For two long hours
You've resisted the captain's powers.
The cargo will soon be ours.

His wife heard him, an' from within she sang back:

Too late, too late, my dear,
He has me around the middle;
Too late, too late, my dear,
You've lost your damned old fiddle.

The Woman Who Married Her Son

(Palestinian Arab)

NCE upon a time there was a woman. She went out to gather wood, and gave birth to a daughter. She wrapped the baby in a rag, tossed her under a tree, and went on her way. The birds came, built a nest around the baby, and fed her.

The girl grew up. One day she was sitting in a tree next to a pool. How beautiful she was! (Praise the creator of beauty, and the Creator is more beautiful than all!) Her face was like the moon. The son of the sultan came to the pool to water his mare, but the mare drew back, startled. He dismounted to find out what the matter was, and he saw the girl in the tree, lighting up the whole place with her beauty. He took her with him, drew up a marriage contract, and married her.

When the time for pilgrimage came, the son of the sultan decided to go on the hajj. 'Take care of my wife until I return from the hajj,' he said to his mother.

Now the mother was very jealous of her daughter-in-law, and as soon as her son departed she threw his wife out of the house. Going over to the neighbour's house, the wife lived with them, working as a servant. The mother dug a grave in the palace garden and buried a sheep in it. She then dyed her hair black and put on make-up to make herself look young and pretty. She lived in the palace, acting as if she were her son's wife.

When he came back from the hajj, the son was taken in by his mother's disguise and thought her his wife. He asked her about his mother, and she said, 'Your mother died, and she is buried in the palace garden.'

After she slept with her son, the mother became pregnant and started to crave things. 'My good man,' she said to her son, 'bring me a bunch of sour grapes from our neighbour's vine!' The son sent one of the women servants to ask for the grapes. When the servant knocked on the neighbour's door, the wife of the sultan's son opened it.

'O mistress of our mistress,' said the servant, 'you whose palace is next to ours, give me a bunch of sour grapes to satisfy the craving on our side!'

'My mother gave birth to me in the wilderness,' answered the wife, 'and over me birds have built their nests. The sultan's son has taken his mother to wife, and now wants to satisfy her craving at my expense! Come down, O scissors, and cut out her tongue, lest she betray my secret!' The scissors came down and cut out the servant's tongue. She went home mumbling so badly no one could understand what she was saying.

The son of the sultan then sent one of his men servants to fetch the bunch of sour grapes. The servant went, knocked on the door, and said, 'O mistress of our mistress, you whose palace is next to ours, give me a bunch of sour grapes to satisfy the craving on our side!'

'My mother gave birth to me in the wilderness,' answered the wife of the sultan's son, 'and over me birds have built their nests. The sultan's son has taken his mother to wife, and now wants to satisfy her craving at my expense! Come down, O scissors, and cut out his tongue, lest he betray my secret!' The scissors came down and cut out his tongue.

Finally the son of the sultan himself went and knocked on the door. 'O mistress of our mistress,' he said, 'you whose palace is next to ours, give me a bunch of sour grapes to satisfy the craving on our side!'

'My mother gave birth to me in the wilderness, and over me birds have built their nests. The king's son has taken his mother to wife, and now wants to satisfy her craving at my expense! Come down, O scissors, and cut out his tongue. But I can't find it in myself to let it happen!' The scissors came down and hovered around him, but did not cut out his tongue.

The sultan's son understood. He went and dug up the grave in the garden, and behold! there was a sheep in it. When he was certain that his wife was actually his mother, he sent for the crier. 'Let him who loves the Prophet,' the call went out, 'bring a bundle of wood and a burning coal!'

The son of the sultan then lit the fire.
Hail, hail! Finished is our tale.

Duang and His Wild Life

(Sudan, Dinka)

MOU was so beautiful. She was betrothed to a man from the tribe. But she was not yet given to her betrothed. She still lived with her family.

There was a man called Duang in a neighbouring village. Duang's father said to him, 'My son, Duang, it is high time you married.'

'Father,' replied Duang, 'I cannot marry; I have not yet found the girl of my heart.'

'But my son,' argued his father, 'I want you to marry while I am alive. I may not live long enough to attend your marriage.'

'I will look, Father,' said Duang, 'but I will marry only when I find the girl of my heart.'

'Very well, my son,' said his father with understanding.

They lived together until the father died. Duang did not marry. Then his mother died. He did not marry.

These deaths made him abandon himself in mourning; so he no longer took care of his appearance. His mourning hair grew long and wild. He never shaved or groomed his hair. He was a very rich man. His cattle-byres were full of cattle, sheep and goats.

One day he left for a trip to a nearby tribe. On the way he heard the drums beating loud. He followed the sounds of the drums and found people dancing. So he stood and watched the dance.

In the dance was the girl called Amou. When she saw him standing, she left the dance and went near him. She greeted him. They stood talking. When the relatives of the man who was betrothed to Amou saw her, they became disturbed. 'Why should Amou leave the dance to greet a man who was merely watching? And then she dared to stand and talk with him! Who is the man, anyway?'

They called her and asked her. She answered, 'I don't see anything wrong! I saw the man looking as though he were a stranger who needed help. So I went to greet him in case he wanted something. There is nothing more to it.'

They dismissed the matter, although they were not convinced. Amou did not go back to the dance. She went and talked to the man again. She invited him to her family's home. So they left the dance and went. She seated him and gave him water. She cooked for him and served him.

The man spent two days in her house and then left and returned home. He went and called his relatives and told them that he had found the girl of his heart. They took cattle and returned to Amou's village.

The man who had betrothed Amou had paid thirty cows. Amou's relatives sent them back and accepted Duang's cattle. The marriage was completed, and Amou was given to her husband.

She went with him and gave birth to a daughter, called Kiliingdit. Then she had a son. She and her husband lived alone with their children. Then she conceived her third child. While she was pregnant, her husband was in the cattle camp. But when she gave birth, he came home to visit her and stay with them for the first few days after her delivery.

After she delivered, she felt a very strong craving for meat. She was still newly delivered. She said to her husband, 'I am dying of craving for meat. I cannot even eat.'

Her husband said to her, 'If it is my cattle you have your eyes on, I will not slaughter an animal merely because of your craving! What sort of a craving is this which requires the killing of livestock? I will not slaughter anything.'

That ended the discussion. But she still suffered and could not eat or work. She would just sit there.

Her husband became impatient and embittered by her craving. He slaughtered a lamb openly so that she and the others could see it. Then he went and killed a puppy dog secretly. He roasted both the lamb and the puppy in smouldering smudge.

When they were ready he took the dog meat to his wife in her women's quarters. He grabbed his children by the hands and took them away with him to the male quarters. His wife protested, 'Why are you taking the children away? Aren't they eating with me?'

He said, 'I thought you said you were dying of craving. I think it would be better for you and the children if you ate separately. They will share with me.'

He seated them next to him, and they ate together. She never doubted what he said, even though she felt insulted. That he would poison her was out of the question. So she ate her meat.

As soon as she ate her fill, her mouth started to drip with saliva. In a short while, she became rabid. Then she ran away, leaving her little baby behind.

Her husband took the boy to the cattle camp and left only the girl at home. She suffered very much taking care of her baby brother. Fearing that her mother might return rabid, she took the remainder of her mother's dog meat, dried it, and stored it. She would cook a portion of it and place it on a platform outside the hut together with some other food she had prepared.

For a while, her mother did not come. Then one night, she came. She stood outside the fence of the house and sang:

'Kiliingdit, Kiliingdit,
Where has your father gone?'

Kiliingdit answered:

'My father has gone to Juachnyiel,
Mother, your meat is on the platform,
Your food is on the platform,
The things with which you were poisoned.
Mother, shall we join you in the forest?
What sort of home is this without you?'

Her mother would take the food and share it with the lions. This went on for some time.

In the mean time, the woman's brothers had not heard of her giving birth. One of them, called Bol because he was born after twins, said to the others, 'Brothers, I think we should visit our sister. Maybe she has given birth and is now in some difficulties taking care of herself and the house.'

The little girl continued to labour hard looking after the baby and preparing food for the mother and themselves. She also had to protect herself and the baby so their mother would not find them and, having become a lioness, eat them.

She came again another night and sang. Kiliingdit replied as usual. Her mother ate and left.

In the mean time, Bol took his gourds full of milk and left for his sister's home. He arrived in the daytime. When he saw the village so quiet, he feared that something might have gone wrong. 'Is our sister really at home?' he said to himself. 'Perhaps what I was afraid of in my heart has occurred. Perhaps our sister died in childbirth and her husband with the children have gone away and abandoned the house!'

Another part of him said, 'Don't be foolish! What has killed her? She is a newly delivered mother and is confined inside the hut.'

'I see the little girl,' he said to himself, 'but I do not see her mother.' As soon as the little girl saw him, she raced towards him, crying.

'Where is your mother, Kiliingdit?' he asked her in haste.

She told him the story of how her mother turned wild, beginning with her mother's craving for meat and her father's poisoning her with dog meat.

'When she comes in the evening,' she explained, 'her companions are the wives of lions.'

'Will she come tonight?' asked her uncle.

'She comes every night,' answered Kiliingdit. 'But, Uncle, when she comes, please do not reveal yourself to her. She is no longer your sister. She is a lioness. If you reveal yourself to her, she will kill you and the loss will be ours. We shall then remain without anyone to take care of us.'

'Very well,' he said.

That night, she came again. She sang her usual song. Kiliingdit sang her response.

As she approached the platform to pick up her food, she said, 'Kiliingdit, my daughter, why does the house smell like this? Has a human being come? Has your father returned?'

'Mother, my father has not returned. What would bring him back? Only my little brother and I are here. And were we not human beings when you left us? If you want to eat us, then do so. You will save me from all the troubles I am going through. I have suffered beyond endurance.'

'My darling Kiliingdit,' she said, 'how can I possibly eat you? I know I have become a beast of a mother, but I have not lost my heart for you, my daughter. Is not the fact that you cook for me evidence of our continuing bond? I cannot eat you!'

When Bol heard his sister's voice, he insisted on going out to meet her, but his niece pleaded with him, saying, 'Don't be deceived by her voice. She is a beast and not your sister. She will eat you!'

So he stayed; she ate and left to join the wives of the lions.

The next morning, Bol returned to the cattle camp to tell his brothers that their sister had become a lioness. Bewildered by the news, they took their spears and came to their sister's home. They took a bull with them. They walked and walked and then arrived.

They went and sat down. The little girl went ahead and prepared the food for her mother in the usual way. Then they all went to sleep. The little girl went into the hut with her baby brother, as usual, but the men slept outside, hiding in wait for their sister.

She came at night and sang as usual. Kiliingdit responded. She picked up her food and ate with the wives of the lions. Then she brought the dishes back. As she put them back, she said, 'Kiliingdit!'

'Yes, Mother,' answered Kiliingdit.

'My dear daughter,' she continued, 'why does the house feel so heavy? Has your father returned?'

'Mother,' said Kiliingdit, 'my father has not returned. When he abandoned me with this little baby, was it his intention to return to us?'

'Kiliingdit,' argued the mother, 'if your father has returned, why do you hide it from me, dear daughter? Are you such a small child that you cannot understand my suffering?'

'Mother,' Kiliingdit said again, 'I mean what I say, my father has not come. It is I alone with the little baby. If you want to eat us, then eat us.'

As the mother turned to go, her brothers jumped on her and caught her. She struggled in their hands for quite a long time, but could not break away. They tied her to a tree. The next morning, they slaughtered the bull they had brought. Then they beat her and beat her. They would tease her with raw meat by bringing it close to her mouth and pulling it away from her. Then they would continue to beat her. As she was teased with meat, saliva fell from her mouth and formed little puppies. They continued to tease her and beat her until three puppies had emerged from her saliva. Then she refused raw meat. She was given roast meat from the bull and she ate it. The brothers beat her some more until she shed all the hairs that had grown on her body.

Then she opened her eyes, looked at them closely, sat down and said, 'Please hand me my little baby.'

The baby was brought. He could no longer suck his mother's breasts.

When the mother had fully recovered, her brothers said, 'We shall take you to our cattle camp. You will not go to the cattle camp of such a man again!'

But she insisted on going to her husband's cattle camp, saying, 'I must go back to him. I cannot abandon him.'

Her brothers could not understand her. They wanted to attack her husband and kill him, but she argued against that. When she saw that they did not understand her, she told them that she wanted to take care of him in her own way. She was not going back to him out of love but to take revenge. So they left her and she went to her husband.

When she got to the cattle camp, he was very pleased to have her back. She did not show any grievance at all. She stayed with him, and he was very happy with her.

One day she filled a gourd with sour milk. She pounded grain and made porridge. Then she served him, saying, 'This is my first feast since I left you. I hope you give me the pleasure of finding it your heartiest meal.'

First he drank the milk. Then came the porridge with ghee and sour milk mixed into it. He ate. Then she offered him some more milk to drink on top of the porridge. When he tried to refuse, she pleaded with him. The man ate and ate and ate, until he burst and died.

A Stroke of Luck

(Hungarian)

E went ploughing. He was a poor man. The plough cut a furrow and turned up a lot of money. When he set eyes on it, he began to speculate about what to say to his wife. He feared that she might blurt it out to the neighbours, and they would be served a summons to appear before the magistrate.

He went and bought a hare and a fish.

When she brought him his midday meal, he said to her after he had dined, 'Let's fry a fish.'

She said, 'What do you think! How could we catch a fish here in the field?'

'Come on, woman, I've just seen a couple of them, when I was ploughing around the blackthorn shrub.' He led her to the blackthorn shrub.

Says the woman, 'Look, old man, there's a fish.'

'Haven't I told you so?' And he flung the ox goad at the shrub so that the fish turned out at once.

Then he said, 'Let's catch a hare.'

'Don't be kidding me. You haven't got a gun.'

'Never mind. I'll knock it off with the ox goad.'

They were going along when she cried out, 'Look! there's a hare on the tree yonder there.'

The man flung his goad at the tree and the hare fell down.

They were working till the day drew to a close, and in the evening they made their way home. When they went past the church, they heard an ass braying.

The man said to the woman, 'You know what the ass is braying? He is saying, "The priest says in his sermon that soon a comet will appear and that will be the end of the world!" '

They went on. When they passed the city hall, the ass uttered another loud bray. The man said, 'The ass says that "The magistrate and the town clerk have just been caught embezzling public funds." '

As time wore on they were making good use of their money.

The neighbours kept asking them, 'Where did that lot of money come from?'

Then she said to one of the neighbour women, 'I wouldn't mind telling you, but you mustn't pass it on to anyone.' And she told her that they had found the money. Their neighbour reported it to the magistrate, and they were summoned to appear before him. And when he was questioned about the money, the man denied it. By no means did they find any money. Not a penny had been found by them.

The magistrate then said, 'Your wife will tell me.'

'What's the use asking her. She's just a silly woman,' he said.

The woman flew into a temper and began to shout at him. 'Don't you dare say that again. Didn't we find the money when we caught the fish under the blackthorn bush?'

'Now Your Honour may hear for yourself. Catching a fish in a bush. What next!'

'Can't you remember how you shot down a hare from the tree with the ox goad?'

'Well, haven't I told Your Honour? It's no use asking that fool of a woman.'

'A fool you are yourself. Have you forgotten that on our way home we heard an ass braying when we passed the church, and you said that the priest was preaching that a comet would appear and that would be the end of the world.'

'Now wasn't I right, Your Honour? It would be better to leave her alone, or she might give offence with her silly talk.'

The woman flew into a rage and said, 'Don't you remember that when we were passing the city hall and the ass uttered a loud bray you were telling me, "that the magistrate and the town clerk have been just caught out . . ." ' The magistrate jumped to his feet and said to the man, 'Take her home, my good man, she seems to have lost her wits.'

The Beans in the Quart Jar

(USA, Hillbilly)

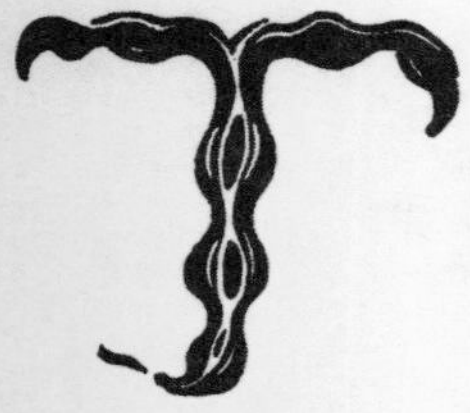

HE old man had taken sick and thought he's gonna die anyway, so he called his wife in and confessed, he said, 'I been stepping out, and I want to be honest with you, and I want to ask your forgiveness before I go.' And she said, 'All right', and 'I'll forgive you.' She forgive him.

By and by, she was taken sick and she called him in and she said, 'No, look, I stepped out quite a lot, and I want to ask forgiveness.' He said, 'Yes, I'll forgive you.' She said, 'Every time I stepped out I put a bean in a quart jar. And you'll find they're all there on that mantelpiece, except that quart I cooked the other Saturday.'

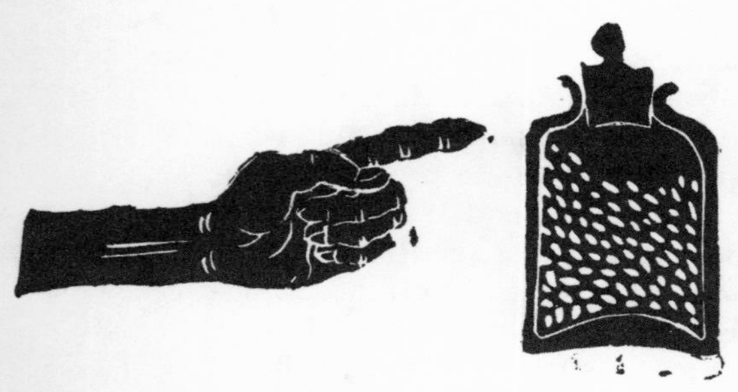

Part Six

USEFUL STORIES

A Fable of a Bird and Her Chicks

(Yiddish)

ONCE upon a time a mother bird who had three chicks wanted to cross a river. She put the first one under her wing and started flying across. As she flew she said, 'Tell me, child, when I'm old, will you carry me under your wing the way I'm carrying you now?'

'Of course,' replied the chick. 'What a question!'

'Ah,' said the mother bird, 'you're lying.' With that she let the chick slip, and it fell into the river and drowned.

The mother went back for the second chick, which she took under her wing. Once more as she was flying across the river, she said, 'Tell me, child, when I'm old, will you carry me under your wing the way I'm carrying you now?'

'Of course,' replied the chick. 'What a question!'

'Ah,' said the mother bird, 'you're lying.' With that she let the second chick slip, and it also drowned.

Then the mother went back for the third chick, which she took under her wing. Once more she asked in mid-flight, 'Tell me, child, when I am old, will you carry me under your wing the way I'm carrying you now?'

'No, mother,' replied the third chick. 'How could I? By then I'll have chicks of my own to carry.'

'Ah, my dearest child,' said the mother bird, 'you're the one who tells the truth.' With that she carried the third chick to the other bank of the river.

The Three Aunts

(Norwegian)

NCE upon a time there was a poor man who lived in a hut far away in the wood, and got his living by shooting. He had an only daughter, who was very pretty, and as she had lost her mother when she was a child, and was now half grown up, she said she would go out into the world and earn her bread.

'Well, lassie!' said the father, 'true enough you have learnt nothing here but how to pluck birds and roast them, but still you may as well try to earn your bread.'

So the girl went off to seek a place, and when she had gone a little while, she came to a palace. There she stayed and got a place, and the queen liked her so well that all the other maids got envious of her. So they made up their minds to tell the queen how the lassie said she was good to spin a pound of flax in four-and-twenty hours, for you must know the queen was a great housewife, and thought much of good work.

'Have you said this? Then you shall do it,' said the queen; 'but you may have a little longer time if you choose.'

Now, the poor lassie dared not say she had never spun in all her life, but she only begged for a room to herself. That she got, and the wheel and the flax were brought up to her. There she sat sad and weeping, and knew not how to help herself. She pulled the wheel this way and that, and twisted and turned it about, but she made a poor hand of it, for she had never even seen a spinning-wheel in her life.

But all at once, as she sat there, in came an old woman to her. 'What ails you, child?' she said.

'Ah!' said the lassie, with a deep sigh, 'it's no good to tell you, for you'll never be able to help me.'

'Who knows?' said the old wife. 'Maybe I know how to help

you after all.'

Well, thought the lassie to herself, I may as well tell her, and so she told her how her fellow-servants had given out that she was good to spin a pound of flax in four-and-twenty hours.

'And here am I, wretch that I am, shut up to spin all that heap in a day and a night, when I have never even seen a spinning-wheel in all my born days.'

'Well, never mind, child,' said the old woman. 'If you'll call me Aunt on the happiest day of your life, I'll spin this flax for you, and so you may just go away and lie down to sleep.'

Yes, the lassie was willing enough, and off she went and lay down to sleep.

Next morning when she awoke, there lay all the flax spun on the table, and that so clean and fine, no one had ever seen such even and pretty yarn. The queen was very glad to get such nice yarn, and she set greater store by the lassie than ever. But the rest were still more envious, and agreed to tell the queen how the lassie had said she was good to weave the yarn she had spun in four-and-twenty hours. So the queen said again, as she had said it she must do it; but if she couldn't quite finish it in four-and-twenty hours, she wouldn't be too hard upon her, she might have a little more time. This time, too, the lassie dared not say no, but begged for a room to herself, and then she would try. There she sat again, sobbing and crying, and not knowing which way to turn, when another old woman came in and asked, 'What ails you, child?'

At first the lassie wouldn't say, but at last she told her the whole story of her grief.

'Well, well!' said the old wife, 'never mind. If you'll call me Aunt on the happiest day of your life, I'll weave this yarn for you, and so you may just be off, and lie down to sleep.'

Yes, the lassie was willing enough; so she went away and lay down to sleep. When she awoke, there lay the piece of linen on the table, woven so neat and close, no woof could do better. So the lassie took the piece and ran down to the queen, who was very glad to get such beautiful linen, and set greater store than ever by the lassie. But as for the others, they grew still more bitter against her, and thought of nothing but how to find out something to tell about her.

At last they told the queen the lassie had said she was good to make up the piece of linen into shirts in four-and-twenty hours. Well, all happened as before; the lassie dared not say she couldn't sew; so she was shut up again in a room by herself, and there she sat in tears and grief. But then another old wife came, who said she would sew the shirts for her if she would call her Aunt on the happiest day of her life. The lassie was only too glad to do this, and then she did as the old wife told her, and went and lay down to sleep.

Next morning when she awoke she found the piece of linen made up into shirts, which lay on the table – and such beautiful work no one had ever set eyes on; and more than that, the shirts were all marked and ready for wear. So, when the queen saw the work, she was so glad at the way in which it was sewn, that she clapped her hands, and said, 'Such sewing I never had, nor even saw, in all my born days'; and after that she was as fond of the lassie as of her own children; and she said to her, 'Now, if you like to have the prince for your husband, you shall have him; for you will never need to hire work-women. You can sew, and spin, and weave all yourself.'

So as the lassie was pretty, and the prince was glad to have her, the wedding soon came on. But just as the prince was going to sit down with the bride to the bridal feast, in came an ugly old hag with a long nose – I'm sure it was three ells long.

So up got the bride and made a curtsy, and said, 'Good-day, Auntie.'

'*That* auntie to my bride?' said the prince.

'Yes, she was!'

'Well, then, she'd better sit down with us to the feast,' said the prince; but to tell you the truth, both he and the rest thought she was a loathsome woman to have next you.

But just then in came another ugly old hag. She had a back so humped and broad, she had hard work to get through the door. Up jumped the bride in a trice, and greeted her with 'Good-day, Auntie!'

And the prince asked again if that were his bride's aunt. They both said, yes; so the prince said, if that were so, she too had better sit down with them to the feast.

But they had scarce taken their seats before another ugly old hag came in, with eyes as large as saucers, and so red and bleared, 'twas gruesome to look at her. But up jumped the bride again, with her 'Good-day, Auntie', and her, too, the prince asked to sit down; but I can't say he was very glad, for he thought to himself, 'Heaven shield me from such aunties as my bride has!'

So when he had sat a while, he could not keep his thoughts to himself any longer, but asked 'But how, in all the world can my bride, who is such a lovely lassie, have such loathsome misshapen aunts?'

'I'll soon tell you how it is,' said the first. 'I was just as good-looking when I was her age; but the reason why I've got this long nose is, because I was always kept sitting, and poking, and nodding over my spinning, and so my nose got stretched and stretched, until it got as long as you now see it.'

'And I,' said the second, 'ever since I was young, I have sat and scuttled backwards and forwards over my loom, and that's how my back has got so broad and humped as you now see it.'

'And I,' said the third, 'ever since I was little, I have sat, and stared and sewn, and sewn and stared, night and day; and that's why my eyes have got so ugly and red, and now there's no help for them.'

'So, so!' said the prince, ''twas lucky I came to know this; for if folk can get so ugly and loathsome by all this, then my bride shall neither spin, nor weave, nor sew all her life long.'

Tale of an Old Woman

(Africa, Bondes)

HERE was once an old woman who had no husband and no relations, no money and no food. One day she took her axe and went to the forest to cut a little firewood to sell, so that she could buy something to eat. She went very far, right into the heart of the bush, and she came to a large tree covered with flowers, and the tree was called *Musiwa*. The woman took her axe and began to fell the tree.

The tree said to her, 'Why are you cutting me? What have I done to you?'

The woman said to the tree, 'I am cutting you down to make some firewood to sell, so that I can get some money, so that I can buy food to keep from starving, for I am very poor and have no husband or relations.'

The tree said to her, 'Let me give you some children to be your own children to help you in your work, but you must not beat them, nor are you to scold them. If you scold them you will see the consequences.'

The woman said, 'All right, I won't scold them.' Then the flowers of that tree turned into many boys and girls. The woman took them and brought them home.

Each child had its own work – some tilled, others hunted elephants, and still others fished. There were girls who had the work of cutting firewood, and girls who had the work of collecting vegetables, and girls who pounded flour and cooked it. The old woman didn't have to work any more, for now she was blessed.

Among the girls, there was one smaller than all the rest. The others said to the woman, 'This little girl must not work. When she is hungry and cries for food, give it to her and don't be angry at her for all of this.'

The woman said to them, 'All right, my children, whatever you tell me I will do.'

In this way, they lived together for some time. The woman didn't have to work except to feed the littlest child when it wanted to eat. One day the child said to the woman, 'I am very hungry. Give me some food to eat.'

The woman scolded the child, saying, 'How you pester me, you children of the bush! Get it out of the pot yourself.'

The child cried and cried because it had been scolded by the woman. Some of her brothers and sisters came, and asked her what was the matter. She told them, 'When I said I was hungry and asked for food, our mother said to me, "How I am worried by these bush children."'

Then the boys and girls waited until those who had gone hunting returned, and they told them how the matter stood. So they said to the woman, 'So you said we are children of the bush. We'll just go back to our mother, *Musiwa*, and you can dwell alone.' The woman pleaded with them every way, but they wouldn't stay. They all returned to the tree and became flowers again, as it was before, and all the people laughed at her. She dwelt in poverty till she died, because she did not heed the instruction given to her by the tree.

The Height of Purple Passion

(USA)

HERE was this sailor walking down the street and he met a Lady Wearing Lipstick. And she said to him, 'Do you know what the Height of Purple Passion is?' And he said 'No.' And she said, 'Do you want to find out?' And he said, 'Yes.' So she told him to come to her house at five o'clock *exactly*. So he did, and when he rang the doorbell, birds flew out all around the house. And they went around the house three times and the door opened and they all flew in again. And there was the Lady Wearing Lipstick. And she said, 'Do you still want to know what the Height of Purple Passion is?' And he said he wanted to find out. So she told him to go and take a bath and be very clean. So he did, and he came running back and slipped on the soap and broke his neck. That's the end. He never found out what it was. My girl friend Alice told me this story. It happened to somebody she knows.

Salt, Sauce and Spice, Onion Leaves, Pepper and Drippings

(Africa, Hausa)

HIS story is about Salt, and Sauce and Spice, and Onion Leaves, and Pepper and Drippings. A story, a story! Let it go, let it come. Salt and Sauce and Spice and Onion Leaves and Pepper and Drippings heard a report of a certain youth who was very handsome, but the son of the evil spirit. They all rose up, turned into beautiful maidens, and then they set off.

As they were going along, Drippings lagged behind the others, who drove her still further off, telling her she stank. But she crouched down and hid until they had gone on, and then she kept following them. When they had reached a certain stream, where they came across an old woman who was bathing, Drippings thought they would rub down her back for her if she asked, but one said, 'May Allah save me that I should lift my hand to touch an old woman's back.' The old woman did not say anything more, and the five passed on.

Soon Drippings came along, encountered the old woman washing, and greeted her. She answered, and said, 'Maiden, where are you going?' Drippings replied, 'I am going to find a certain youth.' And the old woman asked her, too, to rub her back, but unlike the others, Drippings agreed. After she had rubbed her back well for her, the old woman said, 'May Allah bless you.' And she said, too, 'This young man to whom you are all going, do you know his name?' Drippings said, 'No, we do not know his name.' Then the old woman told her, 'He is my son, his name is Daskandarini, but you must not tell the others,' then she fell silent.

Drippings continued to follow far behind the others till they got to the place where the young man dwelled. They were about to go in when he called out to them, 'Go back, and enter one at a time,' which they did.

Salt came forward first and was about to enter, when the voice asked, 'Who is there?' 'It is I,' she replied, 'I, Salt, who make the soup tasty.' He said, 'What is my name?' She said, 'I do not know your name, little boy, I do not know your name.' Then he told her, 'Go back, young lady, go back,' and she did.

Next Sauce came forward. When she was about to enter, she, too, was asked, 'Who are you?' She answered, 'My name is Sauce and I make the soup sweet.' And he said, 'What is my name?' But she did not know, either, and so he said, 'Turn back, little girl, turn back.'

Then Spice rose up and came forward, and she was about to enter when she was asked, 'Who is this, young lady, who is this?' She said, 'It is I who greet you, young man, it is I who greet you.' 'What is your name, young girl, what is your name?' 'My name is Spice, who makes the soup savoury.' 'I have heard your name, young woman, I have heard your name. Speak mine.' She said, 'I do not know your name little boy, I do not know your name.' 'Turn back, young lady, turn back.' So she turned back, and sat down.

Then Onion Leaves came and stuck her head into the room. 'Who is this, young girl, who is this?' asked the voice. 'It is I who salute you young man, it is I who salute you.' 'What is your name, little girl, what is your name?' 'My name is Onion Leaves, who makes the soup smell nicely.' He said, 'I heard your name, little girl. What is my name?' But she didn't know it and so she also had to turn back.

Now Pepper came along. She said, 'Your pardon, young man, your pardon.' She was asked who was there. She said, 'It is I, Pepper, young man, it is I, Pepper, who make the soup hot.' 'I have heard your name, young lady. Tell me my name.' 'I do not know your name, young man, I do not know your name.' He said, 'Turn back, young maid, turn back.'

Now only Drippings was left. When the others asked her if she was going in she said, 'Can I enter the house where such good people as you have gone and been driven away? Would not they the sooner drive out one who stinks?' They said, 'Rise up and go in,' for they wanted Drippings, too, to fail.

So she got up and went in there. When the voice asked her

who she was, she said 'My name is Drippings, little boy, my name is *Batso* which makes the soup smell.' He said, 'I have heard your name. There remains my name to be told.' She said, 'Daskandarini, young man, Daskandarini.' And he said, 'Enter.' A rug was spread for her, clothes were given to her, and slippers of gold. And then of Salt, Sauce, Spice, Onion Leaves and Pepper, who before had despised her, one said, 'I will always sweep for you', another, 'I will pound for you', another, 'I will draw water for you', another, 'I will pound the ingredients of the soup for you', and another, 'I will stir the food for you.' They all became her handmaidens. And the moral of all this is that it is from such common things that our most blessed foods are made. So just as such common stuff may be transformed under the right circumstance, if you see a man is poor, do not despise him. You do not know but that some day he may be better than you. That is all.

Two Sisters and the Boa

(Chinese)

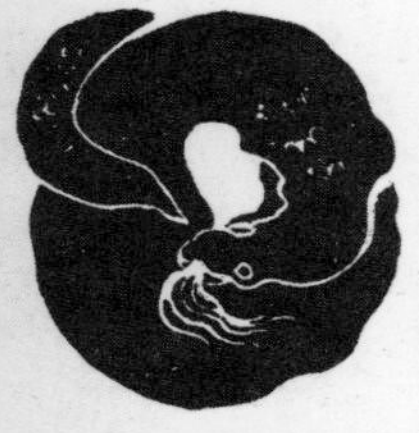

NCE there was an old, Kucong *binbai*, or old woman, who had buried her husband in her youth. Her sole possession was two daughters, the elder, nineteen years old, and the younger, seventeen. One afternoon, she returned home from working in the mountains, feeling thirsty and tired. So she sat down under a mango tree to rest. This mango tree was laden with ripe, golden-yellow fruit hanging down from the branches. A breeze blew from the mountains, carrying the exquisite fragrance of ripe mangoes to her nose, making her mouth water.

Suddenly, the *binbai* heard a swishing sound, 'sha-sha', up in the mango tree, and then thin pieces of bark fell on her. The old woman thought that somebody must be up there, so without even taking a look, she called out, jokingly, 'Who's the young man up in the tree whittling arrows out of mango branches? Whoever you are, if you would honour me by presenting me with a few mangoes, you can have your choice of my two daughters.'

Hardly had the *binbai*'s words escaped her lips, when there came the rustling of leaves, 'hua-hua', and a fully ripe mango fell plop, right on the ground. Feeling delighted and thankful at once, the old woman picked up the mango and began eating it, all the while looking up in the tree. Better for her she had not looked, for she was all agog with what she saw. Coiled all around the mango tree was a boa as thick as a bull's thigh, knocking mangoes free, its tail swishing back and forth. The *binbai* could not care less about picking up any more mangoes, and she scurried down the mountain in leaps and bounds, her bamboo basket on her back.

Wheezing and gasping for breath, the old woman entered her

door. As she saw her two darling daughters coming up to meet her she called to mind what had happened under the mango tree. She couldn't help feeling nervous and confused, as if she were stuck in a briar patch. She walked outside and was met by a strange sight. Though it was already dark, all her chickens were still circling around outside the chicken coop. She tried repeatedly to drive them inside, but they would not go. She went up to the coop and peeped in. Gosh! The very same boa which had been coiled around the mango was right there, lying in the chicken coop! As she was about to run away, the huge, long boa began to speak.

'*Binbai*, just now, you made a promise under the mango tree: whoever picked a mango and gave it to you to eat, could have his choice of one of your two daughters. Now please, keep your promise. Give me one of your girls! If you should go back on your word, don't blame me for getting impolite!'

Seeing that boa in the chicken coop, with its brightly patterned, scaly skin, gleaming eyes, and that long, forked tongue sticking out, the *binbai* shivered from head to foot. She couldn't say yes, but she couldn't say no, either. So all she said was, 'Now don't get mad, boa! be patient, please, Let me talk this over with my girls, so I can tell you what they think.'

The *binbai* went back into the house and recounted all that had happened to her two daughters. 'Oh, my little darlings!' she exclaimed. 'It's not that Mama doesn't love you or dote on you, but I have no choice other than to push you in the burning fire. Now you two sisters have to think it over – who is willing to marry the boa?'

No sooner had the old woman finished speaking than the older daughter started screaming, 'No, no! I won't go! Who could marry such an ugly, dreadful thing?'

The younger sister thought for a while. She saw that her mother's life was threatened, while her older sister was adamant.

'Mama,' she said, 'to prevent the boa from doing you and sister any harm, and so you two can live in peace, I'm willing to marry the boa.' And with that, she cried many a sad, sad tear.

The *binbai* led her second child to the gate of the chicken coop and told the boa he could have her. That very night, the old woman took the snake into her home, and the boa and Second

Daughter were married.

The next morning, when the boa was about to take her second daughter away, mother and child wept in one another's arm. How hard it was to part! Off went the boa, leading the *binbai*'s dear child to the virgin forest, deep in the mountains, where he brought her to a cave. She groped about in the dark, dark cave, following after the boa. On and on they went, never coming to the end. So worried and afraid was Second Daughter, that her teardrops fell like strings of pearls. Rounding a bend in the cave, there was a gleam of light, and suddenly, a resplendent, magnificent palace came in view. There were endless, vermilion walls and yellow tiles without number, long verandas and tiny pavilions, tall buildings and spacious courtyards. Everywhere one could see carved beams, painted rafters, piles of gold, carved jade and wall hangings of red and green silk. Second Daughter was simply dazzled. As she turned around, that terrifying, dreadful boa which had been close by had disappeared. Walking beside her now was a gorgeously dressed young man, looking ever so vigorous and handsome.

'Oh!' she exclaimed, completely outdone. 'How could this be?'

The young man beside her replied, 'Dear Miss! I am the king of the snakes of this region. Not long ago, when I went out to make an inspection tour of the snake tribes, I saw you two sisters. How I admired your wisdom and beauty! I made up my mind right then to have one of you as my wife, and that's how I thought of a way to win your mother's approval. Now, my hopes have come true, Oh, dear Miss! In my palace you'll have gold and silver without end, more cloth than you can ever use, and more rice than you can ever eat. Let us love each other dearly, enjoying a glorious life, to the end of our days!'

As she listened to the snake king's words, Second Sister's heart flooded with warmth. She took hold of his hand, and, smiling sweetly, walked towards the resplendent, magnificent palace.

Second Sister and the snake king lived happily as newly-weds for a time. Then, one day, she took leave of her husband to go back home and visit her mother and sister. She told them all about her rich, full married life with the king of the snakes.

How could the elder daughter not be full of regret? 'Ay!' she thought. 'I'm to blame for being so foolish. If I had promised to marry the boa in the first place, would not I have been the one now enjoying glory, honour and riches in that palace, instead of my younger sister?' So she made up her mind, then and there. 'Right! That's what I'll do. I'll find a way to wed a boa too!'

After the younger sister left to return to the snake king, the elder sister walked deep into the mountains, carrying a basket on her back. To find a boa, she would only go where the grass was tall or the jungles were dense. From dawn to dusk and dusk to dawn, she kept on searching until, at last, after great difficulty, she found a boa under a bush. Its eyes were shut, for the boa was enjoying a good snooze.

First Sister gingerly raked the snake into her basket and left for home in high spirits, the boa on her back. She had only gone halfway when the boa woke up. It stuck out its tongue and licked the back of her neck. Instead of being frightened by what the snake was doing, First Sister secretly felt quite delighted. 'Hey!' she whispered softly. 'Don't be so affectionate just yet! Wait till we get home!'

After getting back home, she laid the boa in her bed, then rushed to make the fire and do the cooking. After supper, First Sister told her mother, 'Mama, I found a boa today too, and I shall marry him tonight. From now on, I can live a rich, comfortable life, just like my baby sister!' And off she went to sleep with her boa.

Not long after the mother went to bed, she heard her daughter's voice, 'Mama, it's up to my thighs!'

The *binbai* did not say a word, thinking all she was hearing was a pair of newly-weds having fun playing around.

After a while, First Sister called out, her voice trembling, 'Mama, it's up to my waist!'

The old woman did not understand what such words could mean, so she did not budge an inch.

Yet more time passed, until this time she heard a mournful voice from the inner room, 'Mama, it's up to my neck now . . .' And then, all was silence.

The *binbai* felt something was not quite right, so she quickly rolled out of bed, lit a pine torch and went to take a look. That dreadful boa had swallowed down her elder daughter, leaving but a lock of her hair!

The old woman felt sad and nervous. She paced back and forth in the room, not knowing what to do to rescue her daughter. In the end, all she could think of doing was to pull down her dear, thatched hut, set it afire, and burn up the boa. In the raging flames a loud 'bang' was heard. As the boa was being burned to death, it burst into many pieces. In a later age, these came to be countless snakes, big and little.

The next morning, the *binbai* picked out of the ashes a few of her daughter's bones that had not been consumed by the fire. She dug a hole in the ground and buried them, holding back her tears.

Afterwards, she declared, 'My elder daughter! This is all because of your greed!' With these words, she went off into the dense jungle, and deep into the mountains, to look for her second daughter and her son-in-law, the king of the snakes.

Spreading the Fingers

(Surinamese)

N the early times Ba Yau was a plantation overseer. He had two wives in the city. But as he found provisions on the plantation, he brought them to his wives. But when he brought things, then he said to them, 'When you eat, you must spread your fingers.' But when he said this, the first one did not understand very well what that meant to say. He told the second wife the same thing, and that one understood. What he meant was that when he brought them things, they were not to eat them alone, they were to give others half.

Now the one who did not understand what that said, in the afternoon when she cooked, she ate. Then she went outside, and spread her fingers, and said, 'Ba Yau said when I eat I must spread my fingers.' Ba Yau brought her much bacon and salt fish. She alone ate it. But when Ba Yau brought the things for the other one she shared half with other people, because she had understood what the proverb had said.

Not long afterwards Ba Yau died. But when Ba Yau was dead, nobody brought anything to the wife who had spread her fingers for the air. She sat alone. But to the other one who had shared things with other people, many people brought things. One brought her a cow, one brought her sugar, one brought her coffee. So she received many things from others.

Now one day, the one wife went to the other, and she said, 'Yes, sister, ever since Ba Yau died, I have suffered hunger. No one brought me anything. But look, how is it that so many people have brought things to you?'

Then the other one asked her, 'Well, when Ba Yau had brought you things, what did you do with them?'

She said, 'I alone ate them.'

Then the other one said again, 'When Ba Yau said to you,

"You must spread your fingers", what did you do?'

She said, 'When I ate, I spread my fingers in the air.'

The other one said, 'So . . . Well then, the air must bring you things, because you spread your fingers for the air. As for myself, the same people to whom I gave things, bring me things in return.'

The proverb, when you eat you must spread fingers, means, when you eat, you must eat with people, you must not keep all for yourself. Otherwise, when you have nothing, nobody else is going to give you, because you had not given people what was yours.

Publisher's Note

About a month before she died, Angela Carter was in the Brompton Hospital in London. The manuscript of *The Second Virago Book of Fairy Tales* lay on her bed. 'I'm just finishing this off for the girls', she said. Virago published her first book of non-fiction, *The Sadeian Woman* in 1979. Her loyalty to us was boundless. When we first heard she was ill, we told her not to worry about this collection, we had published *The Virago Book of Fairy Tales*, that was enough. But no, Angela claimed it was *just* the project for an ailing writer to pursue while lying on the couch. And so she worked on the book until a few weeks before her death.

Though all the stories were collected, put in order and grouped under her chosen headings, and Virago was instructed to print the jacket 'beetroot red', Angela Carter was unable to finish the notes beyond 'The Witches Piper' in Part Two. We are extremely grateful to Shahrukh Husain, editor of the forthcoming *The Virago Book of Witches*, who was able to draw on her own extensive knowledge of folklore and fairy tales to complete the remaining 29 notes, including 'Rolando and Brunilde' and 'The Greenish Bird' from Part One. Shahrukh Husain has included the remarks and notes from Angela Carter's own file of notes wherever they were left.

Notes

Part One: STRONG MINDS AND LOW CUNNING

1. The Twelve Wild Ducks

From the collection of Norwegian folk tales made by Peter Christian Asbjørnsen and Jørgan Moe, in George Webb Darsent's handsome Victorian translation, *Popular Tales from the Norse* (Edinburgh, 1903).

The film-maker Alfred Hitchcock thought nothing was more ominous than the look of blood on daisies. Blood on snow catches even more directly at the viscera. The raven, the blood, the snow – these are the elements of the unappeasable northern formulae of desire. In 'The Story of Conall Gulban' in J.F. Campbell's *Popular Tales of the West Highlands* Conall 'would not take a wife forever whose head should be black as the raven, and her face as fair as the snow, and her cheeks as red as blood'.

Campbell crisply suggests the raven must have been eating something, because of all the blood, and offers a variant from Inverness:

> *When he got up in the morning there was young snow, and the raven was upon a spray near him, and a bit of flesh in his beak. The piece of flesh fell and Conall went to lift it, and the raven said to him, that Fair Beauteous Smooth was as white as the snow upon the spray, her cheek as red as the flesh that was in his hand, and her hair as black as the feather that was in his wing.* (Popular Tales of the West Highlands, *orally collected with a translation by J.F. Campbell, Vol. III, Paisley, 1892.)*

This carnivorous imagery expresses the depths of a woman's desire for a child in traditional stories. 'Snow-White' in the familiar version collected by the Brothers Grimm starts off the same way. Please note that, according to the editors of Palestinian Arab stories, childless mothers in fairy tales wish for daughters far more frequently than they do for sons.

'The Twelve Wild Ducks', with its savage beginning and theme of sibling devotion, forms the basis of the Danish Hans Christian Andersen's lovely literary story, 'The Wild Swans'. Andersen upgraded the ducks to romantic swans although I feel that if wild ducks were good enough for Ibsen, they should have been good enough for him.

2. Old Foster

Collected from Jane Gentry in 1923 in Hot Springs, North Carolina, by Isobel Gordon Carter. Text from *Journal of American Folklore*, 38 (1925), 360–1.

This ancient story of sex murder and serial killing travelled across the Atlantic with the first English settlers of the US in the sixteenth and seventeenth centuries. 'Old Foster' is first cousin to the sinister Mr Fox (see *The Virago Book of Fairy Tales*, edited by Angela Carter, p. 8), and to 'The Robber Bridegroom' of the Brothers Grimm.

3. Šāhīn

From *Speak, Bird, Speak Again: Palestinian Arab Folktales*, collected and edited by Ibrahim Muhawi and Sharif Kanaana, and published by the University of California Press.

These stories were collected on tape between 1978 and 1980 in Galilee, since 1948 part of the state of Israel, the West Bank and Gaza. In the Palestinian tradition, women are the custodians of narrative; if men tell stories, they must adopt the narrative style of women. Since storytelling style matures with age, old women have the edge on everybody else. Tales are told on winter nights, when there is little work in the fields, and extended families gather together for mutual entertainment. The oldest woman usually starts. The gatherings are dominated by women; there is a pronounced pro-woman bias to all these Palestinian stories, although the Palestinian family is, as Muhawi and Kanaana explain, 'patrilineal, patrilateral, polygynous, endogamous and patrilocal'.

In their introduction, they note that the pattern of free mate choice by women 'is so consistently at odds with the facts of social life that we must finally conclude that a deeply felt emotional need is being articulated'.

Nevertheless, 'Šāhīn', with its exuberantly self-assertive heroine, was told by a sixty-five-year-old man from Galilee, a ploughman and shepherd all his life. In another variant, the exhausted hero, newly married, says to Šāhīn, 'Believe me you are the man and I am the bride.' And it is nothing but the truth.

4. The Dog's Snout People

A story from the Baltic country of Latvia collected in the 1880s and published in a majestic collection called *Siberian and Other Folk-Tales:*

Primitive Literature of the Empire of the Tsars, collected and translated with an introduction and notes by C. Fillingham-Coxwell (London, C.W. Daniel, 1925).

Christian culture was slow to influence the people of heavily forested Latvia, who are said to have retained pagan altars as late as 1835. According to tradition, marriage was obtained by abduction, a risky business. Geographically between, and politically at the mercy of, Germany and Russia for centuries, the Letts, according to Fillingham-Coxwell, regarded the Germans and Russians 'with hatred and despair'. Fillingham-Coxwell also thought the enigmatic 'dog's snout people' themselves might contain memories of aboriginal Lettish inhabitants.

5. The Old Woman Against the Stream

Norwegian, again; from the same Asbjørnsen and Moe collection as 'The Twelve Wild Ducks', in a modern translation by Pat Shaw and Carl Noman (New York, Pantheon Books). Originally published in Oslo by Dreyers Verlag in 1960.

6. The Letter Trick

The people who were taken from West Africa as slaves to the place formerly called Dutch Guiana, now Suriname, took with them an invisible treasure of memory and culture. In the late 1920s, the anthropologists Melville J. Herskovits and Frances S. Herskovits collected a vast number of tales and songs, in the coastal city of Paramaribo. The language of the city was a thick, rich Creole; the Herskovits translated their material into English.

The city of Paramaribo possessed a mixed-race culture – Dutch, Indian, Carib, Arawak, Chinese and Javanese people mingled with those of African descent, but, amongst the latter, a strong African influence remained, expressing itself not only in voodoo beliefs and practices but in such matters as the tying of a headscarf. Descent was traced through the maternal line; the men were often absent as migrant workers.

Storytelling had an important place in this community. Tales were told to entertain the dead as they lay in state. And there was a taboo against telling stories in daytime, because, if you did so, death would come and sit beside you, and you would die, too.

(*Suriname Folk-lore*, collected by Melville J. Herskovits and Frances S. Herskovits [New York, Columbia University Press, 1936], p. 351.)

7. Rolando and Brunilde

This type of industrious spinner or seamstress is often rewarded with an illustrious lover simply for sitting at her window sewing or singing. (See 'The Greenish Bird', this volume p. 37.) Here though, she attracts an evil magician who abducts and thereafter deactivates her. Quite unusually, it is her mother who embarks on the Path of Trials as a sort of trickster-heroine. A fairy-hag is her helper and Rolando her assistant. The tale includes some interesting images of the two old women humping heavy bags over a garden wall and breaking into the castle – activities generally reserved for the young.

8. The Greenish Bird

A Mexican variant of the story most familiar in the beautiful Norwegian form, 'East o' the Sun, West o' the Moon', in Peter Christan Asbjørnsen and Jørgan Moe's collection (see *The Virago Book of Fairy Tales*, p. 122).

Like the last tale, this Mexican one begins with an industrious spinner at a window. Luisa is swiftly won over by her bird-wooer and begins an indeterminate sexual relationship. Like the Greek love god, hero of Apuleius' third-century Latin novella 'Cupid and Psyche' contained in the Golden Ass, the greenish bird is magical, generous and wonderful in bed. Luisa knows nothing about him, which does not particularly bother her. Like Psyche's sisters Luisa's too are jealous, and mar the relationship, causing the severely wounded prince to abandon her with an injunction to come in search of him. The iron shoe clad heroine who visits the sun and the moon in search of her offended lover occurs in Eastern Europe too, most notably attempting to redeem a Pig-prince. The Cap O' Rushes ending to this tale is similar to the Egyptian Cinderella story 'The Princess in the Suit of Leather', *The Virago Book of Fairy Tales,* p. 39), when the Prince, having realised his sweetheart is a servant in his palace, demands that she bring his meals to him. (*Folktales of Mexico*, by Americo Paredes, [Chicago 1970], p. 95.)

9. The Crafty Woman

From the Baltic state of Lithuania, again from C. Fillingham-Coxwell's collection. He quotes a Russian variation, from around Moscow, in which the part of the old woman is played by a young Jew.

Part Two: UP TO SOMETHING – BLACK ARTS AND DIRTY TRICKS

1. *Pretty Maid Ibronka*

This popular Hungarian story has been narrated in almost every village in the country in fairly similar form. It is also known in Lithuania and Yugoslavia. Hungarian popular belief has a particular dread of a revived corpse but the terrible lover, with his hat 'graced with a crane's feather' and his cloven hoof is reminiscent of the demon lover who returns to claim his faithless mistress in the great Scots ballad, 'The House Carpenter' (in Francis Child's collection *The English and Scottish Popular Ballads*, 3 vols. New York 1957). The demon takes the Scotswoman away on shipboard and destroys her: But Ibronka gets away with it.

This story was narrated by Mihály Fédics, an illiterate day-labourer, in 1938, when he was eighty-six years old. He had gone to the United States at the time of World War I and worked as a labourer there but soon returned to Hungary. He learned his stories during the long winter evenings, in the village houses where people went to spin together. Later, working as a lumberjack, his stories were the principal source of entertainment in the forest camp. 'It was his custom to interrupt his own story, by calling out "Bones" to his listeners, to see whether they had gone to sleep: if the encouraging answer "tiles" came, he went on with the story, but if there was no answer, he knew that his companions had dropped off, and the tale was to be continued the following day' (p. 130 *Folktales of Hungary*).

This information, together with the story, comes from *Folktales from Hungary*, edited by Linda Degh and translated by Judith Halasz (London, Routledge & Kegan Paul, 1965).

Copyright University of Chicago, 1965. In the series 'Folktales of the World', edited by Richard M. Dorson.

2. *Enchanter and Enchantress*

A witch duel, or transformation contest, tale from tribal Russia. For more about transformation contests see *The Virago Book of Fairy Tales*, p. 235. This story comes from a Finno-Turkish people called the Mordvins, who lived between the rivers Volga and Oka in the heart of Russia when this story was collected in the nineteenth century. The Mordvinian idea of the cosmos was that of the beehive.

Fillingham-Coxwell, p. 568.

3. The Telltale Lilac Bush

As told to Keith Ketchum in 1963 by Mrs Sarah Dadisman of Union, Monroe Country, West Virginia. (From *The Telltale Lilac Bush and Other West Virginian Ghost Tales* collected by Ruth Ann Musick [University of Kentucky Press, 1965], p. 12.)

4. Tatterhood

A Norwegian story from Asbjørnsen and Moe, in George Webb Darsent's translation.

5. The Witchball

An old-fashioned farting story from rural America, as told by seventy-six-year-old V. Ledford, of Clay County, Kentucky. This text is reprinted from *Buying the Wind: Regional Folklore in the United States*, edited and collected by Richard M. Dorson (University of Chicago Press, 1964).

Vance Randolph found another wise woman with access to farting powder in the Ozark mountains in Arkansas; this story may be found in *The Virago Book of Fairy Tales*, p. 73.

6. The Werefox

From *Chinese Ghosts and Goblins*, edited by G. Willoughby-Meade (London, Constable, 1928), p. 123.

7. The Witches' Piper

Narrated by Mihály Bertok, aged sixty-seven, a herdsman of Kishartyan, Nograd County, Hungary, and collected by Linda Degh in 1951.

Once upon a time, the bagpiper provided the music for the Shrove Tuesday dance. Witches would force the piper to play for them and then pay him back with a dirty trick.

8. Vasilissa the Fair

The heroine Vasilissa is as familiar in Russian folklore as the European Ella i.e. Cinderella. (See *The Virago Book of Fairy Tales*, 'Vasilissa the Priest's Daughter', p. 57 and 'The Baba Yaga', p. 151.) The tale contains powerful indicators that the Baba Yaga's origins are probably in the Mother goddess of various mythologies. She refers to the morning, day and night as her 'own' and her mortar and pestle are reminiscent of corn and wheat grinding. In addition, she possesses fire, a basic element. (A more obscure tale tells how she stole fire.) She is stern and harsh in her judgement but just and not devoid of ethics, conforming to the deathly aspect of the Mother goddess. The skulls surrounding her home represent the dead in general, though 'The Witch and her Servants' (*The Yellow Story Book*, ed. Andrew Lang) contains a more specific explanation. When the ubiquitous Iwanich of Russian tales goes to work for a witch, she delivers the following warning:

If you look after them both for a year I will give you anything you like to ask; but if, on the other hand, you let any of the animals escape you, your last hour is come, and your head shall be stuck on the last spike of my fence. The other spikes, as you see, are already adorned, and the skulls are all those of different servants I have had who have failed to do what I demanded (p. 161).

The remaining riddle is that of the invisible pairs of hands. It is clear that the hag is alluding to the secrecy of women's mysteries when she expresses approval that Vasilissa has stopped short of asking the question that would force her to reveal what is inside her house. Her aversion to blessings may well represent the fear of a pagan goddess being driven out by Christianity. Fillingham-Coxwell's note referring to Russian society at the time of collection, says: 'The priest has a difficult, ill-paid and not very exalted position. So superstition and a belief in witchcraft abound, though the efforts of the orthodox church to suppress pagan practices and traditions have not been without a large measure of success' (p. 671 *Siberian and Other Folktales*). A poem entitled 'Russian Folk-Tales' includes the lines:

Cannibal witches will scarcely attack or make ready to eat us
Easily, quickly we conquer if enemies dare approach us.

For details of the Baba Yaga herself, see Angela Carter's note to 'The Baba Yaga' (*The Virago Book of Fairy Tales*, p. 239).

(*Siberian and other Folktales: Primitive Literature of the Empire of the Tsars*, collected, translated and with an introduction by C. Fillingham-Coxwell, London, 1925, p. 680.)

9. The Midwife and the Frog

This story, set in the Magyar Mountains not far from the banks of the Szuscava, was collected by Gyula Orlutory from thirty-three-year-old Mrs Gergely Tamas in 1943. The *gyivak* of this story is glossed in the book as 'a minor devil'.

This tale-type counts as a legend the world over since it continues to be believed. A Middle Eastern variant, in which a midwife delivers a djinn's wife, is always told as if it occurred to an acquaintance of the teller. There the terrified woman accepts a handful of stones which turn to gold when she returns home. A Norse version appears in *Folktales of Norway* edited by Reidar Christiansen (translated by Pat Shaw Iversen, The University of Chicago Press, 1964, p. 105). Numerous variants exist in the British Isles. According to Katharine Briggs, 'the earliest version is from *Gervase of Tilbury* in the 13th C', *Folktales of England*, The University of Chicago Press, 1965. See 'The Fairy Midwife', p. 38 and 'The Midwife', in *The Best-Loved Folktales of the World*, edited by Joanna Cole, Anchor, Doubleday, New York, 1983, p. 280.

(*Folktales from Hungary*, edited by Linda Degh, and translated by Judith Halasz [Chicago, 1965], p. 296.)

Part Three: BEAUTIFUL PEOPLE

1. Fair, Brown and Trembling

This Irish Cinderella was collected by Jeremiah Curtin in 1887 in Galway. The unkind sisters here are Trembling's own. The henwife is the Celtic equivalent of the fairy godmother. Storytellers sometimes preferred to avoid the use of the word 'witch' in Ireland and Scotland. It was too much like 'tempting fate' so they tended to call her a bird-woman or a henwife. Though henwives are usually good (see Duncan Williams's collections, where the henwife is Jack's greatest helper in the Jack tales) they do occasionally let slip a remark that triggers a sequence of malign events (see Frank McKenna, *The Steed of the Bells* [cassette] selected from the archives of the Ulster Folk and Transport Museum). The henwife asks Trembling to stay outside the church rather than going in, perhaps suggesting practices outside the approval of the Church. Magic good, bad or indifferent had the status of the Devil's work in Christianity so magical practices such as the use of the cloak of darkness would have been frowned on. Trembling's husband is the son of the King of the ancient city of Emania in Ulster, called Omania here. He changed his loyalties from Fair to Trembling after seeing her magical regalia. Another story in Curtin's repertoire has the King of Greece marrying an Irish king's eldest daughter then falling in love with the younger, Gil an Og. He curses them both, turning Gil an Og into a 'cat within her castle' and her sister into 'a serpent in the bay'. Gil an Og consults a druid and initiates a series of fights in order to free them both (*Myths and Folktales of Ireland,*

Jeremiah Curtin, reprinted from the 1890 Little, Brown and Co. edition by Dover Publications Inc., Toronto, London, 1975, p. 212).

The golden hair cut adrift occurs as far afield as India (cf. Prince Lionheart, in 'There Was Once a King' (in *Folk Tales of Pakistan*, retold by Sayyid Fayyaz Mahmud, Lok Virsa [Pakistan, undated], p. 117). Strands of Princess Yasmin's golden hair are seen floating downstream by a king, who determines to marry the owner of the hair.

The willingness of the King and Trembling to allow their daughter to marry the cow-herd may have something to do with this statement in Curtin's telling of Kil Arthur: 'In that time there was a law in the world that if a young man came to woo a young woman and her people wouldn't give her to him, the young woman should get her death by law' (Curtin, p. 113).

(*Irish Folk-Tales*, edited by Henry Glassie, Penguin Folklore Library [Harmondsworth, UK, 1985], p. 257.)

2. *Diirawac and her Incestuous Brother*

This story was told by a twenty-year-old man (who was not a member of editor, Francis Mading Deng's family).

Angela Carter notes that the Dinka are cattle herders and subsistence farmers of the Sudan. Their land – about 10 per cent of the Sudan – is crossed by the Nile and its tributaries, making communications difficult. 'The main goal of a Dinka is to marry and have children' (p. 166).

Adults and children sleep together in huts. One person is asked to tell a story, then people tell stories in succession, notes Angela Carter, then quotes from Francis Mading Deng: 'As the storytelling progresses, people begin to fall asleep one by one. Sometimes they fall asleep, wake up in the middle of a story, and then fall asleep again . . . People who wake up in the middle of a story are usually brought up to date briefly. As time passes and some people begin to sleep and perhaps snore, the storyteller starts to ask from time to time: Are you asleep? . . . As long as there are people still awake, storytelling continues. The last storyteller is quite likely to be the last person awake and so the final story will be left incomplete' (p. 29).

The lions in most Dinka stories are clearly not real lions but represent a wild, untamed side of human nature. Neither are the puppies, who according to a footnote, symbolise wildness and therefore merit such brutal treatment in folk tales. The victim is subdued by severe beating and 'teasing'. The animal's partiality to raw meat indicates his wildness and its selection of cooked meat signifies it has been tamed (see 'Duang and His Wild Wife', p. 177 of the present book).

It is mostly women and young people who tell the stories. Stories tend to be associated with bedtime and are geared towards the children, the primary educators of childhood (p. 198).

It is likely that the sibling incest taboo is powerfully reinforced not only from the community but the most insignificant sources, because of the children's communal sleeping environment. It is for the heroine Diirawac who killed her brother that the village mourns, the elderly allowing their hair to grow matted and the young abandoning their beads to signify disaster. Violation of the incest taboo is considered more unnatural than murder. No single entity in the tale disputes the validity of the taboo.

(*Dinka Folktales: African Stories from the Sudan*, edited by Francis Mading Deng [New York and London, 1974], p. 78.)

3. The Mirror

Though this variant is poignant, even tragic, the motif of the mistaken mirror image is generally found in humorous tales. In one version a man quarrels with his wife after buying a mirror he mistakes for an image of his dead father. A nun mediates. This version of the tale is also found in India, China and Korea.

The Sun goddess of Japanese myth once took exile from the chaotic world in the Heavenly Rock Dwelling and was enticed back when the celestial smith fashioned a mirror of iron and told her that her reflection was a rival goddess. Beguiled by its beauty and brightness, she returned to light up the world.

(*Chinese Ghouls and Goblins*, edited by G. Willoughby-Meade [London, 1928], p. 184.)

4. The Frog Maiden

The start of the tale, with its wicked stepmother and two stepsisters is complemented by further echoes of the Cinderella story when the Frog Maiden arrives to see the prince in a carrot coach with mice for horses. Variations of this story are found all over the world. 'The Three Feathers' (Brothers Grimm), 'The White Cat' (France) and 'The Monkey Princess' (Pakistan) are all standard tales featuring the *Dummling* (simpleton) hero. In her *Introduction to the Interpretation of Fairy-tales* (Spring Publications Inc., Dallas, USA 1970), Marie Louise von Franz says that 'the bride is either a toad, a frog, a white cat, an ape, a lizard, puppet, rat, a stocking or a hopping nightcap – not even living objects – and sometimes a turtle'. A few lines down she explains that

The main action is concerned with the finding of the right female, upon which

depends the inheritance of the female and further, that the hero does not perform any masculine deeds. He is not a hero in the proper sense of the word. He is helped all the time by the feminine element, which solves the whole problem for him . . . The story ends with a marriage – a balanced union of the male and female elements. So the general structure seems to point to a problem in which there is a dominating male attitude, a situation which lacks the feminine element, and the story tells us how the missing feminine is brought up and restored (p. 36).

(*Burmese Folktales*, edited and collected by Maun Htin Aung [Calcutta, 1948], p. 137.)

5. The Sleeping Prince

The motive for the princess's journey is provided by the sight of horses' blood on the grass and her comment about its beauty. This seems a strange sentiment except that the blood and the beauty of it on the grass is probably connected with menstrual initiation and fertility. This is borne out by the invisible voice guiding the princess to go in search of a mate. The voice also mentions sticks and the sprinkling of water – elements that never actually materialise in the story – suggesting a sexual initiation which comes to pass only much later. The gory use to which the princess puts the witch's remnants could again be related to puberty – the pain and trauma of sexual deprivation and isolation represented by the witch are now objects of access to womanhood and sexual fruition, particularly the ladder which leads to her bed.

This tale is found in India too, beginning like the famous British tale 'Cap O'Rushes' with the expulsion of the youngest princess who gives an unacceptable response to her king-father's question. The princess asks the prince for some puppets and he overhears her enacting the incidents of her life. The impostor, her maid, is buried to the waist and trampled by horses.

(*Suriname Folk-lore*, collected by Melville J. Herskovits and Frances S. Herskovits [New York, 1936], p. 381.)

6. The Orphan

The motif of the mother feeding her daughter from beyond the grave occurs the world over. An almost exact parallel with this aspect of the tale is the Grimm Brothers' 'One Eye, Two Eye and Three Eye'. Treasure associated with the tree is also a feature of both, focusing primarily on the heroine's imminent rise in social status. She is not a conjurer though her stepmother proves to have access to spells and enchantment. The heroine's own inner magic emanates from her innocence. The second common motif here is the type found in 'The Goose Girl', where an envious woman deceitfully takes the place of the true bride. See 'The Woman Who Married Her Son' and 'The Sleeping Prince' in this volume. A third standard element in fairy tales is the metamorphosis of women into birds, either at will or by enchantment – for example, 'The White Duck' (European), 'The Crane Wife' (Japanese). See also 'The Bird Woman', included in this collection. A more exciting parallel is found in 'Devil Woman', in *Tales of the Cochiti Indians*, collected by Ruth Benedict (Smithsonian Institution, 1930). Here a demon transforms a new mother into a bird – a dove in this instance – by sticking a pin in her head. The removal of the pin ends the enchantment.

(*Tales of Old Malawi*, retold and edited by E. Singano and A.A. Roscoe [Limbe, Malawi, 1986], p. 69.)

Part Four: MOTHERS AND DAUGHTERS

1. *Achol and Her Wild Mother*

Another Dinka story featuring a human lion. This one is told by the daughter of Chief Deng Majok, Nyankoc Deng, who was then aged eighteen to twenty. Perhaps Achol's mother's grisly compulsion to gather wood and forfeit her hands and feet to the lion actually represent some other kind of misdemeanour, such as adultery. Angela Carter's notes copied from *Dinka Folktales* would seem to support this: 'lions are what the Dinka fear most' (p. 25) and 'A person who violates fundamental precepts of the Dinka moral code is often identified in the folk tales as an outsider and an animal' (p. 161). She comments: 'this differentiates the animal from the human, the lions of the stories are not really lions. Hence the emphasis on human interaction with lions. As in the other stories, the lioness is fed nightly by her daughter until her son arrives and beats the wildness out of her' (see 'Duang and His Wild Wife' p. 177 in this collection).

(Deng p. 95.)

2. *Tunjur, Tunjur*

A fifty-five-year-old woman called Fatime, from the village of Arrabe in Galilee told the story of Tunjur, a cooking-pot. Angela Carter's notes quote the description of another teller from *Speak Bird, Speak Again* (p. 31): 'When she came to the part about the man defecating in the cooking pot and the pot closing on him, Im Nabil laughed; then, still laughing she said the pot chopped off the man's equipment.' Angela Carter comments that 'men don't like the stories, partly because some of the mores of which they are guardians, e.g. the "woman's honour" thing, are consistently challenged in the tales – in which *heroines predominate*'. She goes on to quote again from *Speak Bird, Speak Again* (p. 14): 'the ideological basis of the system lies in the father–son bond. The female is identified as the "other".'

In this story, the daughter – a cooking pot – is quite clearly the 'other', but is sparklingly in step with the cunning and playful heroine of Šāhīn (see p. 13 note p. 212) in her ability to match every man in wits and strength. She is a recognisable female trickster of the famous British Molly Whuppie type (a female Jack-the-Giant-Killer), even to the extent of going that little bit further than she has to, for the sake of a bit of fun. The story is well in keeping with the woman's need in society to articulate her capabilities without being in the custody of the male infrastructure, so men are entirely peripheral to this story except as fools.

(Muhawi and Kanaana, p. 55.)

3. The Little Old Woman with Five Cows

A Yakut creation myth tells of a Supreme Being who created a small and level world, which was scratched up by evil demons and spirits making the hills and valleys. The evil spirits were regularly appeased and thanked by Yakut shamans. Today they inhabit the Lena basin and intermarry with Russians.

The magical maiden in this Yakut tale has her origins in what would appear to be a foundation myth of sorts. The 'middle land' inhabited by the human race, here represented by the Yakuts, is clearly in need of honour or redemption and the maiden is sent down as the saviour, duly suffering trials, death and resurrection. Unlike 'The Finn King's Daughter' (Reidar Christiansen, p. 147) and other tales, in which the reader is informed in a phrase or sentence about the metamorphosis, this tale contains the horrific and explicit process of transformation. The demoness herself is, like the *muzayyara*, an Egyptian water-nymph with iron breasts. (*Folktales of Egypt*, edited and translated by Hasan M.El-Shamy, University of Chicago, 1938, p. 180). Angela Carter comments: 'The ancient Indian stories contain many horrible descriptions of Rakshasas' (ogres).

The goddess Kali herself is depicted at her most ferocious, with her tongue hanging from her mouth like the demoness of this story who shoots out an iron tongue. Like the troll-woman in 'The Finn King's Daughter', this demoness is not quite familiar with the social customs of the society she is attempting to infiltrate. There is a cryptic reference to the fact that 'she wrongly fastened her horse to the willow tree where the old widow from Semyaksin used to tether her spotted fox', and this merits the hostility of her husband's clan. The editor of *Siberian and Other Folktales* notes that 'each species of tree has a master of its own except the larch' and it is with a larch branch that the plant maiden kindles the fire when she arrives, suggesting that she is in tune with humans and comes in fulfilment of a greater plan. She also knows of an interesting cleansing ritual vital to get rid of the internal and external pollution of her husband caused by coupling with the demoness. The hanging of the Khan's son from the tree for purification is reminiscent of Christ on the crucifix and other suspended gods such as Attis (Anatolia), Sluy (Wales) and Wotan (Germanic), all of whom returned after a few days.

(C. Fillingham-Coxwell, p. 262.)

4. Achol and her Adoptive Lioness-Mother

In this tale told by a twenty-year-old woman, the incest taboo is once again threatened but maintained through the intervention of non-human creatures. (Cf. 'Diirawac and Her Incestuous Brother' p. 104.) Angela Carter comments: 'Incest taboos are particularly complex and important in polygamous societies. Here for example, Achol and her brother cannot recognize each other, having been separated in early childhood through the deceit of their half brothers.'

Part Five: MARRIED WOMEN

1. Story of a Bird Woman

Angela Carter jotted down some salient quotes from *Siberian and Other Folktales* in her notes. 'Stories of bird-women occur among the Yakuts, the Lapps and the Samoyedes'; 'It is not unknown for a Siberian folktale hero to order a large supply of boots when he undertakes a great feat'; and 'Generally speaking, the Chukchis believe that all nature is animated and that every material object can act, speak and walk by itself.'

The transformations of animal goddesses into human wives is the primary component of this story. Japanese and Chinese folklore abound in these. The journey and magical battle of redemption found here are unusual, though. Generally the husband has to content himself with his children or – possibly – rare encounters with the departed wife. The Welsh classic, 'The Song of Taliesin', includes a series of incidents in which the goddess Ceredwen takes the form of birds, ranging from a mighty eagle to a macabre raven and a lowly hen.

(C. Fillingham-Coxwell, p. 82.)

2. Father and Mother Both 'Fast'

The true purpose of this joke, which challenges the incest taboo, is to rebound on the main protagonist. It contains bawdy references to adultery and illegitimacy, as do most cuckolded husband jokes. It was collected from Jim Alley by Richard Dorson.

(*Buying the Wind; Regional Folklore in the United States*, Richard M. Dorson [Chicago, 1964], p. 79.)

3. Reason to Beat Your Wife

This piece of scatological humour comes from a thirty-year-old peasant woman from a village in the Nile delta, who remembered hearing it from her mother when she was ten. Her husband put up some resistance to her offer of telling the story to the (male) editor Hasan El-Shamy and acceded to his appeal only on condition that her voice would not be recorded. He enjoyed the story though, and joked that his wife had put it to good use.

The editor adds:

> *The climactic event in this humorous anecdote belongs under the general motif 'absurd wish'. The overall motif may be contrasted to 'The Taming of the Shrew', which carries the local title of 'Kill Your Cat on Your Wedding Night'.*

In fact it is the notion of a husband establishing his superiority over an already dutiful wife that gets its comeuppance here, so it is appropriate that the tale comes from a woman who got it from an older woman. The tale seems to advocate indulgence of the weaknesses of men and the fact that being dutiful pays off – but it hints at concealed guile with the robust, earthy humour familiar in Arab tales. For the audacious use of shit, see 'Šāhīn' (p. 13) and 'Tanjur, Tanjur' (p. 139 and note pp. 222–223).

(Hasan El-Shamy, p. 217.)

4. The Three Lovers

The paramour at the window in this tale from south-west Mexico receives a similar fate to Chaucer's character in 'The Miller's Tale', after having his rump kissed.

(*Cuentos Españoles de Colorado y de Nuevo Mejico Vol. 1*, original text by Juan B. Rael [Stanford University Press, 1957], p. 105. This text translated by Merle E. Simmons, p. 427.)

5. The Seven Leavenings

Angela Carter notes: 'Fatime again – two tales woven together by the personality of the old woman. The woman moves from father's house to husband's house and at no time has space of her own – but don't dismiss the *power* of the "other" – expressed partly in telling of tales, embroidery, basket-making, pottery, wedding songs, laments.' Then she quotes from *Speak Bird, Speak Easy*: 'for the female, conflict is inherent in the structure of the system'.

A footnote from the editors of that book reads: 'Inability to get pregnant and have children is the most common theme in all the folktales in this collection' (p. 207). Without a doubt this is one of the anxieties expressed by women in tales, particularly since 'a man is more easily forgiven if he hits a wife who doesn't have children' (loc. cit.).

The woman in this story is clearly an old crone with magical instincts, a wily and wise helper of women who speaks in a cryptic language of her own; for example, 'The land is longing for its people, I want to go home.' Perhaps the fact that the bread doesn't leaven means that her work, the deliverance of women from their husbands, is never finished – except of course when it suits the storyteller to bring the tale to its end. Being an old woman, she is particularly suitable as the companion of a younger woman and unlikely to misguide her. This gives her the space to practise the necessary wiles to improve the lot of her protégée. Angela Carter quotes, 'Older women are thought to be asexual; the husband is therefore more ready to believe in his wife's innocence after the old woman confirms her interpretation of "black on white"' (p. 211). The frame/vignette format is standard in the Middle East (cf. the Arabian Nights).

The 'seven' in the title suggests that it is part of a cycle of seven stories narrated in the same formula.

(Muhawi and Kanaana, p. 206.)

6. The Untrue Wife's Song

Another daring woman teaches her husband a lesson in this story collected by Ralph S. Boggs from B.L. Lunsford aged forty-four, of North Carolina. This tale is based on 'Old Hildebrande', a longer tale originating from Europe and with an anti-clerical bias.

(*Journal of American Folklore*, 47, 1934, p. 305.)

7. The Woman Who Married Her Son

This story was told by an eighty-two-year-old woman from the village of Rafidiya, district of Nablus, in Palestine, notes Angela Carter.

The familiar scenario of a wife being replaced by a rival has a twist here, when a mother replaces her daughter-in-law in her son's bed and even becomes pregnant. Muhawi and Kanaana compare her pica (craving) for sour grapes to the western one for pickles. The same theme appears in 'Rom', in Jan Knappert's *Myths and Legends of the Congo,* London, 1979. Rom's mother's action is in part prompted by pity that unknown to him, his sweetheart has abandoned him, so it is the young man himself who commits a grisly suicide, chanting:

I entered the lap I came out of
My strength went back where it came from (p. 27).

Here though, the mother is motivated by selfishness and lust. In part her jealousy is triggered by sharing status with another woman. Angela Carter quotes a Palestinian proverb: 'The household of the father is a playground and that of the husband is an education. A woman always belongs in one household or another.' She jots down some phrases: *sexuality* – utterly disruptive of social fabric, especially female sexuality; sexes segregated; 'honour'.

The tale certainly demonstrates the fear of disruption caused by this example of female sexuality gone rampant. The slur to family honour – guarded by men but lodged in women – is punished with death by burning. Interestingly, though the editors Muhawi and Kanaana attribute the teller's omission of the detail of this punishment to her quickening of pace and brevity towards the end of the story, it is really more likely to be her way of reducing the punitive consequences of female transgression. As for the segregation of sexes – perhaps that is what makes it easier to believe that a son could mistake his mother for his wife, however well disguised she may be. Of course, a mother-in-law could be as young as thirty.

The brutality of the wife's action in casually cutting out the innocent servant's tongue is not particularly unusual in fairy tales or for that matter in history. Here it indicates her commitment to silence. When her time of silence is up she allows the messenger to keep his tongue. The silence of a woman in fairy tales, through either enchantment or commitment, is a standard narrative device to facilitate plot development. This is a legacy from the early Middle Ages, when women in European narratives lost their voices during the period between betrothal and marriage. The silence of heroines appears as a redemption motif in several German fairy tales, where loquacious heroines never became popular. In Europe, the silencing of heroines for fear of evil spells or the threat of everlasting condemnation was linked to concepts of power and retribution for the original sin.

(Muhawi and Kanaana, p. 60.)

8. Duang and His Wild Wife

This story was told by Nyanjur Deng, another of Chief Deng Majok's daughters, aged twenty. Angela Carter quotes from *Dinka Folktales*: 'The late Chief of the Nyok extended the practice of diplomatic marriage further than anyone else in the history of the Dinka. He had nearly 200 wives drawn from most of the corners of Dinkaland. The family was closely knit, living in several large villages, and all kinds of dialects were spoken and subcultures represented' (p. 99).

Here Duang considers his wife's pica (craving) to be unreasonable since the Dinka deplore the killing of animals for any reason other than ritual or sacrifice. His deceitful act re-emphasises that from Amou's point of view Duang has behaved as an 'outsider'. Having gone through the civilising ritual (see 'Diirawac and Her Incestuous Brother' p. 104 and 'Achol and Her Wild Mother' p. 135) she avenges herself with his death.

(Deng, p. 97.)

9. A Stroke of Luck

One of a body of jocular tales about the inability of women to keep a secret. In some variants the trusting husband gets into trouble; here he turns it to his advantage.

(Degh, p. 147.)

10. The Beans in the Quart Jar

Another cuckolded husband joke, told by Jim Alley to Richard Dorson (see 'Father and Mother Both "Fast"' p. 162 and 'The Untrue Wife's Song' p. 173).

(Dorson, p. 80.)

Part Six: USEFUL STORIES

1. A Fable of a Bird and Her Chicks

A stern and darkly humorous fable about preparation for the tough and persecutory side of life, this story is representative of Yiddish humour and aphorisms.

From *Yiddish Folktales*, edited by Beatrice Siverman Weinreich with a foreword by Leonard Woolf.

2. The Three Aunts

'Old Habetrot' is the English variant of the Norse tale in which the helper presents herself to the lazy spinner's husband as an illustration of what might happen to his wife if she is forced to pursue the crafts of spinning and weaving (cf. Vasilissa the Fair p. 78, who actually does spin, weave and stitch the king's shirts to perfection, so is naturally under no pressure to continue). The lazy spinner, though, resists the pressure of her straitened circumstances to tie her to a spinning wheel. Since the only release from her penury lies in marrying an affluent man, guile and subterfuge are necessary escape devices. What is most enjoyable is the conspiracy of women, which not only conceals the heroine's trickery but saves her from a future of drudgery and rebuke. Not so the post-1819 editions of the Grimms' story which demands of the reader, 'You must yourself admit that she was a disgusting woman.'

(Darsent, p. 194.)

3. Tale of an Old Woman

'Muriwa' is the Bondes word for sycamore. An almost identical story occurs in the South Pacific. These stories indicate that the conditions imposed by magical helpers are binding. If they are not duly respected, the creatures withdraw (see 'Story of a Bird Woman', p. 159). In both these stories nothing is left behind as a reminder of the days of grace.

(*African Folktales*, edited by Roger Abrahams [New York, Pantheon Folklore Library, 1983), p. 57.)

4. The Height of Purple Passion

An unsolved mystery riddle ending in anti-climax. The author collected it from a nine-year-old American girl in the presence of her stunned parents. The source of the joke is probably a French literary story that still survives under various names including 'The Bordeaux Diligence', which occurs in a Hitchcock anthology of horror stories from the late sixties.

(*The Rationale of the Dirty Joke*, Vol. II, by C. Legman [London, Panther 1973], p. 121.)

5. Salt, Sauce and Spice, Onion Leaves, Pepper and Drippings

The power of the name is a fundamental premiss of this story. The password – the coveted man's name – is only gained after a specific and vital test has been passed. Unlike the Tom Tit Tot group (stories like 'Rumpelstiltskin') the test is service and generosity of spirit rather than trickery and contest. As in all *Dummling* (simpleton) stories, the most unlikely candidate triumphs.

(Abrahams, p. 299.)

6. *Two Sisters and the Boa*

A careless joke with a non-human creature results in a scary mistake (see 'The Midwife and the Frog', p. 87). The tale is otherwise of the Beauty and the Beast type. The point that the wicked sister always seems to miss is that the reward lies not in emulating her sister's actions, but in her generosity of spirit. (Source unknown.)

7. *Spreading the Fingers*

A moral tale from Suriname, reminiscent of an oral Islamic tale in which a pauper shares out the food quota allocated him for his entire life and ensures that he never goes hungry. But his game is with God, who is a willing player in it.

(Melville J. and Frances S. Heskovits, p. 355.)

The End

Angela Carter

'Angela Carter's writing is bold, dreamy and startlingly precise. She describes what might be called the real life of fantasy – late twentieth-century culture seen through the looking glass, our obsessions and repressed imaginings depicted with a kind of rival realism' – *Lorna Sage*

'She is always bold. Yet there is, in her writing, a reassuring sense of purpose, a sure-footedness, as if it were not at all hard to juxtapose make-believe with the colloquial, macabre with the commonplace' – *The Times*

Virago publish:

The Virago Book of Fairy Tales

Angela Carter's first pick of Mother Goose's feathers is 'A winner, full of various peoples, wicked and funny and bizarre' – *A.S. Byatt*

'The book is very much a portrait of its maker – it has Angela's deadpan, slightly black humour, and her sexual frankness. Each story gives one an authentic shivery feeling' – *Marina Warner*

Nothing Sacred
Selected Writings

Reissued with five new pieces

Angela Carter's journalism 'exists somewhere in the territory marked out by the Roland Barthes of *Mythologies*, middle period Orwell, and early Tom Wolfe' – *Guardian*

The Sadeian Woman
An Exercise in Cultural History

Provocative, polemical, and always readable, Angela Carter tackles the Marquis de Sade, the most notorious pornographer of them all, wittily and brilliantly enlisting him in an argument about women's sexual freedom.

The Magic Toyshop

Fifteen-year-old Melanie steps into a bad dream when she tries on her mother's wedding dress. Using magic and myth Angela Cater spins a beautifully told story of sexual awakening.

Adapted for a television film.

The Passion of New Eve

'Taut, vengeful allegory of a sex-changed English lecturer in a nightmare America of the near future. Makes Myra Breckinridge look like Danny La Rue' – *Sunday Times*

Fireworks

Short stories and allegorical tales, ranging in settings from Tokyo to South America, from London to strange erotic landscapes of the imagination.

Wayward Girls and Wicked Women

An Anthology of Stories edited by Angela Carter

A marvellous collection of stories about bad girls and wicked women designed to promote the female virtues of discontent, sexual disruptiveness, and to hell with the consequences. Includes tales by Grace Paley, Bessie Head, Katherine Mansfield, Elizabeth Jolley, Djuna Barnes, Colette, Jamaica Kincaid, Ama Ata Aidoo, Jane Bowles and many more.